UsingWomen

UsingWomen

Gender, Drug Policy, and Social Justice

Nancy D. Campbell

Routledge

New York   London

Published in 2000 by

Routledge
29 West 35th Street
New York, NY 10001

Published in Great Britain by
Routledge
11 New Fetter Lane
London EC4P 4EE

Library of Congress Cataloging-in-Publication Data
Campbell, Nancy Duff.
    Using women : gender, drug policy, and social justice /
    by Nancy D. Campbell
        p.   cm.
    Includes bibliographical references and index.
    ISBN 0-415-92412-X (hb) — ISBN 0-415-92413-8 (pbk.)
    1. Women—Drug use—United States.   2. Women—Government
policy—United States.   3. Narcotics, Control of—United States.
    4. Sex discrimination against women—United States.
    5. Social justice—United States.   I. Title.
HV5824.W6 C35   2000
362.29'082'0973—dc21   99-087644

CONTENTS

ILLUSTRATIONS

ACKNOWLEDGMENTS

I gratefully acknowledge the ongoing intellectual, spiritual, and technical contributions of Ron Eglash and the constant companionship of Isaac Campbell Eglash in the project's final months. For inspiration I thank my parents, David and Sandra Campbell, and my extended family, who weathered their own crises and mine while this book was in process. My siblings and their families, Connie Campbell, Tony Diehl, and Alexandra Campbell-Diehl, David R. Campbell and Amanda E. Myers-Campbell, and Gary Campbell have long tolerated their older sister's elusive endeavors. Finally, my friends Giovanna Di Chiro, Kathryn Keller, Deirdre O'Connor, and David Rapkin dissented and empathized but, most important, punctuated the long periods of silence that this effort required.

This book began as a dissertation shaped from the outset by Wendy Brown, Angela Y. Davis, Barbara Epstein, and especially Donna Haraway of the University of California at Santa Cruz. The 1995 "Feminism and Discourses of Power" research colloquium at the Humanities Research Institute, University of California at Irvine, provided a congenial atmosphere for thinking through the conceptual framework. I would like to acknowledge the HRI staff and "fellows": Wendy Brown, Judith Butler, Rey Chow, Nancy Fraser, Angela Harris, Saidiya Hartman, Anne Norton, Jenny Sharpe, Jacqueline Siapno, and Irene Wei.

The Ohio State University Department of Women's Studies provided a unique setting in which to hone my ideas about gender, public policy, and political discourse. I would like to thank the following colleagues for extraordinary efforts on my behalf: Mary Margaret Fonow, Susan Hartmann, Nick Howe, Sally Kitch, Linda Krikos, Martha Wharton, and Ara Wilson. I am indebted to Margaret Newell for contributing the title. Additionally, I have benefited from the support of many people in Columbus, including Michele Acker, Elizabeth Allan, Lu Bailey, Rhonda Benedict, Angela Brintlinger, Hong Cao, Steve Conn, Cory Dillon, Ada Draughon, Lisa Florman, Stephanie Grant, Jodi Horne, Virginia Reynolds, Eulalia Roël, Linda and Brian Rugg, Birgitte Soland, Kate Weber, Judy Wu, Maria Zazycki, Tracy Zitzelberger, and many others.

Most important, I have relied on two extraordinary research assistants, Kate Bedford and Jenrose Fitzgerald, each of whom made the project and its passions their own. For technical triage, I depended on Valerie Rake's expertise and legendary calm. All of my students were generous in allowing me to develop as a teacher and theorist before their very eyes; I thank them for listening and responding to my ideas.

My feminist reading group, PMS, provided pleasure during this process: Suzanne Damarin, Gia Hinkle, Patti Lather, Nan Johnson, Marilyn Johnston, Linda Meadows, Laurel Richardson, Amy Shuman, Pat Stuhr, and Amy Zaharlick. An unusual group of drug policy historians was assembled by David Musto with the help of the National Institute of Drug Abuse, and my efforts seemed less isolated in their company. I would especially like to thank Caroline Acker, John Burnham, David Courtwright, Jill Jonnes, Stephen Kandall, Mara Keire, Joe Spillane, and Bill White for their insights and contributions to the field.

My research was supported financially by a Coca-Cola grant for Research on Women awarded in 1998. For their assistance I thank the staff of the Anslinger Archives at the Pattee Library, Pennsylvania State University; the Library of the New York Academy of Medicine; the New York Public Library; and the National Library of Medicine. I also gratefully acknowledge the Ohio State University's generous professional leave and junior faculty development policies. A fellowship from the OSU Institute for Collaborative Research and Public Humanities allowed me to complete the project in a timely fashion. Lastly, my editor, Ilene Kalish, had faith in this project and steered it to completion with grace and good humor.

Introduction
Drug Policy, Social Reproduction, and Social Justice

Spectacular Failures

Housecleaning has long been associated with legal drug use by white women (see Figure 1). "Mother's little helpers" once pepped up 1950s middle-class housewives afflicted with the feminine mystique.[1] Today a spick-and-span house or too-well tended yard may betray a methamphetamine user.[2] "Meth" or "crank," once the "blue-collar cocaine" of truck drivers and carpet layers, was declared the "pink-collar crack" of the 1990s. "Today, you have the sense that it's moms trying to juggle a job and three kids and day care, and women working on their feet as waitresses for twelve hours a day."[3] Portrayed as a "white woman's drug," meth reputedly numbed the pangs of hunger and postpartum depression (see Figure 2). In 1992 in some areas of the country women tested positive for meth at higher rates than men. "That's the first time we've seen that on any drug," remarked Clinton administration drug czar William McCaffrey. "There may be a piece of it related to weight loss and a piece of it related to enabling prostitution—it's a drug that allows you to deal with your feelings of remorse."

McCaffrey went on to associate crank with "crack," an illegal cocaine-derived drug characterized as being used primarily by African-Americans. Both drugs were characterized as having a particularly powerful attraction for women—the power to "shatter a mother's love for her children." Both were thought to overcome women's intuition, their "natural instincts," and the redemptive power of maternal love. Women's turn to these drugs thus signified that the scope and impact of illicit drug use in the late twentieth century had exceeded a natural limit. By this logic, women who use illicit drugs embody both individual deviance and social failure; the differences between drugs and their users have been racialized and their meanings encoded in the "figures" of drug-using women on which political discourse relies. This book recounts such gendered and sexualized meanings

You can't set her free.
But you can help her
feel less anxious.

Figure 1   Advertisement for antianxiety drug, 1969.

U.S Senate Committee on Commerce. The Relationship between Drug Abuse and Advertising. 91st Cong., 2d sess., 22 September 1970.

of women and drugs in order to show how public constructions are produced, how they circulate, especially in public policy, and the assumptions that shape them.

White women use meth to endure dull and repetitive work, the economic and emotional travails of childbearing and child rearing, and the constant monitoring of their weight. The governing assumptions that undergird McCaffrey's example include white women's overconcern with appearance, their revulsion toward sex

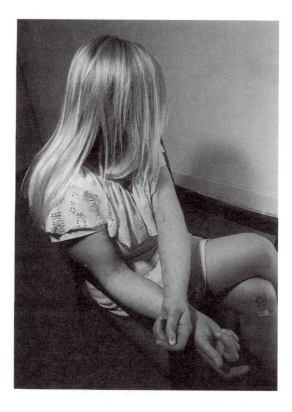

Figure 2   A methamphetamine user, 1997. Photograph by Jeff Green/NYT Pictures.

Reprinted with permission from the *New York Times*.

work, and their feelings of remorse (which at least signal the presence of moral conscience). White women who use illegal drugs are also figured as "cleaner" than women of color who do so. That is, white women are represented as using drugs to remain functional, orderly, and clean, while women of color who use drugs are depicted as the nonproductive inhabitants of chaos, decay, and squalor. Crank enables white women to meet their obligations as mothers and workers—the drug helps them juggle service jobs and child-care responsibilities. Crack-using women are not afflicted with the compulsion to clean, work, or care for their children—they are represented as sexual compulsives, bad mothers, and willing prostitutes who lack even the capacity for remorse that might redeem them.

These contrasts signal social inequalities among women yet disavow the material differences in labor, child care, and health care that structure women's lives. Such rhetoric indicates how thin the veneer of formal equality for women is. When women violate gender norms by using illicit drugs, they are represented as spectacular failures—callously abandoning babies or becoming bad mothers, worse wives, or delinquent daughters. Such "violations" invite attempts to govern women by targeting their behaviors and decisions. *Using Women* examines how the cultural meanings of drug use affect the practices of governance, inquiring into their implications for drug policy and their effects on drug-using women's lives.

Anxious Impulses and Social Injustice

Illicit drug use is used as a barometer of individual character and the health or disease of society. As the quintessential "impulsive self," the drug user is overly receptive to social messages and peer pressure. U.S. ideals of citizenship are based on the converse belief that the autonomous or sovereign self "stand[s] apart from any social relationship in which he or she is involved."[4] Women are problematic in this scheme of autonomy, for women's social subjectivity and citizenship are not predicated on the illusion of sovereignty. Even "impulsive" women remain enmeshed in complex relations of dependency on and responsibility for others. The female addict embodies an "impulsive self" who shirks her duties while giving free rein to her desires.

Ironically, women—themselves prototypical dependents—are culturally assigned responsibility for social reproduction.[5] The daily activities that reproduce "society" and its productive forces are typically unremunerated and unremarked, but they are not absorbed without cost. Women tend to the tasks of social reproduction in their "leisure" hours, at times sharing their joys and frustrations with others but ultimately being responsible for keeping families together and afloat. Drug-using women thus bear the social and economic costs of illicit drug use and the material effects of drug policy to a greater degree than drug-using men do.

Women embody a collision between normative expectations of how citizens should conduct themselves as citizens and how women should behave as women. This paradox presents a conundrum not only for women but also for public policy. What is at stake in drug policy debates and outcomes is the reiteration of women's responsibility for social reproduction and the nature of women's economic, social, and political autonomy. How we regulate women drug users reflects the social expectations placed on women in general. Drug policy debates reveal a pervasive anxiety about how a society composed of self-interested consumers can reproduce itself—and leaves that question for individual women to solve.

Women's rights depend on the degree to which women fulfill their responsibilities as contingent workers, consumers, and caretakers. Women purchase their autonomy at the price of good behavior and social conformity. Most go about the business of social reproduction without resorting to crime and participate in social violence to a lesser degree than they are subject to it. Until recently, drug-using women were effectively governed through disciplinary modes of social regulation such as threats of child removal and social stigma. However, the "happening of crack" in the mid-1980s crystallized a shift from discipline to punishment.

Crack was constructed as the "drug of choice, the escape of choice . . . the drug of preference for young women."[6] The discursive links between women's behavior, crack use, social decline, and the position of the United States in the global economy were articulated in a hearing on law and policy affecting addicted women:

> One of the most tragic and insidious aspects of crack use by a pregnant woman is that it seems to almost destroy the maternal instinct. There are all too many of these abandoned babies, euphemistically termed "boarder babies.". . . [This] is a story of hospitals under siege . . . of foster care systems that are strained beyond limit . . . of a swamped educational and social service system. . . . The long-term implications for America are truly staggering in terms of who will be the earning members of a society in a social security system and whether or not . . . America can remain competitive in the global marketplace.[7]

Tracing domestic disharmony and declining competitiveness to women's drug use, such representations decried the loss of "maternal instinct." The nation, it seemed, was threatened by women's behavior and their social and biological reproductive decisions. While we often dwell on biological reproduction as the wellspring of the drug problem, the underlying issue is: Who will take responsibility for social reproduction?

The number of women using drugs, patterns of law enforcement, and the severity of punishment for drug crimes increased the number of incarcerated women by almost 500 percent between 1980 and 1994.[8] The proportion of women incarcerated for violent offenses simultaneously declined.[9] Women are not becoming more serious criminals; most women in federal prisons are there on drug offenses.[10] "Without any fanfare, the 'war on drugs' has become a war on women."[11] The body count is highest among women of color—nearly half of imprisoned women are African-Americans, who are seven times more likely to be incarcerated than white women. Nearly 70 percent of women in prison were single parents responsible for young children prior to incarceration.[12] Most would once have been placed on probation, but federal sentencing guidelines prevent judges from doing so.[13] Mandatory sentences and "neutral" sentencing are thus women's issues.

Current drug policy is neither fair nor just to women, but the impact of the injustice depends on class and racial formation. For this reason I call for an explicit commitment to social justice as a principle of drug policy. We must recognize that policy decisions—especially the emphasis on incarceration, "neutral" sentencing, and patterns of law enforcement—partly produce the current dimensions of the drug problem. These decisions have accompanied the legislative gutting of social provision and the privatization of social services, including mental health services and drug and alcohol treatment. These forms of social injustice are outcomes of ill-considered policy decisions.

Dynamic Deflections: The Political Stakes of Social Justice

Social justice for women depends on recognizing that women are made responsible for absorbing the costs of social reproduction in ways that men are not. Women's position in low-security, low-wage service work converges with race and sex discrimination to place most women in states of economic and social vulnerability. On top of this, women are expected to be responsible for social reproduction. The pervasive fear that women will refuse these responsibilities is based on realistic concerns that run deeper than the anxiety that women will shift "their" burdens to the state. It has become a full-scale fear that women will refuse to be "women." That is, they will refuse to play their part in the social arrangements that subordinate women to men, women of color to white women, and single, lesbian, or bisexual women to women who inhabit normative family configurations.

Only a broad recognition that responsibility for social reproduction cannot and should not be fully the responsibility of individuals can lead to social justice. If we are serious about building a polity that exceeds the sum of our "impulsive selves," we must share the costs of social reproduction more equitably. As we shall see, drug policy debates often reinscribe women's overaccountability for social costs by constructing maternal responsibility for even those "features of social relations originating outside the mother's immediate experience and not subject to her control."[14] Fearing that women will become unfit or unwilling to serve as they have in the past, policy-makers target women who use drugs during pregnancy as symbolic distortions of maternity and femininity.

Policy-making proceeds as a discursive practice, but the texts and practices that emerge from it exercise material effects that shape the experience and interpretation of addiction. Yet policy-makers disclaim their own responsibility by attributing policy failures to human nature, immorality, or bad behavior on the part of the governed. By deflecting blame onto representative figures, policy-makers avoid addressing the larger structures, decisions, and policies that exacerbate our multiple drug problems. Holding individuals responsible for addiction reproduces deeply held American notions of personal responsibility, risk, vulnerability, and productive citizenship. But not all individuals have the means or the capacities to discharge the responsibilities of citizenship and social reproduction. The uneven distribution of the means to realize autonomy, reduce vulnerability and violence, and carry out responsibilities is simply disregarded in drug policy.

Interrogating this assumption is the basis for proposing social justice as a remedy, and is one of the goals of this book.

The Cultural Practices of Policy Construction and Analysis

Drug policy is based on policy-makers' attempts to know the "truth" of addiction.[15] Policy is embedded in the culture that produces it, and is best seen as a cultural practice of governance. The "truth" of addiction limits how stories about it must be told in the policy-making process and in drug studies.[16] For instance, "drugs" are the main vehicle of addiction narratives—they displace other explanations such as economic dislocation or cultural practices that deny agency and efficacy to many people in social contexts where drug use proliferates. Drugs, it seems, banish all other desires and fundamentally transform their users,[17] an attribution of their omnipotence that grants substances the power to erode individual and communal particularity. The myth of pharmacological omnipotence[18] is a culturally specific "truth" inscribed in U.S. drug policy.

Cultural values are installed in public policy in ways that do not always yield policies that are practical, ethical, or just. Policy-makers, like scientists, function as if they inhabited a "culture of no culture."[19] Both the symbolic and substantive dimensions of policy arise from frameworks of "reigning ideas and values" that filter what we see and how we see it.[20] Policy is not simply symbolic; policy-makers share the collective power to put their ideas into motion through legal, political, and administrative institutions.[21] By reading cultural assumptions back into policy discourse, I foreground the relationship between the processes of cultural figuration and policy-making rather than denying its existence. I contend that a set of "governing mentalities" underlies the shifting policy agendas of the late-twentieth-century United States. Governing mentalities shape the policy process and outcomes in ways that hurt women through the gendered and racialized nature of the liberal state and the effects of capitalism. Women remain problematic subjects who are still not fully integrated as participants in the democratic processes of governance.

Critical policy analysis "reads" public policy for what it can tell us about contemporary political culture. Policy studies is a growing field of feminist scholarship that spans multiple arenas, including antipoverty policy, domestic crime control, immigration, penal policy, reproductive rights, and others.[22] This book joins other feminist policy studies by inquiring into a specific set of obstacles to women's full political, economic, and social autonomy and participation. Feminists occupy an ideal position from which to link illicit drug policy with other "women's" issues such as sexual and reproductive rights and the labor struggle. While feminist approaches vary, they commonly emphasize history, rhetoric and discourse analysis, and cultural studies to a greater extent than conventional policy analysis.

Critical policy analysis differs from conventional policy analysis because it examines the structures of political exclusion, social isolation, and economic marginalization.[23] Policy analysis typically misses the cultural assumptions that I call "governing mentalities," which then exert unacknowledged effects on the policy-making process and policy outcomes. As I demonstrate, these hidden assumptions are historically grounded and culturally specific. The disparate impact of such policies exposes the myths of gender neutrality, race-blindness, and classlessness in the United States. Gender, sexuality, and racial-ethnic formation are crucial to comprehending the position drug addicts have played as cultural others and as politically subversive subjects. Our political discourse on drugs is unreadable without critical theories of difference that address—at a minimum—racial-ethnic and class formation, gender, and sexuality.

Drug policy narratives "underwrite and stabilize the assumptions for decision making in the face of high uncertainty, complexity, and polarization."[24] Policy decisions cannot diverge too far from the assumptions that undergird our stories about drugs and those of the institutions installed to respond to our beliefs. Drug policy narratives perform deflections that are not simply bias or fiction—these deflections are integral to the production of "truth" and a sense of "reality" in a complex, uncertain, and rapidly shifting world. The figures that emerge from these stories embody the characteristics of drug users and encode the meaning, political significance, and presumed incidence of drug use. Many "fantastic figures" have enjoyed moments of hypervisibility in our political imaginary. These figures are multidimensional and cannot be reduced to flat-footed stereotypes.[25] The book proceeds by placing these cultural figures within their historical moment, reading for how the governing mentalities are expressed in the policy process and policy outcomes.

Public policy arenas repress the performative and phantasmatic elements of knowledge by turning to the authoritative discourse of science. Policy-makers project the sense that they "know" what they are doing—that their decisions are based not on fiction or fantasy but on empirical knowledge. Yet the knowledge on which they rely is inevitably the product of time and place, truth claims that are inscribed and bounded by the governing mentalities that prevail in a particular political rationality. The cultural images that "haunt" knowledge claims and political positions are not generally the stuff of policy analysis, but they are my elusive object. To reach them, I rely on cultural theories of representation that result in a richer analysis more useful to developing a politics of drug policy based on an appeal to social justice.

Why Women?

Women addicts haunt the political theater in which public knowledges are staged, identities performed, and policy produced. They appear as witnesses to recount personal experiences of abjection, addiction, revelation, and recovery. Addicted women dramatize endless repetitions of the truths and consequences of drugs in this political theater. Yet each phantasm "presents itself as a universal singularity."[26] When addicts are constituted as a social problem, "women who use drugs" appear as a singular—and often spectacular—problematic. Historical amnesia makes it seem as if the repetition is a "fad" and not a long-standing pattern. This book was written against the historical amnesia of U.S. drug policy and discourse. I invite readers to seek parallels between our current preoccupations and earlier episodes.

Policy-makers have historically capitalized on the "fit" between drug use and nonnormative racial-ethnic, class, and gender formations to achieve their political aims. The passage of the Harrison Act (1914), which effectively criminalized the sale and purchase of narcotics, staged associations between drug use and interracial sexuality.[27] The link between drug use and threatening forms of cultural difference was built into law, policy, popular culture, and scientific discourses, as the old construction of drug use as an aspect of femininity was increasingly racialized.[28] Once an unremarked feature of "whiteness," drug use became a heavily marked aspect of "blackness" over the course of the century. The meaning of femininity, too, mutated from a sexual form that cast women as either sexual predators or victim-prey to a maternal form. Not until the last decades of the twentieth century, however, did these cultural formations collide to yield the demonized figure of the "crack mom."[29]

The governing mentalities that shape how we think, talk, and make policy related to drugs rely on our notions of dependency, femininity, and sexual deviance. Women's social subordination positions them differently before the law in ways that vary according to their sexual identity, racial-ethnic formation, or reproductive status. When racial and gender relations are shifting, drug-using women who are pregnant or responsible for raising children become especially visible. Racial-ethnic and class formations crosscut drug narratives, making drug discourses part of an evolving complex of social policies that target the behaviors of the "dangerous classes" but excuse those of the dominant. Drugs are consistently represented as about to burst their bounds, loose the floodgates, spill over, leak into, or erode the edifice of the dominant culture. Women's thumbs are dramatically caught in the dike.

The Politics of
Women's Addiction
and Women's Equality

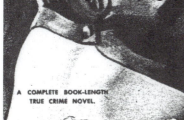

A COMPLETE BOOK-LENGTH
TRUE CRIME NOVEL.

The Politics of
Women's Addiction
and Women's Equality

The American woman is many people. She is a lawyer, doctor, nurse, engineer, secretary, teacher, housewife, student, mother, daughter, and grandmother. She is unemployed, married, single, rich, poor, black, white, Asian, Hispanic, and Native American. She is straight and gay, thin and obese, living in a city and a rural hamlet. She is Catholic, Jewish, Protestant, and Muslim. The typical female substance abuser can be any or all of these women.[1]

Fantastic Figures: Race, Gender, and Addiction

What are "we" talking about when we talk about drugs and women who use them? Illicit drug discourse is an excellent arena for exploring how public policy affects women's lives. Policy is shaped by the underlying assumptions and cultural figures that U.S. political discourse on drugs presumes and reiterates. Drug policy provides a case study of the interplay between political power, knowledge production, and a parade of fantastic figures—the "morphinist mothers" and "opium vampires" of the nineteenth and early twentieth centuries, the "enemies within" and the "girl drug addicts" of the 1950s, the "heroin mothers" of the 1970s, and the "crack moms" of more recent memory.

Shared beliefs, values, figures, and knowledge-production practices are encoded in the governing mentalities that guide domestic drug policy in the late-twentieth-century United States. In turn, public policy configures the social worlds we inhabit, and is thus a consequential form of cultural production. Part I argues that drug discourse, the cultural practices of governance, and the gendered state work to contain women's claims for political, social, and economic autonomy. Where once the state simply ignored addicted women, gender-specific needs are now recognized—but not in ways that address the perpetuation of inequality. Thus this book is not simply about women on drugs. Instead, I seek to explain how, why, and when women drug users become visible or invisible in relation to cultural shifts and public policy.

Feminists in the addiction field called for the recognition of gender and racial difference based on their understanding of social isolation and economic marginalization. A "women's agenda" has supplanted their critique and dampened the political project for women's equality within the field. Chapter 1, "Containing Equality: Biology and Vulnerability," outlines the implications of prevailing constructions of gender difference in addiction studies. The chapter argues through a discourse analysis of an exemplary text that drug discourses reduce women's addiction to biological vulnerability. The chapter analyzes the social relations, cultural assumptions, and emotive resonance of the figure of the female drug addict in contemporary society so that readers have a shared entry point for the historical analysis that follows in Part II.

A substantial community of experts and policy-makers is driven by the governing mentality that women's drug use results from their greater "biological vulnerability." This assumption guides policy toward basic scientific research on sex and gender differences. If addiction was attributed to women's lack of support for raising children alone, policy might veer toward strengthening women's political autonomy and economic security. Deciding how to classify the problem and specify its sources limits the possible solutions. The emphasis on biological difference does not recognize that the differences that matter are men's and women's differential responsibilities for social reproduction.

Drug policy is also driven by a prevailing governing mentality that roots drug abuse in the breakdown of "the family" as a protective social institution.[2] Both behavior and biology "cause" addiction among women to matter more than addiction among men. Women are supposed to keep families "intact," and are routinely blamed when structural and cultural forces weaken or fragment families. The dominant-mother/absent-father model of family dysfunction was advanced to explain drug addiction in the adolescent heroin crisis of the early to mid-1950s, and it continues to "explain" drug use today.[3] In the late 1980s, a major political and cultural crisis ensued when increasing numbers of women of childbearing age formed households without men. Maternal drug use was used to justify coercion—including court-ordered contraception and long-term surveillance of women. Beneath the obsession with drug-addicted babies lies a basic animosity to women's self-governance.

Women's claims for political autonomy are contained through policies that reinforce gender difference and place undue burdens on women. This asymmetry is the legacy of two fantastic figures that inhabit the liberal state. On one side is the masculine figure of the autonomous liberal subject so addicted to self-interest that he disavows all dependency.[4] On the other stands the feminine figure of a relational codependent so thickly bound to others that she is incapable of self-governance. Neither caricature is livable; neither side of the divide is inhabitable. The feminine caricature cannot give up her relational responsibilities; the masculine figure can abstain from his unburdened state of independent autonomy. Entrapped between an impossible equality and an equally improbable difference, women present something of a conundrum for public policy.

My purpose in writing this book was not to disregard the actual harm of women's drug abuse nor to excuse irresponsible behavior in either gender. Instead, I trace how women's drug use has been constructed as a gendered, racialized, and sexualized threat to modernity, capitalist production, social reproduction, and democratic citizenship. The figure of the female drug addict is an overdetermined condensation symbol for a wide and shifting array of cultural anxieties that are translated into public policy. Drug policy targets threatening others—by building institutions to confine them and so limit cultural contact with them, but above all by governing the "known facts" about them.

Modes of Regulation

Mainstream political scientists categorize illicit drug policy as a "valence issue," by which they mean that there is only one legitimate political position for such policy. Just about everyone, or so the story goes, agrees that illicit drug use is bad. An "issue" has but two conflicting sides, obscuring the fact that conversants' positions and goals may not be clear, may be hybrid, or may exceed the immediate issue. For instance, the goals of U.S. foreign policy and response to the Cold War structured the U.S. response to global drug policy well into the 1980s.[5] With the demise of the Cold War construct as a governing mentality, a redefinition of national security discourse ensued.[6] Drug abuse became a bipartisan issue on which there was a much less predictable alignment of left or right.

Drug abuse, alcohol abuse, and child abuse are considered definitive valence issues. Those who differ from prevailing views on these topics are easily discredited as "un-American." Communities of experts can easily cast aspersion on those who dissent from the "uniformly agreed-upon" definition of such problems.[7] Additionally, the "creation of long-lasting and powerful institutions that continue to focus on the problem even decades after public concern has died down" makes dissent more difficult.[8] Those who are experts in the eyes of the state dominate official thinking on the problem and prevail symbolically and practically. Drug policy is an unusual valence issue because of a long-standing agreement to disagree among the experts charged with its control.

Domestic drug policy is divided into two modes of regulation—criminalization and medicalization. Each mode is based on the model of addiction as either a "crime" or a "disease."[9] Based on a market model, U.S. drug policy assumes that drug use is a matter of individual consumer preference, and that pricing the commodity high enough will deter use. The market logic directs drug policy toward reducing supply or demand, delimiting use from abuse, and, more recently, protecting third parties against harms associated with drug use and traffic. Despite different effects, both law enforcement and medical or related public health perspectives buy into the market logic. Thus attempts to reduce supply alternate with attempts to reduce "demand," the individualized and commodified desire to consume illicit drugs.[10] Demand falls to a therapeutic complex comprised of multidisciplinary medical and social services. All antidrug agencies, regardless of their orientation, have expanded since their inception. They have expanded at different rates, however, with public health aspects such as education, prevention, and treatment remaining underfunded relative to law enforcement (especially if the costs of incarceration are factored into the equation).

Ongoing tensions between law enforcement proponents and public welfare advocates have yielded distinct forms of expert knowledge, tactics, and strategies that inform the ideological and institutional division of labor currently exemplified by the Drug Enforcement Agency (DEA) and the National Institute of Drug Abuse (NIDA), part of the National Institutes of Health (NIH). The agencies appear opposed to one another in spirit and purpose. The division of labor was instituted in response to a bifurcation of authority and expertise. Drug addiction research and treatment were the province of the United States Public Health Service (USPHS) from the 1930s until the mid-1950s, when the National Institute of Mental Health (NIMH) assumed jurisdiction over the "disease."

Institutionalized within multiple agencies that appear arrayed against each other to respond to very different needs, the market model arose out of a shared historical context or "episteme." Both the treatment apparatus and law enforcement operationalize similar conceptions of individual behavior and personal responsibility that keep U.S. drug policy in place—and ineffective. In the 1980s the emphasis on the individual demand was translated into public policy. Policymakers sought to change individual behavior under the rubric of "demand reduction"—not to reduce the endemic violence of the drug trade or to improve the economic infrastructure colonized by it. Drug policy is widely acknowledged as a failed set of fragmented policies that escalate that which they seek to diminish.[11] Scholarly examinations of drug policy note that public and policy-makers' response to illicit drug use "cannot be explained by the severity of the problem itself."[12] Acknowledging their frustration at the impotence of the "war on drugs"—the central organizing metaphor for U.S. drug control policy—policymakers devised new modes of intervention aimed to change the behaviors and desires of individuals who used illicit drugs.[13] While evidence mounts that U.S. drug policy is seriously flawed, it has proven immune to charges of failure. This immunity stems from the utility of illicit drug policy in reinforcing class- and race-based social divisions.

"Harm-reduction" drug policy arose as an alternative to criminalization and medicalization. Proponents of harm reduction recognize that drug use will inevitably occur, and advocate small, pragmatic steps to reduce its "collateral damage."[14] Contentious in the United States, harm-reduction measures have gained international support among communities concerned with illicit drug use and HIV/AIDS transmission.[15] Needle exchange is a classic harm-reduction tactic, proven to reduce levels of HIV transmission among intravenous drug users (IVDUs) yet castigated for "condoning" drug use. Attempts to implement harm reduction illustrate an important feature of drug policy. The federal government steers clear of policy decisions such as needle exchange, but local decisions depend on the knowledge and politics circulating in a particular locale—there are successful needle exchanges and unsuccessful ones. Harm-reduction advocates must overcome the very governing mentalities that I foreground, especially the consistent "othering" of drug addicts.

Gender and Drug Policy

Each policy mode implicates women, but they were not prioritized as a "target population" in domestic drug policy until demand reduction came into vogue. Although women are not the majority of drug addicts in the United States, their rates of illicit drug use have escalated, and the strategic interpretation of women's needs, desires, instincts, and the values they embody in political theater played a part in the demand-versus-supply struggle. Policy-makers claimed that increased substance abuse among women represented a novel condition on the horizon of history. The debate centered on how to control women's demand more effectively rather than raising deeper questions about women's empowerment and their responsibilities for social reproduction. Instead of promoting equity, demand reduction led to highly symbolic prosecutions.

Women who use illicit drugs are widely figured as failures of democracy, femininity, and maternity. They are represented as more socially isolated, degraded, and stigmatized even by drug-addicted male subjects.[16] This book explains why through a rereading of drug policy history that reveals how cultural attitudes structure the nation's drug laws. Women's political autonomy is contested, contained, and infringed in the drug policy arena.[17] High rates of addiction among socially subordinated groups raise questions about the social effects of structures of exclusion, disenfranchisement, and marginalization.

Women's advocates—including state-centered or "liberal" feminists and treatment professionals—have criticized punitive drug policy with some success. By defining the problem of prenatal drug exposure as a "women's issue," feminists "reshaped efforts to criminalize drug use by pregnant women as a broader attack on women's autonomy and, especially, their reproductive rights."[18] The feminist consensus against prosecution emerged as a singular exception to the American bias against harm-reduction drug policy.[19] Feminists recognized that expanding women's political empowerment, autonomy, and economic equality could lessen the inroads of addiction and mitigate some of the effects of the "war on drugs."

As women's behaviors came under scrutiny and sanction, women were blamed for producing the very circumstances that actually demonstrate that women are harder hit by the failures of the U.S. government to control drug trafficking or to provide treatment. The number of women who seek treatment but cannot obtain it bears out the persistent calls for gender-specific treatment modes raised by those who work directly with addicted women. For decades, activists, researchers, and program administrators have campaigned for women's increased access to treatment, development of gender-specific treatment modalities, and attention to gender-specific barriers to treatment, such as lack of child care or transportation. There is much to applaud in the belated recognition that gender matters, as attention to gender specificity emerged in clinical applications and addiction research. However, the mode of attention also matters.

Women are increasingly involved with the criminal justice system due to the "war on drugs," despite evidence that punishment does not deter and "zero tolerance" is not successful policy. Harm reduction is no panacea for women, because they are blamed for harm to third parties (often before birth) and understood as primary conduits for harm to children. Thus policies that do not explicitly attend to women's rights, well-being, and autonomy could have the adverse consequences of rendering drug-using women vulnerable to legal interventions that may well offset the good of medical attention. Prenatal care is an indisputable good for any and all pregnant women, regardless of their drug-use practices. But if a poor woman presents for prenatal or obstetric care, she runs the risk of heightened state scrutiny into her drug-using practices. Poor women, who are disproportionately women of color in the United States, are unevenly subject to all drug policy modes including surveillance. This suggests that drug-related harms take place in conditions of social constraint. Women's vulnerability to institutional coercion should be calculated and addressed by taking constraints into account. The harms to which we attend are political matters.

Blaming individual women for the effects of decades of bad social policy displaces responsibility and leads policy-makers down dead-end paths to short-sighted reforms. We have done little to alleviate individual or collective pain and everything to produce the current dimensions of drug problems. I consider the potential of feminist policy studies for solving these problems in Chapter 2, which lays out a theory of how state formation and the policy-making process are gendered and raced, and the cultural and political implications of that differential.

Contentions over drug policy are popularly construed as a polarization between legalization, decriminalization, treatment and/or public health, and criminalization. This poorly maps the possibilities for public discourse on the drug policy debate. Both legalization and decriminalization mask a range of policies beneath words that appear to subsume the nuances of each to a "free market" free-for-all. Many legalization and decriminalization proposals call for further regulation and tighter controls over most (but not all) currently illicit substances.[20] Calls for legalization, criminalization, or a public health framework are calls for different *modes of regulation*, each of which invokes a different set of "facts" and "values," expertise and experience. Part I is about the intersections and divergences between modes of social and political regulation—how they came to be, what they have to do with cultural figurations of drug use and drug users, and how they can be changed.

Containing Equality
Biology and Vulnerability

The Science of Susceptibility
Vulnerable Abusers

Social justice concerns—the exploration of women's economic, political, and social vulnerability—are displaced by the emphasis on biological and endocrinological activity. Gender-specific drug research investigates women's greater "biological vulnerability" to addiction by studying interactions between sex hormones and neurotransmitters.[1] Biological reductionism prevents us from attending to questions of value, judgment, and bias in gender-specific research and treatment, and obscures other social formations—race, ethnicity, sexuality, and class—that intersect with gender in both the experience of addiction and scientific research. Gender difference is conflated with biological sexual difference in recent gender-specific studies on the pharmacological effects of illicit drugs.

These studies are the type of research that feminist scholars of science have subjected to substantive critique.[2] Feminists have criticized numerous studies in a variety of fields in which men were the "steady state" to which women were compared. Once preoccupied with pregnancy and fetal development, drug studies now focus on developing gender-specific drug treatment modalities. "Although issues related to childbearing and child-rearing are still important areas of drug abuse research, researchers are questioning whether treatment strategies that were developed through research conducted largely on male subjects are appropriate for women."[3] The studies concentrate on metabolic differences between men and women, which apparently make a more credible case that women's needs differ from men's than sociological demonstrations that addicted women suffer greater social exclusion, stigma, and isolation than male addicts. The question arises: Is it possible to recognize that addicted women face gender-specific problems without reducing them to matters of individual metabolism?

The exclusive focus on women's biological vulnerability yields problematic findings. Consider a recent NIDA-funded study by Scott E. Lukas at the Harvard-affiliated Alcohol and Drug Abuse Research Center.[4] The study found that cocaine affects men and women differently because "hormonal fluctuations play an important role in women's responses to the drug." Performed on only six volunteers from each gender, the study neglected race, previous drug experience, or social location—anything other than gender that might have made a difference in the results. Male subjects were tested once; females were tested at two stages of their menstrual cycles. Both times the women were tested, they showed lower blood levels of cocaine and higher levels of cocaine metabolites than the men, despite receiving equivalent doses relative to body weight. The interpretation of this finding was that women were "much less sensitive" to cocaine. Curiously, men were not "much more sensitive" despite more rapid effects and "significantly more episodes of euphoria, or good feelings, and dysphoria, or bad feelings" than women. Women were not, say, "better at metabolizing cocaine"—their "decreased sensitivity" was a liability. Because women needed more cocaine to achieve the "same effect as men," women "could be more vulnerable to relapse at different points in their [menstrual] cycle." Craving and withdrawal fluctuated for women because "the response to cocaine will be different at different times of the month and not a steady state as it is for men," according to Elizabeth Rahdert, a research psychologist at the NIDA Division of Clinical and Services Research. Men's hormones also fluctuate, but no reason was offered for the presumption that male cycles would be any less significant. Testing women twice and men once built into the experimental protocol an unexamined assumption of gender difference as a biological vulnerability. This assumption then emerged tautologically as a "finding."

Treatment and research are limited by practical and ethical bounds; funding decisions are often made on the basis of extramural concerns. If women metabolize cocaine differently from men, the question is what we make of that difference. What can addiction science tell us about our social values and ethical commitments? Answering these questions requires a deeper reading of how scientific constructions of addiction are used in drug policy discourse and in social interactions between networks of experts, addicts, and policy-makers. The remainder of this chapter is an analysis of an influential report, *Substance Abuse and the American Woman* (1996), issued by the National Center on Addiction and Substance Abuse (CASA) at Columbia University.[5] The report represents "mainstream" addiction discourse at the end of the twentieth century, purporting to be a compendium of all "scientific" knowledge, despite its exclusive focus on research that yielded identifiable gender differences achieved through a restricted range of research protocols.[6] The text is replete with examples of how drug discourses reduce political claims in force and scope to an exclusive focus on women's biological vulnerability.

The CASA report is a selective meta-analysis of more than 1,700 scientific and technical articles, surveys, government documents, and books. It claims to be the "first comprehensive assessment of the impact on women of all substance abuse—illegal drugs, alcohol, tobacco, and prescription drugs." CASA is a high-profile, media-savvy organization headed by Joseph A. Califano, Jr., former Secretary of Health, Education, and Welfare during the Carter administration. James Burke, chair of the Partnership for a Drug-Free America, initially approached Califano to head the research center, which is financed by the Robert Wood Johnson Foundation and affiliated with Columbia University.[7] The board of directors spans labor and the corporate sector, including luminaries Betty Ford and Nancy Reagan. Corporate donors ranging from Disney to Mobil Oil fund the organization. As a nongovernmental entity that exerts a form of quintessentially postmodern power, CASA attempts to control the terms of political discourse through textual mediation and publicity. As enclaves of expertise, entities like CASA are useful to state actors such as those I consider in Chapter 2, but conduct their cultural work in ways that reach "beyond the state."

The "Wrong Way" to Equality

"Substance abuse" serves as a condensation symbol among those who argue for a medical approach.[8] The concept signals that biomedicine will be narrowly privileged, but that all licit or illicit, presently or potentially used "substances" can be considered. Anything can serve as a "substance"—compulsive use determines whether a thing or an activity such as exercise is "addictive" or not. Repetitive activities such as commuting or assembly-line work are not addictive—they are "productive." Repetitive sexual activity, eating, television watching, reading, or exercise are addictive—they are "consumptive." Expanding the definition of what counts as a drug could yield insight into the social context and cultural meanings attributed to addictive activities. Instead, such activities are studied to see how they change brain chemistry by altering the flow of information via neurotransmitters. Neurophysiological changes are an increasingly important component of our narratives about addiction. However, the capacity to make valid neurophysiological claims does not reduce the importance of social and cultural claims. Rather, empirical claims provide grist for the cultural and political mill.

The CASA report calls for a "women's agenda for substance abuse research," meaning prevention and treatment programs targeted at specific factors that place women and girls at higher risk for illicit drug use.[9] These feminine factors include widespread sexual abuse, "the overriding importance women attach to being thin," "stress or sexual dysfunction," and the "likelihood that girls are more responsive to peer pressure than boys."[10] Women's symptoms are "inner-directed—depression, anxiety, and low self-esteem," hidden by "intense shame." The early pages of the report supply a set of assumptions about femininity as a cultural condition and how it produces a gender-specific form of substance abuse in women and girls. This unprecedented degree of attention to gender specificity appears to vindicate feminist advocates of drug-using women.[11] However, the call for a "women's agenda" is not a call for a feminist agenda, as is illustrated by the following quote from the report's conclusion:

> Effective prevention and treatment of substance abuse and addiction among women requires eroding the special stigma of the female alcoholic and addict without suggesting that the risks of smoking, alcohol abuse, and illicit drug abuse among women and men are alike. . . . With preventive education about women's greater susceptibility to the consequences of alcohol and drugs and the potential harm to the fetus of such use during pregnancy, we can preserve cultural attitudes that maintain differences in female and male drinking norms and fully inform women about the risks they take when they smoke cigarettes, abuse alcohol, and use drugs. For women, the path to equality may offer equal access to the tragic consequences of substance abuse and addiction. But they do not have to go as willing victims. With effective prevention strategies they do not have to go at all.[12]

According to this position, the preservation of gender-differentiated social and behavioral norms would prevent women from becoming "like men" and taking the "wrong way" to equality.

By focusing on women's biological susceptibility and fetal harm, the CASA report narrows expansive feminist claims for social justice to a thin demand for woman-centered treatment. The preface sets up an analogy between "equality" and "addiction" that suggests that American women are closing the "gender gap" in both the best and worst of ways. The "best" ways appear as stable and productive forms of middle-class employment—American women are "filling posts as corporate officers, law firm partners, doctors, academics and in other professions once not open to them."[13] Yet women are also becoming "like men" "in the worst of ways,"[14] destabilizing the nation by threatening the preserves of gender difference. The "women's agenda" sets out to nurture and positively value gender differences and biological vulnerabilities.

Pursuing equality leads to addiction; accepting gender difference is the key to avoiding it. According to CASA, the pursuit of equality has made women as likely to abuse substances as are men—but women get drunk, addicted, and diseased much sooner. "In substance abuse and addiction, women are represented not as having come a 'long way' but as having come the wrong way."[15] The "gender gap" is typically used to analyze and represent differences between male and female political behavior. Widening gender gaps metaphorically suggest that women are becoming "mature" or "independent" political actors. The CASA report indicates that women are becoming less mature, less law-abiding, and less conforming to gendered social expectations: too much equality too fast is generating addictive behavior in women.

Substance Abuse and the American Woman advises prevention and treatment programs to take into account "the ways in which a woman is not like a man,"[16] and prevent the further collapse of gender distinctions in U.S. society. The report paints "equality" as especially troubling in adolescents: "Girls and boys are often indistinguishable in their rates of drug and alcohol use."[17] Once it was considered unlikely that women would become regular drug users because they were "more mature and less vulnerable to the temptation and pressure to smoke and get high or drunk."[18] By the 1990s, girls emerged as the more impressionable group: "girls and boys are now wading into drugs, alcohol, and tobacco at the same early ages."[19] The CASA report identifies both social change and biological vulnerability as catalysts for women's addiction, but emphasizes the need for changes in women's behavior toward men and children to solve it. The idea that changing gender roles, familial or sexual arrangements, or other aspects of social transformation generate increased addiction among women—who in turn relay it to others—underlies the logic of blame. Under this formulation, "woman-centered treatment" begins to look like the training ground for gender-normative behavior and cultural conservatism.

To its credit, the CASA report attempts to counter wrongheaded stereotypes about addiction. The report criticizes addiction research for hiding substance abuse among whites and the upper and middle classes while exposing the addiction of low-income, primarily African-American women. White and/or middle-class patterns of drug use are widely represented as less problematic and persistent than those of low-income persons of color, a disparity that creeps into addiction research. By contrast, CASA reports that white women are more likely to use drugs and alcohol than women of color.[20] Yet the report also states that white women are more likely to "use," while black women are more likely to "abuse."[21] Similarly, working women's drug use concerns the authors more than that of women who work only within their homes. The visibility of women's substance abuse shifts relative to patterns of social change. Once women confined to the private sphere were the problem; today it is women's participation in the public sphere that is questioned.

The policy distinction between licit and illicit drugs also comes under criticism, as CASA documents the "complex and common reality" that more newborns are "Virginia Slims babies, Newport babies, . . . beer babies, wine babies or other alcohol babies" than "crack babies."[22] While researchers have been largely unsuccessful in isolating the effects of particular drugs on babies, nicotine and alcohol are the most widely used drugs during pregnancy. The licit/illicit divide is racialized: according to CASA, African-American women are twice as likely as white women to use illicit drugs while pregnant, but pregnant white women were more likely to use licit drugs.[23] Despite the message that licit drugs can be just as harmful, the perception that illicit drugs are more harmful exerts a powerful pull in the social context in which these messages are decoded. The idea that illicit drugs "cause" social problems and licit drugs "solve" them is a major governing mentality encoded in racial patterns of use and abuse.

A "women's agenda" might situate women's drug use in the context of women's subordination and social constraint. This outcome is unlikely, as CASA's research agenda explains the root of substance abuse among women in the following ways:

- women's vanity—weight concerns, the pursuit of glamour, and the "culture of thinness";
- women's greater biological and endocrinological vulnerability;
- women's inability to handle the stress of employment;
- age and/or widowhood;
- racial-ethnic differences that result in different patterns of use and "attitudes toward treatment."

These causal explanations generate research "needs," such as the need to assess the long-term damage of prenatal exposure; the need to assess the role of maternal drug abuse in child abuse and neglect; and the need to assess which treatment and prevention strategies "work." The list presumes much about the causes of women's drug use as well as interpretations of what drug-using women "need" and who they are. Widowed and adolescent women who are not attached to men emerged as at "high risk," their vanity their main risk factor. Heterosexual marriage appeared to militate against substance abuse by making women less concerned with appearance and taking them off the "sexual auction block."[24] This heterocentric bias pathologizes lesbian and bisexual women, whose sexual orientation appears as a causal factor for substance use and abuse.[25] CASA's agenda normalizes a particular type of womanhood and womanly virtue. A reader gains the distinct impression that addiction would not be a "woman's issue" if all women behaved like white, middle-class, heterosexual, married mothers who resist the seductions of advertising and fashion, and accept their bodily appearance and station in life. These social concerns are naturalized by the appeal to women's biological vulnerability. While the report focuses on women's natural susceptibility to addiction, much of the research summarized conveys social messages and cultural anxieties about what women ought to be and do.

"What's Use for Men Can Be Abuse for Women"
Falling into the "Gender Gap"

The CASA report asserts and stabilizes gender difference as a metabolic difference under the section heading: "What's Use for Men Can Be Abuse for Women."[26] The section emphasizes that the consequences of substance abuse "strike women with a special vengeance" of "magnum force" that exceeds all other forms of violence to which women might fall victim.[27] The force of physiological effects—metaphorically figured as a poisonous snake or natural disaster—naturalizes gender difference.[28] This claim also separates addiction from other forms of violence against women. While CASA speculates on a possible link between men's drug use and "spousal" violence, the center finds little exploration of this "extra-maternal factor" in the research. Rather, drug abuse is constructed as a form of violence that women commit against themselves and those closest to them. This section of the report also establishes an enormous distance between biomedical expertise and "what is known and acted upon by women, their husbands and friends, their doctors and other health professionals."[29] Women, the report implies, lacked knowledge about themselves and their bodies and fail to keep pace with biomedicine. Thus are women constructed in a state of denial and ignorance, and biomedicine positioned as the agent of enlightenment. Women fail to comprehend that "what's good for the gander may not help the goose."[30]

Popular culture, legal discourse, the scientific discourse of addiction research, and therapeutic discourse exhibit a series of assumptions about addicted women's characteristics and needs. "Different drug and alcohol combinations, such as alcohol and prescription drugs, or alcohol and cocaine, appear to characterize different populations of women."[31] "Targeted" prevention and treatment involve strategically modifying the mode of address to appeal to specific populations and gender differences in "risk factors, physiology, psychology, and patterns of abuse and addiction."[32] Drugs are not so much the targets as are the users, depicted as consumers whose desires can be manipulated through mechanisms developed for that purpose. Users are understood as gendered and raced in ways that make them unresponsive to "universal" interventions. Women, it seems, require that their specific needs and risk factors be acknowledged through an apparatus of difference and "cultural sensitivity." Difference has become a weapon in the "war on drugs."

Within the combat context, the metaphor of a strategic strike recalls the "smart bombs" of recent wars, which supposedly lacked the "side effects" of so-called collateral damage (although they have since been found to go astray of their marks). Similarly, Prozac, a "designed drug, sleek and high-tech," is a "tailored molecule" represented as potent and effective because it is "clean"—that is, specific in its effects.[33] Illicit drugs are portrayed as less specific and thus more difficult to control. The equation between specificity and potency is central to the illusion of effective control, implying a high degree of efficacy without invoking the negative associations of social engineering. This form of social control evokes the flexibility of post-Fordist economic strategies—not crude modernist conformity but the diversity of democracy-by-design. Consumers are understood to have specific desires and preferences according to which they "select" their "drug of choice." The drug-of-choice metaphor likens the changing demographics of drug use to fashion trends or fads. Women are represented as highly susceptible to such cycles, adjusting their preferences to embrace the drug of the moment and the always inevitable "next drug."[34]

The discourse of women "at risk" recognizes that women are "at risk" differently from men. For instance, a disproportionately high history of physical and sexual assault among girls and women who use illicit drugs suggests that the social context of violence plays a significant role in generating addiction. Risk factors such as mental health disorders (especially depression) or eating disorders are more prevalent in female addicts than in addicted men. Constructing these widespread social problems as individual "risk factors" removes them from the realm of accident to the realm of purpose. Such behaviors come to appear as if they were "calculated risks" that respond to an understanding of cause and effect.[35] The result is a "delirium of rationality":

> Not just those dangers that lie hidden away inside the subject, consequences of his or her weakness of will, irrational desires, or unpredictable liberty, but also the exogenous dangers, the exterior hazards from which the subject has not learned to defend himself or herself, alcohol, tobacco, bad eating habits, road accidents, various kinds of negligence and pollution, meteorological disasters, etc.[36]

Prevention is structured for those who "display whatever characteristics the specialists responsible for the definition of preventive policy have constituted as risk factors."[37] Risk, then, is that against which we have not yet learned to defend ourselves.

The CASA report cites an array of risk factors: biological sexual difference; the form of women's equality; domestic violence; child abuse and childhood sexual abuse; the "cultural bias towards thinness"; age, race, ethnicity, and marital status; women's greater susceptibility to peer pressure and advertisements; and the greater pitfalls of "work outside the home" for women. Nonmedical use or "misuse" of prescription drugs is prevalent among young, white, low-income women who are unemployed or working part-time; female addicts are "sicker" than male addicts and twice as likely to be unemployed.[38] Both employment and unemployment are risk factors for women; similarly, both employment and receipt of public assistance place women at risk. Women's substance abuse is said to "trigger" substantial health care and welfare costs, despite the lower proportion of health care spending on that item among women relative to that among men. (In 1995, it comprised $68 billion or 12.3% of all health care spending for women, compared to $72 billion or 19.2% in men.) According to CASA estimates, 20 percent of women on Aid to Families with Dependent Children (AFDC) are "frequent binge drinkers or regular drug users," behaviors that "trap" them on welfare.[39] Using more stringent criteria from the *Diagnostic and Statistical Manual of Mental Disorders* (DSM-IV), the National Institute on Alcohol Abuse and Alcoholism (NIAAA) found that the percentage of substance abusers among welfare recipients was "virtually identical" to the percentage in the general population.[40]

The CASA report typifies the differences between a "woman's agenda" and a "feminist agenda" in its insistence that the changing conditions of women's lives—including those for which feminists pushed—were "risk factors." By representing addiction as an obstacle to women's otherwise unfettered progress out of the home and into the workplace,[41] the report states that women are moving in the wrong direction, taking the "wrong way."[42] While social change has "given [women] unprecedented opportunities," it has also "planted land mines on their road to success."[43] The report rebuts earlier claims that women in "traditional gender roles" were at higher risk for substance abuse, a feminist claim designed to curb tranquilizer use among middle-class white women.[44] Indeed, the CASA report leads readers to question whether women should be working outside the home at all. Rather than address gender discrimination, the "wage gap," or occupational segregation as precipitants of women's addiction, CASA calls for a wholesale reassessment of the "stress and benefits of employment" for women. The figure of the drug-abusing housewife is rendered as quaint as the notion that housewives need "liberation."[45]

The claim that women's demands for equality generate "gender role conflict" or "identity confusion" and so propel women into addiction recurs with remarkable regularity. In the early 1970s, licit and illicit drugs were portrayed as "the subtle betrayer of the feminine mystique."[46] Addiction discouraged women from cultivating the mature femininity necessary to adapt to rapid change in cultural norms and too much freedom:

> With the emphasis on sexual equality, there is an increasing acceptance of drugs by females, for they, too, seek subjective experiences. Therefore, the housewife who chain smokes, equates "figure" with reducing pills, cures "tension headaches" with tranquilizers, relies on an afternoon cocktail to get her through the day, or relieves "blues" by barbiturates is as much an addict as the adolescent girl who thrives on marijuana or the more severely addicted narcotics user.[47]

According to this logic, the once-hidden addictions of middle- and upper-class women were caused by repetitive and conflicting female roles. The CASA report is merely the most recent statement of the idea that social transformation generates addiction in women. It is significant because it places women's biological vulnerability at the root of their social nonadaptability.

Iconic representations of women's "equality," such as cigarette smoking, come under severe criticism in the CASA report, which castigated advertisers for depicting smoking as a "sign of spunk," trumpeting the link between thinness and smoking, and "add[ing] to the rebellious spirit of the independent woman who might flout the evidence that nicotine is addictive and deadly."[48] CASA couched its counternarrative as biological revenge—osteoporosis will rob women of the very independence they thought they gained through smoking. Women's misplaced priorities were at fault: "Many female smokers clearly care more about their appearance than health."[49] This mistake backfires as "smoker's face"—the "lines or wrinkles, gaunt facial features, grayish skin, and a plethoric complexion" found among 46 percent of smokers. Women who erroneously thought alcohol was sexy were "more likely to get breast cancer, to be infertile, and to suffer violent abuse at the hands of their partners."[50] Adolescent girls who drank were more likely "to attempt suicide, to have sex and have it without a condom, which can lead to unplanned pregnancies and STDs such as AIDS and gonorrhea."[51]

Advertisers' seductive fictions lure women into such illusions—yet women are also cast as unable to resist these messages. Once a target of feminist activists, advertising is now construed as a major threat to women's health. The Second Wave feminist critique of the "objectification" of women, however, once accompanied a left critique of the profit margins of pharmaceutical companies and the women's health movement's focus on doctor-patient relations. Absent the materialist critique, women and girls are represented as individually susceptible to the seductions to which they should be more immune. Girls and women are "particularly reliant on what they learn from [the] media," and more responsive to it than men: "Teenage girls are often obsessed by weight. The desire to be thin motivates girls far more than boys."[52] Individual women's enthrallment to fashion is also a culprit in women's increased substance abuse. CASA advises women's magazines to "take more responsibility" in breaking "their own addiction to tobacco advertising revenue," and suggests the fashion industry "ease off its adulation of social x-ray thinness and display [its] wares on healthier women."[53] The feminine propensity to internalize these images directly threatens women's health. By constructing women as not only biologically vulnerable but also cultural dupes, the gender-specific drug discourse of the CASA report contains rather than advances feminist work. Drug discourses work as discourses of containment through which expansive political claims are bounded in scope or reduced in force.

A Window on Women's Addiction

Before women's addiction emerged as a public problem, it was largely viewed as "hidden": "A woman's substance abuse has traditionally been tucked behind the curtains of private homes while a man's is often a public event at bars, athletics events, and fraternity parties."[54] CASA understood that health care professionals and family members might not recognize the "markers of female substance abuse," mistaking these "signs" for emotional disturbances.[55] The difficulty of diagnosing women is due to gender differences in the display and performance of addiction: "Friends, accustomed to seeing the public displays of male abuse, such as crime and violence, often overlook developing inner-directed symptoms among women."[56] Families might discourage women from seeking treatment; physicians might "miss" the signs of addiction due to their patients' duplicity.[57] This picture contrasts with studies that show physicians overlook the signs of addiction in white women, but not in women of color.[58] Racial difference translates into varying capacities to keep the public/private divide intact.

Pregnancy is portrayed throughout the CASA report as a moment when the "hiddenness" of women's addiction is suspended and a "window of opportunity" opens: "The origins, patterns and consequences of substance abuse are different—often far more devastating—for women than for men. What motivates a woman to seek—or not to seek—treatment is likely to be different from what motivates a man."[59] Thus pregnancy is used to make the case that public policy should recognize that women's needs differ from men's, despite the "grim consequence" that "women who smoke, abuse alcohol, and use illegal drugs like men, will die like men who smoke, abuse alcohol and use illegal drugs—from cancers and heart disease, from violence and AIDS."[60] Men and women also comprehend the causes and consequences of drug use differently: women report "internal and personal correlates," while men cite "outer-directed problems, such as trouble at work, financial difficulty, or drunk-driving arrests."[61] These differences find their way into behavior: girls are depressed or suicidal while boys act out.[62] The internal nature of women's addiction makes it "harder to nip in the bud or recognize, given the lower visibility of the problem."[63] The spectacular quality of masculine addiction contrasts with the more muted quality of feminine addiction. Gender differences in "expression" are represented as women's learned responses to the higher levels of social stigma and the harsher "truths of addiction, illness, violence, and death" they face.

The political consequences of the presumptions and conclusions of the CASA report are best seen in light of the construction of addiction as an effect of social change. Readers gain a clear sense that women's biological vulnerability innately inclines them toward substance abuse. The nagging sense that social change exacerbates these innate factors is implicit. Drugs are positioned as agents of social change that force the reconsideration of women's rights in relation to "human service delivery" systems (prevention, treatment, adoption, foster care, and orphanages).[64] Larger political claims are deflected through intense scrutiny of women's behavior, which throws their rights into doubt and strains the very systems established to assist them. Significantly absent are policy proposals to strengthen women's economic security, access to child care, health care, and insurance, or reproductive rights. These are women whose unhealthy habits cost too much: *Substance Abuse and the American Woman* estimates the health and social welfare costs of women's substance abuse at $10 billion annually.

Women who turn to licit or illicit drug use are figured as ill equipped for the demands, risks, and "mixed messages" that result from cultural ambivalence toward women's "proper" or "traditional" roles.[65] Women's drug use (licit and illicit) has been consistently linked to changing gender performance expectations since the 1950s, as illustrated by Figure 3. The accompanying text emphasized the pressure of social change on this coed and prescribed an antianxiety drug to relieve feelings of insecurity and oversensitivity to "unstable national and world conditions." The drug would channel the student's energy into more efficient and productive activities—coping with everyday problems rather than larger issues. A licit antianxiety drug would enable women to respond to their new freedoms without resorting to illicit drugs. As the CASA would put it three decades later, "Women, far more frequently than men, point to a specific life crisis as a precipitator. . . . The problems most frequently cited are those which threaten their role as wife and mother. . . ."[66] Women's addiction is constructed as the product of individual women's inability to cope with changing versions of normative femininity.

Veiled once by invisibility, women's addiction is now viewed through the heavily tinted windows of pregnancy and normative femininity. The social stigma that addicted women experience is portrayed as a direct attack on the very core of their feminine identity. Anxious to avoid the assault, addicted women use gendered tactics such as secrecy, duplicity, and deviousness. CASA views these tactics as futile because women's biological susceptibility and physiological markers will eventually give them away. Finally, women's addiction is represented as more complicated than men's due to the sheer "complexity of the moral, ethical, and legal questions raised by women's substance abuse and addictions—questions our nation has not considered sufficiently."[67] Complicated by women's hormones, gender politics, and psychological attributes, the complexity of women's drug use is mirrored by its constructed simplicity among men.

Drug Policy and Social Justice

The discursive arena in which the CASA report performs its cultural work is also an arena for the containment of women's legitimate claims for rights and freedoms

A Whole New World... **of Anxiety**

The new college student
may be afflicted by
a sense of lost identity
in a strange environment.

Today's changing morality
and the possible consequences of
her "new freedom" may provoke
acute feelings of insecurity.

She may be excessively
concerned over competition
—both male and female—
for top grades; unrealistic
parental expectations
may further increase
emotional tension.

Her newly stimulated
intellectual curiosity may make
her more sensitive to and
apprehensive about unstable
national and world conditions.

Exposure to new friends
and other influences
may force her to reevaluate
herself and her goals.

Figure 3   Advertisement for antianxiety drug, 1969.

Courtesy of Hoffman-LaRoche Inc.

extended to reproduction, freedom from assault and abuse, and freedom from discrimination. Women's claims for equality and political autonomy are contained by constructions of women's unique biological vulnerabilities. A drug policy based on the principles of social justice does not naturalize sexual difference as a form of vulnerability. Instead, the recognition that women face economic insecurity and social vulnerability due to their uneven responsibility for social reproduction should be translated into a socially just drug policy. Such a drug policy would not be focused solely on drugs but would be cognizant of the need for a transformed economic and political geography in the terrain now colonized by the illicit drug economy. Until this nation prioritizes those who are politically vulnerable and economically marginalized, drug treatment and prevention will remain underfunded stopgap measures directed toward normalization. Until then, "women-centered treatment" rests on flawed premises about who women essentially are, how they should behave, and what labors they ought to perform.

Governing Mentalities
Reading Political Culture

Politicizing Policy Studies
Knowing Experts: Feminism and the Sociology of Knowledge

Illicit drug policy became a domain of feminist thought and action as it began to impact vast numbers of women. Gender matters for understanding political discourse on drugs in the sense that women's drug use encodes broad anxieties about biological reproduction, child rearing, sexuality, and the potential for social reproduction in a society composed of "impulsive selves." By tracing how the figures of drug use have been historically gendered, sexualized, and racialized, we can come to terms with who "we" have become as a public and from there work out who "we" want to be.[1] Feminist policy studies incorporates a variety of approaches designed to analyze how women get "used" in public policy—and how women might "use" public policy to achieve a fuller measure of social justice.

Political discourse is an interesting species of realist discourse that employs a rich set of narratives, tropes, and metaphors. Through the twin concepts of "discursive practice" and "governing mentalities,"[2] I will analyze the parade of tropic figures and the cascades of metaphors that we use to represent drug-using women in political discourse. "Tropics is the shadow from which all realistic discourse tries to flee. The flight, however, is futile; for tropics is the process by which all discourse constitutes the objects which it pretends only to describe realistically and to analyze objectively."[3] Drug discourse both embraces its tropic nature and represses the fantastic quality of its visions by cultivating the effect of realism.

We can learn something of ourselves—as policy-makers and witnesses, parents and children, teachers and students, activists and theoreticians, experts of the behavioral and biomedical sciences—from our governing mentalities, our fantastic figures, and the form and content of our policy negotiations. In this chapter, I introduce theories and methods to "read" law and policy as forms of cultural production that structure experience, interpretation, and reality. By placing historical and cultural studies in dialogic tension with policy studies, the governing mentalities emerge as the frames in which truth-claims make sense. The assumptions and images that compose the governing mentalities also structure the apparatus of knowledge production. Illicit drug policy is a prime arena for working out a conceptual framework to link knowledge production, cultural figuration, and the material effects of policy.

Feminists are engaged in rethinking the structure of democratic institutions through the analytic categories of gender, racial-ethnic formation, class, and sexuality. These power differentials affect women's lived experiences and shape the knowledge claims, interpretations, and images that find their way into public policy. Feminist theory takes both "materialist" and "figurative" form, an epistemic break that sometimes takes on the quality of a political schism. "Politics is not the mere effect of discourse," writes Kathleen Jones. "Talking about words will not make this reality go away. For most of the women and men in the world talking about, endless talking about, is all that has been forever."[4] Mere talk is counterposed to real power—legal systems, economic inequality, the military, or the police. Materialists contrast the fixity of structural inequality and the concrete knowledge of "those who have felt the state's inscription of rules on their bodies" to the fluidity of mere words and unreal knowledges—"fantasies of parodic floating signifiers."[5] Stubbornly realist, the materialist mode sometimes overlooks the very processes by which the state inscribes rules on bodies.

On the other hand, the theory of cultural figuration refuses the oversimplifying comforts of the material-discursive divide by emphasizing how practices of cultural figuration "organize interpretive practice" and create "performative images that can be inhabited."[6] Figures provide a metaphoric mechanism "through which people enroll each other in their realities."[7] "A figure collects up the people; a figure embodies shared meanings in stories that inhabit their audiences."[8] The governing mentalities inhabit "us." As material-semiotic hybrids they cannot be captured through analytic strategies that mistake the material for the simply real or the semiotic for the merely fantastic. Embodied in a series of figures, the governing mentalities guide the realist and rationalist discourses through which policy-makers approach their work.

Policy-makers are in the business of enrolling others in their realities—not only by way of technical reason, realism, and a staunch commitment to the "rationality project," but through persuasion. Public policy is made through a discursive negotiation between contending ideological positions, rhetorical figures, and material interests. Cultural representations and interpretations of value are as significant as positivist knowledge claims to the policy-making process. Making sense of this significance requires a conceptual framework that refuses to separate the material world from the symbolic, discursive, or narrative technologies that produce the categories and images with which we think. A feminist sociology of knowledge provides that framework, especially when joined with postpositivist policy analysis.

Postpositive Policy in a Positivist World

Public policy is both an instrument and an effect of power. It encompasses a range of texts and social practices that may be imposed from above but work more seamlessly by influencing how people govern themselves.[9] Good, self-governing subjects absorb the metaphors, rhetorical devices, gatekeeping practices, and narrative conventions integral to the policy-making process. This seemingly democratic process embeds the governing mentalities of some individuals and groups in policy while silencing others. The policy-making process restricts the knowledge claims that can be made, the problems that can be solved, and the solutions that can be offered. Once policy has been enacted and accepted, it becomes difficult to see it as a made thing, as a social construction, much less as a way of managing populations that systematically enfranchises some and disenfranchises others. Policy becomes part of the "self-evident" world, and social norms, "facts," and values are embedded within it.

The policies we pursue and the knowledge on which they are based tell us something about who we are as a polity. Basically, how we "know" drug addicts matters for how we govern them. Knowledge producers vary from social scientists to therapeutic professionals to addicts themselves. Their accounts are based on a positivist tradition in which the knowing subject largely disappears from the process of truth production. Knowledge claims are not granted truth status unless they are externalized: the knower cannot be too close to the known without suffering a loss of credibility, authority, and objectivity.[10] For knowledge to be useful to the projects of governance, it must be authoritative in positivist terms—based on sensory data but purged of all subjectivity, values, or recognition of power differences. Positivism conflates all knowledge with instrumental reason; knowledge cannot be too political, or it is "biased." This chapter centers on how ethics, images, and values enter knowledge production and the policy-making process in the form of the governing mentalities. I offer a conceptual framework for "reading" public policy in order to expand the theoretical repertoire of policy studies and to extend the range of feminist theory.

Bias inhabits value neutrality and objectivity—especially the "gender-neutral" structures of professional hierarchy and discursive authority. Feminist theory supplies a way to see how ethics and values enter knowledge production and knowledge-based policy-making. There is more going on in the policy-making process than meets the eye. Drug policy rests on a restricted form of technical reason that masks the phantasms percolating beneath its surface. Overreliance on narrow forms of technical expertise tends to obscure the effects of social context, undermining our capacity to change the circumstances that produce the drug problem — or to even imagine doing so. The flat voice of positivist social science can only mock the fantastic figures and mobilizing metaphors that form the cultural repository of images that inflect our policies. The governing mentalities work through gender-coded and racially marked structures and processes — policy is both their product and a means through which they guide and govern. The empirical and theoretical task of comprehending the governing mentalities requires a mode of analysis capable of mapping both the figural and realist dimensions of public policy. Together feminist theory and postpositivism form a powerful tool kit for illuminating the fields of social power in which knowing takes place.

Just as important as investigating the production of positivist knowledge claims is interrogating the uses to which they are put in political discourse. For example, rational claims are pitched to cultivate the effects of facticity, realism, and morality.[11] Discursive frameworks shape which facts are considered credible, and hence what policy alternatives are considered realistic.[12] Positivists treat the infiltration of factual claims by values as an annoying form of bias. By contrast, postpositivists seek to restore normative values within the projects of reason and thus share common ground with feminists seeking politically useful hybrids of "fact" and "value."

Feminist philosopher Mary E. Hawkesworth reminds us that positivism draws a false dichotomy between "fact" and "value," sorting knowledge and values into separate spheres.[13] The feminist critique of the dominant form of positivist objectivity has opened the way for a "stronger" objectivity.[14] Similarly, postpositivists emphasize the limits of technocratic decision-making by contrasting it to social constructionist theories of knowledge, dialectical modes of argument, and interpretive methods that expand what is taken into account.[15] Both feminism and postpositivism integrate normative claims and interrogate basic assumptions in ways that positivism forecloses, thus generating complex hybrids of "fact" and "value" better suited to achieving democratic goals. Feminist science studies, sociology of knowledge, and rhetorical studies of science offer model investigations of the interplay between knowledge production, politics, and cultural figuration.[16] This work, like mine, takes seriously the need for fulsome accounts of the dynamic social and historical processes at work in the culture of knowledge production and knowledge-based policy-making.

A feminist postpositivism would differ from the "relativism" of which postpositivist analysts often stand accused. Normative commitments form the basis for a multivocal feminist ethics that slips neither into relativism nor moral absolutism. For instance, feminists recognize that the gendered materiality of suffering and subordination may work through cultural forms of representation or actual policies that harm vulnerable groups. As a "pedagogy of suffering," an analysis of gendered materiality is an "antidote to administrative systems that cannot take suffering into account because they are abstracted from the needs of bodies. When the body's vulnerability and pain are kept in the foreground, a new social ethic is required. The challenge is to state this ethic in terms that remain multivocal. A multivocal ethic does not imply relativism; it suggests the recognition of difference . . . the need to recognize multiple voices and afford each full legitimacy."[17] Multivocality is partly the product of a postmodern moment that has strained many modern administrative systems, in which many voices speak multiple and conflicting stories from myriad social locations. However, multivocality is also the outcome of the hard work of social movements organized to compel the recognition of cultural difference within modernity. Therein lies the potential of postmodernity as a paradigm for social action and theory that promotes democratic participation.

Feminists are dedicated to discerning, defining, and changing structures of exclusion, marginalization, social isolation, and subordination based on gender wherever and however they occur.[18] By attending to how social structures, cultural practices, and discursive formations impinge on individuals, they cast the desirability of much policy into doubt. For example, although we might "know" that some drugs harm the developing human fetus, we can also see that pregnant women do not maliciously intend such harm. Thus we could conclude that supportive social policies—such as universal health insurance—better facilitate healthy births, and might decide that our democratic goals and responsibilities are better met through such measures. We would be forced to reconsider our current reliance on incarceration as a response to the widespread use of illicit substances in the U.S. population. Incarceration would no longer accord with our values or our facts, and thus could no longer be considered a viable solution. It might even come to be seen as a form of irrational vengeance that is counterproductive to our goals.

Postpositivist policy analysis derives its justification from its capacity to illuminate the contentious and figurative dimensions of policy questions, to explain how some policy debates have become "intractable," to identify defects in "self-evident" assumptions and arguments, and to elucidate the implications of contending prescriptions. By systematically scrutinizing the assumptions that sustain perception, cognition, facticity, evidence, explanation, and argument, postpositivist policy analysis surpasses positivism because more is examined and less is assumed.[19] Postpositivist policy analysis provides more useful answers to the questions of why and how policy problems are constituted and the cultural uses to which they are put because it better fits the field of social relations in which policy-making takes place.

Policy-makers are no more but no less subject to the governing mentalities than those they seek to govern. Their agency, too, is produced, constrained, and sustained by the structures and discursive formations through which they become political subjects. For the most part they are not intentionally misinformed, malicious, or out to blame women for all social problems. Rather, they act within a set of discursive structures specific to their elite status, ideological affiliation, and social location. Individuals may resist or reinforce the episteme in which they are embedded, but they cannot act outside it. The cultural practices of figuration shape the governing mentalities by which we know and navigate our social worlds. If diverse populations were better represented among policy-makers and their advisers, the cultural frames of reference invoked might possibly shift to resist prevailing social codes and ways of thinking. Such a shift would not inevitably follow, however, because the differences between policy-makers are political differences—they are differences of analysis and interpretation, attitude and belief, political judgment, and ethics and moral values.

Policy-making is contentious, speculative, and incremental. Because policy-makers cannot know the effects of their work in advance, they must rely on experts, nongovernmental organizations, public perceptions, and the media to decide which problems are worth working out—and what solutions to propose. These actors seek to control the range of possibilities through a process of knowledge production, distribution, and consumption. Thus epistemological and ethical questions are embedded in the work of policy-making as surely as political calculations. It is the job of feminist and postpositivist analysts to raise and answer these questions.

Rationalizing Risk and Blame: Narrative, Confabulation, and Definition

Domestic drug policy centers on preventing or reforming individual behaviors such as demand for drugs, childbearing, or sexual practices. The narratives of drug discourse do not proceed as simple discussions of "fact," but instead assess the moral and symbolic value of particular paths and patterns of risk and blame. These stories must achieve the rhetorical effect of realism—"facts" must overshadow the values and images they inflect. Facts change—there is always a "next drug," a set of emergent harms, a more alarming group of users, a cyclic sense of urgency, and new numeric confabulations to document the escalation of drug use beyond the controls designed to contain it. Policy narratives contain these elements but are especially concerned with identifying "cause," defining the problem, and quantifying its current scope.

Counting is a form of classification. Numbers work as metaphors, selecting and tallying one feature in order to draw analogies between unlike things.[20] For example, perinatologist Ira Chasnoff's extrapolation of 375,000 "crack-addicted" babies born in the United States was widely reported early in the crack-cocaine crisis. Chasnoff, director of the National Association for Perinatal Addictions, Research, and Education (NAPARE), pioneered cocaine-exposure prevalence studies on newborns. Later studies estimated less than 100,000 as the high and 37,000 as the low figure, but these studies were not reported until after the epidemic had passed.[21] The main problem with the earliest studies was that prenatal cocaine exposure rarely occurs in contexts where crack is the only adverse effect on the fetus. Longitudinal studies, including Chasnoff's own, controlled for shared environmental factors, and showed little difference in cognitive abilities between cocaine-exposed children and children who grew up under similar circumstances but were not exposed to cocaine *in utero*.[22] Indeed, "the greatest impediment to cognitive development in young children is poverty."[23] This latter message, however, was not translated into a confabulatory equation.

Confabulations figuratively encode the lack of self-governance exercised by poor, urban residents—especially women. Drug use is a puzzling behavior within a prevailing political rationality in which all individuals supposedly operate as "self-interested maximizers."[24] Users have long been constructed as individuals maladjusted to the economic and cultural processes of modernity, as Part II shows. Their failure as productive citizens has been linked to other forms of differential citizenship. Women's assigned responsibility for social reproduction bars their admission to the sphere of "self-interested maximizers." While all addicts appear to contradict the subject formation of the modern capitalist subject, female drug addicts appear to deviate even further from that "ideal." Positioned as nonproductive, contingent citizens, women and persons of color join the maladjusted in occupying an ambivalent status.

Drug policy hearings regularly lament women's irrationality and stubbornness. Social controls over (some) women's reproductive capacities are cast as necessary to counteract the immense burden that women of reproductive age place on society. The degraded and unruly figure of the potentially pregnant drug addict is a condensed exemplar of bad behavior compounded by maternity, because mothers are expected to regulate and condition the behavior of others. The degree to which juveniles come to the attention of the police signals that mothers have failed to integrate their families into the state's utility. When the state must attend to mothers, pregnant women, or even "potentially pregnant" women, this signals a breakdown of women's capacity to manage themselves and others and shows the production of a world of antisocial disorder—the world as writ by commentators on the decline of the family.[25] The "weak family" explanation comes to seem commonsensical as blame for lack of social cohesion falls on women.[26] These governing mentalities become basic assumptions of drug policy-makers and the public.

Confabulatory knowledge claims are thus more usefully thought of as political claims rather than as "facts." When joined to numeric confabulations, the governing mentalities serve as political tools to make palpable an ethos of threat. Ultimately, these condensed images blame women and invite heightened surveillance. They legitimated the crack-baby problem in a certain form that made alternative constructions less possible to entertain. Confabulatory numbers make realist appeals that often pave the way for bipartisan policy-mongering where conflict over social provision might have otherwise arisen. The timing of the crack-cocaine scare, which accompanied an ideological convergence between neoconservatives and New Democrats on welfare reform, augmented the political effect of the numbers. They are artifacts of political life.

Policy-relevant confabulations rely on a rhetoric of escalation: the drug problem appears unmanageable yet still subject to policy-makers' manipulations. When a policy problem is constructed as intractable, those blamed for producing it are written off as incorrigible, irrational, and beyond the reach of public policy. The pattern of public need and provision (always under dispute) is a society's "signature."[27] The United States devotes major social resources to protecting abstract victims from potential harms and risks, but does not address basic and concrete needs. The very discourse of risk and insurance sets up a scenario in which women rationally and consciously weigh the "choice" between children and cocaine. Cause and effect appear tightly linked and predictable when, in actuality, the links between knowledge, intent, risky behavior, and pregnancy outcome are poorly understood.

Vague yet staggering figures are bandied about as confabulations reply to the persistent difficulty in obtaining accurate counts of drug users. Policy-makers grab on to these figures and produce narratives about their cultural significance, fully aware that they are engaging in imaginative acts of speculation by playing the numbers game.[28] Seeking "hard" evidence in a hearing, Senator Christopher J. Dodd (D-CT) ventured that six million people in the United States needed treatment. Witness Mitch Rosenthal, a Phoenix House administrator, explained that six million was misleadingly high, but failed in his attempt to rein in the confabulation. The committee later calculated the "astronomical" costs of treatment, multiplying six million by the annual cost of Phoenix House ($18,000 per patient per year) to show that the bill for treatment would exceed $108 billion each year. This confabulation generated enthusiasm for low-cost treatment, described by sociologist Robert A. Lewis, who touted a twelve-week outpatient dose of the Purdue Brief Family Therapy (PBFT) based on family systems therapy.[29] Rosenthal was pessimistic about the model's potential for the "hundreds of thousands of out-of-control and dysfunctional kids that are in our cities."[30] The exchange on the value of family systems therapy provides an excellent example of how knowledge claims travel and transmute in policy-making networks. It is also an instance of a tautological claim in which "the family" is both the cause of and solution to the problem of drug addiction.

Academic research enjoys a lengthy half-life in congressional hearings, especially when it verifies common sense.[31] The family systems model attributes addiction and recovery to the power dynamics enacted between family members.[32] Family relations are "resources" in this therapeutic modality: "One of the strongest motivations for eliminating drug use may be a drug-abuser's desires to maintain his or her love and family relationships." One year later, in a hearing before the Senate Committee on Labor and Human Resources, Senator Dan Coats (R-IN) credited Lewis's previous testimony as the basis of a family drug treatment program bill.[33] The earlier hearing debated the effectiveness of family systems therapy, and witnesses raised criticisms of it. In the second hearing, Coats indicated that a large body of research corroborated his own view that "systematic treatment of the entire family" was the most effective "treatment of choice" for the underlying tension and stress that caused family members to use drugs to "gain attention" or "escape family problems like unemployment or domestic violence."[34] Addiction, unemployment, and domestic violence were rendered the problems of individuals in "weak" families. Both cost-effectiveness and this built-in deflection onto individuals make the family systems model attractive to policy-makers.

Knowledge claims generated from the family systems model accord perfectly with underlying ideological commitments to "family values," a political agenda that preceded the call for an "objective, rational analysis of what works and what does not."[35] At the outset, Senator Coats stated his fervent belief that the family is the key to the drug problem—thus only an analysis of the family as cause and cure could count as rational, objective, and pragmatic in this hearing.[36] Family values discourse and family systems therapy share a nostalgic longing for structure and systematicity and a construction of the heterosexual, nuclear family unit as an antidote to all social ills. According to this logic, "strong" and "intact" families counteract addiction.[37] "Families that are fractured, or do not function properly, are a fundamental cause of drug abuse. . . . Families are the key to any effective program of rehabilitation. Families are the key to tackling this problem. Strong ones will give us a fighting chance. Weak ones will make our job impossible."[38] The family systems model makes problematic assumptions about gendered dynamics, power distribution, and family configuration.

Rising incidence of female-headed households and drug use among women reinforced the "family values" ideology. William J. Bennett appeared for the first time in his capacity as director of the Office of National Drug Control Policy in the second hearing. He spoke to the scope of the drug problem among women after noting that some populations had understood the risks of drug use and changed their behavior, resulting in a general decline in drug use "with the exception of young women, teenage women, and certain small, targeted groups and minorities."[39] Here women and "minorities" appeared as irrational, self-destructive, and ignorant of the risks and effects of their behavior. Bennett believed that the drug problem resulted from a "tangle of social factors that contribute to the self-destructive behavior of drug use."[40] Echoing the Moynihan Report's infamous phrase, the "tangle of pathology," such code words implicate communities of color, and especially women, at the center of this tangled web.

Like numeric confabulations, definitions of addiction identify cause, symptoms, and forecasts for the future. Definitions of addiction shifted in the mid-twentieth century from an older psychoanalytic lexicon involving psychic states of desire to a cybernetic vocabulary in which addiction served as a "coping mechanism." In the 1960s, the euphemism "drug dependence" was offered as a way to rid "addiction" of pejorative connotations. New definitions of addiction as a "chronic, relapsing disorder" were advanced in the 1990s by neuroscientists and critics of U.S. social policy who sought to scale back basic social provision under the guise of "American enterprise."[41] The now defunct U.S. Office of Technology Assessment (OTA) reported that addiction's "pattern of relapses and remissions resembles other chronic diseases, such as arthritis and chronic depression."[42] Thus treatment is not disease eradication but "amelioration" and "symptom-free intervals."

Redefining addiction as a "chronic, relapsing disorder" has profound implications for public policy. Definitions themselves do not determine the direction of policy, but political contestation over their meaning does. For instance, witness Douglas Besharov reaffirmed Bennett's advocacy of a return to orphanages. Elsewhere Besharov called for "substitute care" in "large congregate institutions,"[43] and an abandonment of the "medical model of drug treatment, which posits that crack addiction can be 'cured.' The plain fact is that—even with the best treatment services available—most crack addicts cannot be totally freed of their addiction. Instead, drug addiction must be seen as a 'chronic, relapsing disorder' (to use a phrase often repeated by treatment professionals) and current child welfare programs must be radically reoriented."[44] If cure is elusive and relapse the rule, the public and policy-makers may well write off addicts, worsening the social isolation, exclusion, and marginalization that researchers consistently find sustain women's illicit drug use.[45] Cloaked as a "realistic agenda," this resignation to the chronicity of addiction would adversely affect maternal and child welfare. Yet the project of redefinition could just as well force the recognition of the unrealistic nature of abstinence as a social policy and fuel the adoption of inclusionary impulses if it was linked to a politics of social justice.

Similarly, how the harm of drug use is defined matters for the type of policy considered realistic. If the source of harm is located in individual behavior, the larger social patterns and structures in which that behavior is situated do not come under scrutiny. Cumulative harms or broader harms that affect whole communities would still be permitted, while individual harms are prohibited.[46] Demand-side drug policy reflects a cultural preoccupation with individual accountability, delegitimating broader forms of social responsibility. It strategically recenters the individual as the ultimate social arbiter. This example shows that the narratives, confabulations, and definitions embedded in drug policy discourse are but loosely based on positivistic knowledge claims. They owe more to the shifting symbolic values of U.S. political culture and the "rugged individuals" who inhabit it.

Drug policy provides an arena for the display of symbolic values and attempts to regulate individual behavior on the basis of specious determinations of worth.[47] This is not to say that social science offers nothing to policy-makers, but rather that positivism cannot and should not be taken to guide the policy-making process. Hopes that drug science will evolve to drive drug policy are misplaced but common.[48] An ideology of rationalism is at work in the idea that scientists will subject addiction to systematic scrutiny and provide a set of "facts" to accord with dominant values.[49] To give politics over to scientism is a temptation to which policy-makers periodically succumb. However, they have other loyalties, shaped by calculations of interest, constituency relations, chances of reelection, personal views, or even their sense of responsibility or lack thereof.[50] Another way of knowing enters their cognitive practices—the governing mentalities are shaped by the cultural processes of figuration and highly suspect calculations of social value.

Women play specific roles in the political imaginary of policy-making, for women are burdened with the special responsibility of transmitting the values, attitudes, and beliefs thought to immunize against drug addiction. Moralistic positions on women's drug use abound—in fact, expert discourses of legal, scientific, biomedical, and sociological drug knowledges are often designed to counter moralism. The structure of elite classes in modern democracies leads to class conflict between those who claim their politics are based on objective facts, and those whose politics are represented as the result of subjective preferences, opinions, or moral values. Recently, a convergence between scientism and moralism has emerged, in which scientific facts are selectively rallied to support particular moral values.

Facts are conveyed in moral containers that naturalize certain configurations of value and reinstate the fact/value dichotomy: "The consequence of the repudiation of all valuation as subjective preference is not only that the nature of policy analysis cannot be rationally assessed, but that there can be no rational debate on any personal, professional, or political questions that involve values. A consistent commitment to a positivist conception of reason, then, precludes the possibility of rational deliberation on the most important political issues confronting contemporary politics."[51] Ultimately, a zealous commitment to "scientized politics" stimulates the growth of a combative sphere of "moralized politics."[52] Neither science nor morals alone can answer the political question of whose social problems are worth solving.

Governing Mentalities
Reading Congressional Hearings as Rhetorical Spaces and Political Sites

Investigative hearings dramatically illustrate how discourses of power constitute the objects they seek to govern and provide spaces in which the governing mentalities are aired more explicitly than usual. They represent a species of political discourse produced in the regulatory context of governance yet lacking law's imprimatur. They are often candid, even off-the-cuff, and always somewhat inchoate. The activity of the congressional hearing is both exemplary and performative—hearings appear to do something about the problematic subjects they proceed to constitute as governable within their terms. They are performative arenas in which meanings exceed individual intent. Witnesses and interrogators stage their sexual and racial politics, revealing their political stakes and commitments through rhetorical strategies and narrative constructions. The embodiment of the witness provides a crucial relay for the deflection from social to individual responsibility.

The policy-making process is a dual process of subject formation that simultaneously constitutes those who govern and those who are governed. To understand this process requires analyzing the social antagonisms that render the state a site, space, and species of class struggle.[53] Hearings occur free of the constraints and standards of evidence of judicial proceedings, academic debate, or scientific study. While they do not lack discursive and material constraints, they allow rather unconstrained expressions. Policy-makers serve as brokers of a politicized morality easily glimpsed in "just say no" or "zero tolerance" campaigns; they are subject to a constant compulsion to "other" those with whom they are confronted. Explicit instances of racism, sexism, or homophobia are not my interest here. Rather I want to understand how arguments based on racial and sexual difference construct political positions and finesse the acceptance of claims like those I considered in the previous chapter.

"Knowledge does not force the hand of governance,"[54] but the state invests in certain ways of knowing. Politically speaking, it is important to contest the state's "tacit managerial ambitions" and the presumption that what unruly actors need most is regulation of their individual choices and behaviors.[55] The testimony of friendly and resistant witnesses in congressional hearings is constrained within the bounded terms on which the hearing is based. Because hearings are generally thematic, subjects cannot stray too far nor can they introduce views at odds with the prevailing political rationality. Conflicts like those between pro-choice and right-to-life proponents are predictably balanced and scripted. There are few surprises that cannot be contained. Policy shifts do, however, take place as "policy monopolies" are built, contested, and displaced over time. These shifts are the product of material and discursive configurations.

Policy Monopolies: The Power of Ideas and Images

"Policy monopolies" denote a form of governance in which "long periods of domination by elites [are] punctuated by bursts of rapid social change."[56] Political scientist John Kingdon described periods when new ideas, political clout, or moral authority destabilize existing policy monopolies.[57] He also attended to the discursive domain, including interpretive paradigms and institutional arrangements as means by which those in power delegitimate oppositional views in order to maintain their monopoly. However, his influential model separates elite, expert, or official agents from the extrainstitutional social movements that shape how issues get to be issues. For Kingdon, elite power is based on a position within an institutional "structure." Elites are thus passive recipients rather than active participants in the contest for cultural and political hegemony. The "agents" in the system are social movements and political pressure groups. Rather than see the relationship between elites and social movements as one of dynamic interaction, the model downplays elite agency and the role of social antagonism. Finally, Kingdon detaches ideas from both structure and agency, thereby eviscerating them of their force in mobilizing social movements or motivating policy-makers.

My conceptual model does not detach ideas and images from social structures, institutions, and movements that aim to change them. Social bonds are formed, institutions built, and identities conferred even through apparently simple acts like classification or memory.[58] The governing mentalities are ideas and images that are integral to the formation of social subjectivity. For instance, those in power deploy images of threat and ideas of risk in order to police threatening others, deviant relations, violent settings, or unnatural contexts in hopes of maintaining a policy monopoly. These activities in turn reassure elites that they prefer their circumstances for good reason, that their relationships are "normal" and "natural," and that their patterns of life are superior. The governing mentalities work through the subjects they produce.

There is no better example of how ideas and images work in public policy than the two seemingly oppositional frames that structure U.S. drug policy: "crime" and "disease." Both frames encompass multiple political perspectives, varieties of professional expertise, official discourses, and popular appeals. The existing policy monopoly forecloses alternatives or hybrids, effectively colonizing the entire political spectrum. Crime versus disease proponents are now relatively dissociated from the political positions of left or right, and from "objective" characteristics that might translate into political behavior. Thus we are ill served by a model of the policy-making process that does not take into account the governing mentalities of those who govern. By "mentalities" I mean epistemological frames, interpretive paradigms, standards of evidence and proof, and what drug scientist Norman Zinberg called "set"—the personal, psychological, and emotional response to a deeply charged subject.[59]

As the social group authorized to pronounce the rules by which we are governed, policy-makers construct drug use as an intentional flouting of the law. Everyone knows illicit drugs are prohibited—according to this logic, those who use them do so out of willful disobedience. This is the fallacy of a naïve legalism: "To consider regularity, that is, what recurs with a certain statistically measurable frequency, as the product of a consciously laid-down and consciously respected ruling, . . . or as the product of an unconscious regulating by a mysterious cerebral and/or social mechanism, is to slip from the model of reality to the reality of the model."[60] Policy-makers prefer to explain drug use as the outcome of individual "bad choices" because that explanation authorizes them to act as they do. Public policy is monopolistically engineered (in ways often hidden from public view) to suppress the contingency and performativity of politics beneath a managerial mantle. Theorizing the power of policy images and ideas works to expose the prevailing modes of reason and behavior that govern what we as reasonable subjects are expected to embody.

Proof Positive: The Testimony of Unreliable Witnesses

Testimony is an ambiguous sort of evidence that links emotion with authenticity to produce an affective realism different from the empirical realism of those whose claims to authority are not grounded in the evidence of experience. The spoken truths of testimony pass through a social process of validation and acquittal, or condemnation and dismissal.[61] The testimonial moment is but one component of the production of truth: a series of moments prepare the way for it, and a series of interpretive moments when credibility will be ascribed or withheld follow it. Social-political mechanisms and epistemological issues disadvantage women witnesses by rendering their testimony literally incredible in certain rhetorical spaces, such as the U.S. Senate confirmation hearings of Clarence Thomas.[62] However, the truth-value of all witness testimony is highly unstable—it is both a highly contested truth and based in the "unassailable" evidence of experience.[63] A witness can achieve credibility and stabilize the interpretive process if her story accords with the prevailing "facts" and "values." Narrative form matters in the construction of truth and credibility—the more conventional the form, the less contestation of the truth-claims advanced within it.

Drug policy hearings elicit cautionary tales, often in the form of recovery narratives that warn listeners of the inevitable "hitting bottom," and convey the precariousness of subjectivity in a "remission society," Arthur Frank's term for the mode of relationality through which we construct intimacy and commonality in the late twentieth century.[64] Building on Frank's idea that sickness and wellness are always becoming each other, I suggest that we inhabit a "relapse society"—we are all about to succumb to the cultural contagion of addiction. We hold addiction at bay by continually restaging our resistance to this threat. Witnesses who embody this threatened contagion are convenient others—even for themselves. Recovery narratives attest to the threatening possibility of an embodied state beyond redemption. Because of this, testimony typically consolidates prevailing relations between socially dominant and subordinate groups, keeping their positions intact relative to one another.

Recovery discourse—a confessional mode perfected by Alcoholics Anonymous—has become a major cultural modality through which subjects "become the self of the stories one tells."[65] Recovery talk is highly exclusionary—its scripts stay within the limits of a modern morality play. The confessional ends on an upbeat note but follows the "hitting bottom" script—and if it does not, it does not count as a recovery narrative. The testimony of addict witnesses is often made more credible by the presence of the administrator or caseworker who accompanies the witness to testify at her side. These teams attest to one another's truths—neither one alone could be so convincing. The witness whose life is devoted to rescuing others from drugs bolsters the witness who testifies to the embodied experience of using drugs.

Feminists interested in social policy argue that women should serve more often as witnesses in hearings on social policy that affects them.[66] They predict this would lead to more inclusive, democratic, and thus better social policy. However, the power dynamics of such arenas tend to reduce the authority of speakers and grant cognitive authority to listeners. The question arises: "How [can] feminists and others, who know they are not operating on a level playing field, . . . negotiate the legitimate demands that they (we) take one another's experiences seriously, and yet resist the temptation to substitute a new tyranny of 'experientialism' immune to discussion for the old and persistent tyrannies of incredulity, denigration, and distrust."[67] When speakers must recount their own "deviance," power differences are pronounced because they must confess to lacking moral authority at least in the past. The recovering addict splits herself between the irresponsible and immature life she once lived and what she represents in the testimonial moment. No matter how sincere and strong, recovering addicts are unreliable witnesses, because the status of their recovery remains uncertain.

Feminists who expect that the revelatory power of female experience narratives will shift social policy discourse are sadly mistaken. Witnesses encounter acute problems of credibility—unless their testimony accords with what policymakers want to hear. They then encounter praise, as did 21-year-old recovering alcoholic Melissa Bell: "We always save the best for last. . . . You have great writing ability. I don't understand what you have been through because I haven't experienced it. But your story is a very touching one and I think it is again proof positive that if given the right breaks, the right counseling, the right support, all the other things, that confidence-building, self-image building young people can overcome drug addiction."[68] The proof positive was the fairly conventional recovery narrative written and delivered by Melissa Bell, which illuminates the discursive constraints on witnesses. Miss Bell's statement follows the general contours of the recovery narrative:

> My name is Melissa Bell, and I am an alcoholic. I'm also addicted to marijuana, LSD, and every other mind-altering substance I have ever tried. I suppose I could say that I am chemically dependent, but somehow that sounds too sweet. The truth is that I'm a drunk and a drug addict. Thank God, however, because I am recovering day by day from the chronic, progressive, fatal disease from which I suffer. My story is not unique. Thousands of people have been through the things I have. The miracle is that I have lived to tell it.[69]

Recalling her youth in a "dysfunctional/broken/alcoholic family," Miss Bell turned to drugs as her solution to the dilemmas of adolescence and femininity—"when I was drunk, I was no longer fat. I was no longer ugly. I was no longer different. I was no longer scared to be around anybody."[70] Five years sober, she told of her miraculous recovery from a "chronic, progressive, fatal disease."

Melissa Bell narrated how her childhood rendered her a prime candidate for the intergenerational transmission of addiction through learned alcoholic attitudes and behaviors. These behaviors were deceptive—"if a person is nice and acts right in public and always keeps their house clean, everything must be all right."[71] She compared her "insides to everyone else's outsides, meaning the way I felt with the way they looked," drawing a dichotomy between "normal" outward appearances and "abnormal" inner turmoil. Her childhood evenings were spent with an abusive and alcoholic stepfather and a younger brother for whom she was responsible while their mother worked as a waitress. She sought freedom from "the bondage of all of the responsibilities," and used sex to get whatever she wanted.[72] This deterioration continued until her mother placed her in detox and Melissa was able to accept her alcoholism.[73] Once she "confessed," the "miracles" began—Melissa made friends, became close to her mother and brother, graduated from high school, got a job, learned how to "earn money in a responsible manner," and refrained from stealing and prostitution.

The young Melissa moved through a series of familial and social obstacles on her path to sobriety and "maximum service to God and my fellow man."[74] These obstacles sprang from the everyday lives of adolescent girls and their working mothers. The norms of femininity and the "peer pressure" that emanated from them were the only social problems in the narrative—body shape and size, relationships, appearance, low self-esteem, and insecurity. There were a few openings in the prevailing narrative, such as when Melissa criticized private "scared straight" programs because it was "sad that poor kids can't go to treatment because they don't have insurance."[75] Observing her peers in prison or "unmarried on welfare with kids," she detailed their narrow options in ways that made potentially political connections between individual and social responsibility. Instead her story provided "proof positive" that individuals who want to rid themselves of addiction could do so without significant social support or public policy—and this belief confirms what policy-makers know.

Policy-makers construct investigative hearings as opportunities to gain information and determine "what the people want." Neither are constituted prior to the question; both are shaped to fit prevailing cultural interpretations. "Sometimes knowledge comes first, and needs belief to establish—to 'complete'—it."[76] What are policy-makers looking to confirm as they listen to women's stories of addiction and recovery? Who is a credible witness in their eyes, and to what truths do good witnesses attest? The experiences that witnesses relate are regarded as instructive data that add an element of "human interest" and the rhetorical dimension of pathos. The stories of women addicts who testify before congressional bodies share the features of therapeutic discourse, including long-term sexual and psychological abuse, often at the hands of a father or male relative; a persistent illness, addiction, disappearance, or untimely death of a mother; and a history of foster care. The witness must confirm and complete the policy-maker's knowledge with her truth—the truth of experiential knowledge. The common presumption that "giving or hearing testimony invokes no more significant moral-political issues than do acts of perceiving tables and chairs" obscures the witness's role in constructing the version of truth on which the policy-maker will act.[77] This presumption suspends power relations as if "the truth will out"— rather than seeing truth as produced, transcribed, reported, and legislated through a process thoroughly inflected by differential power dynamics. Unreliable witnesses do not produce truth; rather, truth is relayed from "unreliable" witnesses to "reliable" ones. Along the way, unwanted assumptions are discarded and expertise becomes a vehicle by which to convey the "information." Truth is ultimately disengaged from the speaking subject.

Congressional hearings are far from Habermasian ideal speech situations:

> Liberal-democratic societies that take some version of post-positivist empiricism implicitly for granted foster the belief that if people just "tell it as it is," "speak the truth," "stick to the facts," then they will be heard and believed; their experiences will be taken seriously into account in deliberative processes that follow upon their testifying. Moreover, the tacit rhetoric that shapes such societies promotes the assumption that would-be knowers are equally distributed across the epistemic terrain; and that everyone has equal and equivalent

access to the discursive spaces where knowledge is claimed, corroborated, and contested.[78]

Thus we need a multifarious notion of "counterpublic" spheres to change the conditions of social inequality.[79] Differences of knowledge and politics between speakers and listeners, witnesses and policy-makers, cannot be wholly attributed to gender, racial-ethnic, or class differences. Witnesses, however, embody "difference" and generalize their experiences to other members of the category they represent; their stories act as exemplary tales.

Drugs offered a "place in life" to ex-addict Elaina Wilcox after her mother died of multiple sclerosis.[80] Wilcox, herself a drug-addicted mother, regarded motherhood as a common bond between women: "Drug addicted mothers love their children just like any other mother. But it is not easy to stop using drugs. It has taken a long time and a lot of treatment for me to reach this point in my recovery. Recovering from any kind of addiction is a long-term process, fraught with relapse. It takes a tremendous support system. I feel lucky because I have support. I have my children—that means more to me than I can say."[81] Representing herself as strong, Wilcox portrayed other addicts as overwhelmed and weak. Addiction provides a narrative by which significant numbers of women make sense of their lives and differentiate "their" story from that of countless others. For legislators, addiction provides an exemplary narrative that compels belief.

Conclusion
Theorizing the Governing Mentalities

Governing mentalities animate the conceptual practices and material institutions of power; they guide prevailing interpretations of events and evidence. Although figurative in nature, they are materialized in institutions, policy-making cultures, and bureaucratic-administrative programs and procedures. Governing mentalities derive their power to compel from both symbolic and material registers.[82] They are the cultural processes of formation and figuration that shape public policy debates and outcomes. By attending to material and discursive practices and their consequences for women's lives, the governing mentalities model expands the possibilities for feminist cultural studies and policy analysis.

A process of "scientization" has occurred in policy-making spheres across the twentieth century that legitimates certain forms of expertise. First consolidated in New Deal social insurance schemes, policy expertise was formalized to an unprecedented degree in the policy sciences movement of the 1950s.[83] Harold Lasswell, who regarded history as a "succession of personality forms," sought to diagnose the styles of thought beneath the "working attitude of practicing politicians."[84] He argued that "true" political personalities used the public world to alleviate individual stress: "The politician displaces his private motives upon public objects, and rationalizes the displacement in terms of public advantage. When this emotional and symbolic adjustment occurs in combination with facility in the acquisition of manipulative skills, the effective politician emerges."[85] In Lasswell's landscape, the person who manipulated policy was invariably masculine. Born into a "maternal environment," masculine peer relations later displaced the relationship with the mother. This acknowledgment of emotion, childhood experience, and the psyche in the formative activities of the "political self" was brief. Policy analysis foreclosed questions of subject formation as the field became extremely narrow, atheoretical, and technocratic.

Through the Great Society programs and the Vietnam conflict, policy analysis was professionalized and a new "politics of expertise" emerged.[86] Postpositivist policy analysts seeking a place for ethics in public policy have only recently recognized the limits of technical reason.[87] Postpositivism is significant not only for the ethical and epistemological questions it raises, but also for its practical relevance in expanding participation beyond the positivist model of expertise. "The postpositivist orientation thus depends on the equally difficult political task of building new policy institutions that permit the public to engage in a much wider range of discourse."[88] To accomplish this goal, postpositivists advocate participatory democracy through organizations modeled on think tanks. Feminist policy research organizations offer an excellent example of this model as they generate alternative political discourses. Conservative think tanks offer an even more effective example, suggesting that discursive possibilities may be tightened as well as expanded.

As policy analysis became increasingly specialized, it became more public. The drama of the policy-making process was displayed through television broadcasts and popular reportage to a national audience beginning in the early 1950s. Witnesses in congressional hearings were not confined to a narrow focus, but were asked to give a "true picture" of what it was like to get "high" or to be a drug addict in more broadly accessible terms. The political drama became detached from the scientism of policy analysis as the twentieth century progressed. Witnesses provided testimonial moments crucial to the affective realism that hearings cultivate. Sense-making is not an entirely rational enterprise, for emotion, experience, social bonds, and political goals enter it. The policy-making process takes place by way of persuasion and conversion, often working through analogies and metaphors that strike deep affective chords, the symbolic powers of discourse, and the constructs of risk, threat, vital interests, and other categories we invoke to give us an illusion of control or a sense of its limits.

To avoid the psychologizing register of Lasswell and his lineage, I turn to Foucault's concept of "governmentality," which relates the process of subject formation to the material and discursive practices of governance. "My problem is to see how men govern (themselves and others) by the production of truth."[89] Governmentality relies on technologies, or "ensemble(s) of practices" that consist of contradictory strategies but make up a political rationality. The cumulative effect of the governing mentalities is a political imaginary of discourse on drugs. The disjuncture between the knowledge of real-life behaviors and the dreams, utopian schemes, and imaginary productions that find their way into the programs of governance is the distance between the imagined outcome of a policy intervention and its actual consequences. The managerial dreams of the positivist social sciences often assume that technical knowledge will someday drive policy, politics, and even ethics. Postpositivists insist on a more critical role for knowledge in politics—to craft a substantive account of how truth is produced in a particular political rationality and its accompanying political imaginary.

Policy-makers are positioned to relay stories whose rationales compel a particular outcome, engender identification, and elicit consensus. Some have a "feel for the necessity and logic of the game" of governance—imbued with a form of metacapital derived from the power and reason of state, they make the rules the rest of us supposedly follow.[90] Policy-making itself is not a set of explicit rules but a form of practical logic or a *habitus*—"society written into the body, into the biological individual."[91] Regularity and repetition, rather than radical breaks or discontinuity, are the stuff of governing mentalities, the practical logics of gender relations, class conflict, and racial formation that may interrupt and contradict, but also consolidate and propel, the "game" of governance. This does not mean that policy-makers lack individual agency or responsibility, but rather that individuals are dwarfed by the fields of meaning and power in which they play. In theorizing how governing mentalities perform their cultural work, I hope to get at this habitus, this "social body" of the body politic.

The habitus is central to the French regulation school's theory of society as consisting of a network of contradictory social relations prone to crisis.[92] The regulation school is preoccupied with the question of why, given this crisis-prone state of affairs, social reproduction takes place smoothly for long periods of time during which individuals align with the "needs of the particular regime of accumulation."[93] They argue that two factors are responsible: "The first operates as habit, or *habitus*, as Bourdieu would say, in the minds of individuals with a particular culture and willingness to play by the rules of the game. The other is installed in a set of governing institutions that vary widely, even within the same basic pattern of social relations. Wage relations, market relations, and gender relations, for instance, have changed greatly over time. Such a set of such behavioral patterns and institutions we call a *mode of regulation*."[94]

Social relations and institutions are dynamic in regulationist thought—"we quickly tried to get rid of the notions of structures without subjects, without contradictions, and without crisis."[95] Still, the regulation theorists' link between subjects and structures remains functionalist, whereas the governing mentalities assume a dynamic and contingent relationship between subject formation and cultural figuration. How you play the game is in a complex and unpredictable tension with your position on the playing field. While some actors exercise greater influence, their power does not derive from and cannot be reduced to their social position. Nor can power be reduced to cognitive differences, beliefs, attitudes, preferences, or values—all concepts that conventional political scientists use to comprehend the positional power that institutions confer on legislators, judges, bureaucrats, advisory bodies, or commissions convened to handle specific problems of governance.

Domestic conflict is the outcome of contestation between values and beliefs, but conventional policy analysts do not recognize these as political constructs. They appear instead as cultural characteristics or individual attributes constituted prior to the political contestations in which they are expressed. Congressional hearings resignify and consolidate interpretive frameworks, as policy-makers fit new knowledge into previously held constructs and tacit knowledge. The knowledge frameworks and fantastic figures they bring to bear—the governing mentalities—shape policy outcomes as much or more than the "focusing events" through which Kingdon understands symbolic power.[96]

As a conceptual framework, the governing mentalities capture a more dynamic sense of the patterns of thought formation and discursive practice than is available in policy science. Knowledge is a dimension of politics; the theory of knowledge a dimension of political theory. "The specifically symbolic power to impose principles of the construction of reality—in particular social reality—is a major dimension of political power."[97] Value judgments enter the production of demographic data (which "variables" count when and for whom) but lie hidden beneath the cloak of positivism. This is not the case when narrative interpretations of "data" are advanced in the context of public agenda setting. Public discourse is value-loaded to overcome the limits on what is sayable or unsayable, possible or impossible, and compelling or not. I turn to public discourse because that is where "facts" and "values" converge or collide. Kingdon's metaphor of the "policy primeval soup" is similar—ideas float around policy communities, firm up or dissolve, bump against one another, and recombine. Those that prosper survive a "natural selection process."[98] Ideas are the tools with which policy officials spring such traps and persuade others to do so. Endlessly reiterated, ideas mutate and are recombined, often showcased in congressional hearings not tied to any particular proposal. Hearings entrain policy-makers' vision of what is possible and impossible, as statements, understandings of cause and effect, or assessments of risk and blame become governing mentalities in the course of debate over concrete policy proposals. The translation of an idea into policy is a measure of its effectiveness and, in the case of drug policy, its tenacity.

The game of governance is a cultural production that requires a mode of analysis that recognizes this. Ideology theory or the historical study of the "mentalit[ies] of government,"[99] ideas, or "systems of thought," is similar but not the same as the history of the material and discursive practices of governance. Foucault's later work, which concentrated on the "triple domain of self-government, the government of others, and the government of the state," is useful here.[100] Rather than fetishize the state or the economy, Foucault saw the "governmentalization" of culture percolating through the political arena and into the minute crevasses of the ethical self. The cultural processes of "governmentalization"— how we become well-governed and law-abiding citizen-subjects—are a deep and pervasive form of discipline.

Policy-makers rely on a set of discursive practices to enroll subjects in a bounded political imaginary. Discursive practices are those "things and activities that we speak of, . . . the rules which prescribe distinctions we make, distinctions that reside in our language in general and speech practices in particular, . . . the commitments to meaning that we make [which] have the effect of allocating power, authority, and legitimacy."[101] To study these commitments requires a mode of analytic attention that does not divide social structure from discourse, and proceeds with a historical contextualization of our political rationality. What is the history of our policy choices? Why were our choices delimited as "crime" versus "disease," understood in congressional debate as "sanctions" versus "treatment"? How did these institutional modalities come to be our "only" possibilities?

Gendering
Narcotics

A COMPLETE BOOK-LENGTH
TRUE CRIME NOVEL.

Gendering Narcotics

Historical Amnesia: Late-Twentieth-Century "Heroin Chic"

"Heroin chic" emerged in the 1990s as a trend in the fashion world. Emaciated, blue-tinged models stared out of deep-set, blackened eyes, their features sharp and their whiteness starkly emphasized (see Figure 4). Many images produced by the Partnership for a Drug-Free America (PDFA) rely on white female models to depict heroin use as socially unacceptable. The PDFA's ostensible goal is to reach everyone in the country at least once a day with public service announcements that "unsell drugs."[1] Leading licit drug sellers—alcohol, pharmaceutical, and tobacco companies—are the major contributors to the nonprofit PDFA. A 1998 PDFA commercial depicts a young, white woman smashing raw eggs with a cast-iron frying pan and then rampaging through a well-stocked kitchen. The audience, presumably disgusted by the oozing eggs and the narrator's evident sarcasm, is shown the complete destruction of self, family, and friends that awaits heroin users.

The nasty young woman represents the consequences of loving an unworthy object—or of harboring her in your home.[2] This frenzied and feminized agent of destruction destroys the quintessential scene of social reproduction—the middle-class kitchen. The figure's whiteness, youth, and middle-class status remind us that this commercial would not "work" if it depicted an always-already-unlovable woman of color, a poorly equipped kitchen, or a razed inner-city neighborhood. The destruction of nurture and domesticity, of women's "rightful" place, and of the physical surroundings of a middle-class kitchen suggest that white women who use drugs fatally disrupt the process of social reproduction. Drugs have driven this young woman beyond the reach of the trappings of middle-class life and those who love her.

The "heroin chic" phenomenon juxtaposes bodily decrepitude with privilege. In the view of cultural critic Susan Bordo, heroin chic was a form of "being be-

Figure 4   Advertisement
captioned "Heroin is a
religious experience," 1997.

Courtesy of Partnership for a
Drug-Free America.

yond needing, beyond caring, beyond desire."[3] Women who use drugs represent
a threat to orderly social reproduction and civilization itself. White women who
use drugs display the end of respectability as a form of social control and the failure of modernity's "civilizing mission" (a task with which white women have typically been charged). The multiple and shifting meanings of white women who
"do" drugs in the late twentieth century play on a repository of images drawn
from earlier representations of white women who used narcotics. Part II works
against the historical amnesia that pervades our nation's discourse on illicit drugs
by examining this cultural repository.

The "Age of Dope": Consequence and Antithesis of Western Civilization

Narcotic drug use was constructed as both Western civilization's opposite and its
ultimate outcome.[4] During the "age of dope"[5]—the period between the abrupt

closure of the maintenance clinics of the early 1920s, and the point when street supplies "dried up" during World War II—drug use served as both primitive other and a threat propelled by the very speed and velocity of modernity and urbanization. A 1928 silent film, *The Pace That Kills*, began:

> Since the dawn of creation race after race has emerged from the dim shadows, flourished, then faded away into the mists of obscurity. History teaches us that each nation, each race perished miserably when they ignored their problems and failed in their struggles against debauchery and sin. Today we—the highest civilization the world has ever known—are faced with the most tragic problem that has ever confronted mankind—a menace so threatening, so all embracing that if we fail to conquer it our race, our people, our civilization must perish from the face of this earth! What is this octopus—this hideous monster that clutches at every heart. Creeping slowly, silently, inexorably into every nook and corner of the world? It is the demon DOPE! In its slimy trail follow misery, degradation, death; and from its clutching tentacles no community, no class, no people are immune regardless of birth, training, or environment.[6]

Addiction was visually represented as the insidious effect of foreign decadence—the octopus resided elsewhere, but strangled the nation from within. The logic that drug use was a "curse of civilization" positioned the United States as the largest crusader against addiction, the nation most vulnerable to it, and the most "civilized" nation on earth.

That logic was central to a 1925 hearing before the House Committee on Education, part of a successful effort to enlist the federal government in the First World Conference on Narcotics Education, held in July 1926 by the World Narcotic Defense Association (WNDA). The WNDA broadcast its message—that U.S. drug consumption exceeded that of all other nations—by radio and newspaper campaigns in 1925 and 1926. Headed by temperance reformer and Spanish-American War hero Richmond Pearson Hobson, the WNDA organized witnesses for the House hearing and mailed thousands of letters to school officials, parent-teacher organizations, distinguished citizens, and textbook publishers. The magnitude of the response should not be underestimated in an age before direct-mail solicitation was common—the record of the hearing reprinted 1,200 replies, which took up 130 pages of the testimony.

"The curse of civilization is the rapid spread of narcotic drug addiction, which is the overshadowing menace of the country," intoned Frederick A. Wallis, former U.S. Commissioner of Immigration at Ellis Island and then Commissioner of Correction in New York City, at the hearing.[7] Despite his knowledge that most drug users were native-born,[8] Wallis argued that the solution was an "uncompromising crusade" to its source. Through eugenically informed immigration control—"scientific selection" and "intelligent distribution"—he pro-posed to seal the borders against addicts rather than drugs. He urged a united effort to eradicate the evil: "Every nation is highly sensitive and intensely jealous of the health of its people and no nation responds so quickly and so generously to the imperative needs of humanity as the United States. When some pestilence or disease is threatening the life or the social well being of our people, the whole Nation rises courageously to thwart the evil. There is no cost too great and no sacrifice too extreme."[9] Wallis echoed these remarks at the conference the next summer, delivering two papers, "The Criminology of Drug Addiction" and "The Curse of Civilization."[10]

Despite the energetic popularization of its agenda, the WNDA failed to build a seamless consensus. Its style and methods did not appeal to the U.S. Public Health Service or professional associations. Early in 1926 Hobson invited the prestigious New York Academy of Medicine to the conference. Heroin addic-tion, he wrote, "menace[d] the future of the nations of the west" and struck at the "very foundation of the social order."[11] The academy discreetly checked with H. S. Cumming, U.S. Surgeon General, who gave assurances that the WNDA did not have the imprimatur of "serious students of narcotics."[12] "Frankly," Cumming wrote, "the relations between its president and this office have not been congenial" due to Hobson's methods, which the Surgeon General adjudged "mistaken and more likely to do harm than good." In March the acad-emy refused Hobson's invitation, stating that the New York Academy of Medi-cine, the United States Public Health Service, and the Philadelphia College of Physicians "do not agree . . . as to the truth of the facts upon which [the Associa-tion's] activities are based."[13] For decades the New York Academy of Medicine would play the voice of reason in the debate over whether addiction should be treated as a "crime" or a "disease."

The meaning of public health was contested in the 1920s. The WNDA offered a public health framework that modeled addiction on contagious diseases such as foot-and-mouth disease, cholera, or plague.[14] Addiction was also considered a disease that could be contained by limiting social interaction and association:

Schools close, factories shut down, amusements cease, business suspends until the evil is safely eradicated; everything else is secondary to the importance of meeting the situation. . . . It seems to me that human life is of far greater value than livestock. Is not life more than meat, and the body more than rai-ment? Of all the plagues that visit our land, drug addiction is by far the most horrible and most deadly. It kills body, soul, and spirit. It destroys not only the person who acquires the habit, but that person immediately becomes the medium of transmitting the habit to many others, thus rapidly spreading the curse from family to family and from community to community.[15]

Here drug addiction operated as "civilization's other"—that which would devalue human life to the status of meat. Addicts served as passive vehicles for the spread of contagion, but were also thought to act as "mediums" who sought to make more of their kind. The mystical constructions of contagion that circulated in the orbit of the WNDA did not appeal to the scientific rationalists of the New York Academy of Medicine.

The conference itself displayed a national purity discourse that depicted white women as contaminants.[16] The decadent, perverse, and feminized populace of Europe, where middle-aged women and young boys worshipped in the "cult of Morphia," was contrasted to the masculine vigor of the United States. The typical worshipper of Morphia was an absentminded, elegant woman whose "statuelike indifference and rigidity tell us she is a morphine addict."[17] She was a mistress of orientalized artifice who transmitted her addiction to the not-quite-masculine boys she lured into drug use. I examine this figuration of female addicts as sexual predators in Chapter 3. Here I want to remark on the depiction of Europe as the site of feminized indulgence and fatigue. In the eyes of the American narcotics reformers, the Old World was the "germ of vice." Europe had undergone a "morbid spiritual disintegration": "Hope is no longer there, it is across the ocean. The land of hope is America, the land of youth. Europe is old, skeptical, and cynical."[18] We may wax moralistic against "heroin chic" in the 1990s, but narcotics use by rich, idle, and, above all, thin white women has long signified a modern—if "foreign"—femininity, exoticism, and artifice.

The vice of addiction was a hybrid construct that linked physiological predisposition to the social dislocations of the modern West. "Drug addiction is a consequence of modern life," stated Dr. Julius Cantala, who outlined a hierarchy of racial immunity and susceptibility to it.[19] Westerners, he noted, turned to the Orient's artificial pleasures because "our overwrought nerves needed something to enliven our tired brains" in the wake of World War I.[20] Immune to simple pleasures, "civilized" nerves "require[d] the deeper stimulus of active poison."[21] As artificial sensations displaced the natural buoyancy of a moral life, the "craze of pleasure" fundamentally altered drug addicts, constituting them as an "exotic species" that threatened modern Western civilization itself.[22]

The threat of narcotics impinged from two sides—a "primitivizing" register and an "orientalizing" register. Early-twentieth-century drug discourse linked the age of dope to the practices of the "oriental" through the figure of the "white slaver."[23] The primitivized subcultural styles and sites of jazz clubs and dance halls, and the domestic and leisure activities of the working classes, recent immigrants, and African-American communities were also associated with the drug threat.[24] The primitivizing rhetoric applied to the lower and working classes; the orientalizing register applied to the self-indulgence of the upper and middle classes—native-born women supplied by unscrupulous physicians, traffickers in

Figure 5 Illustration from
"Trapped by the Poison Gas in
Her Jeweled Vanity Case," *The
American Weekly*, 1931.

Courtesy of the Hearst Corporation.

women, and "oriental drug smugglers."[25] Thus a rich tapestry of characters developed during the 1930s and 1940s. The oriental dope problem was visually depicted as a Fu Manchu villain, dragon, octopus, or reptile grasping Hawaii and
about to engulf the West Coast of the United States. Editorial cartoons represented the dope traffic as the "three [*sic*] horsemen of the apocalypse"—from the
Orient, Central America, and Europe.[26] The Orient was represented as poised
to flood the West with cheap dope, often through dope traffickers' "woman
lures," white women who posed as glamorous travelers but turned out to be
smugglers[27] (see Figure 5).

Antidrug reformers believed that white women preceded all others into the "age
of dope." Prizewinning author and WNDA member Sarah Graham-Mulhall presented the stunningly condensed figure of the "opium vampire" in a popular book:

Opium is among the women who are rich in idleness and money, among the ambitious girls who are well-born but who are trapped by the opium trafficker in college dormitories, in business colleges, in their hospital training for nurses. They become drug scouts, they capture the young man whose outlook on life is still romance, whose respect for women is yet what it should be. They coax the older men in order to rob them. Under the influence of the drug they stop at nothing in their adventures in opium; and those who are caught in the golden mesh of their drug nets, find themselves dragged down to death with them.[28]

The decadent artifice of upper-class white femininity was orientalized, while addiction among men of color and the lower classes was primitivized. Both forms of atavism threatened to undermine modern civilization from within.

Maladjustment to Modernity: Primitivizing Rhetoric in the 1940s

Psychoanalysis and anthropology drew parallels between narcotics use and the "magical systems of the primitive man or sorcerer," "cannibalistic interests," and pregenital or oral libidinal interests.[29] During World War II, narcotics supplies diminished because the Federal Bureau of Narcotics (FBN) stockpiled opiates as strategic materials. This news reached the public through popular magazines such as *The Family Circle*, which ran a story on the dangers of paregoric (tincture of opium) that quoted Harry J. Anslinger, director of the FBN from 1930 to 1962 and chief architect of U.S. drug policy: "Like opium and heroin, the paregoric slaves are everywhere, and I knew a minister's daughter who had the craving so badly that on her way from the drugstore she would slip into the alley separating our houses and take a pull at the bottle before entering her home."[30] This furtive figure domesticated the threat of dope. Anslinger was a master of public relations, narrating stories to heighten his readers' vigilance against the encroachment of illicit drugs on their daily lives—and those of their children.

Commenting on the strange practices of addicts, Anslinger reported on recent military studies of marijuana users: "[The Army's] latest report declares them to be under compulsion of destructive tendencies toward both themselves and others. Case histories were marked with delinquent and criminal behavior, and the men were described as feeling and acting like enemy aliens toward society."[31] The construction of drug users as "enemy aliens" reinforced the enduring association between illicit drug use and sexual and racial deviance. The studies primarily involved men of color, most of whom came from the "poor delinquent colored section of the city," an environment consisting of "broken homes," people on public assistance, and "delinquent brothers and sisters."[32] Marijuana use was but one aspect of their difficulty in "mastering everyday tasks of social living": "They seem to have no technic [*sic*] available. . . . They have no roots in the social order. They are declassed persons who have never held a job consistently but have always been on the fringe of society, delinquents who live by petty gambling, frequently without any visible means of support. They feel themselves alienated from the rest of the world and express this in various ways. They distrust the world and everybody in it, with a strong feeling that everybody is their enemy."[33] "In effect," the authors noted in that memorable phrase, "[the subjects] felt and acted like enemy aliens toward society."[34]

Modernity's challenges exceeded the subjects' undeveloped, "primitive" instincts; marijuana tipped the balance toward asocial behavior in individuals of "poorly integrated social conscience."[35] The army studies found that family configurations in which strong, moralistic mothers dominated weak fathers produced maladjustment.[36] Unable to control their behavior "in a socially acceptable manner or . . . direct their energies toward a goal which would provide 'normal' satisfactions,"[37] maladjusted individuals regressed to infantile states such as an "unending search for pleasure in the most primitive terms," aggression, hostility, or "running amuck."[38] Habitual marijuana users were "emotionally immature individuals who are constantly frustrated in their attempts to find adequate instinctual expression."[39] Charen and Perelman, authors of a study of 55 African-American and five white male marijuana users at Fort McClelland (where whites outnumbered men of color by a ratio of seven to one), speculated that marijuana served a "peculiar need" for African-American men.[40] "Marijuana, insofar as it removes both anxiety and submission and therefore permits a feeling of adequacy, enables the Negro addict to feel a sense of mastery denied him by his color. The white psychopath or neurotic not faced with the dual problem of personality and environmental frustration finds alcohol or other forms of satisfaction more acceptable."[41] Unlike the marijuana studies, which pathologized the drug and the user, the army studies on alcoholism assumed a continuum between social drinking and chronic alcoholism and did not identify psychosis among alcoholics.[42]

The marijuana studies clearly exhibited a full set of racialized and sexualized associations between marijuana use and "deviance," especially homosexuality. One African-American described parties at which he "found himself in odd positions, performing some sexual perversion."[43] Others were incapable of emotional relationships without a "distinct homosexual coloring," and were indifferent toward women.[44] Many claimed they did not experience heterosexual desire without marijuana; with it they enjoyed "sexual satisfactions without emotional ties" and "all sorts of perversions," including eating feces and "swallowing of leukorrheal discharges."[45] Subjects themselves adopted the construction of moral perversion: "Nothing seems wrong any more. . . . You see lots of queer things going on that you never dreamed existed."[46]

Such practices signaled the presence of "social outcasts living in a world of different standards."[47] Marijuana users were represented as infantile, searching for immediate gratification (ever a signifier of low social class), and directed entirely by the strength of their desires. "The personality pattern of these men is one of strong libidinous desires resulting from early home conflict, a weak ego which identifies with an undesirable father image, and a superego created by a moral mother. The superego is unable to prevent undesirable behavior but is able to create intense anxiety. Use of marijuana removes the superego, which in turn strengthens the ego and enables it to satisfy the libidinous desires at various levels of infantile behavior. Homosexuality is evident in many of these men."[48] In psychoanalytic thought, civilization requires the superego; without it there is no possibility of an individual's integration into the project of civilization.

Both inadequacy and heightened suggestibility concerned policy-makers because of the view that enemy nations plied the U.S. population with drugs. During World War II, Japanese smuggling was portrayed as a "new form of chemical warfare": "Pestilence and war are historically associated with each other but it has been left to the Japanese to find a way of making a pestilence, the opium traffic, pay for war. The drug habit spreads swiftly and devastatingly. The Japanese have used this weapon effectively in the Far East. They cannot use it in this country because we were in this war against narcotics ten years ago and conducted a vigorous unheralded battle which effectively stopped the infiltration of Japanese poison into the veins of our American people."[49] The FBN circulated a widely published photograph of a "Japanese woman" smuggling heroin taped to her dark thighs that echoed earlier sketches of white women smuggling drugs beneath their skirts (see Figures 6 and 7).[50] Anslinger's claims about Japanese heroin smuggling also prefigured his allegations of Chinese "Communist narcotic aggression" in the 1950s, which I detail in Chapters 4 and 5. Such claims often appeared in stories that centered drug use among school children and adolescents, whose suggestibility stood for the nation's vulnerability to the "enemy within."

Later in the 1950s and 1960s, the threat of narcotics use impinged from an ultramodern, dystopian side represented by Russia and Asia, especially Communist China. The residue of orientalism tinged the post–World War II threat. Communism menaced modern democracy with "brainwashing" or "Pavlovian mind control" achieved through drugs.[51] Both atavistic and futuristic constructions positioned the United States as a "victim nation," which failed to explain why the nation was the world's most voracious drug consumer. Justifying why the United States was the nation best suited to direct the global restriction of narcotics required the figure of an "other." Drug addiction thus became the province of problematic individuals who responded poorly to social change and could not adapt to the rigors of modernity, capitalism, and democracy. Trained on subversives, the sciences of difference elaborated specific formations of mid-century

The New Mode of the Long Skirt
Will Facilitate This Form of
Smuggling Dope into Prisons.

Figure 6 Illustration from "Exposing the Traffic in Dope," *The American Weekly*, 1930.

Courtesy of the Hearst Corporation.

Figure 7 Photograph captioned "A Japanese woman tried to smuggle heroin in this unsightly fashion."

Reprinted from *Liberty* magazine, 1945.

U.S. addict identity as if they were universal attributes of addicts or general patterns of addiction. Drugs were associated with liberation of the true self and drives and desires not channeled toward civility and self-governance. Drug discourse began to work as a technique of normalization that applied to broader segments of the population than the tiny ranks of addicts warranted. Primitivism and orientalism continued to perform cultural work, serving as foils against which the modern Western subject was constituted.

Primitive Pleasures, Modern Poisons
Femininity in the "Age of Dope"

Addiction and Progressive Modernity
Public Health and Private Practices

Drugs mark the discontents within the "civilizing process" to an extraordinary degree in U.S. political culture. Popular and political concerns about the rising tide of drug addiction often accompany anxiety-provoking cultural shifts. Drug policy thus operates as "symbolic policy" to index social disorder. Like other symbolic policies, such as child abuse, drunk driving, or teen pregnancy, drug policy discourse uses claims about the scope of individual "deviance" to justify expanded governmental intervention.[1] In the 1910s and 1920s, immigration, urbanization, industrialization, and the northward migration of African-Americans precipitated white middle-class anxieties that were channeled into an array of reform projects.[2]

Progressive addiction research generated a model of public health expertise, a typology for categorizing addicts, and an institutional template that presaged federal mental health policy and science policy in the post–World War II period. The transfer of policy-making and administration to state and federal government bureaucracies modeled on capitalist enterprises was a key political achievement of the period.[3] Public health became a recurring object of public policy, a framework that bolstered addiction research despite the attempts of law enforcement agencies to overpower it. Modern medical and scientific works that dealt with drugs as a matter of mental "hygiene" developed beside the antidrug discourse of the moral purity movement, which targeted narcotics after Prohibition. This chapter demonstrates the convergence of these forces on the idea that addicts were inadequate to meet the demands of modernity, democracy, and capitalism.

The 1920s was a pivotal decade during which policy-makers explored a variety of directions, ranging from public health measures such as detoxification and maintenance clinics in 44 cities across the nation to heightened law enforcement in the wake of the Harrison Act (1914).[4] After the clinics were abruptly closed in 1923, there was no federal action on treatment until the Porter Bill of 1929, which created a Narcotics Division in the Public Health Service and two "narcotics farms" at Lexington, Kentucky, and Fort Worth, Texas.[5] Both treated federal prisoners and voluntary patients; the enabling legislation stated that "any person who submits himself for treatment shall not forfeit or abridge any of his rights as a citizen."[6] The USPHS operated the narcotics farms with the military and the Bureau of Prisons. They were based on "fundamental psychiatric, psychoanalytic, psychological, and sociological principles," and offered educational, vocational, spiritual, occupational, recreational, and psychiatric treatment.[7] They also served as living laboratories, although research was primarily carried out at the Lexington facility.

Narcotics law enforcement stepped up with the 1920 creation of a Narcotic Division within the Treasury Department, charged to enforce the Harrison Act. Processes of cultural domination are formally rooted in institutional structures. The Narcotic Division implemented the act by targeting poor addicts dependent on the "black market" and physicians or pharmacists who supplied lower-class persons. This shift exposed a highly vulnerable, newly criminalized, and increasingly visible population of the urban poor to prosecution.[8] Although the Harrison Act's constitutionality was still not fully tested, by mid-1928 nearly one-third of federal prisoners were serving time on Harrison Act violations.[9] The act and the two 1919 Supreme Court decisions that upheld federal enforcement powers, *U.S. v. Doremus* and *Webb et al. v. U.S.*, dampened physicians' willingness to treat addicts or prescribe narcotics to the nonaddicted population. The pattern of enforcement divided addicts into two classes—the "respectable" medical addict and the "nonrespectable" criminal. The class division was in turn gendered and racialized. Respectable white women addicts were constructed as tragic and innocent victims of unscrupulous doctors, while prostitutes and careless mothers were condemned. The dichotomy between "predator" and "prey" was embodied in two intertwined figures of addicted women: "opium vampires" who preyed on unsuspecting men and boys, and "white slaves" victimized by unscrupulous men.

White Women in "Dopeville"

White women were considered the population least resistant to the pleasures and deteriorations of narcotics by the late nineteenth century.[10] "A delicate female, having light blue eyes and flaxen hair, possesses, according to my observations, the maximum susceptibility," physician H. H. Kane agreed in 1880.[11] Addicted white women comprised a higher proportion of addicts in some regions well into the twentieth century.[12] Drug addiction was then viewed as an individual aberration among whites, while persons of color appeared more "naturally" or "organically" addicted as a group. Dr. Julius Cantala painstakingly reviewed susceptibility by race at the WNDA conference.[13] He concluded that dope fascinated whites but their bodies protested against it in ways that repelled organic damage. Drug addiction among African-Americans was limited by the group's disinclination to begin narcotics use. However, once addicted, "negroes" quickly reached the "lowest state of bodily degeneration" due to their "low organic resistance."[14] No less than a "hereditary immunity" protected the "yellow race."[15] Addiction among whites was thus constructed as an individual psychological problem, while addiction among persons of color was a physiological problem that applied to the group. Cantala's racialized mind/body dichotomy voiced one of the "governing mentalities" through which Americans understood addiction in the twentieth century.

Racial mixing troubled this hierarchy. Drug policy was constructed by dominant groups who responded to changing cultural conditions by seeking to preserve white women's innocence and to emphasize their corruption by men of color through the trope of miscegenation. White women's assumed susceptiblity to narcotics use was extended to the seductions of nonwhite men. Fears of miscegenation were often expressed through a parallel drawn between the white female population and men of color (African-Americans, Chinese, and white ethnics). For instance, the American Pharmaceutical Association (APA) acquired influence over drug legislation by emphasizing the illegitimacy of interracial associations. The APA Committee on the Acquirement of the Drug Habit reported high susceptibility of Negroes and "women generally" to cocaine in 1902.[16] The committee noted that the quantity of smoking opium imports to the United States indicated that the practice of opium smoking was no longer confined to the Chinese but had seeped into the rest of the population. Already considered susceptible, white women personified these fears.

Associations between racial mixing and narcotics use emerged in the legislative campaign that led to the passage of the Harrison Act. The ill-fated Foster Bill, defeated in 1911, was an attempt to reduce the profit of retail sale of narcotics—most pharmacists and pharmaceutical manufacturers were understandably unfriendly to it. However, Christopher Koch, M.D., vice president of the Pharmaceutical Examining Board of Pennsylvania and chairman of the Legislative Committee of the Philadelphia Association of Retail Druggists, was deeply involved in the struggle against drug use by children. He testified on behalf of the bill, differentiating between legitimate and illegitimate use. He associated illegitimate use with racial mixing: "In the Chinatown in the city of Philadelphia there are enormous quantities of opium consumed, and it is quite common, gentlemen, for these Chinese or 'Chinks,' as they are called, to have as a concubine a white woman. There is one particular house where I would say there are 20 white women living with Chinamen as their common-law wives. The Chinamen require these women to do no work, and they do nothing at all but smoke opium day and night."[17]

Often from "good" families, the girls progressively declined from "sporty boys," alcohol, and cigarettes to Chinese restaurants and opium smoking. Though they were initially seduced out of curiosity or "pure devilishness," the pipe eventually failed to satisfy them; they progressed to intravenous morphine. Ultimately, they needed cocaine in order to function at all. Such girls, Koch implied, contributed to the United States' exceedingly high per capita consumption of opiates; they were the only specific population he mentioned other than Chinese men. Koch reinforced his verbal representation of orientalized decadence by demonstrating how to smoke opium. Adding racial details to his description, he began: "Usually, a white woman lay on one side of a bunk beside a Chinaman" in order to prepare opium for smoking.[18] Elaborating further, Koch explained that "opium becomes like food" to racially mixed couples, who then conducted "all sorts of orgies."[19]

U.S. State department employee Hamilton Wright, an international antidrug crusader who campaigned for domestic antinarcotics legislation after serving as a delegate to the Shanghai Opium Commission in 1909, reinforced Koch's remarks on the debauchery of opium use.[20] Wright warned that morphine use was no longer confined to the "criminal classes and the lower orders of society" but was "creeping into the higher circles of society."[21] He quoted "reliable information that the crime of rape in the South is largely due to the cocaine habit"—particularly the "use of cocaine among the Negroes in the South in the last 10 or 15 years."[22] While the Foster Bill did not pass, the discursive confinement of the U.S. drug problem to dangerous populations—white women who associated with men of color and "colored" persons themselves—became a keynote in drug discourse.

While Koch claimed that the cocaine habit was "essentially an American vice," he associated specific patterns of drug use with the "colored" population, and other patterns with (white) professionals.[23] Cocaine use marked the inadequacy and self-delusion of Negro men: "It is a very seductive drug. . . . Persons under the influence of it believe they are millionaires. They have an exaggerated ego. They imagine they can lift this building, if they want to, or can do anything they want to. They have no regard for right or wrong. It produces a kind of temporary insanity. They would just as leave rape a woman as anything else and a great many of the southern rape cases have been traced to cocaine."[24] Such assertions were already racialized; although white physicians used drugs "when they are run down and have a lot of work to do," cocaine did not, apparently, incite them to rape.[25] By figuring addicts as racial and ethnic others, Koch could insist on the "Americanness" of addiction and yet reinforce its association with alien or foreign elements. Although Koch and Wright did not prevail in the Foster Bill hearings, Wright later capitalized on the images of interracial sexual relations and rape in the testimony leading to the Harrison Act. Condensed images that connected drug use and traffic to "white slavery" and racial mixing were recycled to justify laws, policies, and bureaucratic moves among policy-makers and the general public.

Federal opiate controls finally passed with the Harrison Act of 1914,[26] which overcame significant obstacles from white Westerners and Southern Democrats loathe to increase federal police powers.[27] Wright stimulated fears of interracial contact and emphasized the "large number of [white] women who have become involved [with drugs] . . . living as common-law wives or cohabiting with Chinese in the Chinatowns of our various cities."[28] He again stressed the threat of African-American men's cocaine use to white Southern womanhood. Racist fears of cultural contamination from sexual proximity between white women and men of color effectively overcame political resistance to the State Department agenda, a strategy that gained legislation where it might otherwise have foundered.

Drugs were coded as a threat to modern civilization through their construction as a threat to white women, who occupied an ambivalent state. Antidrug reformers strategically linked the "age of dope" to the practices of white women by portraying them as predatory transmitters of addiction. Reformers also invoked the need to protect white women and children, hoping to rally support for their legislative agenda, a uniform state narcotics law. A consortium of federal bureaucrats, the press (especially the Hearst newspapers), and reform organizations such as the Women's Christian Temperance Union (WCTU), the General Federation of Women's Clubs, and the Congress of Parents and Teachers pushed model legislation. Reformers advocated federal restriction of drugs by drawing associations between drugs and crime, and racial mixing. Drug policy scholarship has underplayed the cultural processes of racialization and sexualization that shaped the reformers' legislative and social agenda. By delving further into the reform discourse at the 1926 WNDA conference on Narcotics Education, the governing mentalities that shaped early-twentieth-century drug discourse become clear.

The Drugged Nation: Social and Biological Reproduction

Addiction emerged as a hybrid construct of vice, disease, and crime, a catchall category for moral, mental, or social inadequacy and sexual deviance. Drugs threatened civilization by working to level the naturalized hierarchy of distinctions between the sexes and races.[29] The socially leveling aspects of drug use threatened a heterosocial order, based on strong sexual differentiation, class distinction, and racial segregation, which reformers sought to preserve. They observed addicts operating according to inscrutable ethical codes, which bolstered their sense that addicts were an "exotic species."[30] The "unnatural distinctions" of the "special world of dope" bound addicts to one another in an order in which "sex loses its disparity; men and women mingle without manifesting any of the distinction that exists in normal life."[31] The social bonds developed in drug cultures "create[d] an artificial world with fictitious values and false standards."[32] The breakdown of social and sexual differentiation meant that addicts perceived the artificial as the real and could not even distinguish between men and women. Addiction interrupted the "natural" processes of social reproduction and differentiation.

More importantly, drugs threatened freedom and were counterpoised to slavery, a state of "social death."[33] Addiction appeared as a form of bondage modeled on slavery that affected whites: at the WNDA conference, Hobson warned, "political bondage is not the worst form of human bondage."[34] According to him, the number of "slaves to habit-forming narcotics" outweighed the number of "chattel slaves in the past" by a ten-to-one ratio. Compared to "white slavery"— the "crime of trafficking in the virtue and chastity of women"—chattel slavery was trivial.[35] This view resembled House debate on the Mann Act (1910), the Progressive legislation designed to regulate "white slavery": "It is indeed appalling to know that, in this day of enlightenment, we have had for several years a species of slavery a thousand times worse and more degrading in its consequences and effects upon humanity than any species of slavery that ever existed in this country."[36] Mann himself maintained that the "truthful or fanciful" horrors of the black slave trade would "pale into insignificance as compared with the horrors of the so-called white slave traffic."[37]

Narcotics posed a threat to freedom through its link to "white race suicide": "[Addiction] destroys the seat of those very attributes upon which all the institutions of freedom and civilization must rest, and the blow goes so deep that it strikes at the germ plasm of the species and impairs and destroys its power of procreation. The profits that spread human slavery in the past were small indeed compared to the vast profits that are now driving this latter slavery into the tissues of mankind."[38] Hobson's speech constructed narcotics use as a weapon of biological warfare deployed against the very "germ plasm" of the white race.

The analogy between addiction and the traffic in women achieved several goals. The whiteness of "white slavery" obscured the victimization of women of color. As one antiprostitution tract put it, "The phrase, white slave traffic, is a misnomer, for there is a traffic in yellow and black women and girls, as well as in white girls."[39] Secondly, the analogy diminished the impact of chattel slavery on persons of color by extending the slavery metaphor to any form of submission to a higher force. The fear that loyalty to drugs subsumes all others is a perennial feature of political discourse on drugs. Coupled to the fear that white women might submit sexually—willingly or by force—to nonwhite men, submission was constructed as the sexual coercion of white women by men of color. Thirdly, the analogy positioned white women as prey, thereby rescuing them from the position of predator.

To Progressive reformers, drugs, "deviant" sexualities, and the market structure of sex work appeared as similar threats. White men became the moral arbiters of white slavery, rendered vigorous, moral, and masterful through their protection of white women. Indeed, Sarah Graham-Mulhall argued: "It does not seem possible that the white man would become enslaved in this fashion . . . the white man seems to be an entity that is rising up now in history rebelling against this form of human slavery."[40] The antidrug crusade's imperialist motives were striking where addiction was considered an impediment to the efficient extraction and accumulation of profit. Graham-Mulhall noted that "vastly more profit can be gotten out of China undrugged and India undrugged than out of China and India drugged."[41] Drugs were seen to undermine economic productivity as well as the procreative powers.

The construct of the United States as a "drugged nation" owed much to Graham-Mulhall, who derived her authority from her brief stint as deputy commissioner of the Department of Drug Control during the six-month period in 1919 to 1920 when the New York Clinic operated. "In our New York State Department we had so many baby addicts that we had to set up a special procedure for infant addiction. We had college men and college women addicts. We had mother and grandmother addicts. Yes; we had capitalist addicts, editor addicts, lawyer addicts, writer addicts, and addicts engaged in preaching against addiction or professing to have been cured. . . . [There was need to show] civilization how to protect itself against all these addicts and how to protect these addicts against a civilization that sells addiction."[42] Like many reformers, Graham-Mulhall grappled with the paradox of a "civilization" that sold addiction yet constructed itself as its chief victim.

The anxiety about the pervasiveness of addiction among whites was projected onto white women, who were viewed as responsible for reproducing addiction. One quarter of addicts registered at the New York City clinic were women, three quarters of them white. Graham-Mulhall claimed that over half of the 1,532 registered female addicts were pregnant when the clinic closed, registering alarm about the extent of addiction and amplifying its threat by depicting addiction as reproducible across generations. Her concerns, too, encoded anxieties about white racial decline. Addiction was figured as a feminine attribute despite the demographic shift to men, as women addicts were the "tragic figures" who dragged young men and innocent babies along the path to addiction. A U.S. District Court judge who spoke at the WNDA conference dramatically recounted a story of a 27-year-old, white, female narcotics user sentenced to prison.[43] Her syphilitic infant was discharged to charity; her parole was delayed and made conditional.

The judge also told the story of a lightly sentenced, 19-year-old man who would not have been in court "if it were not for the girl and the drugs." His dramatic accounts illustrated how blame was directed toward women—and away from men.

Antidrug rhetoric established that babies born addicted would have a "poisoned" attitude that would undermine the progress of modernity, freedom, productivity, and civilization. Wallis explained that the children of addicted mothers did not inherit addiction so much as a predisposition to it.[44] Education could overcome this inheritance.[45] In his congressional testimony and his speech before the WNDA, Wallis stated: "Babies are born in drug addiction, and horrible as it may seem, they actually begin life under the influence of narcotic drugs, and many of them at their mother's breast. . . . What can society expect of children whose father and mother, or both, are criminal addicts? What will be the children's attitude towards society? How many generations will be poisoned by the offspring of this man and woman who are given entirely to the use of drugs and its attendant evils?"[46] He maintained that addiction threatened the nation's "civic health" through intergenerational transmission.[47]

Drug-related films of the period conveyed to a wide audience the tenacious governing mentality that women are responsible for "reproducing" addiction. In *The Pace That Kills* (1928), a young, white, female prostitute named Fannie initiated "Country Boy Eddie" into cocaine, opium, morphine, and heroin use. Soon after telling Eddie she was pregnant, she drowned herself.[48] Such representations were common in exploitation films despite the prohibition against depictions of drug use by the Motion Picture Production Code of 1930. Dwain and Hildegarde Esper released the film *Narcotic* (1933) amid controversy from state and local censor boards. Billed as an "unusual fact-story," the film told the story of an addicted physician, but the publicity stills centered on "the women who worshipped him." A newspaper story titled "Dope Makes Strange Creatures of Beautiful Women" began: "The happy, normal laughter of physically adorable girls gives way to the hysterical outbursts of dope-maddened, sexually perverted women under the sinister influence of drugs, as disclosed in the amazing 'dope party' scene from the new talking picture 'Narcotic.'"[49] A caption beneath a widely reproduced still of the doctor injecting a beautiful blonde read, "Only a tiny red spot on her arm but it blackened her soul forever." Another story attributed white women's fascination with the drug to curiosity, the "downfall of women, . . . since the beginning of time."

Narcotic was promoted as starkly realistic, unadorned, and uncensored—an alternative to the "usual sugar and water situations disclosed in the average film." Attempting to pass the censors, Dwain Esper publicly advocated uniform state narcotics laws and called the 1931 Geneva Anti-Narcotics Treaty the "most important international law of the civilized world." Three years later, the Espers released *Marijuana*, a film in which a white, female heroin addict aptly named Burma gave birth, lost her husband, and became the "ice queen of the snow peddlers" by selling headache powders to society matrons.[50] *Marijuana* marked the last directly drug-related film plot until after World War II.[51] These films positioned addicted white women as relays between the underworld and the "straight" world, between civilization and its discontents.

Narcotics use was constructed as a maladaptive—if ubiquitous—response to modernity, of which complexity and efficiency were key elements. The presence of "deviance" stimulated the fear that modernity required more than some individuals could give. Reformers sometimes portrayed the economic effects of drugs as more significant than their moral effects. They linked productivity concerns to assessments of moral worth and mental fitness, marking the fear that some individuals simply could not contribute to the project of social reproduction. For example, Arthur Woods, a New York City police commissioner and assessor to the League of Nations Committee on Traffic in Opium and Other Dangerous Drugs, asserted that drugs gave inadequate men "synthetic courage" that allowed them to master risks they otherwise could not. Narcotics were weapons—"coefficients of power"—that eroded self- and social discipline. Tapping the primitivizing register, Woods opposed simple premodern societies to complex civilizations:

> In civilized society, since members of groups are highly dependent upon one another, there must be self-control, and the individual must be ready to accept limitations of his freedom of action for the sake of the welfare of the body politic. Whereas the social body needs members who face and accept responsibility, narcotics produces shirkers, searchers for privilege and self-gratification. Modern society faces evil days indeed if people cease paying heed to the obligations that they share as members of groups. In a complex civilization like ours, where the highest pitch of social efficiency is requisite, we cannot risk the lowering of standards which is involved in this baleful deflection of interests and ambitions.[52]

Drug users were thus disqualified from membership in civilized groups. Narcotics use was the antithesis of the effort required of a productive member of the "civilized" social body.

Reformers believed that narcotics dampened worldwide economic activity. Frederick Wallis maintained that opium consumption was already excessive in the United States:

> What does this mean? Startling as it may seem, it means the entire nation paralyzed, and practically out of existence for seven whole days of each year. Can you imagine every railroad train at a standstill, rusting on the tracks for a

week? Every streetcar stalled? Every automobile "dead"? Every plow motionless in the furrow? Every vessel in our lakes and every steamship in our ports of entry tied fast? No lights in the streets, in the office or home; all industry shut down; every human being in a state of coma; the country dead for over seven days? And who can figure what eight grains of opium per capita constitutes in economic, physical, and moral disaster?[53]

Similarly, WNDA conference speaker L. A. Higley, a chemistry professor from Wheaton College, Illinois, claimed, "We have now reached the point in narcotic consumption where the majority of the people of each of the principal nations are under the influence of narcotics all the time. . . . We now have instances of whole nations coming under the influence of narcotics."[54] Women were implicated in the intergenerational reproduction of addiction, an emphasis that was both sexualized and racialized in the remarkably condensed and seductive figure of the "opium vampire" in Graham-Mulhall's 1926 book *Opium: The Demon Flower*. In the book, "Dopeville," the drugged nation, was figured as a feminine nation in need of protection and a vigorous masculine defense.

Predators and Prey
Victims, Vectors, and Opium Vampires

There was no more "exotic" addict than white women who used opiates to "ensnare [their] prey" and extend the seduction of opium to "all grades of society."[55] White, deceptively fashionable, pretty, and sexualized, the figure of the "opium vampire" typified the orientalizing register (see Figure 8). Opium vampires inhabited a mythical realm founded "ages ago by good old American stock whose American descendents have made it Dopeville—drugged, dazed, dying."[56] In this drugged nation, "self-confessed addicts, self-confessed former addicts, and former addicts who claim they are cured, insist that 'every soul in this town's an addict.'"[57] Closely related to the New Woman and "flapper" figures, opium vampires preyed on men and children; the latter were both victims and vectors of addiction.

Opium vampires were clearly predators, in contrast to the innocent "child addicts" they sometimes produced. Graham-Mulhall believed "no addict mother [should] be allowed to care for her addict baby, no matter what the tragic consequences of their separation and exposure."[58] Children "must be immediately taken out of the addict home, without scruple, just as anyone must be removed from contagion of an incurable disease, and the state must make proper clinical provision and care for child addicts because fortunately they are all curable."[59] Otherwise the contagion of addiction would spread from "nerve-exhausted, neurotic, drug-poisoned" parents whose "cells and nerves . . . are so impregnated

Figure 8   Illustrations captioned "Swanky Sin" and "Woman in Kimono," from "A Show Girl's Road Back from the Drug Habit."

Reprinted from *True* magazine, 1937.

with the poison of the narcotic—auto-intoxication—that it is impossible for them to beget a healthy child."[60]

Opium: The Demon Flower unfolded as a series of cautionary tales, warning men and boys against the feminine. Reputable colleges were scandalously awash in drugs: "Young girls returning from a vacation to resume their studies can spread the drug habit they may have acquired in a short interval of absence. As to our boys in colleges and universities, too many are the unfortunate prey of dissolute women, who bind them to shameful secrecy of illicit relations, by the hideous fascination of drugs."[61] Addicted college boys were portrayed as victims of corrupt older women; college girls might appear "fit and normal" but they, too, unwittingly passed on addiction. Their addictions often originated from a physician's misplaced effort to "quiet the fulmination of . . . complicated femininity," and suppress the "high-strung mentality," pride, and "feminine arts of deception" they exhibited.[62] Even medical addicts exhibited a sexualized deceptiveness (see Figure 9). Addiction among women was caused by a "morbid psychology" and the "modern whirl of sensational, overstrained habits of life."[63] While modernity "caused" women's addiction, *women* "caused" addiction among men.

Opium vampires embodied a particular brand of upper-class, white femininity—decadent, deceptive, and exotic. Devious, pretty, and luxuriously dressed, they were "actresses in the great drama of opium."[64] Their charm, cleverness,

Figure 9 Illustration of physician injecting seductive woman, from "Exposing the Traffic in Dope," *The American Weekly*, 1930.

Courtesy of the Hearst Corporation.

and brightness deceived even the resolute Graham-Mulhall. She reserved her sympathies, however, for the "young men they have ruined and the girls they have drawn into the drug net." Their duplicity most piqued Graham-Mulhall: "A slender little girl, with a clinging femininity about her that appeals, or a woman whose beauty is of the dazzling stage type—these are the most dangerous opium vampires. In the upper strata of a society where money is plenty, where gayety and pleasure are the chief aims of life, the opium vampire is often bred."[65] Gradually, charming women metamorphosed into the predatory mistresses of opium dens and "apartments where men who are reported missing are often found."[66] Long associated with femininity, deception was lodged in the feminized "lying body" that preyed on men and boys.[67] The society women who were the opium vampires were symbolic sisters to their lower-class cousins—prostitutes who lured men into drug use and working mothers who doped babies to keep them docile.[68] Such deflections and divisions were integral to Progressive campaigns, which sent moral messages to the public about when "normal" behaviors crossed the line to "deviance."

Both tools and allies of unscrupulous men, opium vampires purveyed a "new form of white slavery, which begins and ends with the power of opium."[69] Well-bred, dainty, young, and smartly gowned women were more valuable to men than "hardened criminal types," brutal in their "feminine callousness."[70] Observing class differences in generations of "white slaves," Graham-Mulhall noted that earlier generations were comprised of immigrant women of peasant stock, while the current generation consisted of native-born "daughters of good families, young women of intelligence and breeding." The latter pursued opium out of their hunger for romance: "A warning against the opium vampire is all that can be done to save the boys, the young men, from her entanglements."[71]

The opium vampire of the 1920s was a temptress, a seductress whose appeal lay in her sexuality, her femininity, and her whiteness; she was a grandmother to "heroin chic." Her deceptive sexuality still haunts our political-cultural imaginary. The figures who today encode the "curse of civilization" are no longer the orientalized figures of decadent white women but the primitivized figures of women of color. They bear the burden of representing both the physiological reproduction of addiction and the social dislocations of (post)modernity.

Researching Addiction Prior to World War II

The lurid imagery of *Opium: The Demon Flower* contrasted to the flatly scientific efforts of addiction researchers, whose efforts were summarized in an encyclopedic compendium produced under the auspices of the Bureau of Social Hygiene by Charles E. Terry and Mildred Pellens for the Committee on Drug Addictions of New York City. The first report of its kind, *The Opium Problem* exceeded 1,000 pages and cited some 6,000 sources published between the 1880s and 1928. Lawrence Kolb undertook the first systematic federal research on addiction in 1923 at the Hygienic Laboratories of the U.S. Public Health Service in Washington, D.C. Working for the Immigration Service at Ellis Island in 1914, Kolb became intrigued with alcoholism and drug addiction. In 1925 he published three papers, including one that set out the K-classification scheme, used to categorize drug addicts for decades to follow.[72]

Kolb sought to dispel the association between drugs and crime, already a stock discursive resource in the teens and 1920s, arguing that opiates inhibited aggression and made "psychopaths less likely to commit crimes of violence."[73] Reviewing 225 criminal cases and statistics from "morphine cities" and "heroin cities," he demonstrated that increased law enforcement was responsible for the sudden increase of addicts behind bars—not an increase in narcotics use. Already he illustrated a racialized pattern of drug law enforcement that benefited whites and targeted African-Americans.[74] Alcohol, Kolb claimed, was involved far more in the commission of crime than opiates or cocaine. Drug users were responsible for few serious crimes: most of his subjects committed minor crimes of "disorderly conduct" (drunkenness, fighting, and petty theft). Narcotics charges, used to legislate morality as early as the mid-1920s, predominated.

Addiction resulted in "moral deterioration" and lethargy because opiates soothed disturbed individuals, sapped their vitality, and reduced violent tendencies.[75] "Habitual criminals are psychopaths, and psychopaths are abnormal individuals who, because of their abnormality, are especially liable to become addicts. Addiction is only an incident in their delinquent careers, and the crimes they commit are not precipitated by the drugs they take."[76] Kolb undoubtedly pitched his scientific claims to defend against the popular association of drugs with crime, yet he also established a hierarchy of susceptibility based on class formation and "professionalism." He explained that the "highest type of citizen [was] a moral individual with superior intellect balanced by a normal flow of emotions and with a personality undisturbed by nervous instability of any kind."[77] Such individuals— who might be physicians or lawyers—rarely became addicted and evidenced little deterioration when they did. Their respectability exempted them: "The criterion for lack of deterioration in individuals originally useful and in good standing in the community has been continued employment in useful occupations, the respect of associates, living in conformity with accepted social customs, avoidance of legal prosecution except those brought about by violations of narcotics laws, undiminished mental activity, and unchanged personality."[78]

An exception that is of interest because of its gender implications occurred in the case of a 53-year-old physician who descended from a "fastidious, foppish parasite" to a "slovenly, dirty dependent without ambition, pride, or honor."[79] According to Kolb, his susceptibility was due to the "pernicious pampering influences of his mother," who moved him from a public hospital to a posh resort. "The next meeting with his mother was a love feast; he embraced her with childish happiness, and it was plain how her blind coddling had contributed to his ruin."[80] Such subjects "suffer[ed] in manliness,"[81] and became "outcasts, idlers, and dependents" rather than the "fairly useful citizens" they might have been.[82] "The psychopath, the inebriate, the psychoneurotic, and the temperamental individuals who fall easy victims to narcotics have this in common: they are struggling with a sense of inadequacy, imagined or real, or with unconscious pathological strivings that narcotics temporarily remove; and the open make-up that so many of them show is not a normal expression of men at ease with the world, but a mechanism of inferiors who are striving to appear like normal men."[83] Addicts were an inferior species masquerading as "normal." Addiction signaled maladjustment for most researchers—Kolb considered it a form of adjustment for inadequate individuals.

Few studies of female addicts appeared prior to the 1950s. Between the Harrison Act and the 1930s, the ratio of male-to-female addicts changed from two-to-one to three-to-one, according to a 1935 study by Bingham Dai, a University of Chicago graduate student.[84] Dai's sample consisted of 1,400 male addicts and 533 female addicts, many intensively interviewed. Most addicts in his study (77 percent) were white and native-born, discrediting the "popular notion that opium addiction is a vicious habit peculiar to a certain race or nationality."[85] The female sample was drawn from the Women's Reformatory, where many claimed to be iatrogenic (medical) addicts. He found that women comprised approximately 15 percent of drug peddlers, a rare clue that women took part in drug traffic. Two thirds of addicts in the sample did not have children; thus "the family as an integrating influence played a rather insignificant role."[86] Fully half the women had left their home of origin prior to the age of sixteen. Significant numbers had married to escape "unpleasant" homes of origin, but were single, divorced, separated, or widowed. They were "free of the social responsibilities usually borne by married people, but at the same time were denied the kind of instinctual as well as other emotional satisfactions that can be obtained only in a normal married life."[87] Addicts were marked as sexually "alternative," if not downright "deviant."

The maternal relationship was especially fraught for both male and female addicts. While the absence of the father may leave its trace, the presence of the mother was highly influential in the etiology of addiction. Dai presumed the "broken home" hypothesis, indicating that it was prominent prior to his study. However, broken homes of origin (due to separation or divorce) were not found in higher proportions among drug addicts than in the general population. Dai offered psychological and social explanations for the "failures" of sexual and marital adjustment he encountered, the inadequacy of personality makeup, and the inferiority, instability, and insecurity his subjects described.[88] Thus addiction research from the 1920s and 1930s emphasized individual maladjustment, whether it was attributed to poor social and economic circumstances or psychological disposition. Such efforts supplied a counternarrative to the construction of addicts as predators but ultimately did not displace the dichotomy between predator and prey.

White Slave Narratives and Masculine Adventure Stories

While the federal mental health apparatus was gradually assembled, the law enforcement apparatus had consolidated its powers earlier, thanks largely to the untiring efforts of Harry J. Anslinger, a true crusader who became the nation's foremost authority on drug law enforcement. A diplomat to the United Nations, his name remains synonymous with repressive drug law enforcement today. He was a prolific writer of popular fiction, speeches, radio addresses, articles in law, criminology, and medical journals, and loosely factual narratives about the heroics of drug law enforcement. Soon after Anslinger became chief of the Federal Bureau of Narcotics (FBN) in 1930, a proposal was advanced to merge the FBN and the Prohibition Bureau and move them out of Treasury and into the Department of Justice.[89] Suggested as a federal cost-cutting move (it was, after all, during the Depression), the merger would have reduced the newly appointed director's authority. In response, Anslinger cultivated the press and exposed horse-doping at race tracks.[90] As a Republican, however, he soon needed a new and more compelling issue to maintain his post in a Democratic administration. His office released a rash of reportage on the "white slave traffic," one of the "disastrous effects of the government's 'economy' program with respect to narcotics law enforcement."[91]

For Anslinger, narrative functioned as "direct manifestation[s] of reality" and words were accorded a transparent status.[92] His moral discourse depended on direct—and emotionally charged—correlations between words and things. He advocated against "contagious" representations of drug use as strenuously as he protested anything that tolerated or "condoned" drug use. In his stories, the sympathetic main character's misery results directly from lack of policy (such as a uniform state narcotics law), a budget cut, or other bureaucratic maneuver. His characters were allegorical figures that encoded a symbolic threat to the existing moral order. They figured in parables about the effect on adolescent girls and their parents of drug laws and policies, enforcement agencies, and budget appropriations. They were hybrid "fact-fictions" based loosely on actual narcotics cases.

These "fact-fictions" indicate the depth of the racism and misogyny of this influential policy-maker and policeman. To merely reiterate blatant examples of "bias" or "stereotypes" would accomplish little, for the governing mentalities perform a deeper, more persistent, and dynamic form of cultural work. Anslinger's prodigious paper trail contributed much to the repository of narratives from which we draw our cultural imagery of drugs. While inadmissible as historical evidence, his "fictions" aligned with his "facts." Anslinger's influential "fact-fictions" structured policy across a career that spanned bipartisan administrations from 1930 to 1962 until he became a political liability to the Kennedy administration. They were not his alone—the same tenets were echoed in testimony, the popular press, and scientific studies. We cannot dismiss these representations as Anslinger's idiosyncrasies; I am less interested in his imaginary than ours. The narratives rely on common images of racial and sexual difference—the "Dragon Lady," the emasculated "oriental,"[93] conniving upper-class women who think themselves beyond the law, and innocent white girls and their scandalized parents. Women occupy only two positions in this imaginary—total guilt or complete innocence, predator or prey.

One of the earliest "fact-fictions" surfaced in a series of articles published in Hearst-owned newspapers in November 1933 on a northern California "white slave ring." Quoted officials criticized the government's "penny wise and pound foolish" decision to cut FBN appropriations. Article after article linked "federal powerlessness" to the exploitation of white women and girls, placing the masculine state in the position of protecting feminine innocents.[94] William G. Walker, chief of California narcotics enforcement, said: "My hands are tied so far as interfering seriously with this terrible traffic in young girls." Citing manpower shortages and slashed budgets, he continued, "This enslavement of young girls, while we stand helpless, is only one phase of the whole penny-wise and pound-foolish policy." He warned that the price of narcotics would fall; law enforcement officers would turn mothers away rather than "save" their daughters. "Decent young girls seeking work, [would be] transformed within a week into dope-saturated, cringing slaves by something that takes possession of them, body and soul," according to the chief, who described dope gangsters hiring women to convert "young and reasonably pretty" girls into "dazed, helpless thing[s]" for one hundred dollars a head. "And I can't follow through with this thing because I lack a few dollars to employ operatives to do the detective work and gather the evidence," Walker concluded.[95] The chief requested emergency appropriations from the state legislature to make up the federal shortfall.

Another article in the series alleged that 63 young women were admitted to the San Francisco Hospital "to conquer the octopus that has sunk its tentacles into their body and brain—the drug habit."[96] The girls were described: one "fair-haired with the look of the country about her," another "dark and more sophisticated," and presumably urban. Some were educated and cultured; all sank to the same level—an "advanced state of social disease." Battling the "four horsemen of the apocalypse"—here named narcotics, prostitution, disease, and crime—narcotics agents were figured as saviors of civilization. At times, racialized male addicts—"a Chinaman, an Irishman, a Mexican"—appeared to concretize Anslinger's warning that "peddlers and addicts are headed toward the Pacific coast as the new Utopia of the drug user." Attempting to whip up fervor among Californians, Anslinger noted that the budget cuts made it "humanly impossible for us to do any more than skim the surface."

A similar series by society matron Winifred Black was released later that month. She appealed to parents, emphasizing young girls who went "down to the levee where giant black men buy cocaine to make them 'step lively' when the mate calls orders," into alleys "where the human wreckage seems to gather by some weird and evil instinct," into flower shops, up to a famous hotel where a woman waits, "hardly [able to] bear the strain until she hears the knock at the door, which tells her the poison is there, waiting for her."[97] Dwelling on racially and gender-coded locations, Black sniffed out the dope traffic: "I saw a woman in a Chicago beauty parlor once—a pretty woman she had been, too, before she took to dope—you could tell that by her features even in her wan face—she had

a little girl with her, a gay little creature with bright eyes and a laughing mouth—
how long was it, I wonder, before she understood what made her mother so tired
and listless, and why she was always so gay after she had come to the beauty parlor?" America, according to Black, was about to be flooded by a "tidal wave" of
dope if the budget directors did not give the FBN sufficient funds.

These accounts suggest that young girls and women served as representative innocents in mobilizing public sentiment (see Figure 10). The figure of the addicted
white girl as "prey" worked like lynching narratives in which the raped body of
the white woman served as the occasion for white racist violence against African-
American men. The bodies of addicted girls sold into sexual slavery worked to direct law enforcement toward men of color. Sometimes that connection was literal,
as in a January 12, 1932, report from Honolulu that appeared in the *New York
Evening Journal* on a Hawaiian dope ring that brought about "lawlessness and li-
cence, culminating in wanton attacks on white women." "Impotent" in the face of
these attacks, the police chief commented, "Women have not been safe for years.
They are open to attack by hop-heads and justice can't be obtained because of the
narcotic clique."[98] The stories construct white women and girls as a national resource in need of protection from threatening foreigners—in this case, the narcotic ring consisted of "Japanese, Chinese, half-breeds, and renegade Americans
who import from Mexico" who formed a recognizable social "clique" of users.

"White Girl Trap!": The Frank Gin Case

A 1931 narcotics case in Cleveland, Ohio, loomed especially large in Anslinger's
imaginary. The Detroit Division of the FBN arrested Frank Gin, alias Quack
Sang, and Ruth Miller Hohlfelder, a 25-year-old white woman and self-described
artist arrested previously on a narcotics charge. The case unfolded from an
anonymous tip that a Chinaman was "selling heroin and smoking opium to
white women and young girls."[99] Narcotic officers staked out Frank Gin's apartment and were questioning him when Hohlfelder entered. Hohlfelder turned
over the heroin she was carrying and offered to give the agents an additional cap-
sule she had left behind at her apartment. Several material witnesses were ar-
raigned, including Ruth Stull, "a dancer who is a familiar figure in the city's night
life."[100] Stull offered to testify as a material witness before the grand jury; she,
too, had been previously arrested with Hohlfelder.

The agents seized photographs of Stull and other white girls from Gin's bed-
room. Two young white girls, Agnes Taylor and Doloris King, who were not addicts but who lived in the apartment building, were called as material witnesses.
Gin often cooked Chinese food for them, which the girls appreciated "due to the
fact that with the present condition among waitresses in the City of Cleveland,
they were making very little money." They alleged that Gin had offered them

Figure 10   Illustration of book cover, *Dope, Dames and Sudden Death*, depicting white slavery.

Reprinted from *True Crime Detective* magazine, 1947.

money in return for engaging in sexual relations with him. This round of interviews turned up more white women who frequented the Gin apartment. Gene Nash and Marie Jay Vecchio were also called as material witnesses. Vecchio alleged that Frank Gin offered her free drugs "if she would endeavor to induce young, white girls to come to his apartment where he could induce them to use drugs."[101] The case report was primarily devoted to the women's sworn affidavits, quoted in full "for the purpose of showing the relationship which existed between these young white women and this Chinaman."[102] The women were identified consistently as both "young" and "white," indicating that the author, narcotics agent Ralph H. Oyler, drew quite consciously on the white slavery narrative.

The girls testified to the sale of heroin and smoking opium, the odor of which the agents had detected. The Nash affidavit stated that other white girls stopped by the apartment to purchase heroin—"Frank Gin would take them into a back bed room for the purpose of making the sale."[103] Girls who arrived without enough cash were sent out to solicit prostitution. Vecchio stated that Nash had introduced her to both Frank Gin and the heroin habit, and corroborated Nash's observations. Contact between the girls and Chinese men took place in Chinese groceries, restaurants, and homes. Stull described smoking opium at a New Year's Eve party in 1928 at the home of Ruth and Alfred Hohlfelder and had apparently undergone a cure for heroin addiction at the Cleveland City Hospital. She too corroborated the allegation that Gin had asked her to recruit young girls who were not yet addicted to induce them to use drugs.[104] She also described an incident in which Gin offered her additional heroin "if she would consent to enter into sexual relations with him."[105] Agent Oyler noted that Gin "repeatedly requested [the girls] to induce young white girls to come to his apartment and use heroin, in order to cause them to become addicted to the same and become regular customers."[106]

Despite the girls' affidavits, which attested to their familiarity with heroin for as much as two and a half years previously, press accounts and fictional narratives maintained the innocence of the "unsuspecting girls" (with the exception of Hohlfelder, who was sentenced to eighteen months at the Federal Industrial Institution for Women in Alderson, West Virginia). Chinese men were the villains in all versions of the story—they inhabited "celestial vice dens" in the midst of the Depression, and ensnared white women in a "sinister web of oriental sex desires." The girls' respectability was emphasized—these "high-class girls" did not "look like scum."[107]

Frank Gin was sentenced to five years in the Atlanta Penitentiary and was later moved to the federal penitentiary in Lewisburg, Pennsylvania. "This is precisely what every citizen is afraid of when he thinks of the Chinese quarter," commented federal judge Samuel H. West.[108] "People in Cleveland are inclined to overlook this peril because of their relations with respectable Chinese," he continued. The judge intended his decision to "stand as a warning to others who would entice girls." Soon after his release from Lewisburg in December 1937,

Frank Gin was again arrested in Cleveland on August 8, 1938, and September 14, 1938, for dispensing heroin to a woman named Marie Wonderling. This time he was sentenced to ten years on eight counts, pleading guilty to the purchase, sale, and distribution of narcotics.[109] Gin wrote to the Honorable Judge Paul Jones from his cell on November 16, 1938, to protest the length of his second sentence, stating that he had no lawyer and assuring the court that he would return to California upon release.[110] His case was destined to live in infamy through several thinly fictionalized renditions. All versions, however, allow the characters to voice moral positions on addiction and "white slavery."

"Dream Girls": "Fact-Fictions" about the Frank Gin Case

The Gin case had a lasting impact on Anslinger, who revisited it in his 1961 book *The Murderers,* in a section provocatively titled "Embryo." Earlier drafts appeared in his papers along with the press coverage, the case file, and an unpublished manuscript titled "Chinese Bluebeard" by a Cleveland-based reporter named Jack Heil.[111] Anslinger appears to have used Heil's manuscript as the basis for his own narratives. Heil maintained that "the use of drugs by young girls was increasing at an alarming rate, indicating that some agency was promoting, very successfully, the use of dope, in various forms, among young women in Cleveland."[112] Narcotics agents noticed "an increasing number of girl addicts, artists, dancers, stenos, and just plain working girls." Heil also published a short piece, "White Girl Trap!" in 1937 that Anslinger saved.[113] "White Girl Trap!" was explicitly racist, beginning with an account of a "fawning Quack Sang," "fat-faced and grinning," serving a bevy of "comely girls in their teens or early twenties" amidst a "fragrance with an oriental tang." In this account, several Chinese men nervously awaited the administration of "sex inflaming drugs" to the girls. The agents noted, "opium and heroin isn't enough—they feed them [love pills]."

Establishing the girls' lack of sexual desire for the Chinese and casting aspersions on their masculinity was important to all of the narratives. "Ruth Stallings," as Ruth Stull was named in "White Girl Trap!" articulated the white girls' revulsion for Chinese men. "Many times when I got dope from [Gin] he asked me and begged me to bring him girls to enslave. He and his companions had an insatiable lust for white girls. Many times he tried his wiles on me, but he was repulsive and I told him so. On one occasion he tried to force me to accede to his bestial desires. I've always been somewhat of an athlete and we had a real roughhouse battle. Guess I beat him up pretty badly before he quit." In "Chinese Bluebeard," Marie Jay (Vecchio) said, "I frequently bought heroin from Frank Gin. I have witnessed the wild dope parties in Gin's suite participated in by his Chinese friends and numerous white girls. The usual procedure was to get the girls hopped up by hitting the pipe or on heroin and then get them to remove their clothing and pose for him."[114] Heil also revealed an "unusual relationship" between Ruth Hohlfelder and "Ruth Jones"—"neither cared particularly for male companionship."[115] The specter of sexual deviance loomed.

Prostitution and interracial sex held considerable fascination for Anslinger as a writer. His female characters ranged from the naïve embryos to the handmaidens of the underworld.[116] His earliest rendition of the story was an unpublished manuscript later titled "Underworld Slaves," apparently redrafted in the 1940s.[117] Frank Gin/Quack Sang appears as "Sang Gin," and the judge addresses him: "This is the most shocking condition I have ever heard of. To think that it could exist in the heart of the community is almost beyond human comprehension. This is the sort of thing that every decent citizen fears when he thinks of the Chinese quarters of the city. It is responsible for the feeling that now and then rises against the most honorable upright Chinese. The most horrible feature of it is the enticement of respectable young girls to the orgies of your criminal den."[118] Anslinger emphasized the girls' entrapment in the very "heart of the country." In his second version, concerned parents worry their daughters might be using dope. One father trailed his daughter to a "certain corner" of the city where she disappeared for the night. She had been "hitting the pipe," a recent fad among the young.[119] The father's distress spurred an investigation of addicts from the "Roarin' Third" precinct, Cleveland's "hotbed of crime and vice."[120] New male addicts were nowhere to be found; however, stories about young girls from good families abounded.

Anslinger implicated Chinese tongs and family associations in the seduction of white teenage girls: "Chinese seduction of teen-aged girls and prostitution presented serious problems to our Bureau in the years immediately after 1930. The Chinese not only dealt with prostitutes imported from Asia; many of their customers developed a liking for Caucasian girls. The result, I learned, was a primitive Chinese-American call-girl organization loosely interlaced through Chinese Family associations and the tongs."[121] The second chapter of *The Murderers*, "Slavery, Inc.," reinforced the organized nature of the vice business. The "dream girls" illustrated the racialized and sexualized progression from innocence to blame in Anslinger's imaginary. The tale began in impenetrable mystery. Dazed white girls from upper- and middle-class families alarmed their parents, who became suspicious of their daughters' "listless, blurred lethargy." The parents alerted FBN agents to the existence of a Chinese businessman who sponsored sex-and-drug orgies for Chinese men, into which their daughters were unwittingly conscripted. Anslinger assigned a brilliant agent to the case—"a lean, full-blooded Cherokee Indian who sometimes passed as a Chinese, sometimes as an Indian, Mexican, Negro or Eurasian."[122]

"Our Cherokee 'Chinese'" agent soon discovered "a scene of unspeakable sexual depravity" populated by a "cowering" naked Chinese male customer. "Joe Sing," the Frank Gin character, was an elusive businessman who accepted his arrest with

"Oriental calm," and was accompanied by four white eighteen-year-old girls. "Girl after girl in a pitiful repetition related essentially the same story and sequence of events"—their unwitting involvement in an organized business network that plied young white girls with opium, aphrodisiacs, and heroin to ease their physical and mental distress at being forced to have sex with Chinese men.[123] The drug device maintained the white girls' innocence—nothing was real to them or their parents, who maintained a state of shock. Their dream-girl daughters were granted another chance to fulfill a destiny more befitting of their race, class, and gender.

In Anslinger's account, the agents narrowed their search by looking for previous cases with a "feminine angle."[124] He mentioned an incident described only in Heil's manuscript in which a young, nude, female body had turned up in Gin's apartment years before, but police were unable to ascertain Gin's role in her death. In Anslinger's version, the agent in charge passed for a Chinese immigrant, being acquainted with the "sing-song language of the underworld Chinese."[125] In a handwritten page, Anslinger elaborated on the agent's ethnicity, this time described as "full-blooded Cherokee Indian" though he passed for addict, peddler, African-American, Chinese, or "just plain hoodlum." The agent searched the apartment of a Chinese man in a "respectable building," at which point a "comely, well-dressed girl" arrived. She was not disappointed to see the agents because she "wanted to stop but couldn't."

When questioned, the girls played up their naïveté: "I realized suddenly he was kissing me. And I was kissing him as I had never kissed anybody before."[126] Anslinger listed these entries into the litany of the girls' innocence without attributing them to a particular character. He described the girls as startled at strange objects or nude pictures, but undaunted until they discover themselves in "reckless mood[s]" from eating candy containing what laboratory analysis reveals to be Spanish fly.[127] The Heil manuscript used less clinical and more florid language, describing how "low and sensuous music" led girls to the "acme of abandon" in this "garden of Eden" in which "passion reigned supreme."[128] Despite the "unspeakable happenings" in which they participated, these girls—joined sometimes by "respected wives from reputable sections of greater Cleveland"—retained their innocence. Even Hohlfelder, the guiltiest among them, was lightly sentenced because she was "honestly desirous of throwing off the bonds which had enslaved her to drugs."[129] The affidavits revealed young women who knew what they were doing and had been doing it for some time; the fiction reveals innocent girls unwittingly enslaved.

The fictional raid delivered these "victimized" girls from "the tortures of a thousand purgatories."[130] Although Anslinger cut a sentence describing Gin as an "oriental sex monster," Gin is characterized as wily, crafty, evil, and beyond redemption. The last paragraph of "Underworld Slaves" reads: "Some penologists and sociologists feel Gin can be rehabilitated. He will be caught at the same thing again. Congress felt very strongly that the death penalty should be applied in such cases, but public opinion forced them to withdraw the provision. What do you think?" Readers are positioned to side with Commissioner Anslinger—the alternative would consign innocent white girls to the predatorial clutches of men of color. The last paragraph illustrates the narrative use to which the allegorical figures of Anslinger's imaginary were put. The characters encode arguments, sociological claims, and political positions that justify the policies that Anslinger advocates, and convince the public that his path is righteous.

The images that Anslinger amassed in his scrapbooks and displayed in his masculine adventure stories indicate the extent to which cases from the 1920s and prewar 1930s guided him. They illustrated a pattern by which threats of subversion, deception, and disorder were coded as feminine and foreign. Addiction was consistently characterized as threatening to modernity, democracy, and capitalism—rather than produced by them or endemic to them. The effects of these larger forces and social processes on individual lives were left unexplored in favor of a lurid fascination with narcotics and the construction of drug use as a form of political subversion. The figures of addicted white girls and women embodied the governing mentalities about women's role in transmitting, reproducing, and sexualizing addiction. Women played only two roles—the calculating predator or the unwitting prey.

"Dope" was one mode of miscegenation between races, classes, and sexes—a mode that was primitivized and orientalized through reference to non-Western persons and practices.[131] The racialization and sexualization of the drug problem was consistently used to overcome political objections, narrow professional interests, and winnow out dissenting views. These cultural processes kindled a lingering emotional charge, an aura of urgency, and the sense that democracy, capitalism, and modernity—the foundations of the United States of America itself—were under siege. The leveling, intermixing, and disinhibiting aspects of drug use remain staple concerns in drug discourses.

The figures of white women encoded "natural" propensities to addiction in drug discourse of the 1920s and 1930s. Addiction was a quintessential effect of what Michel Foucault called "biopower," an indispensable element in capitalist development, which would "not have been possible without the controlled insertion of bodies into the machinery of production and the adjustment of the phenomena of population to economic processes."[132] Women are differentially located in relation to the "machinery of production," economic processes, and population pressures. Women are situated as the responsible agents of social and biological reproduction—the "social adjustment" mechanisms that reproduce both the labor force and the capitalist class. Addiction in women mitigates against the orderly and controlled "insertion of bodies" into the processes that reproduced capitalism, democracy, and modernity. The idea that white women were fascinated with dope and so vulnerable to it persisted. Addiction remained the province of modern femininity as the "age of dope" came to an end with the onset of World War II.

The "Enemy Within"
Gender Deviance in the Mid-Century

Addiction Comes of Age
The "Troubled Individual"

Addiction—once a private matter—was redrawn as a national, public burden through the figure of the adolescent addict in the 1950s: "the drug addict cannot succeed: a nation of addicts would perish."[1] In the mid-twentieth century, the "troubled individual" was tagged as a social deviant and political subversive. Addicts began to be figured within the domestic social order as enemies whose unnatural needs and desires could not be satisfied through the "normal" channels of work and family. Maladjustment was the main explanatory framework in New York City's first post–World War II heroin "epidemic." The public events recounted in this chapter involved participants from many professions, political perspectives, and academic disciplines. Together they crafted a discursive shift away from older psychoanalytic narratives of desire, craving, and moral deterioration to the new concept of addiction as a pathological response to stress.[2] The New York City drug crisis affords a rich opportunity to study the process by which moral indignation and cultural figuration creep into "scientific" proceedings and policy decisions.

Mid-century articulations of drug users as "enemies within" acknowledged drug use as an ambivalent cultural practice that subverted notions of unitary identity, natural purity, and bodily integrity. Drugs are both natural and artificial, a practice of the self and a technique of othering. Their use entailed the incorporation of foreign substances, rendering addicts self and other, male and female, white and black. In the 1950s these threatening hybrids were conflated with anti-American political ideology. Scientific and popular representations of 1950s drug addicts cast them as a foreign presence, a signal that trouble from elsewhere was infiltrating American cities and psyches.[3] The heroin crisis centered on adolescents, who occupied a newly problematized, liminal state.

Political meanings are attributed to illicit drug use through interpretations of the symbolic figure of the drug user. These meanings vary according to substance, user population, and techniques of use. Policy responses range from inclusion to exclusion, quarantine to reintegration, normalization to demonization. They are based on interpretations of the meaning of drug use and the nature of drug users as well as assessments about the role of the liberal state in regulating individuals. The decision to exclude or include addicts—as human beings, members of a culture, and persons deserving of social benefits—was at issue in mid-twentieth-century social policy, and remains so today. Were addicts to be cast out—segregated through quarantine, incarceration, or "civil" commitment—or reintegrated into the communities from whence they came? Did it matter who they were—young or old, male or female? Addiction was constructed both as an expression of alienation and a source of potential infection to be contained through moral resolve, interdiction, repressive force, or an escalating series of punishments. Others argued that addicts deserved treatment, which has varied in content and form. These disagreements, acrimonious as they were, arose from different conceptualizations of addiction. The New York gatherings cast the inadequacy of the "crime versus disease" framework into high relief. The actual diversity of views demonstrates how basic assumptions about addiction and drug users govern policy decisions and political discourse.

Experts in the new field of adolescent psychology cast young people as especially open to subversive political ideologies, personality reversals, and "peer pressure," and fastened on parents as the cause of this susceptibility. Individualism was the vaccine that regulated the subject's relationship to social groups, including parents—especially mothers—who were overly invested in maintaining their children's dependence. According to this theory, an insidious need for social approval compelled teenagers to subordinate their individuality to an unconscious, peer-dominated "chain reaction," which could only be subdued by strengthening the individual adolescent's resistance to the peer group.[4] The emphasis on parenting, and especially the mother-son relationship, obscured the role of poverty, structural unemployment, the cultural impact of consumer capitalism, and other social precipitants of addiction.

Protecting Innocence: The Kefauver Hearings and the Boggs Act (1951)

National attention to adolescent narcotics use arose in the first nationally televised congressional hearings before the Senate Crime Investigating Committee and the Subcommittee to Investigate Juvenile Delinquency (see Figure 11). The hearings stimulated intense fervor among an estimated 20 to 30 million viewers. Chaired by Senator Estes Kefauver, the hearings lasted from May 1950 to August 1951, during which time they dominated the evening news and housewives held

Figure 11   Photograph of the Kefauver hearings, 1950.

Courtesy of ACME Photo/UPI.

daytime "Kefauver parties."[5] Kefauver was "everything a politician wasn't." His popular book *Crime in America* "uncovered the ugly, dirty truth about the infection of politico-criminal corruption that is eating away at the strong, healthy tissues of our nation."[6] He had a prescient eye for public relations. As the "nation's number one crime buster," Kefauver was a *Time* magazine cover boy on March 12, 1951. However, rival junior senator Joseph McCarthy eclipsed Kefauver's rise to national prominence.[7] Organized crime and anticommunism served the two junior senators as the means to gain political currency and national publicity.

The mention of teenage drug addiction before the Kefauver Crime Committee primed the pump for the November 2, 1951, passage of the Boggs Act, which mandated minimum sentences for the first time in U.S. history.[8] The debate that led to the Boggs Act drew on sensationalistic themes that emerged from the Kefauver hearings and the New York hearings on teenage narcotic addiction chaired by State Attorney General Nathaniel L. Goldstein in the summer of 1951.[9] The impetus for the New York State hearings was Goldstein's "suspicion that right here in New York City [there] was a great incidence of narcotic addiction, especially amongst girls."[10] Addicted women were amply represented in the press coverage of the New York hearings, which was reprinted in the *Congressional Record* the summer before the Boggs Act passed.

Mandatory minimums aimed to deter drug trafficking by escalating its risks through enhanced, predictable sentences. They were supposed to make the "enforcement machine" run smoothly by feeding recidivists back into jail and providing new grist for the mill of justice. The transformation of "wholesome women" into lowly harlots and petty criminals was frequently invoked as an example of how productive citizens became "parasitic criminals" by calculating the low risk of getting caught.[11] A *New York Times* story reprinted in the *Congressional Record* in July 1951 featured an "attractive blond girl" from Cincinnati who lured men into back rooms and put "knockout drops" in their drinks, robbed them, forged government checks, and described the physical effects of withdrawal. Narcotics peddling was not considered an impulsive or opportunistic crime, for it depended on "deliberate and calculated scheming and diligently developed sources of supply, on carefully cultivated outlets and customers," according to Malachi Harney.[12]

The New York State hearings highlighted female witnesses who recounted "gruesome case histories" from the women's prison in Bedford Hills, New York. The national coverage centered on two cases. The first was that of a 25-year-old prostitute who was a former model and a graduate of Oberlin Conservatory; the second a sixteen-year-old high school girl from the Bronx. In the "current addiction wave of hurricane force,"[13] adolescent addict voices were frequently female. A *Time* article emphasized the "misdirected sense of adventure" that enticed youth into heroin use in the "same spirit in which they might have tried a high dive, swallowed a gold fish or taken up a fad for wearing pink bobby socks."[14] Another recurring theme was the transformation of ordinary spaces such as "the ladies' room," subway stations, schools, and drugstores into "heroin hunting grounds" that harbored prostitutes who scoured the city for drugs. A *Newsweek* article excerpted several girls' tape-recorded case histories under the heading "degradation in New York." Most detailed accounts of the drug experience came from women, who embodied the threat of addiction. Support for mandatory minimums was partially mobilized on the basis of gender—these girls were prey who became predators.

The Boggs Act made drug possession "sufficient evidence to authorize conviction" unless the accused could explain it to a jury's satisfaction. Some subcommittee members protested the burden this placed on innocent defendants. Others argued that only the guilty would suffer and felt that juvenile addicts would never suffer because "everybody has sympathy for the poor drug addict." Law enforcement would protect "little boys and little girls"—"they are not going to drag the high-school boys and girls before the criminal courts." Emotion entered the House debate with an impassioned speech by a father of six, Representative Edwin Arthur Hall (R-NY). He argued for hundred-year minimum sentences to "guarantee . . . our young Americans security from drugs and dope and narcotics of all kinds for all time. Only by taking a strong stand for the right can we hope to make this great country strong enough to resist its foes from outside and, as important, from within our borders."[15] Parents were depicted as innocent, shocked, and law-abiding in the political debate. Representative Thompson (D-TX) worried that fathers might commit crimes against dope peddlers who led their daughters astray. While some found addicts insignificant, others attributed grave danger to them.

Depicted as preying on the white population, drug addiction was called a "white death" or "white plague." Those "little white packages" carried a "form of contagious degeneracy which, with cancer-like malignancy, breeds the decay of decency," according to Representative Yates (D-IL). He favorably compared the proposed mandatory minimums to the Mann Act (1910), which he claimed made "white slavery" and kidnapping "too hot to handle."[16] The "traffic in human flesh" drew on a politically potent analogy between adolescent drug use, prostitution, and kidnapping. The "social monster" of drug addiction was thriving— "fattening itself because of short penalties and tall profits." Those who argued for mandatory minimums amplified the metaphoric conflation of addiction with "white slavery."

Those who argued against mandatory minimums were distinctly less hysterical. They included Representative Celler (D-NY), who argued that mandatory sentences would result in the miscarriage of justice and prison overcrowding (already a concern). He cited the "pitiful cases" of veterans, physicians, nurses, and physicians' wives who would be "prejudged" by the imposition of inflexible sentences. Thus the figure of the typical user informed policy-makers' positions on mandatory minimums. If a legislator was exercised by parental sentiment or paternalistic duty to protect innocent girls or vigilantly guard against "enemies within our borders," he supported mandatory minimums. If he was instead concerned that the prisons were about to be filled with "pitiful" professionals, he argued against them.

Women and girls were enlisted to persuade legislators of the drug trade's inherent debauchery. They were depicted as abject victims of "conscienceless," "heartless," and otherwise nefarious individuals who preyed on them. There was scant acknowledgment that the development of drug markets responded to larger political-economic patterns and social conditions—such as urban poverty, undereducation, and youth unemployment. Addicts were understood to come from places where schools were inadequate, housing and recreational facilities deteriorated, and living conditions wretched. The frustration of social deprivation was widely understood to provide an opening for drug markets. Policy-makers acknowledged that there was not enough prison space, nor enough room in the

federal narcotics treatment hospitals, nor enough appropriations to customs officials to deal with the ongoing problem. The Boggs Act disregarded these problems in favor of the policy of incarceration. The FBN realized its ambition to
obtain mandatory minimums in the Boggs Act.

Legislators understood that a certain amount of political theater was central
to how juvenile delinquency played on the national stage. Many felt that the
Kefauver Committee was a just publicity gimmick.[17] Arguing to extend his appropriation in the mid-1950s, Kefauver cited the subcommittee's finding of a direct correlation between juvenile delinquency and narcotics use.[18] He claimed
that young girls were turning to prostitution to support $20-to-$30-per-day
habits; 80 percent of all Spanish-American boys had "contact with narcotics";
and 25 percent of girls in Iowa reform schools used marijuana. He cited no
specifics on the habits of white boys, although they were presumably among the
"tens of thousands of youngsters from southern California [who] pour over the
border in search of this excitement." The absence of attention to majority-pop-
ulation boys deliberately overlooked their participation in drug use and traffic.
Girls and persons of color were simply sexier, more exotic, and more intriguing
subjects of vice.

Undertaken in the name of youth—"the very lifeblood of our Nation"—Kefauver's strategic deployment of the narcotics issue indicated that its symbolic
significance outweighed its actual practice. Where white women once symbolized addiction, youth now played that role. According to Kefauver and
Anslinger, mandatory minimums had taken older drug peddlers off the streets,
leaving teenagers to perform criminal actions. Rather than use this insight to
argue against the unintended and deleterious effects of mandatory minimums,
they used to bolster attention to juvenile delinquency, which was dwindling by
the mid-1950s. The Kefauver hearings instead relied on another discursive resource in the "war on drugs"—the connection between organized crime, drug
trafficking, and communism.

Organized Crime, Juvenile Delinquency, and Communism

Historical periods when the U.S. government mobilizes around domestic subversion often coincide with renewed attention to drug addiction.[19] Citizen anti-
crime committees formed around the belief that crime would rise after the war's
end because youth were left unsupervised while fathers fought and mothers
worked. The committees charged the federal government with ignoring its responsibility to reduce crime and railed against "anti-American" vices—communism, drug traffic, gambling, and prostitution. They also blamed communism
for increased drug traffic and use in capitalist democracies. One member of the
California Citizens' Advisory Committee on Crime Prevention testified:

While every American is affected directly by the narcotics evil, it has more than a casual bearing on the future of the free world. . . . With the end of World War II and the full control of China by the Communists, the United States and other nations suddenly found an alarming rise of heroin addiction. It is well known that heroin of almost pure strength became a principal export of the Communists from Red China; that the manufacture and export of enslaving drugs has been vigorously encouraged by the Communists where they gained control of satellites. Drug addiction in the free nations is a subtle and diabolical form of conquest in which the victims pay for their own enslavement. This is even more cruel and mind destroying that [sic] the techniques devised by the masters of the Kremlin to force the innocent to confess crimes punishable by death. The export of narcotics brings about mass self-destruction among peoples marked for slavery by the Red imperialists.[20]

Illicit drug use relaxed subjects, opening them to communist "brainwashing," and leading them to submit to foreign powers. Narcotics export was "part of the Kremlin pattern of aggression" and part of a plan to engineer communist hegemony over the "free world."[21] These fears were condensed in Kefauver's investigations into organized crime and juvenile delinquency.

Addiction was metaphorically constructed as a form of slavery that bound its subjects to a master personified as "communism" and the organized crime syndicate. Although the older "white slavery" register resonated with this usage, the construction of "enemies within our borders" associated new meanings of political and ideological subversion with narcotics use. Both communism and organized crime implied a subject loyal to a shadowy syndicate that would stop at nothing to undermine democratic law and order. While the Kefauver Committee initially concentrated on narcotics trafficking, its quarry soon became "the sinister criminal organization known as the Mafia."[22] The committee adopted Anslinger's fervent belief that an organized crime syndicate called the Mafia "domina[ted] the dope trade." Historians speculate that rivalry between FBI chief J. Edgar Hoover, who did not believe in the "Mob," and Anslinger influenced the latter's zealous attempts to persuade the committee of the seriousness of the drug problem. Most famous for its Mafia exposé, the committee also inquired into comic books, pornography, baby-selling, "delinquency among the Indians," venereal disease, and "confidence games."

The Kefauver Committee allowed Anslinger's views on drug and crime policy considerable sway, publicity, and popularity. Anslinger painted his opponents as anti-American, communist sympathizers who were soft on crime, thus hindering the effectiveness of arguments from more tolerant quarters. The Kefauver hearings solidly situated the narcotics traffic in the context of domestic fears of communism, juvenile delinquency, and organized crime. The idea that communism inspired illicit drug use has passed into relative obscurity and nostalgic amnesia,[23] but addiction's political subversiveness did not. Addicts were and are represented as "enemies within our borders," a perception that affects knowledge production, political discourse, and policy outcomes by failing to recognize that addiction is endemic to mainstream U.S. institutions. Instead addicts are viewed as a fundamentally separate class.

The Cold War structured drug policy, science, and culture through an enduring discourse of siege. The debate over whether addiction was a crime or a disease was a debate over which authority was to preside over it. Those who believed drug addiction was a crime or a disease might without contradiction agree that it was a form of "communist narcotic aggression." Illicit drug use became an index of Western "willpower" to withstand alternate ideologies and ways of life. The cultural figuration of drug users was also complicated by differential racial, economic, and sexual histories. Long before the infamous Moynihan Report, the nuclear family was the site of a struggle between the production of characteristics of democratic self-governance and those of "dependents" susceptible to communist or totalitarian ideology. Concerns about absent fathers, the effects of African-American "matriarchy," and the corruption of youthful bodies arose. In the Cold War context, the restoration of paternal authority, maternal submission, and normative heterosexuality were antidotes against addiction. They continue to serve as our "solutions" long after the thaw.

New York City: The Locus of the Postwar Heroin Crisis
Local Efforts to Comprehend and Curb Juvenile Addiction

Warnings of a "frightening wave" of addiction about to engulf thousands of boys and girls spurred the New York City Welfare Council to action after the war's end.[24] Surveys of the extent of the problem began in several metropolitan areas.[25] A series of *World Telegram* and *Sun* articles by Edward Mowery about heroin use in Harlem appeared in the spring of 1950. Reporting rising narcotics use among adolescents, the New York City Probation Department and the Welfare Council sought to arouse popular interest in drug treatment. The Police Department increased the number of drug enforcement officers from eighteen to over 50 that year. In September, the supervisor of the New York State Training School for Girls sought help for four girl drug addicts, tipping the balance toward a full-scale public inquiry. Several public events showcased expert knowledge and guided the formation of public policy responses in 1950 and 1951.

The Mayor's Committee formed in December 1950; it was considered a "weak link" because it had no power to implement directives.[26] The Welfare Council drew representatives from 58 organizations to form a Committee on the

Use of Narcotics among Teen-Age Youth. Finally, the Committee on Public Health Relations of the prestigious New York Academy of Medicine held conferences titled "Drug Addiction Among Adolescents" on November 30, 1951, and March 13 and 14, 1952. The academy conferences were designed to overcome the weaknesses of the previous efforts, which were considered cursory by Hubert S. Howe, chair of the New York Academy of Medicine's Subcommittee on Narcotics.[27] The academy conferences were the most authoritative venue, attracting support from the Josiah Macy, Jr., Foundation, then working with the World Health Organization (WHO) to broaden concepts of health to include psychological and social deprivation.

Collectively, these public events aired many views on the causes and consequences of drug addiction and the cultural significance of adolescent addiction. Each event circulated a set of representations, scientific constructions, and expert discourses that constructed the "adolescent drug addict" in ways that shaped policy outcomes, and, eventually, their effects. The spread of addiction to "innocents"—especially to children—allows the construction of crisis to hold sway. Thus the discursive construction of addiction among women and children is meaningful in a way that its construction among men is not. Because men have comprised most addicted persons in the twentieth century, the repetitive return to the figure of the female addict to encode declining morality, the uncivilizing effects of drugs, and alarm for the future is striking. It is based less on demographics than on the meanings at play in our particular regime of truth. If drugs express something of the truth of the self, drug-using women and children express core cultural concerns about social and biological reproduction.

The national political consequences of the academy conferences outweighed the more local efforts because Howe's report recommended voluntary treatment and/or narcotics maintenance. The academy recommendations contradicted the direction of federal drug policy established by the Boggs Act and the FBN, which moved Anslinger to arrange a congressional inquiry headed by Senator Price Daniel (R-TX) to contain the report's potential public impact.[28] The legislative outcome of the Daniel hearings was the Narcotics Control Act (1956), which stiffened the mandatory minimum sentences leveled by the Boggs Act (1951). The 1956 act was so punitive that it galvanized a joint effort to "humanize" the drug addict by the American Bar Association (ABA) and the American Medical Association (AMA), two bodies formerly hostile to one another. In turn the ABA/AMA report prompted a fierce rejoinder from the FBN.[29] The 1950s can thus be seen as a decade of escalating animosity between law enforcement and a fragile alliance of legal experts, scientists, and physicians committed to humanitarian treatment and further research.[30] Whether drug addicts were considered criminals or sick human beings would ultimately determine the levels of social tolerance, access to treatment, and public expenditure on which they could rely.

The Alarmists: The New York City Welfare Council

United on the moral urgency of its task, the Welfare Council Committee was divided on how to go about its work. The report declared narcotics an "emotional release" that "insulate[d] thousands of youngsters in a nightmare world, drugs impairing temporarily—and in some cases, forever—their physical and moral fiber."[31] Accurate numbers simply did not matter—even one teenage addict presented a grave threat as a source of infection to others. Predisposition to addiction was found among children whose parents "distrust[ed] social institutions." Locating addiction among the distrustful classes amplified its threat.

The Welfare Council recommended psychotherapeutic "readjustment" for addicts, which appealed to both crime and disease advocates. Thinking or talking about drug use was considered an act of disloyalty in and of itself: the short slide from talking about drugs to becoming addicted was a persistent theme. Psychiatrist James Toolan, of the Bellevue Psychiatric Division, suggested institutionalizing even "normal boys" until their susceptibility passed because drugs might liberate unconscious drives that would channel them away from normalcy. An architect of the "heroin addict type,"[32] Toolan speculated that poverty and racial discrimination magnified the effects of deprivation in families of origin, which then produced maladjusted individuals whose internal economies were organized by external forces. The drug epidemic was thus an "acute emergency, requiring collective security. While we occupy ourselves with civil defense preparations against a possible enemy attack from abroad, we should not ignore the enemy within our borders."[33] The "enemy within" was an enduring trope by which the threat of narcotics to civil society became intelligible to the "free world."

Direct educational assaults were proposed. In a letter reproduced in the appendix to the Welfare Council's report, Clare C. Baldwin, assistant superintendent of New York City schools, wrote to Anslinger on behalf of the Welfare Council. Baldwin urged lifting the "aura of mystery and secrecy" surrounding drug use, which he categorized as a public health menace, not a diffuse threat of moral deterioration. Anslinger in turn encouraged Baldwin to support five-year mandatory minimum sentences and a quarantine ordinance: "These two actions will do more to curb addiction than an educational program, which will only arouse curiosity. We find that most young people who have become addicted acquired this habit not because of ignorance of consequences, but rather because they had learned too much about the effects of drugs. When young people gather and talk about the horrors of narcotics, addiction usually follows because of the tendency to try it for a thrill. Warning does not deter them, it merely places it in their thoughts."[34] Baldwin found Anslinger's attitudes backward—like those that shielded venereal disease, tuberculosis, and cancer from "educational analysis and attack."[35] The FBN could not dictate local school policy within New

York City. However, the idea that thinking or talking about drugs was an act of disloyalty that encouraged these "enemies within" permeated the Welfare Council conference.

The Rationalists: The New York Academy of Medicine Conferences

The New York Academy of Medicine offered a public health framework that exemplified the spirit of postwar scientific optimism and the vogue for interdisciplinary inquiry.[36] The academy relied on the expert facilitation skills of Frank Fremont-Smith, medical director of the Josiah Macy, Jr., Foundation,[37] and a leader in the World Federation for Mental Health (WFMH).[38] Fremont-Smith considered addiction, gang warfare, promiscuity, truancy, and delinquency to be symptoms of social deprivation. Drug use was simply "one symptom of the social and personal malaise of adolescents," the result of their unmet needs—housing, schools, recreational facilities, freedom from racial or religious discrimination, spiritual values, and communities of responsible adults.[39] He presented himself as a concerned parent and a voice of reason in opposition to "an hysterical public and press."[40] He advocated a systematic effort to tap addicts themselves for information about addiction.[41] As a facilitator, Fremont-Smith was well situated to amplify the flexible refrain that echoed throughout the conference: "Drug use is a symptom or sign, not the primary disease."

Maurice Seevers, professor of pharmacology at the University of Michigan, and the only recognized pharmacological expert present, introduced the notion that drug use was an abnormal psychological symptom of a "primary" disease. He bridged the older psychoanalytic construction of drug habituation as a "condition of desire," and the new, more scientific concept of stress. Drug use indicated emotional instability, psychoneurosis, frustration, or psychopathic deviation: "The adjustment of these individuals to society is in inverse relation to the stress to which they are subjected." The shift from a vocabulary of inner desire to one of external stress was accomplished partly through the cultural figure of the adolescent drug user. For Seevers, the primary disease was magnified levels of social stress in excess of adolescent coping skills. Epidemic drug use among postwar adolescents was no surprise, as Seevers viewed adolescents as insecure, unusually susceptible to outside influences, and "dominated by herd instincts." Drug use was a maladaptive, individual response to a modern world characterized by "fear of the future, fear of impending war, fear of atomic bombs, and fear of military service."[42] Addiction, in other words, was a pathology specific to modernity.

Social psychiatrists theorized addiction as a "deficiency disease" caused by "excessive overprotection, excessive exploitation, deprivation, and rejection" by an overprotective but paradoxically rejecting mother.[43] Addiction arose from a "general dependence in [the addict's] character, producing a kind of moral lethargy.

Frequently the result is a well-nigh spineless being in whom the sinews of personality are flaccid at best."[44] Notions of dependent character or "status frustration" (a code word for low socioeconomic class in a "classless" society) located lack within the addict and the addict's mother. Maladjustment resulted from low degrees of moral resistance and immunity imbued by the mother. The figure of the adolescent drug user exemplified immaturity and inadequacy—but also encoded a particular threat that was gendered masculine except in a few venues.[45] In the next section, I consider addiction among women and girls before proceeding to a detailed reading of the landmark social-psychiatric study of addiction undertaken in the mid-1950s crisis.

The Aftermath in New York City: The American Bar Association

New York City and state were a locus for addiction and talk about its causes and effects throughout the 1950s. The ABA was drawn into the drug policy debate for several reasons, among them the threat that mandatory minimum sentences represented to judicial autonomy. In a public hearing of the ABA Joint Legislative Committee on Narcotic Study in 1957, some 35 key players from the earlier scare testified to their experience over the past seven years. The question of female addicts was more directly addressed in this hearing than in any other public gathering of the 1950s. State Attorney General Nathaniel Goldstein, who convened the first state hearings in 1951, noted his "suspicion that right here in New York City [there] was a great incidence of narcotic addiction, especially amongst girls."[46] A survey of more than 300 girls in New York State prisons and reformatories was conducted and identified 65 girls as narcotics users. They were segregated and subjected to a psychiatric and sociological treatment regimen that included occupational therapy and after care. When this regimen failed to end the girls' addiction, Goldstein averred that the drug problem was of "ancient vintage" and could not be cured "overnight." Henrietta Additon, superintendent of Westfield State Farm, a New York State women's prison, noted that the segregation attempt was incomplete: the "drug girls" were housed where they could evoke the "curiosity and interest of the non-drug girls."[47]

Some used the Westfield experiment as evidence that treatment would inevitably fail. Additon felt the experiment simply did not address drug users' desire to get others to use drugs in order to "build up their belief in themselves" and allay their "despondency and fear."[48] She pointed out that most "drug girls" came from poor neighborhoods, had no vocational training, were of Puerto Rican descent, and learned the habit from their boyfriends: "They have no stability. They have no real family life or supervision. Their family is working outside the home."[49] Additon also opined that "a great deal of drugs are coming in from

Communist China,"[50] an allegation later echoed by Anslinger's testimony.[51] A pattern of associations was set—narcotics addiction in girls took place only in ethnic enclaves or as a result of a communist plot.

At the Women's House of Detention, Judge Anna Kross, Commissioner of Correction for the City of New York, noted that addiction had displaced venereal disease as the main problem of incarcerated women. "During my twenty years on the bench [1933 to 1954], I gradually saw this constant growing, continuous growing, increase of narcotics as far as women were concerned."[52] Rates of addiction among women prisoners were now as high as 50 to 60 percent. Kross stated that the prison conditions made "better criminals" of women.[53] Thus she supported the controversial New York Academy of Medicine report, concurring that addicted women are "sick people" who became criminals "because of the inadequate way in which they are treated."[54] Many public officials who dealt closely with addicts argued that criminalization exacerbated the problem. Indeed, Judge Kross bravely stated her belief that the maintenance clinics of the 1920s were medically and philosophically sound, although badly administered.[55]

Others argued against the dichotomy between punishment and treatment or rehabilitation: "Punishment is a normal process in the State's structure, and there is no reason it can't be done in a rehabilitative way, the same way as when a parent punishes a child."[56] Parole, according to Paul Travers of the New York State Division of Parole, bridged the gap between enforcement and rehabilitation by "promoting health and normal social living."[57] Acknowledging the punitive element of parole, he endeavored to get parolees "emotionally attached" to "values the community considers acceptable."[58] Users lived "undisciplined lives," in the words of probation officer Arch Sayler: "Probationers and parolees must live clean, honest, temperate and industrious lives. They must remain in approved homes, support their dependents, report as directed, and answer all questions put to them by their supervising officer."[59] Social discipline was a stay against the "self-indulgence" embodied by drug addicts. The officers did not shirk from arguing the importance of reestablishing control over these individuals.

In a rare mention of children born to drug-addicted women, another set of addicts emerged in the ABA hearing: "out-of-wedlock" children born of "mothers having the habit."[60] "This," said John Stanton, Chief of the Narcotic Bureau in the City of Buffalo, "causes not only a police problem but a welfare problem."[61] While women were recognized as a growing part of the ranks of the addicted, their presence was seemingly confined to prisons or ethnic enclaves. Women entered drug discourse primarily as mothers in the problematic family configurations that generated addiction.

The Focus on Adolescent Boys
Absent Fathers and Overpresent Mothers on The Road to H

Adolescent boys were considered particularly prone to drug addiction. Youthful be-havior was closely scrutinized in the public and policy-making panic of the early 1950s, which focused on urban males of African-American, African-Caribbean, and Puerto Rican descent. The possibility that male adolescent addicts might someday become productive citizens diverted resources and attention from the majority of drug users—who were not adolescent boys. Older populations were written off as intractable or incurable.[62] The message that reached the aroused citizenry—parents, teachers, administrators, legislators—was that drug use was predominantly the province of young, urban, ethnic males whose sense of mas-culine identity was fragile. The emphasis on addiction as a male pathology gov-erned resource allocation, admissions quotas, patterns of scientific inquiry, and cultural representations.[63] Gender formation and sexuality proved to be signifi-cant categories of difference through which to analyze the history of drug dis-courses, sciences, and control policies. The rest of this chapter analyzes the relationship between addiction and masculinity in relation to femininity within *The Road to H*. The classic study was one of the only studies to address addiction among women and girls, and I address its implications for knowledge about fe-male addicts in Chapter 6.

Articulating social tensions around issues of dependency and autonomy, the figure of the drug user—gendered and racialized—served cultural functions be-yond those of drug control. Global fears and shifts in social-economic relations contextualized the rise in adolescent addiction. While it was unclear whether drug use was a cause or an effect of such shifts, increasing addiction was strongly associ-ated with changing social conditions and child-rearing practices. Vague fears about "social contagions" such as homosexuality or communism fueled the concern with youthful suggestibility and personality reversals in the face of peer pressure. Within the prevailing economy of normativity and the desire for security, parents were supposed to optimize individual adjustment and autonomy by suppressing depen-dency. The discourses in which "security" functioned as a desired—if obscure— object stretched between secure sexual orientation, strong gender identification, and "national security."[64] The drug issue was part of a national paranoia about young men who could not function apart from their mothers. Anxieties converged on the figure of the male drug user, his "gender troubles," and his mother.

Between Psychiatry and Sociology

A team at the Research Center for Human Relations at New York University conducted the classic social-psychiatric study of heroin use among adolescents in the 1950s. Published as *The Road to H* (1964),[65] it still reads as a "remarkably compelling" analysis of the social, economic, and cultural contexts of 1950s adolescent heroin use among boys and girls.[66] Considered definitive for decades, the study was conducted in three boroughs of New York City between 1949 and 1954. The authors insisted "we are all implicated in the life story of the addict."[67] They were especially troubled by the direction of drug policy, because they believed it was based on confusion between a minor symptom and a major epidemic. As drug policy critics, Chein and coauthors appeared to offer knowledge in an attempt to forestall the policy-making panic that struck New York City in the early to mid-1950s.

Personality maladjustment was integral to the social-psychiatric model of addiction that the book offered. Its social complement was the diagnosis of "trouble within many individuals in our society."[68] The book contrasted "normal" drug-using personalities with those who sought to deny or relieve deep-rooted, serious personality disorders through heroin use.[69] *The Road to H* relied on deeply gendered conceptual frameworks that made explicit assumptions about gender and sexual difference. These governing mentalities were assumed but left unstated in later drug discourse. Thus the study usefully maps underlying assumptions about father absence, maternal overidentification and "dominance," the failure of compulsory heterosexuality, and the importance of gender normalization in producing drug addicts as subjects and objects. These assumptions undergird contemporary drug knowledges, public policy, empirical studies, and addict self-representations. This section contains a gender analysis of the structural and psychodynamic perspectives on addict personality in *The Road to H*, concentrating first on the portrayal of masculinity and mother-son relations.

Adolescent addiction was used as an index of social trouble and an indication that the United States was developing "ungovernable" or "unproductive" populations. Stress and anxiety occupied a positive, productive, and adaptive role in *The Road to H*: "We regard anxiety as a significant value in human development and growth, as a stimulus calling for adaptive responses."[70] Because drugs camouflaged and relieved anxiety, psychiatrists sought to displace drug use with "superior forms of adaptation" that helped "every person achieve the fullest development of his capacities to love, to work, to play, and to conduct himself as a reasonably responsible member of society."[71] Addiction worked counter to these plans, transforming normal victims into "monstrous" life-forms.[72]

Neither "crime" nor "disease" quite fit the personality maladjustment model, which localized social trouble within individual psychology and brought drug addiction into the therapeutic domain of mental health through a classification scheme.[73] The "personality disturbance" schema partook of the shorthand convenience of all psychiatric nosologies. It included several degrees of psychopathology: (1) schizophrenia; (2) incipient or borderline schizophrenia; (3) delinquency-dominated character disorders, including pseudo-psychopathic delinquents and oral characters; and (4) inadequate personality. Adopted to dispel the idea that addiction resulted from one set of personality characteristics or conflicts, the schema emerged from clinical observation, interviews, and psychological testing. The results were cast into a psychoanalytic framework the team used to categorize behavior, generate hypotheses, shape interpretations, and support speculations. Thus research design, fieldwork, and presentation of data, case studies, tables, and classification systems depended on psychoanalytic theory, a debt somewhat obscured by the methods of experimental psychology.

Personality-oriented explanations of addiction were rendered suspect by the emergence of a heroin "epidemic" without a concurrent increase in psychopathology. Those who held psychiatric explanations were put on the defensive. Donald Gerard, who joined the NYU team in 1954, and Conan Kornetsky of the NIMH first advanced the classification schema in a study of 35 African-American and Puerto Rican male addicts. Completed under the auspices of the U.S. Public Health Service (USPHS) Laboratory for Socio-Environmental Studies, the study served as proof positive that deep-rooted psychiatric malfunction preceded addiction.[74] Addiction itself was a "successful, albeit malignant, technique" by which addicts managed their preexisting psychiatric disturbances. Gerard and Kornetsky argued that sociological explanations downplayed the role of psychiatric maladjustment, but they did not turn directly to psychoanalysis.[75] Instead, they subjected addicts and controls to psychological tests drawn from experimental psychology—including Rorschach tests, IQ tests, and human figure drawing.[76] Addicts, they observed, responded differently to stressful situations than did the controls. When confronted with novel, difficult, or unstructured situations, addicts regressed, functioned below their intellectual capacity, and exhibited weak object relations.[77] These very categories appeared as "personality disturbances" in *The Road to H*.

Sociological factors were not completely ignored. Gerard and Kornetsky recognized that racial discrimination played some role in "stimulat[ing] development of inappropriate patterns of relating," but did not recognize the ethnocentrism, gender-blindness, or lack of statistical validity of their "clinical observations." Somewhat casually, they mentioned "ambivalent, mutually destructive, excessively close and dependent relationship between a case study named Jay and his mother as a major dynamic factor in his opiate use."[78] Impressed by the frequency with which they clinically observed this family configuration, they promised to follow up on its occurrence. That promise was fulfilled in *The Road to H*.

"Queering" Addiction

Three case studies closely resembling Gerard's and Kornetsky's appeared in *The Road to H*. The first case was Jay, who was peculiarly preoccupied with his mother.

Willie, who resumed heroin use on Mother's Day after leaving Riverside Hospital, was the second. Finally, there was Harry, who returned to his mother after treatment and resumed drug use when he felt "something missing." Each patient's mother was described in decidedly antitherapeutic terms; all were "domineering persons who limited their sons' self-assertion, used them unfairly for their own emotional and physical needs, and gave them little in return."[79] The mothers indulged their sons, failed to discipline them, and were generally inconsistent except at "doing the most wrong things at the most crucial moments." Addict sons were not responsible for their own narcissism; rather their mothers maintained their sons in states of dependency. The overt hostility toward mothers was striking in a text so tolerant of addicts themselves.

These dynamics were holdovers from psychoanalytic explanations of the genesis of drug addiction as a state of primary narcissism. While the researchers were skeptical toward psychoanalytic techniques and diagnostic categories, they also depended on the explanatory power of psychoanalysis. They smuggled unconscious processes, defenses, and "psychophysiological reactions" into social categories of experience. *The Road to H* advanced four psychoanalytic concepts essential to understanding drug addiction: ego pathology, narcissism, psychosexual pathology, and superego pathology. Addicts were "constricted individuals" whose impoverished inner and outer lives made them incapable of "ego synthesis" or "purposeful action."[80] When addicts regressed to the state of primary narcissism, they could identify only with their mothers, who served merely to gratify their infantile impulses. Narcissism, however, had to be reconciled with "low self-esteem," then coming into vogue as an explanation for drug use. Self-esteem, now purged of its psychoanalytic past, once referred to the Oedipal transition from the simple physiological mechanisms of infants to the complex symbolic interactions of adults.[81] Chein and coauthors stressed addicts' incapacity for object relations, classifying them as problematically pre-Oedipal.[82] Social psychiatrists grouped autoeroticism, male homosexuality, and drug addiction as similar patterns of "perverse and infantile strivings."[83]

Gender and sexual identity were considered central components of mature identity. Addicts were disturbed in terms of their gender "belonging." Unable to fulfill their prescribed gender and sexual roles, they remained arrested at "primitive," pre-Oedipal levels. Unable to establish trust or predictable gratification, they could not successfully negotiate the complexities of sexual identification to become "a man like father or a woman like mother." The evidence for this claim included an analysis of expectations for the performance of American masculinity; case histories of sexual behavior; and observations of the addict persona. The results of clinical observation aligned with familiar psychoanalytic narratives. This was not merely a bias to be avoided; rather, this psychoanalytic narrative marked the research as a product of its time.

Gender identity did not emerge as a fully articulated sociological category until the 1950s, and thus the gendered analysis that Chein and coauthors worked into *The Road to H* was prescient. "Desire for drugs" interrupted the gendered process by which the cultural intelligibility of gender proceeds. Judith Butler's investigation into the gender matrix illuminates a process similar to that traced by Chein and coauthors: "'Intelligible' genders are those which in some sense institute and maintain relations of coherence and continuity among sex, gender, sexual practice, and desire. . . . The cultural matrix through which gender identity has become intelligible requires that certain kinds of 'identities' cannot 'exist'—that is, those in which gender does not follow from sex and those in which the practices of desire do not 'follow' from either sex or gender."[84] Addiction disrupted coherent gender and sexual identity, displacing and substituting for (hetero)sex and rendering ambiguous what counts as a sexual practice and what does not. Addicts on *The Road to H* articulated the lack of fit between sex, gender, sexual practice, and desire; these dimensions simply did not align for them.

Essential ingredients of masculinity were found lacking among male addicts, who were oriented toward passive dependency rather than active agency. Male addicts were not confident of their "power, strength, competence, effective and appropriate assertiveness," nor were they becoming "responsible provider[s], father[s], or head[s] of household[s]." They remained little boys who wasted energy playing the "giving and taking game."[85] Direct concerns with sexual performance included a preference for homosexuality; a taste for oral sex; "passive acceptance" of impotence; heterosexual disinterest; and maternal relations bordering on the incestuous. While heroin was sometimes used to enhance (hetero)sex, addicts claimed they used it to prolong their engagement in an activity they did not quite desire. Chein and coauthors concluded that male addicts were insufficiently masculine: "On one side is the big man who exploits women; on the other is the little boy preoccupied with thoughts of the insufficient masculinity of his body, the insufficient recognition of his masculinity by his peers, and the fear (wish) that he be hurt and attacked (sexually invaded) by other men."[86]

The researchers described the addict persona as fluid and shifting, marked by weak masculine identification and an inability to adhere to "sex-appropriate" behavior, dress, gestures, speech, recreational interests, occupational goals, and levels of assertiveness, independence, and aggression.[87] The "crux of the matter" lay in the "naturalness" with which boys adjusted to styles regarded as "sex-appropriate" and "age-appropriate": "The basic feature, then, of an adequate sense of masculine identification is an unostentatious commitment to the masculine identity and, within the framework of the culture, to the age- and status-appropriate behavioral prescriptions that such an identity implies."[88] Effective socialization depended on a primary commitment to the masculine group that could not be too "ostentatious" for fear of arousing suspicion. The primary commitment to masculinity preceded the adequate formation of all other social bonds: "A man, for example, is in our opinion hardly likely to be comfortable with himself as an American (i.e., not simply as a person who happens to be a legal resident and citizen of the country, but as a member of the total community) or as a member of a religious or ethnic group if he has not yet succeeded in making himself comfortable in his masculine identity."[89]

Basically, *The Road to H* found that male adolescent addicts acted and appeared more like adolescent girls than boys. The boys' feminine identification overpowered their thin veneer of masculine identity. They compensated for gender insecurity and sexual vulnerability by engaging in delinquent behaviors. Their "gender troubles" culminated in early adulthood. According to the researchers, it was no coincidence that narcotics addiction often coincided with intensified pressures toward marriage, family, and employment in a culture that placed a premium on "phallic prowess."[90] The weak masculine identification observed in addict subjects resulted from absence of a strong masculine role model, a "vacuum of masculinity" that resulted in sons overidentifying with their mothers or sisters. They were thus unsuited to the social reproduction of masculinity and normative heterosexuality.

By emphasizing the adaptive function of drug use for "abnormal" individuals, *The Road to H* provided a counterweight to the emphasis on dysfunctionality and maladaptation. Those whose desires were abnormally stimulated or frustrated in childhood were attracted to the "cool" detachment of drug use.[91] "Normal men," Chein and coauthors stated with authority, do not aspire to states absent of desire, just as average persons were not satisfied by pills. Addicts could not be "normal men," for the addict's "high" was contrary to the "positive pleasure" valued in Western societies—intense sensory input, orgasmic activity, or creative experience.[92] Addicts were constituted as "queer" along multiple dimensions.

Family Configuration, Femininity, and Addiction

The Road to H displaced moral opprobrium from the addict to the family and, perhaps not surprisingly, to female elements within the family. "The family background of the male adolescent opiate addict is such that it interferes with the development of a well-functioning ego and superego and with his sense of identification as a male. Furthermore, his family background discourages formation of realistic attitudes and orientations toward the future and trustful attitudes toward major social institutions."[93] The key to the "malignant familial environment" was the gendered power imbalance between "weak or absent fathers" and overly present mothers. Eighty percent of addicts experienced weak relations with their fathers, although only half of the fathers were actually absent. The fathers presented "immoral models," hostility, "impulse-oriented" behaviors, unstable work histories, and "fatalism" more often than the fathers of controls.[94] Discordant marital relations were found among fully 97 percent of addicts' parents. Marital discord allowed mothers to expand their domination in the home, yet fully 40 percent of addicts experienced "extremely weak" relations with mothers. Even the researchers noted the lack of evidence for atypical relationships between most addicts and their mothers.[95] Despite this they concluded that 70 percent of addicts experienced "maternal complications" serious enough to lead them to the mother as the source of pathology.

Adolescent addiction was the site for a disciplinary struggle between psychiatry, psychiatric social work, and clinical psychology over the personality structure and sexual psychodynamics of the male adolescent addict.[96] The 40 percent of underinvolved mothers were dismissed, while the overindulgent and protective mothers were accorded undue significance. The case histories were selected according to Gerard's familiarity with the addicts' family configurations—mainly their mothers. He described how the mothers manipulated addicts as "objects" through seduction and rejection. The cases revealed a pattern of rhetorical sacrifice depressingly familiar in drug studies, whereby women are held responsible for producing environments to which addiction was an adaptive male response. The account of heroin's functional qualities in "malignant familial environments" deplored the absent father but ruthlessly blamed the overpresent mother.

The Road to H demonstrated that the incidence of drug use correlated with the sex ratio—rates of addiction, delinquency, and behavioral disturbance were higher in areas where adult females outnumbered adult males.[97] "Addicts have been described as having passive personalities and, even more to the point, being confused with regard to their masculine roles. We thought it possible that a preponderance of females in the environment might, if not cause such personality orientations in the first place, at least contribute to their maintenance."[98] Although the researchers emphasized cautious interpretation, they found that the "percentage excess of adult females over males" in the fifteen-to-nineteen age group was very high in "Negro" and Puerto Rican areas where the "epidemic" was concentrated.[99] Yet the density of young adolescent males was higher in "epidemic" areas. So, too, were adult male unemployment and underemployment, rates of divorce and separation, and numbers of working mothers. Finally, household income, years of education, rates of home ownership, and rates of television ownership were lower, and family "disorganization" and overcrowding were endemic. Rather than attribute the "epidemic" to poverty, structural unemployment and underemployment, or institutional racism, the researchers explained addiction as a matter of family configuration and the "inadequate masculine identification" that flowed from it.

Without women—mothers, wives, sisters, or girlfriends—to inculcate social norms and standards in men, social maladjustment might reign unchallenged.

Ultimately, *The Road to H* directed hostility toward girls and women who failed to perform their normative roles. The "preponderance of females in the environment" produced addiction in two ways:

1. Dominance of females in the family environment and in the life of the boy tends to encourage dependency on and identification with females, the development of feminine tastes, styles, orientations, and the like.
2. The presence of a weak, unstable, or hostile father may interfere with the ability of the child to form a dependency relationship with a male and to wholeheartedly identify with him. This situation (or the absence of male figures in his environment) diminishes the opportunities for the taking-over of masculine standards and behavior patterns.[100]

Women and girls were supposed to perform the adjustments necessary to integrate men into the mid-century social order. They were assigned the tasks of social reproduction, and failure to perform them invited blame in the form of concerns about family configuration, the inadequate state of femininity and inadequate masculinity, or skewed sex ratios.

Representing the "Real"
Girl Drug Addicts Testify

Cold War Compulsions
"Lurches and Lulls": Policy Images and Imaginaries

Drug policy is haunted by the eternal return of notions that addicts comprise an alien species. The popular concerns about domestic crime and subversion that emerged in the wake of World War II associated drug use with deviant sexuality, failures of normative gender, and racial mixing through the figure of the addicted adolescent. Adolescent addicts were liminal figures representing the familiar and the foreign—you might harbor one in your home without knowing it. The postwar experience of addiction filled in previously drawn lines of racial and sexual alterity. Few recall the proliferation of popular culture depicting addiction in the 1950s—the pulp fiction novels, magazines for women and parents, soft-core porn, educational filmstrips, and the entertainment industry's output. I have often been asked, "*Was* there drug addiction in the 1950s?" The official story credited the punitive policies of the 1950s with eliminating the traffic.

When the drug problem emerged as a widespread cultural phenomenon in the 1960s, the previous decade's experience faded into oblivion. Even Anslinger, who retired in 1962, failed to anticipate the resurgence of drug use in the 1960s because of his faith in the power of mandatory minimums and intolerance.[1] Retrospectively, Robert DuPont, director of Nixon's Special Action Office for Drug Abuse Prevention (SAODAP) and later director of NIDA, noted: "The 1950 epidemic is poorly understood and most of the data relating to it is only now being analyzed. It appears to have been serious and to have produced long term negative effects for many of those caught in it. It would be tragic if we were to conclude that because we survived that much smaller epidemic without a major response, that heroin epidemics were inherently self-limiting and therefore no response was needed. Heroin epidemics are far too destructive to warrant such a complacent attitude."[2]

The 1950s heroin epidemic seems remote and insignificant—even, perhaps, quaint—from the vantage point of the twenty-first century. The mental health apparatus and the criminal justice system waged a contest over the ownership of domestic drug policy during the decade. The Boggs Act (1951) instituted mandatory minimums, preventing judges from placing drug offenders on probation, suspending sentences, or paroling second offenses.[3] The 1956 Narcotics Control Act increased fines and upped the minimums; gave Customs and FBN agents authority to carry guns, serve warrants, or make arrests without them; and required drug users to register when crossing international borders. Narcotics offenses became grounds for deportation, and the death penalty could be applied to those convicted of selling heroin to minors. The nine Senate hearings on the Illicit Narcotics Traffic that led to the 1956 Act were a significant episode in the construction of a U.S. drug policy "monopoly."[4] In this chapter, I focus on the testimony of female addict witnesses in these hearings, which were chaired by Senator Price Daniel (R-TX).

Widely reported and sometimes televised,[5] the Daniel hearings crystallized congressional support for punitive sanctions. The subcommittee saw itself as shielding society from dangerous individuals who spread addiction through association and its feminine form, prostitution. Civil commitment, probation, and quarantine were considered benevolent "treatment alternatives." Law enforcement offered a more confident moral stance and a distinct identification of addiction which resonated with anticommunism. At the time, the biobehavioral sciences did not provide an authoritative or predictive model. Angry legal reformers such as Rufus King and Alfred Lindesmith allied with medical researchers such as Robert Felix and Lawrence Kolb, who arrayed themselves against law enforcement and criminal justice professionals.[6] The dichotomy between tough law enforcement and those "soft on addicts" was politicized as the defense of the free world versus "communist sympathies." The Daniel hearings staged the conflict between these two groups before a national audience, ultimately depicting law enforcement as effective in contrast to "impotent" medical approaches. These debates ultimately yielded a potent apparatus of social control that worked through two different but intersecting modes.

Fights over problem definition were acrimonious in the 1950s, involving the stakes of professional authority and personal credibility. Policies were posed in simplified and symbolic terms that appealed at both empirical and emotive levels.[7] Policy images combine elements from available discursive resources and cultural representations. The fight to define the problem of addiction—and solutions to it—took place as much within the cultural domain as the political. Indeed, the inseparability of these domains suggests that cultural studies and policy studies

are practiced most productively together. This chapter investigates the relationship between the practices of governance and the processes of cultural figuration
by studying the figure of the addict prostitute. We gain interpretive purchase by
using gender and race as analytic categories for understanding policy debates.

U.S. policy-making proceeds through periods of "punctuated equilibria" in
which new ideas and alliances destabilize policy monopolies.[8] Change proceeds
through the constant redefinition of prevailing policy images; policy-making can
be usefully thought of as a series of lurches and lulls.[9] Lurches are spurred by
media attention and popular concern; government inquiry tends to follow the
crest of reportage but politicians manipulate both to advance their agendas.[10]
Empirical studies repeatedly demonstrate that media attention declines as institutional inquiry gains momentum.[11] Considerable time elapses before the felt
impact of policy changes, and in this lull institutional authority is built and consolidated largely outside the public eye.[12] Experts from various fields compete for
funds and authority, a process in which law enforcement has met with more success than prevention and treatment professionals.[13]

Drug policy logic was institutionalized and politicized in ways that rendered
substantive change, problem redefinition, or new solutions unlikely. While there
have been attempts to redefine prevailing policy images, lack of a solid political
constituency has been a long-term liability in drug reform politics. Mobilized
constituencies can engage in a politics of articulation and rearticulation: "Where
images are in flux, one may also expect changes in institutional jurisdictions."[14]
Additionally, lack of a clear jurisdictional monopoly over the drug problem made
for a détente in which both the criminal justice and mental health systems enjoyed fluctuating degrees of authority over it. The division of labor was drawn
between two figures—the abject and pitifully ill person and the nefarious criminal trafficker. The figure of the "girl drug addict" acted to condense the multiple
and contradictory meanings attached to addiction. The testimony that women
offered was complicated not only by their status as addicts but by their gender.

The Testimony of the Addict

The truthfulness of the drug addict's testimony became a concern of the court
soon after Harrison Act prosecutions became common. In 1924, George Rossman
traced the ongoing debate on the status of addict testimony.[15] Witnesses must
possess "testimonial equipment" to observe, recollect, and narrate their experiences, all of which are central to the production of truth.[16] Attacks on credibility
or character generally assail at least one of those capacities. Addict witnesses embodied both confusion and coherence: "In the course of time these ideas become
real to him; there is a confusion in his mind between the dreams and the facts.
This leads to a complete disorientation of the man. It disturbs his concepts not

only of material facts, but also of moral facts. He becomes both delusional and false. But in the great majority of these cases there is preserved a certain coherence of ideas—a certain balance of the mental faculties—which gives the patient the misleading appearance of normality."[17] This deceptive "normality" troubled those concerned with eliciting truthful statements from addicts, who, they charged, were prone to memory lapses and a pathological mendacity: "They have been so often narcotized, and thus cut off from actualities, living in a dream state, that they do not seem to be able to recognize realities when they see them."[18] The reproductive function of the capacity for "trustworthy" recollection was based on the witness's consciousness of identity, location in time and space.[19] A witness's capacity for "truthful" narration depended on the strength of his or her character. In common law, "it was believed that a witness possessed of good character would be more likely to tell the truth than one possessed of an inferior character."[20]

Common law questioned women's capacity for truth-telling; women were considered less credible witnesses, whether addicted or not. Rossman used a gendered metaphor to convey the significance of characterological difference in measuring the worth of a witness—the metaphor of the feminine prostitute and her masculine client or "john."[21] If a "common prostitute" served as a witness, the courts concluded that she would be unlikely to speak the truth because "no woman could stoop to a life of shame unless she was utterly lacking in moral principle."[22] By contrast, evidence of a man's "want of chastity," demonstrated by "repeated visits to a prostitute would not necessarily show bad character in the man, and thus adversely affect his testimony."[23] The feminine character was ontologically defective; she could not be trusted to observe, recollect, or narrate the truth of her experience. The always-masculine client was not defective at the level of character—he merely engaged repeatedly in "vicious acts," and his truth-telling capacity was not tarnished.

This distinction between character and act held in relation to drug use. Addicts whose moral character was defective differed from those who simply engaged in "vicious acts." A reliable witness had to be able to maintain the difference between fact and fiction. Contrary to Rossman, who argued that addict witnesses should not themselves be put on trial, other contemporaries said of addicts: "The truth is not in him, especially with reference to himself and his habits."[24] The question of where to locate truth, how to know it, and how to distinguish it from falsehood surfaced in the Daniel hearings when addicted persons claimed to know what should be done in response to their self-defined needs. They were easily discredited, cast as unreliable witnesses even as they attested to the truth of addiction. As with needs interpretation within most bureaucratic social organizations, a process of "depoliticization" ensues as governmental organs translate needs into existing channels and resources.[25] Truth is translated into the known and recognized registers of meaning and relevant policy jurisdictions.

The truth-telling problem and this translation process were evident through-out the Daniel hearings. The translation of the self into an object of knowl-edge—or of an identity into an object of study—is central to the "deflection dynamic" that assigns blame or cause not to social-structural conditions but to the character and behavior of individuals who embody those conditions. The translation process resembles ventriloquism—in hearings, subcommittee mem-bers parrot addict testimony but mold it to their political purposes, be they de-fending "moral education," Christianity, or mandatory minimums. The translation process takes self-defined needs, cultural styles, and forms of indige-nous knowledge, and translates them into terms intelligible to the state apparatus charged to respond to them. By amplifying addicted women's voices, we hope to discern what they can tell us about their historical moment—and ours.

The "Illicit Narcotics Traffic": The Daniel Subcommittee Hearings, 1955–1956

U.S. vulnerability to dope from Communist China, Lebanon, and Mexico was the stated impetus for the Daniel hearings, which began on June 2, 1955, with Senator Daniel's tribute to witness Harry J. Anslinger as the world's leading au-thority on narcotic drugs. Within the field of the history of U.S. drug policy, Anslinger casts a long shadow of blatantly racist, sexist, and anticommunist cru-sading, and his beliefs continue to "color popular thinking on drug abuse and trafficking."[26] As the U.S. representative to the United Nations Commission on Narcotic Drugs, Anslinger first detailed Japanese and then Communist Chinese narcotics traffic. Diplomatically, the narcotics issue cemented the U.S.–national-ist China alliance against the Eastern Bloc in the United Nations, where Anslinger waged his own Cold War. Like Anslinger, the nationalist Chinese as-serted that the Red Army intensified opium cultivation and expanded foreign markets in an effort to undermine the West. Nationalist Chinese and South Ko-rean police corroborated Anslinger's version, claiming to have arrested dozens of communist Chinese refugees "with heroin in one hand and gold in the other for the purpose of spreading addiction and corruption."[27] Since refuted, Anslinger's allegations leaked into popular culture, domestic hearings before the Daniel sub-committee and HUAC, and onto the Senate floor.[28] His biographer stated: "The commissioner's perception of the Chinese as evil purveyors of narcotics may have had an impact on the American media and congressional Appropriations Com-mittees, but no evidence supports his theory of a communist-organized heroin invasion originating in China."[29]

Nothing short of obsessed with "Red Chinese" drug trafficking, Anslinger painted the purchase of heroin as direct financial support for communist regimes. He painted addicts as communist sympathizers and political subver-sives—not because of their political beliefs but simply because they bought heroin from communists who sold drugs "not only to make money to prosecute the efforts of their Government but also to cause destruction and deterioration among people in the free countries to which this drug is being sent."[30] Always sensitive to the public, Anslinger stated: "we are now sending young men to the hospital at Lexington as a result of that problem."[31] By casting all opposing views as "within the Communist orbit," he red-baited his domestic enemies—especially King, Kolb, and Lindesmith, whom he labeled "arm-chair intellectuals" susceptible to the prolegalization propaganda of the addict.

The FBN was integral to shaping U.S. and international drug policy, and Anslinger's name was synonymous with the bureau. Constructing himself as a representative patriot, Anslinger considered attacks on him as attacks on the U.S. government. The antidrug crusade was a definitive part of his self-identity and the means by which he identified his morality with that of the nation. He was an extremely canny government employee who used available cultural frameworks to make drug traffic intelligible, instilling familiar fears about unfamiliar substances. No one effectively opposed his views, larded as they were with indignation and bolstered by a persistent inability to recognize his fabulated truths as fictions. Strategically, he calculated the political effect of each press release; significant questions about his motivations and intelligence gathering activities persist.[32] Although there is little proof, Rufus King, then chair of the ABA Narcotics Committee, speculated that Anslinger handpicked Senator Daniel to head the Senate inquiry because he would support the FBN's desire for increased mandatory minimums.[33] Daniel was hardly Anslinger's only convert—even addict witnesses mouthed FBN positions, admitting to the purchase of Communist Chinese heroin.

Racial difference and sexual deviance were equated with political subversion in this potent cultural figuration of internal difference in the United States. Anslinger's popular writings exhibit a xenophobic and misogynist pattern of allegations, associating narcotic drug use with prostitution, foreign trafficking, and communism.[34] Constructing a homology between addiction and prostitution, he linked drug trafficking to women's groups in China, Japan, and the United States. He claimed that female Japanese communists worked as drug traffickers and prostitutes through the "Society for the Protection of Health and Peace," which targeted "hotels, cabarets, bars, and other establishments patronized by American personnel in the Tokyo area." He also blamed Japanese prostitutes for intentionally spreading addiction to unwitting American men stationed in South Korea, then depicted as a conduit for Chinese heroin. Chinese Communist heroin was allegedly seized on both U.S. coasts and in St. Louis, Missouri, frighteningly close to the heartland. Anslinger made these allegations with little basis, for the FBN had no agents stationed in the Far East. These "facts" were indisputable only in the context of the Cold War.

The Meaning of Addiction in Cold War Culture

Drug users were figured as controlled subjects of communism; addiction was a technique that communists used to gain access to the minds—and wallets—of democratic subjects. Behavioral scientists, too, linked addiction to nondemocratic ideologies and ways of life,[35] as addiction became convenient political shorthand for figuring democracy as itself under siege. At the federal level, it proved crucial to resignify illicit drug use as a sign of political subversion—and not as a sign of ineffective policy or policing. The Cold War climate directly served the political ends of law enforcement. An advanced industrial nation in the midst of a Cold War, the United States portrayed itself as the vulnerable target of unruly communist nations exporting narcotics to cause the decline of the capitalist West.

The United States' isolation in the war against communism made vigilance a requirement of democratic citizenry.[36] The House Committee on Un-American Activities (HUAC) heard testimony from Anslinger and other cold warriors on the tensions that made citizens "psychologically weary." They claimed communists insinuated that: "there is no need for anxiety, sacrifices, or fear since there is no danger of any war: relax. . . . While Communists speak about peace, disarmament, and brotherhood, Americans have to talk of vigilance, danger, sacrifices."[37] The fear that addiction weakened the United States' resolve against communism rendered the threat of narcotics addicts disproportionate to their actual presence.

Narcotics law enforcement understood drugs as an "effective and subtle tool of war" used in the vanguard of military attack as "forerunner to an advancing army."[38] Law enforcement thus emerged as a bulwark of democracy.[39] Mental health professionals, on the other hand, were constructed as un-American unless they could cast their testimony into politicized terms. For example, Charles Winick, director of the Narcotic Addiction Research Project in New York City,[40] found that addiction, communism, and schizophrenia stemmed from common factors: "absence of a stable father figure in the family, exposure to the overtly exploitative use of sex, repeated frustrations of affectional needs, rebuffs related to minority-group status, and a host of more subtle influences. The consequences are seen in frequent manifestations of personal insecurity, problems of sexual identification on the part of males, rebellious attitudes towards authority, and various defensive maneuvers and tendencies to escape through gambling, intoxicants, and other 'kicks.' "[41] Addicts regressed to infancy—calling adult men "daddy" or "baby," and suppliers "mother," and substituting drugs for mature heterosexual activity.[42] Communism was aligned with immaturity, mental illness, nonnormative sexuality, minority status, criminality, and addiction.[43] This formulation appealed to those who believed that addiction was best treated as a crime.

Abnormality was the common factor in constructing addiction and communism as similar threats to the American way of life. Psychiatrist James Lowry also presented heady claims to a congressional hearing, painting drug use as the "ulti-mate in hedonistic experiences which combined the pleasures that other persons derive from work, love of wife, family, or friends, personal or group accomplish-ments, or service to others" with the "ecstasy of the adult at orgasm and the som-nifacient satisfaction of the satiated infant at the breast."[44] Addiction was due to the "absence of any constant person with whom identification could occur," which "retarded" the development of inner controls and caused the addict's psy-chic system to function at odds with normally sanctioned systems of reward and punishment. Addicts did not seem to want to be "normal," which both defined and offended the "normal" men who studied it. They conveyed this meaning through a clear distinction between the "normal" and the "pathological."

The Cold War context shifted some of addiction's older meanings, such as those discussed in Chapter 3.[45] The ninth exhibit of the Daniel hearings was a Philadelphia Police Department pamphlet titled "The Menace of Narcotic Drugs," which drew liberally on Frederick A. Wallis's 1926 speech "The Curse of Civilization."[46] The putative author of the pamphlet, Lt. Glasgow Driscoll, re-cast narcotics law enforcement as a Cold War front by updating the temperance reform vocabulary in which addiction was "a living death, insidious in its ap-proach, terrific in its reactions" that was "eating at the very vitals of the Nation." The new version depicted Red Chinese communists exploiting the U.S. public in a "cold, calculated, ruthless, systematic plan to undermine by creating new ad-dicts while sustaining the old." The police bulletin illustrated continuity and dis-continuity between post–World War I views and Cold War concerns.[47] While the original version gestured toward addiction as a "problem of foreign importa-tion," the later version blamed it on Red Chinese communist exploitation of the free world's susceptibility and China's eagerness to finance the spread of aggres-sive warfare, depravity, and human misery. The only way to stave off commu-nism's "living death" was to strengthen democratic citizens against the allure of communist drugs.

The Philadelphia hearing drew vague parallels between communism and drug addiction. W. Wilson White, U.S. Attorney for the Eastern District of Pennsylva-nia, observed a similar reluctance among communists and narcotics peddlers to cease their illegal activities while on bail. Both groups went on "as if they hadn't been charged at all."[48] According to White, persons who "want to ruin the Gov-ernment of the United States or spread narcotics around to schoolchildren" should not be offered bail. His evident frustration with disobedient communists and drug traffickers led him to believe that drug traffic and use were "about like Communist conspiracy, both are dedicated to destroying our Government." Ac-cording to White, "They are . . . the type of viciousness which goes on day by day, and every day that more of that activity is carried on, there is more harm to our country and to our institutions."[49]

Construed as a clear and present danger, addiction was politicized as an index of the relative health of democracy and capitalism. The idea that dependency on a drug rendered one susceptible to communist ideology persisted into the 1960s as addicts came to be represented as an alternative counterculture. Addicted individuals embodied a form of political subversion compounded by—but not reducible to—racial, sexual, or gender difference. Like communism, addiction was a danger inherent in individuals who were not firmly anchored to the consensual moral order. Drug policy was articulated in a climate in which the interpretive framework of the Cold War answered all political questions. Critics were easily marginalized by red-baiting or appeals to fear in a political culture preoccupied with the detection of subversion. This climate prefigured later links between U.S. foreign and domestic drug policy in efforts to roll back communism.[50] The notion that drug use and traffic subvert the United States of America—the "epitome" of Western civilization—politicized drug use long before it was understood as a form of countercultural politics.

Legislative changes and research mandates responded to a congerie of social panics in the 1950s—there was widespread fear that crime, communism, homosexuality, gender breakdown, and narcotics use were contagious forms of subversion about to overwhelm American society. The cultural proliferation of subversive behavior is usually located in the context of the 1960s rebellions; the 1950s appears as a period of entrenched conformity. The heightened local, state, and federal policing and the concurrent development of a "mass approach to mental health" at the federal level that occurred in response to the drug issue in the 1950s reveal otherwise.[51]

Most U.S. drug policy history focuses on interactions between professional groups and U.S. government agencies.[52] My readings of discursive events such as hearings and conferences indicate that the expert witnesses on whom policy-makers relied diverged politically but converged on moral grounds. Secular democracies encourage the display of conventional moral character as a technique for gaining political capital, credibility, and consensus. Public hearings are performative spaces where alternative moral viewpoints are staged in ways that shore up the hegemonic perspectives of public figures. Yet moral and emotional impulses are inadmissible to most histories of "normal" science and policy. By studying the pattern of interaction between policy-makers, drug scientists, and addicts, we gain insight into the policing of the bounds of normativity through the national politics of juvenile crime and drug control in the 1950s.

Witnessing Expertise and Guaranteeing Truth
Expert Enclaves: Addict, Doctor, Lawyer, Police

An imposing array of USPHS expert witnesses assembled for the fourth session of the Daniel hearings in New York City on June 2, 3, and 8, 1955.[53] The obvious

Figure 12   Photograph of Women's Building, 1950.

Reprinted, with permission, from the *Lexington Herald-Leader*, Lexington, Kentucky.

hostility between the subcommittee and the USPHS doctors contrasted to the subcommittee's rapport with law enforcement officers, judges, and reformed addicts. The New York hearings were most responsive to the New York Academy of Medicine's controversial report, which reputedly advocated "a clinic system of free drugs" to keep addicts comfortable and "gratify their desires."[54] Such a system starkly contrasted to the "narcotics farms" maintained by the USPHS, which housed felons and volunteers in prisonlike conditions (see Figures 12 to 15). The USPHS employed the leading scientific authorities on drug addiction, clinicians and researchers who worked with a marginal population and were themselves marginalized. They could not count on public support or scientific accolades, but a frontier ethos compensated for their political vulnerability. These experts were the most experienced professional group in regular contact with addicts, which made their position unstable, for they spoke for the population they studied.

The USPHS witnesses voiced the federal government's opposition to dispensing narcotics but did not outright refute the Academy of Medicine report. Senator

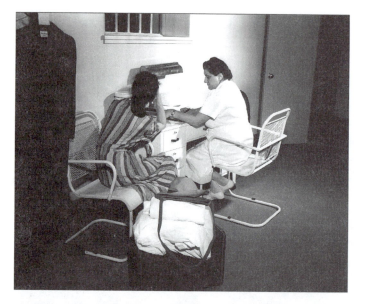

Figure 13   Photograph of an addict entering the hospital, 1950.

Reprinted, with permission, from the *Lexington Herald-Leader*, Lexington, Kentucky.

Figure 14   Photograph of addicts entering Women's Building, 1950.

Reprinted, with permission, from the *Lexington Herald-Leader*, Lexington, Kentucky.

Figure 15 Photograph of an addict leaving Lexington, 1950.

Reprinted, with permission, from the *Lexington Herald-Leader*, Lexington, Kentucky.

Daniel first established the panel's professional authority and credibility, but became agitated by their insistence on further research: "It would seem to me that for you now to come and recommend that more study be given to the matter under a national council is inconclusive. If you men have not got something definite to recommend after all the years you have worked with it, how is some national council which has not worked with 25,000 drug addicts going to be able to come up with a better recommendation?"[55] The panelists were circumspect because they thought it was possible that their colleagues at the New York Academy had encountered a different set of addicts from those with whom they worked (many USPHS patients were felons). Senator Daniel tried many tactics to get them to say what he wanted them to say, including taunts and sarcasm. Eventually, they found common ground in the abnormality of addicts.

Witness Robert Felix, NIMH director and chair of the American Medical Association Committee on Narcotic Drugs, testified that addicts were abnormally disordered on or off drugs.[56] Thus experiments in ambulatory maintenance were doomed because addicts "retreat[ed] from the province of reality." Normal people achieved satisfaction through work and family; abnormal people sought refuge in drugs. Felix held out hope for rehabilitation, arguing that if even one in a million addicts could be made into a good citizen, husband, father, or workman, a governmental and medical obligation to rehabilitate the addict remained.[57] His statement evidenced both humanitarian concern and the profoundly gendered construction of addiction—there is no mistaking his pronouns for the generic. Treatment worked in the service of gender normalization, heterosexual citizenship, and labor discipline.

Exhibiting no qualms about his opposition to giving drugs to "weak individuals," Harris Isbell testified that addiction was an infectious disease. According to him, addicts were poor treatment prospects because they wished to "have their cake and eat it, too."[58] Isbell conducted numerous experiments on both unwitting and "consenting" human subjects at Lexington, for which addicts were paid in their preferred drug.[59] Distribution of drugs for the sake of science did not come under congressional scrutiny until the 1970s, when Isbell testified on U.S. violations of the Nuremberg code against human experimentation. He noted that ethical codes in the 1950s "were not so highly developed and there was great need to know in order to protect the public in assessing the potential use of narcotics."[60] In the Daniel hearings, Isbell characterized addicts as restless, emotionally immature "grownup children" who were incapable of deferring satisfaction, forming stable relations, or developing "the kind of control the rest of us have."

James Lowry, who asserted that male addicts lost their male functions and female addicts became "sterile and unable to have any children," brought addicts' abnormal sexual and reproductive functions to the Daniel subcommittee's attention. He believed that individuals used drugs to satisfy needs for "sensations akin to sexual orgasm," a dominant psychoanalytic interpretation of the etiology of addiction. Because addicts sought something others found in "normal" sexual and reproductive roles, they could not occupy familiar gender roles. According to Lowry's testimony, addicts had "lower resistance than normal to the disagreeable aspects of living and a higher than normal resistance to pleasure. Little things annoy this individual. He becomes almost hysterical at some incident that would not even disturb a normal person, and he does not enjoy simple pleasures."[61] Senators and scientists alike shared the suspicion that most addicts do not desire normalcy and were not satisfied by so-called normal states. Drug addicts were depicted as dissatisfied with what these "normal men" defined as reality.

The friction between subcommittee members and expert witnesses derived partly from lack of shared models for understanding and treating mental illness. Felix advocated federal provision of care to mental patients and drug addicts. He opposed the kind of criminalization that Senator Daniel espoused because it further stigmatized addicts and made them seem untreatable.

Senator Daniel: Some of the enforcement officers think it is best to get [addicts] in the jails temporarily. . . . I would like to see us at the same time that we set up our laws to take them off the streets, set up some place to have them go and get a chance for treatment, and then if they won't take it, and you cannot do anything with them, then, it seems to me, it is just as humane to put them into some kind of colony or some kind of farm or institution like you do mental patients. It is just as humane as the way we treat mental patients, it seems to me, after you have decided that there is just no way to help them any further; you cannot treat them anymore.[62]

Felix sharply pointed out that treating the untreatable was his "special hobby." Despite their disagreement over whether addicts were mentally ill or criminally wayward, witnesses and subcommittee members converged on the view that only abnormal persons could become addicted. Policy responses were another matter—there the researchers diverged sharply from the subcommittee.[63]

The USPHS witnesses were as reluctant to decide policy issues as they were to refute the New York Academy report. The chief policy topic in the New York City hearing was whether responsibility for drug addiction lay with the states or the federal government.[64] Senator Daniel sought to bring addiction under federal purview and legislate a mandatory reporting system to cross-register addicts with health care providers and the criminal justice system. The subcommittee considered several justifications for federal intervention: information gathering; combating interstate commerce in drugs; and the communicable nature of the disease. The subcommittee worried that drug regulation was no more legally justifiable than alcohol regulation, deciding that the two differed because "addicts communicate and spread addiction more than the alcoholics do." The physicians, on the other hand, saw alcohol as responsible for far worse damage than narcotics.

Few scientific or medical experts testified in the remainder of the Daniel hearings, but law enforcement views were prominent at each site. At Philadelphia, the second site, the witnesses were primarily police officers, judges, or recently arrested addicts. The senators, some from law enforcement backgrounds themselves, were noticeably more at ease with the police witnesses than with doctors or researchers. Civil liberties were a different matter in the mid-century; the concern was not how to avoid infringing on addicts' civil rights, but *how* to do so. They openly discussed use of wiretaps for "types of crime that are trying to destroy the nation," forms of police entrapment, and the necessity for stiffer mandatory minimum sentences. Judge Vincent A. Carroll of the first judicial district of Pennsylvania opposed mandatory sentences *except* in narcotics cases. Considered a tough judge,[65] Carroll argued for public condemnation of the addict and scorned treatment on the grounds that it "coddled" addicts and because psychiatrists could not tell when an addict was cured.[66]

Science and medicine were murky, but the law was clear. Lt. Thomas McDermott of the Philadelphia Police Department testified that he could "pick an addict out of a parade" by gait or appearance. His confidence contrasted with the scientific experts, whose circumspect answers made them appear confused, naïve, and amateurish. Where the doctors qualified their claims, the police were unequivocal. McDermott attributed his department's drug enforcement success to its close ties to the FBN. He regaled the subcommittee with crime stories that had little to do with drugs. Addicts would do anything to get drugs, he said, including dismemberment.[67] He recounted the high-profile Black Widow murder in Los Angeles (a case of dismemberment that did not involve drugs, addicts, or traffickers). Although he had never seen a case like it, he stated: "I know this, and the average person does not know it, that the addict is a vicious person. I mean a habitual addict, a man that is a confirmed addict. I think he can be responsible for doing anything. And he has only one thing in mind, and this is to satisfy his habit, and he will satisfy it, no matter how he gets his money." Picking up on the average American's ignorance of "something that might well destroy the human race," one senator responded that he would pursue legislation leading to mandatory life imprisonment or the death penalty for *addicts*, not just traffickers.

The star witness in the Philadelphia hearing was a 25-year-old Native American woman named June Gibbon, who testified under the pseudonym "Beverly Lee Roman." According to the lieutenant, she was "the biggest user . . . ever seen," and a girl who could give the committee "a true picture of what a drug addict is, and what drug addicts can do to you."[68] His statement foreshadowed the prominent place that Beverly Lee Roman's testimony occupied as she spoke the "truth" of addiction.

Witnessing the Truth of Addiction

Female addicts who testified in the Daniel hearings voiced both dominant and countercultural discourses. The hearings staged "alternative" voices, but the subcommittee contained their implications when they contravened its own moral judgment. Witness testimony worked as a form of ventriloquism as the female subject negotiated the distance between the interrogators, who incited her discourse *as if it was her own*, and the site from which she performed a coherent life narrative. While it may be tempting to privilege resistant moments over the direct mouthing of dominant positions, no one set of voices is more truthful than the other. The performances of the female addict witnesses had little discernible effect on policy outcome but served instead as physical evidence of moral failure. They embodied abjection so that the committee could voice pity and appear paternalistically concerned about their "broken homes" and declining moral values. Male witnesses were not displayed as failures of masculinity, used as evidence of moral deterioration, or castigated for their lack of spiritual values. The uses to which testimony was put varied by gender.

The assumed connection between prostitution and addiction preoccupied the subcommittee when they questioned female witnesses. The committee sought to establish the exact chronology of when women witnesses initiated either activity in order to determine whether one "caused" the other. Prostitution went "hand-in-hand" with drug addiction, according to Judge Carroll: "There is no doubt that where there are houses of prostitution, there are also drug peddlers in the shadows of those houses, there is no question about it."[69] As evidence, he called "Beverly Lee Roman," already convicted but not yet sentenced in his court. She was referred to as "Beverly" throughout her performance, which was as remarkable for its insight as for her rhetorical skills and sharp critique of U.S. drug policy. Her story, told from the position of "the biggest user ever seen," served the senators as the "best possible type of evidence." Beverly's narrative also confounded the senators and contradicted expectations despite her obvious material need to cooperate. She and the senators engaged in a repeated struggle over the meaning of her statements, which the senators adopted and later reiterated as "insider" knowledge of the drug-using subculture. She skillfully deflected their attempts to use her testimony to establish their hazy theories, vague connections, and moral condemnations as the truth of drug addiction.

Beverly told several contradictory accounts of her initiation into adolescent drug use, but dismissed attempts to establish marijuana use as the inevitable gateway to addiction and prostitution. She framed drug use as a matter of social learning rather than a physiological phenomenon:

> *Miss Roman:* So I said, "What do you mean, 'get high'?" So he showed me this white powder. So I said, "What shall I do with this?" And he showed me the needle. And I was scared, and I said, "You are not going to stick a needle in me." And he told me to snort it up my nose. So I did. And about 5 minutes later I got this very warm feeling through my body, very relaxed. And I sat down and I felt like going to sleep.[70]

Once the senators heard their first phenomenological account of heroin use, they were hooked. They confessed that Beverly was the first addict to come before them "voluntarily," and seemed eager to hear her story:

> *Miss Roman:* Well, it starts out—you see, I left home when I was 14. My father was an alcoholic, and my mother died when I was 5. So there was nothing to keep me there. And I suppose I always felt sort of unwanted, or something, escapist. So I suppose when I used drugs it made me feel like I didn't care.

Senator Daniel: From there tell us about how you happened to become addicted to the drug.

Miss Roman: I didn't realize at that time it was so easy to become addicted. And I didn't use it every day. But once in a while when someone had one and they came up to me and asked me if I wanted to get high. I would take it. And then it got to be an everyday affair. And pretty soon I woke up one morning and I was sick and I didn't know what was wrong with me. And I called up this girl that I knew and I told her, "I don't know what is wrong with me but I don't feel very well." I explained my symptoms to her. And she told me, she said, "Well, you have got a drug habit." So then I knew. So from then on I was using drugs every day.[71]

The behavior preceded the acquisition of an addiction narrative that rendered it intelligible. This narrative structure ascribed innocence to the subject that evaporated with knowledge. The emphasis then shifted to establishing Beverly's descent into moral and physical deterioration.

Reluctantly, Beverly confessed that she had engaged in prostitution and promised to give the senators a "full picture." After this tantalizing admission, however, she redirected the conversation toward the appalling treatment of female drug addicts: "I saw two girls die in the House of Detention in New York. I met a lot of girls that were drug addicts, and they were all prostitutes. So you can draw your own conclusions."[72] Focused on prostitution, the senators ignored the deaths and her statements about the inhumanity of this form of treatment, which "broke more than the habit." She persisted: "I think it is a very animalistic way to treat a human being. I have heard an awful lot of people talk about drug addiction, but I think the only people who have a right to talk about it are drug addicts, because we are the only ones who know what it is like. And I think from my own experience that 95 percent of the drug addicts are sick, and they shouldn't just be thrown in a hole somewhere and left to lie there and die. And I have seen them die."[73] Miss Roman described conditions in the "tank" with drug addicts who were "sick" (withdrawing). "And naturally if one girl is sick all the girls are interested. And I personally saw this girl lying on the floor—I don't want to make anyone sick, but I am going to tell this—she was throwing up and it was actually black. . . . The matron said, 'Let her alone, she will be all right, all those junkies are the same.' The doctor in charge there said she didn't like drug addicts anyway; she used to say right to our faces that we were the lowest type of humanity—which I don't think is fair."[74] Despite Senator Daniel's persistent attempts to cast aspersions on her account, Miss Roman insisted that abrupt withdrawal caused death.

Beverly commented on policy matters whenever she could divert the senators from their curiosity about the bodily effects of heroin and the conditions of prostitution. She elaborated on her idea of medical probation and underscored the benefits of treatment—"Well, I think they need psychiatry, all of them, myself included, I think we all need psychiatry." She advocated fresh air, good food, and rehabilitation, none of which she had encountered in prison. Senator Daniel taunted her with her inability to stay off heroin, and emphasized her lack of Sunday school attendance, moral training, and church membership. When Beverly described being placed as a domestic worker while on parole (a job for which she considered herself ill suited), the senators appeared more disturbed that addicts were in close proximity to middle-class children than at the restrictive opportunity structures working-class women and women of color faced in the 1950s.

Clearly, Miss Roman attempted to dispel misconceptions and convey her truth.[75] She countered the assumption that addicts lie, cheat, and steal, listing the legitimate occupations of those she knew. The senators corrected her, "You do know as an old pro in this business that any of those users had to steal and violate different laws of society to sustain their habit and also to sustain you." They decided she was susceptible to addiction because "Indians" lacked "moral immunity" and "spiritual training."[76] When she related her decision to flee a "broken home" in the wake of her mother's death and her father's remarriage, she encountered their condescension as they sought to extract "something about the failure of humanity, society as a whole, to meet people who have been in distressed conditions and help them start anew" from the story of "poor Beverly's" broken home.[77] She was asked: "Did you feel alone? Had you had a place in life to go, a place to work wherein you could do your work honestly and fairly, do you think you would ever have gotten back in the habit after you were released from the house of correction?" Miss Roman was sure she would not.

Asked to describe the "thrill" of heroin, Beverly rejected the request until, after repeated interrogation, she asked the senators to put themselves into the frame of their worst mood. She then described heroin as lifting that mood to the "normal" level. Rather than describe a magical "thrill," she explained that heroin use was a relief and necessity. It did not provide, as the senators believed, "a way out of the present": "You merely seek the drug when you become badly addicted because without it you can't stand it, you can't stand anything, yourself or anyone else, the pain, the misery, you're sick, that is all."[78] In contrast to their desire to hear an account of the "thrill," the senators did not encourage her to describe pain, misery, or sickness. Their voyeurism for the state's sake had limits. They expressed gratitude for Miss Roman's honesty, saying, "I think you are very gracious to come here, and I know what a beating you are taking in testifying, and I know something of the suffering you are enduring in telling the American people this story. We want to hear the full story, because this is the first time we have ever had a witness come before any senatorial committee and unburden herself like you have. It isn't any disgrace not to have had a great deal of education."[79] The tone of moral upmanship in the Daniel hearings reached a high-water mark with female witnesses.

The unburdening of Beverly Lee Roman represented the transmission of knowledge from a marginal position to the more socially central positions the senators occupied. Her story gave the senators grounds to claim they "knew" drug addiction. No other witness throughout the entire set of hearings was treated in quite this manner. The senators integrated her testimony with elements from their own truth.

Associating Addiction and Prostitution

The hearings often began with Senator Daniel intoning: "I believe you have had the unfortunate experience of having been addicted to heroin, is that correct, and I understand you were willing to cooperate with this committee in its investigation by giving us your account of the damage caused by this drug, am I correct in that?"[80] He then explained that the committee sought firsthand information about narcotics and was "simply trying to make a record as to how it works, what gets people started on it, what it costs per day, and all of that. We are not calling you in here for the purpose of trying to prosecute you, or to in any way embarrass you," but to "wipe out the traffic."[81] The interactions between women witnesses and the senators differed markedly from typical exchanges with male witnesses. Instead of being bullied or cajoled into answering questions of uncertain legality or propriety, male witnesses who wanted to plead the Fifth Amendment were respected. Male witnesses were interrogated simply about their activities as drug users or traffickers, not their sexual preferences, moral education, marital status, living arrangements, or involvement in prostitution. The senators' prurient interest in female addicts' psychosexual habits was patrolled but evident in the kinds of questions they posed and the line of inquiry they pursued.

Testimony from female witnesses was used to analyze subjective states of desire and to establish the bodily effects of moral distortion, as in this testimony from an addicted woman from New York: "Your values are completely displaced. You are disintegrated morally. I believe that very strongly, because I know, looking back on myself, shortly before I was arrested, I know that I would go long stretches without getting in touch with my mother . . . things that had a lot of meaning to me, I just tossed aside very lightly."[82] Women were asked to exhibit marks on their arms, which were described for the record.[83] The committee actively sought physical evidence of addiction or evidence of moral decline, directing witnesses away from other issues. Some resisted—a cagey witness from Chicago, Marie Batiesse, refused to answer questions about her personal associations with addicts. She twice reminded the chair that "once you get in trouble for narcotics, every time you get picked up they put the same thing on your paper, you don't have to have no narcotics."[84] Senator Daniel was not interested in that line of inquiry: "What this committee is interested in is what kind of trouble [drug use] gets people into."[85] Batiesse consistently denied that association with addicts "caused" addiction. "People use [drugs] because they want to use them . . . there don't know [*sic*] one entice them to use them," she stated.[86]

Female witnesses were often trapped into admitting they practiced prostitution. Leading questions like, "Did it cause you to go into some kind of calling that otherwise you would not have gone into?" painted female witnesses as prostitutes and thus de facto law violators. They were used to establish prostitution as a state of moral disintegration, unconscious desire, and bodily need similar in structure to addiction. Senator Daniel believed that marijuana and cocaine caused the body to *need* heroin. Ethel Gore, a Washington, D.C., witness, corrected him by noting that drug control policies made marijuana and cocaine less available than heroin.[87] When addicts refused to corroborate addiction's contagious quality (as did Miss Gore), the subcommittee prompted them: "This is exactly what I was getting at when I was talking to you about addicts spreading it to other people who see him [*sic*] and associate with them. It is sort of like leprosy. In the case of lepers we got them away for treatment and isolation, but in the case of narcotics addicts we don't."[88] Between leprosy and prostitution, addiction was constructed as a social disease that women transmitted.

Women's presence was not limited to testimony concerning their own addictions. They were blamed for the habit in sons, husbands, lovers, or pimps. Their maternal motivations were questioned.[89] One witness, a Polish national threatened with revocation of citizenship, was told: "This committee has had whole families through which mothers have spread the addiction to their children."[90] Threatened with deportation, loss of citizenship, stigma, or humiliation, female witnesses were badgered until they confirmed prevailing beliefs. These activities call into question the common assumption that women and girls "naturally" conformed to social ideals and norms. Rather, I would argue, their experiences were shaped to fit conceptual frameworks with which their own interpretations did not concur. Their testimony was used to substantiate points with which they explicitly disagreed. This was especially the case in the subcommittee's construction of drug maintenance policy as a form of prostitution because both spread addiction through "association."

Maintenance was discredited via its association with prostitution. The subcommittee asked female witnesses detailed questions about their sexual contacts, their route to addiction, and how they thought addiction was spread. Many women asserted addiction was not contagious by way of association, but their answers were parlayed into a metaphoric homology between drug maintenance and prostitution. For instance, Diana Marcus, a former nurse addicted to morphine and later heroin, became a prostitute after losing her nursing job.[91] She suggested that a federal dispensary would decrease the influence of the "heroin business," which was the real problem in her view. Senator Daniel flatly replied that a black market developed "everywhere this free system has been tried. But the main thing is, whenever free drugs were given like that, drug addiction increased. . . . They didn't try to treat them, and they spread the addiction to their friends and families."[92] Citing the clinics of the 1920s, he insisted that maintenance would inevitably fail because addiction spread by association. He used Miss Marcus's own experience to prove this point—her roommate had suggested she use morphine as a hangover cure. "You started using it because she did—right? So therefore if we had addicts, thousands of them—some say there are 7,000 of them in Chicago—so long as we have these addicts out on the streets, whether they are buying from the black market, or getting from a Federal dispensary, they would be associating with other people and spreading that addiction, wouldn't they?"[93] By conflating the "black market" with a "federal dispensary," he made it seem as if each had the same effects.

Association was also the theme of testimony by Joseph D. Lohman, Cook County Sheriff, who considered addiction worse than a contagious disease. Unlike bugs and germs, "what moves from one man to another has the added impetus of the person himself who is addicted, which is to create for himself a community of comfort and interest on the part of others, so he gives purpose to this transmission, which you do not have in disease."[94] Senator Daniel, too, grappled with the problem of intentionality. He asked: "Is that why you think so often addicts spread the addiction to other members of their family, people they really would not want to be hurting, but still they spread it? I know we found one mother spreading it to every child, and even to the in-laws." Lohman explained that unintentional transmission resulted from emotional dependency, disorganization, or shame in the user's psychology. Drugs imparted an "artificial strength" that attracted others who lived in similar misery.

Actress Lila Leeds, arrested with Robert Mitchum on marijuana charges in 1948, was arguably the most famous witness in the Daniel hearings. Upon release from two months in prison, she made an antidrug film, *Wild Weed* (1949), which later appeared under the title *She Shoulda Said No.* The film feminizes drug use from its opening shots of painted fingernails lighting up to the girlfriend who teaches Leeds's character, "Ann Lester," how to inhale. A lengthy sequence superimposes Ann's face on a series of shots of champagne, flames, dresses, dancing girls, dressing room lights, and cans of "Aztec tomatoes" containing marijuana (see Figure 16). Narcotics agents arrest her in their attempt to gain her cooperation in their pursuit of her dealer-boyfriend, Markey. They take her on a Dickensian tour of her future, displaying white women in various stages of addiction. At the first stop a prison matron displays a female prisoner beyond hope of youth or beauty—photos taken at her arrest mere months before revealed an attractive

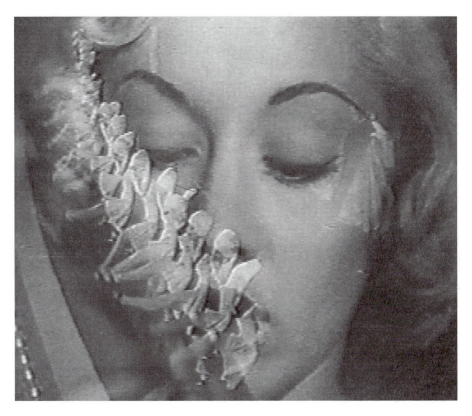

Figure 16 Movie still from *She Shoulda Said No*, 1949, depicting dancers superimposed on woman's face.

24-year-old. When this portrait of abjection fails to overcome Ann's stubbornness, they visit Gladys, a jailed inmate whose arms are hideously marked with bruises and needle tracks. Ann is next forced to gaze through a peephole at a straitjacketed woman screaming hysterically in a cell. Finally, she is taken to the morgue and shown a corpse as the agent intones: "This girl was lucky. She committed suicide. Her name could have been Ann Lester." Still resistant, Ann goes to jail, where thoughts of her younger brother's drug-related suicide turn into hallucinatory voices that accuse her of being a "kid killer" (see Figure 17). The film charts the character's decline from attractive blonde to hardened psychotic.

Leeds testified that the film project exploited the publicity surrounding her arrest and was not a vehicle for antidrug education. Senator Daniel asked her to explain how a mother of two had gotten into "so much trouble with heroin."[95] She replied that loneliness, the pull of association, and the need for momentary

Figure 17 Movie still from *She Shoulda Said No*, 1949, depicting chain superimposed on woman's face.

escape was the main impetus. "Getting back with the group—your friends are on it and you get back on it? Is that the way it was?" inquired Senator Daniel.[96] Leeds corroborated the senators' suspicions of treatment, stating she had become "dependent" on therapy while at the Lexington "narcotics farm."[97] Her reconstruction of emotional dependence spurred Senator Daniel to ask, "Even though you get it out of your body and blood, isn't the addiction something that stays in your mind?" Treatment was portrayed as a mental compulsion, an addiction in and of itself.

Women witnesses made way for Senator Daniel's own views. When Leeds suggested that immigration was the problem because "we do not raise poppies in this country,"[98] he listed producer nations: Red China, Mexico, Turkey, and Iran. His position on the question of "crime" or "disease" emerged in the last hearing in Cleveland, Ohio, when a witness named Miss Alston claimed that addicts "ought to be treated as sick people."[99] Senator Daniel argued that because she was first a prostitute, she "violated the law before [she] ever started using heroin" and could not argue that addicts were sick.[100] "I don't like to call it a sickness, myself," he said, because "people misunderstand when we talk about it as a sickness."[101] Daniel admitted that addiction could bring on "severe mental or physical illness," but he emphasized its criminality. When Miss Alston, who had been raised in a state-run orphanage, dared to suggest follow-up care in order to prevent treated users from returning to their previous activities, Senator Daniel did not take kindly to her suggestion. Where, he asked, "do you think we ought to let these addicts who are out violating the law go?"[102] When addicts focused on social and economic constraints, Senator Daniel shifted the conversation back to vicious associations, criminality, prostitution, foreign suppliers, and the need for mandatory minimum sentences.

Conclusion: Gender, Sexuality, and the Cultural Patterns of Addiction

Women were constructed as calculating agents of addiction, men as unwitting subjects. Links between prostitution, association, sexual deviance or "psychopathy," and addiction helped to focus blame for the underlying psychological causes of drug-related deviance on female presence. Even the emphasis on Red Chinese Communism as a vehicle for addiction in the free world played up women's role in transmitting addiction to the West. There was curiously little emphasis on male response or responsibility, treatment, or rehabilitation; these questions came up primarily with female witnesses. Women's responsibility for spreading addiction through "association" was extensively remarked upon. While prostitution was considered a contagion of association akin to addiction, normative heterosexuality was played up as the salvation from it.

Social workers recognized the substitution of healthy heterosexual social activities for narcotics use as necessary for boys. Seeking to deter heroin addiction among white adolescent gang members, social worker Patrick Kelley believed "the only guys who ever kick it do it by getting a girlfriend."[103] Kelley, who worked with adolescent addicts between 1956 and 1959 in New York City,[104] attributed male aggression and heroin use to "heterosexual anxieties": "Some of the heightened physical activity during this period was probably caused by a bursting out of body energy that had been saddled by the depressant qualities of heroin. Underlying psychological disturbances, also suppressed by heroin, could explain the more aggressive behavior such as 'bopping.'"[105] Drugs were "inadequate problem-solving devices" that replied to the problem of masculine "ineptness in heterosexual relationships." This explanation made girls appear as vehicles to reorient boys toward heterosexuality, the accepted substitute for drugs. Girls were simultaneously outside drug cultures and incorporated into their causal structure.

Addicted women and girls were positioned paradoxically in the 1950s. Symbolically, they could witness and reproduce the truth of addiction; politically, they were situated as knowing agents of its spread; materially, they commanded little attention; discursively, their "truths" were regarded as less credible. The assumption that girls "naturally" conformed to social expectations meant that girl drug addicts were seen as more stubbornly addicted and more deviant than teenage males. Moral outrage directed against addicted women was stimulated by the expectation that most women resisted the temptation of drugs. When this was not the case, they were cast aside from the natural processes of social reproduction. Theirs was an unredeemable susceptibility—as if the presence of female addicts indicated that the forces of addiction were about to overwhelm all "civilized" cultural formations.

Perhaps the "girl drug addicts" of the 1950s are most usefully read as indicating where the parameters of normalcy were giving way, shifting, and reconfiguring in relation to larger social, economic, and political constellations. As women's addiction became more visible in police and probation records, case studies, and statistics, it became "objectively known" within models that were ill suited for analyzing the actual situations of girls and women. The mid-century inquiry into adolescent drug use linked the "truth" of addiction to failed formations of normative masculinity and femininity, thus promoting self-control and the foreclosure of sexual and social deviance as "solutions" to the problem. What might have been learned about young women's resort to drugs to modulate the actual conditions of their social, emotional, and economic lives in the 1950s passed instead into obscurity.

Mother
Fixations

A COMPLETE BOOK-LENGTH
TRUE CRIME NOVEL.

Mother Fixations

Questioning the Subject on Drugs

Drugs have long been an acceptable register for claims about the irreducible otherness of persons who use them, as Part II amply demonstrated in the case of "opium vampires," male adolescent addicts, and "girl drug addicts." Male drug users may be written off, but women's reproductive capacities and responsibilities place them in a more complex position. Addicted women are understood to reproduce their own (in)humanity, as well as offspring who are not fully human. In the last decades of the twentieth century, drug-addicted babies were constructed as nonsubjects lacking the "central core of what it is to be human."[1] The discursive process that unfolded in the 1980s appeared to be one of sober scientific assessment replete with statistical data and rational confabulations outlining an escalating crack-cocaine epidemic. These confabulations were the basis for questioning the very status of drug-addicted babies and their mothers as subjects. By the late 1990s, a note of regret crept into media portrayals of the crack epidemic as it dwindled to an "underground" presence.[2] The dire predictions failed to materialize, and so we must ask what cultural work they performed then and now.

Part III addresses our responses to women's drug use within the context of late-twentieth-century U.S. political culture and gender history. Where addicted women were once constructed as sexual predators or the prey of white slavers, by the mid-century they were positioned as gender nonconformists and sexual deviants. The transition posed a problem for addicted women who were pregnant or mothering; an emerging emphasis on neonatal addiction in the late 1950s focused on maternal behavior. Chapter 6 traces the variety of mothering practices once thought to "cause" addiction. It provides the historical backdrop against which the morality play of late-twentieth-century drug policy unfolded. While in the past women addicts who were pregnant or mothering were constructed as poor mothers who violated feminine norms by dominating their households, in the latter decades of the century women who biologically "reproduced" addiction played stunningly demonized roles. Chapter 7 is based on a close reading and discourse analysis of congressional hearings on maternal crack-cocaine and heroin use in the late 1980s and early 1990s. It closely reproduces my method for reading for what the governing mentalities can tell us about who "we" are as a polity.

Wars within Multiple Arenas

Both women's rights and fetal rights advocates used maternal drug use figuratively. Addicted women show up as "limit cases" in feminist discourse, which frames addiction as a public health problem compounded by gender difference. Pregnant addicts signal women's needs for universal health coverage, equal access to decision-making, or a working social safety net. As they do in my own narrative, pregnant addicts represent a call for social responsibility and policies of social justice. By contrast, fetal rights advocates use them to call into question the "traditional values of parental autonomy." Their prevailing logic is that drug-using women cannot govern themselves, and thus produce unruly children who ultimately reproduce an ungovernable society. Therefore, it is "as American as apple pie" for the U.S. government to protect "potential human life."[3] They array social versus individual responsibility as if they are at odds with one another and at war within the figure of the pregnant addict.

Fetal rights advocates seek to cement a very restricted form of maternal responsibility, which I demonstrate through an analysis of a congressional hearing that was published as *Born Hooked*.[4] The political agenda of drug policy remains up for grabs. Proponents of fetal rights use drug policy as a means to an end, a way to justify limiting women's rights while expanding a culturally conservative agenda. This politic move on the part of antiabortion advocates forced feminists to defend "unfit" mothers and occupy an almost (but not quite) indefensible position. Feminists repeatedly and forcefully contested the qualification of individual reproductive choice—but they did so in ways that left little rhetorical room for them to weigh in on matters of familial responsibility and the well-being of children. The deflection of social problems onto individuals who embody them holds back a feminist analysis of larger social patterns and was singularly unhelpful in the variety of interlinked political arenas in which "personal responsibility" became a governing mentality.

"Responsibility" is a key word in current political discourse and a driving refrain in many spheres of social and political life.[5] The turn to "parental responsibility" was occasioned by the attempt of private think tanks such as the American Enterprise Institute and conservative legislators to deinstitutionalize

U.S. government responsibility for social provision. By deflecting "responsibility" onto the individualized figure of the "parent," they detached social from individual responsibility; thus employers and the government were not responsible for providing individuals with the means to meet their responsibilities. Individual "parents" are assumed already to possess the ways and means to reproduce society in a vacuum of support. The gender-neutral figure of the "parent" belies the fact that mothers remain ultimately responsible for social reproduction. Parenting emerged as a concern in the postwar panic over juvenile delinquency, and was consolidated as an activity of nuclear families in which heterosexual "sex roles" were clearly delineated in the sexual division of labor. Parental deviation from this recommended pattern was thought to generate delinquent behavior—the concept held "parents" as much in place as children.

Today the logic of parental responsibility limits maternal autonomy and reproductive rights. Although recent public policy advances "paternal responsibility" by holding fathers accountable for economic responsibility, it does so in ways that too often compromise mothers and negatively affect women's autonomy.[6] The primary responsibility still devolves to the mother:

> Despite clear evidence that extramaternal factors can be a significant danger to the mother and the fetus, in a democratic society the woman, at times perhaps unfairly, bears responsibility for her actions. She alone is the direct link to the fetus and she alone makes the ultimate decision as to whether or not to smoke, use alcohol or other drugs, maintain proper nutrition, and so forth. Although emphasis here on the responsibility placed on the woman could be interpreted as sexist, the actions of the mother, not the father, do in fact more directly affect the fetus.[7]

This construction of maternal responsibility divorces it from substantive considerations of what women might need to realize "their" responsibilities—much less an exploration of shared responsibility for social reproduction.

Late-twentieth-century U.S. drug policy was novel in its focus and effects on women in the criminal justice system. Women's incarceration results from particular patterns of arrest, conviction, and sentencing which take place in highly uneven ways that disproportionately impact the poor, racial-ethnic minorities, and people who live in certain places. The growing political movement against the incarceration of women benefited from the early success of the feminist movement against punitive drug policy. Much drug policy criticism and feminist legal scholarship reiterated the unfortunate examples of Pamela Rae Stewart and Jennifer Johnson, two women who became figurative martyrs for the punitive political rationality. Their stories testified to the irony that pregnant addicts have vainly sought treatment, only to be turned away to face criminal charges. Such narratives use the most extreme victims of drug policy to indicate the social vulnerability that shapes the majority of drug-abusing women's lives. The most important political arenas in which the drama of maternal crack-cocaine use played out were the reproductive rights struggle, the imposition of policies of "personal responsibility," and the movement against the criminalization of pregnant addicts. The governing mentalities scripted each of these postmodern morality plays.

Babies or Drugs? The Pitfalls of Bad Choices

Pregnant addicts, their babies, and their children play a specific role in political discourse. Criminologists Zimring and Hawkins, proponents of "rational drug control," used babies and children to question the type of policy problem represented by the health and custody issues of newborn "crack babies." Although the problems of such babies were clearly "drug-related," drug control agencies would be of little use in responding to their needs. Rather, Zimring and Hawkins argued, agencies that deal with babies would be better situated to meet this responsibility. Being good rationalists, they stated both ethical and practical reasons for their position. Ethically, they reclassified drug-addicted babies as a problem of child welfare: "there are compelling nondrug values at risk in dealing with these infants" that outweigh the values and interests of drug law enforcement. Both ethically and administratively, then, the needs of "crack babies" exceed the "skills and perspectives . . . associated with drug enforcement."[8] Child welfare values should always trump drug law enforcement. Practically speaking, they suggested, "aggressive concern with child welfare" might lead treatment programs to tolerate relapse and guard addicted women's privacy more stringently than "the drug treatment philosophy of most drug enforcement agencies" allowed.

Babies and children represent innocent third parties who cannot speak for themselves, who are directly harmed, and who are relatively helpless. For rationalists, crack babies represent a choice between two conflicting sets of values—the beneficent values of child welfare and treatment, and those of drug law enforcement. Law enforcement constructs abstinence as the only legitimate goal—even in cases where abrupt withdrawal between the fourteenth and twenty-eighth week of pregnancy would adversely affect a fetus. "The argument is thus that drug control agencies give too much weight to drug issues. The capacity for peripheral vision may be a significant advantage even if no single nondrug interest is regarded as compelling."[9] Zimring and Hawkins sought to admit more values and interests than those narrowly centered on drugs—basically, to admit more elements to the story and allow the characters more room to chart their course. This path, of course, accords well with a feminist postpositivist policy analysis designed to move beyond the "facts" to take account of values embedded in political discourse.

"Rational drug policy" does not accord well with feminist postpositivist positions in other ways. Political tensions over the practice of "child protection" and "child welfare" are gendered and racialized. By failing to consider the values, interests, problems, and custody issues central to the lives of these children's mothers, Zimring and Hawkins "forget" that women are differentially vulnerable and have unequal access to social space, political effectivity, and the basic resources that purchase privacy and protection. Their rationalist case thus lacks something that a feminist postpositivist analysis would provide. Feminists have questioned whether child welfare and protective service agencies are fair, tolerant, and concerned with the well-being, civil liberties, and basic rights of their clients.[10] Studies of the interactions between "clients" and state agencies shift the terrain and reveal the flaws in an otherwise compelling argument. Solving drug problems means redirecting our attention beyond the obsessive focus on drug restriction and child removal as a form of "protection"—and toward issues of social justice.

The rationalist argument counterpoises an out-of-control addict to the "reasonable woman" who weighs drugs against children and makes the "right choice." The argument founders on the shoals of all rational choice theory. Drugs and children are simply not of the same order of value—addicted women do not consciously choose cocaine over kids. Indeed, drugs and children are part of two different value-systems that are linked only by a discursive reduction of drug use and childbearing to matters of individual choice. This individualizing move obscures the political-economic structure of drug use and traffic and fails to recognize that drug use patterns are predictable over time, space, and population. Even a cursory glance at the conditions of women's lives reveals the social constraints on individual women's agency. We therefore gain analytic clarity by emphasizing the stratified social contexts of women's lives. This move does not deprive women of agentic power so much as point to how conventional policy analysis presumes away constraints on women's agency. The effect of this presumption, of course, is to cast addicted women as stubbornly and irrationally making bad choices.

Policy and Maternity

All women are now considered "potentially pregnant" for the purposes of law (regardless of the actual condition of pregnancy or the individual intent to become or remain pregnant). As addiction in women has been constructed as a "biological vulnerability" (see Chapter 1), it is rendered "natural" in the biological sense. This "biologization" covers up the true stakes of drug policy debates—the gendered division of labor and the distribution of social responsibility. Just as the figure of the masculine criminal renders politically progressive work on crime difficult, the maternal figure of the addict and the construction of addiction as individual choice or biological vulnerability obscure the structural forces at work in producing criminals and addicts. The "deflection dynamic" illustrated throughout *Using Women* relies on women as links between self and society. How women perform their social positions as wives, girlfriends, mothers, and grandmothers—that is, how credibly their gender performance fits normative expectations—shifts over time and space, and varies within and between communities. Women do not perform the tasks of social reproduction in the same way everywhere. These practices, as feminist scholars have documented, vary across racialethnic, class, and sexual lines. Certain aspects of femininity, however, remain staples of political discourse.

Maternity is a widely used "mobilizing metaphor" often adopted in public policy to "express emblematically the tensions women experience in their lives."[11] Political discourse uses "maternity" to invoke the material contradictions of everyday life—and at the same time disavow them. Maternity is understood as a state of constraint by the real—a form of labor from which the subject cannot responsibly escape. It is also a productive space that evokes generative power and the capacity for social reproduction. These ambivalent understandings grant maternal metaphors enormous range and flexibility; their political valence is always up for grabs and highly subject to individual interpretation.[12] The maternity metaphor both acknowledges and quickly disavows the material conditions of mothering.

Reproducing
Drug Addiction
Motherhood, Respectability, and the State

Narcotics and Maternal Influence
A Short History of Congenital Addiction

Women's reproductive decisions and practices periodically come under state and social scrutiny. The intensity and techniques of surveillance vary, but the cycles have something in common: "respectable" women become invisible, while their less respectable counterparts become hypervisible and even spectacular. Figured as unfortunate but innocent victims, white women were protected from addiction's consequences by marriage, motherhood, racial privilege, or class membership. Given the myriad changes in early-twentieth-century women's lives—opposition to suffrage, a moral panic about "white slavery," pronatalist and eugenic concerns about "white race suicide," and a campaign against infant "doping"—it is remarkable that public attention to addiction among pregnant women did not surface sooner.

During the Progressive era, the state scrutinized mothering practices in the name of a new focus on maternal and infant health.[1] Maternalist influences on early-twentieth-century social policy exhibited (some) women's increasing influence on government, but also permitted negative comparisons between the mothering practices of poor women, African-Americans, and recent immigrants, and those of white, middle-class mothers. Opposition to maternalism developed in tandem with the refinement of political and cultural mechanisms to contain women's autonomy.[2] One such mechanism is an optics of surveillance that renders mothers "fearfully susceptible to the 'gaze' of others."[3] Another mechanism is the basic idea of eugenics—the idea that controlling poor women's sexual behaviors and decisions about reproduction and family formation can solve social problems.[4] White, middle-class mothers, who formed the majority of addicted women prior to the Harrison Act, were relatively shielded from the "gaze of others."

Figure 18   Illustration captioned "Don't give soothing-syrup to children" from *Children's Health Primer*, 1887.

Reprinted, with permission, from the New York Public Library.

Congenital addiction to opiates was recorded as early as the 1830s. Restlessness, moral and mental weakness, and "blue baby" syndrome (cyanosis) were known outcomes of maternal opiate use. While maternal addiction did not elicit public outrage in the nineteenth century, some mothers and their "help" were criticized. For example, an 1832 dissertation by William G. Smith condemned the "youthful, inconsiderate mother and the idle nurse" who quieted infants with opiate-laced proprietary medicines "rather than forego the pleasures of a crowded assembly, or the gaudy charms of a dramatic scene, a single evening."[5] Mothers who "drugged" children later came under public scrutiny in the campaigns to regulate advertising and sales of patent medicines (see Figure 18). The campaign against "ignorant mothers, stupid nurses, and careless women" who drugged children cited mothers' laziness and backwardness.[6] "Regular" physicians employed such warnings as a strategy of professionalization to consolidate their market through control over pharmaceutical opiates.

Nineteenth-century physicians practiced gradual withdrawal techniques, keeping infants alive by weaning them with paregoric. *The American Textbook of*

Applied Therapeutics (1896) went so far as to applaud the poor prognosis of "infants born of mothers who are morphinists" because "the moral and mental strength of these children is so far below par as to make them liable to much subsequent suffering."[7] "Morphinist mothers" were depicted as direct threats to their babies when, in 1913, a physician found that babies' blood was "as much saturated with the drug as the blood of the mother," thus confirming that narcotics crossed the placenta. "Morphinist fathers" were also thought to impair their offspring: "How could it be otherwise, since every influence within the body tells in the upbuilding of protoplasm, and since the composite protoplasm of the germ borrows its qualities from every form of protoplasm in the parental organism?"[8]

Addiction among mothers and children was rarely mentioned, and there were long periods when very little was known about how to treat it. When Terry and Pellens surveyed physicians in the 1920s, they concluded that most lacked accurate and rational knowledge about congenital addiction.[9] The "opium vampires" of the 1920s and 1930s were rarely maternal figures, although they might be castigated for drugging babies for the sake of a night on the town. By the late 1940s the cause of addiction shifted from the sexualized figure of the "opium vampire" to mothers who maintained children in dependent states. Any form of dependency on a larger structure, institution, or authority figure was considered harmful. Even the military bred dependency by allowing soldiers a "feeling of ephemerality, a living from day to day, [and] a quest for momentary pleasures" to escape from "war tensions, the emphasis on destruction, and the fear of atomic attack."[10] As recounted in Part II, drug use was associated with youth—and returning World War II veterans—by early 1950.[11] Women and especially mothers played a starring role in conveying this threat to all children in the mid-twentieth-century United States.

Normativity and Deviance: Girls on The Road to H

"Dope" was part of an everyday world found in "streets adjacent to high schools" and "the shadows of chop-suey joints, skating rinks, dance halls, drugstores, bus stations and the like."[12] The heightened attention to narcotics use in the 1950s did not focus on reproduction among addicts but on the ubiquity of addiction, the availability of drugs to teenagers, and the role of parenting in producing delinquency. Most of the female subjects in *The Road to H* study had children of their own, yet only their relationships with their mothers were studied. Their relationships with their own children were barely mentioned. State-level civil commitment programs, which recorded the ratio of women to men as one out of five, took no account of pregnancy or motherhood. I found almost no mention of pregnancy in the popular press coverage of the heroin epidemics of the 1950s, despite the inquiry into the sexual practices of adolescent female addicts recounted

Figure 19   Cover illustration by Al Rossi, 1953.

Reprinted from *Junkie: Confessions of an Unredeemed Drug Addict* by William Lee (William Burroughs), published as an ACE Original.

in the Daniel hearings. Cultural representations of addicted women were highly sexualized and so differed from those of male addicts.

Addicted women were portrayed as more desperate and furtive than their male counterparts, hiding their secret vice beneath the trappings of domesticity and femininity (see Figures 19 and 20). Although their number remained small, an important demographic shift was under way. Prior to the war, most addicted

Figure 20   Cover illustration, 1953.

Reprinted from *Narcotic Agent* by Maurice Helbrant, published as an ACE Original.

women were white, middle-class, native-born Protestants.[13] Postwar addicts were younger, poorer, more "delinquent," and more likely to be women of color. For instance, white women addicts in the New York City House of Detention out-numbered women of color by four to one before the war. By the late 1950s the ratio was reversed, a rapid transformation that became more robust over time.[14] Not until the 1960s, however, was "race" employed as a salient analytic category through which social scientists, policy-makers, and the public comprehended the social patterns of drug use.[15]

The postwar addicts were depicted as more racially and sexually deviant than their forerunners in the steady trickle of films on drugs that appeared in the late 1940s.[16] Antidrug films separated addicts from the "emotionally normal person [who] will find no attraction to drugs."[17] Although the educational film *Drug Addiction* revolved around a white boy, Marty Demelon, one of the first addicts pictured was an African-American teenage girl. She was the only female addict in the film—and the only African-American addict. When she appears, the voice-over says, "Addiction to drugs, too often acquired with tragic carelessness, may take control of a life, and force actions not dreamed of before." These words primitivized addiction and located it as a form of external control. The teaching script that accompanied the image noted: "This film begins by showing how youth, normally a gay and happy time, may be blackened by the grim spectre of drug addiction."[18] This enigmatic African-American teenager haunted the film's pretense to grim realism by embodying the "blackening" of youth. In the last frames of the film, white girls link arms with white boys to enact the prescription for conquering addiction—psychological adjustment to heterosexual normalcy.

Restoration into heteronormativity was offered as the cure for addiction in adolescents of both genders. A pulp novel, *Marijuana Girl* (1960), told the story of Joy, a white, college-aged girl who descended into heroin addiction and prostitution through an affair with Frank, an older man with a taste for jazz (see Figure 21). Through him, Joy became overly familiar with the ways of African-American musicians, the minor pleasures of marijuana, and, eventually, a major heroin habit.[19] The "marijuana girl" exhibited "unquestioning obedience" and "slavish devotion to . . . orders and desires," but was also the incarnation of juvenile delinquency and feminine insubordination.[20] Father absence was the explanation for Joy's habit; Frank, a substitute father figure, was only a temporary remedy. Tony, a more age-appropriate boyfriend, was the cure. As Frank explained: "When you establish a certain habit as a kid . . . it somehow gets built into your personality, and without knowing it, you more or less keep repeating variations of the habit all through your life. . . ."[21] According to him, "She doesn't really want a father. She really wants a lover—a man of her own. And that's where you fit in, and I don't. Dig?" Tony responded, "I dig. The normal-er it is, the better. And the thing I've got to do is convince her I really love her—no matter what, but more when she's good than when she's bad."[22] As the book jacket indicated, the way beyond degeneracy—the "vile device of trading herself body and soul for the drugs she had to have"—was to reinstall Joy within the economy of heterosexuality, the "normal-er," the better. This portrait of "our ravished youth," the "hopped-up, sexed-up kids who are America's shame and disgrace," blamed addiction on parental failure, personality disturbance, and gender deviance.

The press played up the lurid and novel aspects of the 1950s epidemic, but professionals referred to it as the "second peak of an old problem."[23] Lauretta

SHE TRADED HER
BODY FOR DRUGS—
AND KICKS!

Marijuana Girl

N. R. DeMexico

S75124
75¢
MAC

NEVER WAS THERE
SO OUTSPOKEN A NOVEL
AS THIS . . . TELLING THE
PLAIN, UNCENSORED TRUTH
ABOUT TEEN-AGE
ADDICTS—AND THEIR
DESPERATE
SEARCH FOR
THRILLS!

Figure 21   Cover illustration, 1960.

Reprinted from *Marijuana Girl* by N. R. DeMexico, published by Softcover Library.

Bender, head of the Bellevue Hospital Psychiatric Division from 1934 to 1956, was "unimpressed" by the so-called epidemic and claimed it was "unimportant in the lives of children with many other real problems."[24] She felt that attention to adolescent addiction deflected from problems such as "gross social neglect," family breakdown, increasing numbers of people without resources, and the "boredom, neglect, and social malaise that characterizes our age."[25] She indicated there were no known research studies on female adolescent addicts, citing the remarks of Dorris Clarke, Chief Probation Officer of the New York City Magistrate Court, who raised the "question of the girl" in the New York Academy of Medicine hearings:[26] "There is absolutely no question but that more and more females are turning to the use of drugs and more and more females are going into prostitution to support their drug habit. . . . We have to give serious consideration to the fact that more and more of our girls, *in contrast to our boys*, are turning to the use of narcotics.[27] Clarke was convinced that young women initiated drug use at higher rates than adolescent males. Bender concurred, indicating that most girls who used narcotics were not caught and citing the fact that since 1950 more narcotics cases had been heard in the Women's Court and the Girl's Term Court than in the male courts.[28] Few were convinced. The frameworks through which drug use was known implicated women as causative agents in male addiction but did not construct women as themselves susceptible to it.

Certainly, male addiction rates exceeded those of women. Some thought this meant that "females are less likely than males to express their tensions in ways that are detectably and flagrantly violative of prevailing social codes."[29] *The Road to H* identified three neurotic character disorders among women that were absent from men: the "sadomasochistic," the "angry-aggressive," and the "cool psychopath."[30] The sadomasochists appeared more masochistic than sadistic, prone as they were to accidents, beatings, teasing, and abuse. The researchers experienced the assertive independence of the angry-aggressives as "a defensive denial of their wish for passivity and dependence." Women addicts in general externalized their troubles, but angry-aggressives' "worlds were out of joint, not they."[31] The psychopaths were "apparently free of anxiety and facile at rationalization."[32] Relations between female addicts and their parents alternated between gratification and deprivation, intensity and weakness.

The family background study subjects differed from those in the clinical study: eighteen were African-American females, who were compared to ten African-American males. Male-female differences were slight but significant: parents did not appear to communicate unrealistic aspirations or distrust of social institutions to daughters. Marriage was considered a realistic aspiration for one's daughter, corresponding neatly to the goal of heterosocial normalization. Criteria for "realistic" aspirations were coded according to gender, racial, and sexual economics. For instance, the families of female African-American addicts were at greater economic disadvantage than those of African-American male addicts. But the women's families were "better integrated"—they were ideologically middle-class. No more and no less than appropriately racialized middle-class aspirations were considered "realistic." The only valid cross-gender comparisons the researchers could make were among African-American drug users, due to the preponderance of African-American females in both studies.[33] Both male and female drug users came from "socially disorganized" areas. Interestingly, although the families of female drug users were more assimilated, their daughters were considered more aberrant and maladapted.

Pregnancy and addiction were both considered symptoms of a gendered psychopathology. *The Road to H* explained that, unlike men and boys, females "have available to them another technique of 'acting out' which is not available to males . . . the out-of-wedlock pregnancy," a drama "enacted largely in the life of the female."[34] Like addiction, pregnancy was considered a symptom of psychological maladjustment. The prevailing social-psychiatric theories of the time located responsibility for drug-addicted sons and daughters with their mothers, and these relationships were central to the study. Female addicts, most of whom had children, were not asked about their experiences of pregnancy, birth, child loss, or child rearing. Out-of-wedlock pregnancy and addiction were merely vehicles for girls' expression of antisocial hostility to authority. Normal girls did not get high or pregnant; those who did were neurotic, psychopathic, or "inadequate personalities" (neither "good delinquents" nor "good schizophrenics," in the researchers' words). Despite the lack of controls, small sample size, time-bound quality, and explicit sexism, the study's gender ideology established an enduring pattern. Addicted white women were diagnosed with personality disorders; addicted women of color were "sociopathically disturbed" and hence more "deviant."

Gender is a dynamic relationship between prevailing codes of masculinity and femininity. Later studies claimed that women who used drugs "act and dress like callous teen-age male delinquents."[35] Conversely, adolescent male addicts were portrayed as too feminine, as illustrated in Chapter 4. Girls were also implicated as agents who transmitted addiction, often through prostitution. As a teenage informant in a journalistic collection put it:

Girls are a big factor in making boys dope addicts. . . . You take a quiet guy, a little backward and shy, the potential raper [sic]. . . . It's easier for a girl to secure a habit and to keep it under control, because all she has to do is lay down on the bed. . . . She can put any price she wants on that, see? Because she's a woman, and men will buy women. Those girls take a plain ordinary joe that doesn't know too much, and they say, look honey, you can sleep with me and live with me and I'll take care of you. They give this guy his first taste of sex.

And believe me, he's at their beck and call. They'll make him anything they want to make him. They'll make him a dope addict, eventually.[36]

This peculiar power of women and girls to induce addiction in men and boys is a perennial feature of the governing mentalities of discourse on drugs.

Mothers' failure to optimize autonomy in their sons led to excessive dependency needs discharged toward "improper objects" (drugs, their mothers, persons of the same sex, persons of a different color). Family configuration produced addiction, which was considered an *adaptive* response for young men in "unnatural" circumstances where fathers were weak or absent and mothers dominant. Addiction was never considered "adaptive" for females. The figure of the "out-of-wedlock mother" paralleled that of the male addict: both represented young people impelled by abnormal needs and desires to live out their deviance in gendered terms. When girls "expressed deviance" through drug use or promiscuity, they did not express "ignorance, but rather *disregard* for what they knew about the long-range probabilities of harm and trouble in the quest for immediate pleasure."[37] Women were portrayed as using heroin willfully and maladaptively—heroin was not the adaptive or unconscious mechanism for girls that it was for boys. Addicted girls were described as unmotivated and resentful. They lacked insight, made trouble, refused work, complained without basis, incited affairs with one another and male patients, hazed patients, drained hospital resources, and underutilized opportunities for therapy. "Unlike the males, who generally try not to attract attention from the hospital staff, the female *gets* herself noticed. Perhaps this reflects a characteristic difference between men and women in our culture. Whatever the basis of the difference, female adolescent addicts are unquestionably far more demanding of the time and energy of the staff than are male patients."[38]

The Road to H found that typical female drug addicts were raised with "congeries of pathogenic features," the most pathogenic being their mothers. "The mothers were usually insecure women, concealing their conflicts and insecurities behind a facade of efficiency, responsibility, and excessive mothering; they were usually religious and prone to preaching; they were opinionated, judgmental, rigid, authoritarian, and dictatorial."[39] Addicts were not individually responsible for their psychopathologies—their domineering mothers were. The mothers who inhabited the "female-dominated households" of the 1950s were not addicts themselves, but therapeutic discourse held them responsible for generating addiction within race- and class-specific family configurations. The level of aggression and hostility expressed toward female addicts and addicts' mothers in studies, conferences, and policy hearings suggests that they fell short of normative femininity. Women embodied the reproduction of addiction in drug policy discourse, a burden they continue to carry.

Gender Failures
Femininity, Sexuality, and Addiction

Women's drug use is located in the circuits of racial and sexual economics, defined as the production and distribution of goods, services, labor, health, and welfare according to sex/gender and racial positions.[40] The cultural processes by which acts or identities become freighted with moral value and political meaning within these cultural-economic systems renders some subjects more visible and audible than others. The "panic logic" of the early 1950s drug crises did not direct sustained attention to female drug use.[41] Still, some illuminating accounts of women's addiction appeared in qualitative social science, federal drug policy hearings, and psychiatric case histories. Autobiographical and fictional accounts of female drug use indicated that women and girls involved in drug worlds intended to act in nonconventional ways.[42]

Addiction among young women was constructed as more pathological, less knowable, less predictable, and therefore less controllable than among men. Situated as extreme departures from normativity, female addicts marked the limits of tolerance for deviance.[43] Adolescent girls often eluded attention until they had used drugs for some time; by then they were thought to be beyond the reach of therapy. Authorities considered girls less reliable witnesses, claiming that they lied to get special attention or privileges.[44] Women's drug use showed up in popular culture as a symptom of other feminized forms of female deviance such as prostitution or lesbianism (see Figure 22). The very conceptual models of adolescent male drug use rendered adolescent female drug use uninteresting to researchers and authorities, who thought the "real" drug problem was among boys. Girls were simply acting out their problems becoming women.

Gender failure—the social or psychological incapacity to perform within the constraints of normative femininity and heterosexuality—aligned with the idea that addiction was a form of moral breakdown. However, gender and sexuality cannot be isolated from race, ethnicity, and class in the construction of deviant subjects. A relational economics attributes meaning to and distributes the material consequences of drug use.[45] Adolescent girls themselves attributed illicit drug use to events in their affective, sexual, or reproductive lives such as out-of-wedlock pregnancy, revulsion toward heterosexuality, perceived expectations, or impatience with normative constraints on their behavior. The "girl drug addicts" of the formative epidemics of the 1950s represented themselves as using illicit drugs to negotiate complex sexual, economic, and social relations.[46]

Absent significant research other than *The Road to H*, I turn to an audiotaped self-representation transcribed at the Chicago Area Project from dictation by the pseudonymous Janet Clark. Lauretta Bender remarked on this "bona fide case with a taped autobiography by a gifted girl" recorded by an unnamed research

Figure 22   Photograph
depicting association
between women as
initiation into heroin
sniffing, 1951.

Courtesy of *True Story,* New
York, New York.

sociologist.[47] Bender described Clark's life: "She had a maladjusted childhood,
with a sociopathic narcissistic mother, an immature ne'er-do-well for a father
who was divorced from the mother when the child was five and died when she was
seven. . . . The story contains all the ingredients and coloring of the drug addict's
life."[48] I present Janet Clark not as an "authentic voice," but to render visible the
"complex social constructs which are the products of pre-given discourses, in
effect 'written' in advance as scripts made available by the dominant culture for
their teenage speakers."[49] This is not a history of the teenage girl drug addict as
an empirical entity, but an account of how one young woman produced her version of the truth in the drug subculture of 1950s Chicago.

A Feminist Reading Of The Fantastic Lodge: The Autobiography of a Girl Drug Addict

Sociologists of deviance represented drug use as a "male" problem. Labeling theory
was based on ethnographic studies of largely male drug users, with the exception of

a tape-recorded life history narrative dictated by a white adolescent female addict published as *The Fantastic Lodge: The Autobiography of a Girl Drug Addict* (1961).[50] Presented as a communique from the "secret margin" between the respectable world and the underworld, the recordings were made at the behest of sociologist Howard Becker and edited by Helen MacGill Hughes. "Janet Clark" narrated her negotiations through the "Negro 'sporting' world, intellectual bohemia, and . . . the world of drugs and drug addicts."[51] Despite its highly mediated nature, her account was presented as a "direct" link between the drug world and the straight world. She reconstructed emotions, social relationships, and situations for her readers, gaining a measure of agency by subjecting herself to the apparatus of knowledge production that was mid-century sociology. Without Becker's efforts, Janet Clark would have been yet another anonymous drug addict who lived fast and died young, leaving little record of her existence.

Instead, Janet Clark played a significant role in the sociological construction of drug addiction by testifying to one girl's lived experience of drug addiction. Despite her indigent status and untimely suicide, her published story was the narrative of the "normal," white, middle-class daughter gone wrong. Janet was reluctantly heterosexual: she often rejected heterosexual relations and maintained that heroin helped her perform as a heterosexual in the marriage that was her own road to H. Addicts and staff at the Lexington Hospital regarded her as a "female homosexual" because she did not follow the one-woman-to-a-bed rule.[52] While living with her widowed mother prior to the onset of drug use, she became pregnant out of wedlock, an event that revealed her mother's love to be uncertain and conditional. Thinking she was a prostitute, her family tried to separate her from her friends, which intensified her affective life to an unbearable degree. To survive, she dissociated: "It's as though I put myself in a suspended state, as though I don't feel anything, really."[53] This painful state resembled "one little ice cube, as though that's me and there's a mechanical brain working inside and somehow or other it keeps going, in spite of all the misery. It's a very unreal sort of world, however, and not my choice as far as worlds go."[54]

Responses to illegitimate pregnancy and therapeutic interventions varied by race during this period. Where white out-of-wedlock pregnancies manifested psychological problems, black out-of-wedlock pregnancies were "biologized" in ways that reinforced the "distinction between a white culture of the mind and a black culture of the body."[55] Janet's mother insisted she put her illegitimate daughter up for adoption, an event that confirmed Janet's sense that "all society was out to kill me, just because I had a child."[56] Janet's first encounter with morphine (M) occurred when she went into labor and asked a nurse to call her mother. Replying that Janet did not "deserve" her mother, the nurse instead injected her with M, a literal substitute for mother love.[57] Janet's interpretation of this event demonstrated the availability of psychoanalytic interpretations.

Drug narratives rely on a tension between characters (and readers) who know the pharmacological properties and cultural semiotics of drugs, and those who do not. Janet related several drug initiations—morphine by the nurse, marijuana by a girlfriend, heroin by her husband. Addiction was revealed at the dramatic moment when the drug-using subjects acquired a *narrative* for how, exactly, heroin addiction works. Janet "knew" in retrospect to blame her mother for her addiction because she possessed psychoanalytic scripts; but she did not "know" she was "hooked" until her husband Bob told her the "whole story" of heroin addiction.[58] Once he incorporated her—self and symptoms—in an addiction narrative, she recognized that she was hooked. Heroin use served as a "technology of the self," but became meaningful through the transmission of a finite set of cultural scripts that linked the self to others.

The addict argot of the time gendered drugs, with heroin playing masculine to cocaine's feminine. "Boy," Janet's term for heroin, "plays havoc with your menstrual cycle. It just stops the most important cycle in a woman's life."[59] Heroin made Janet whole, but also interrupted her sense of femininity. She experienced "girl" (cocaine) as superficial and superfluous because she was "already flipping and frantic" without it. Janet felt no need for cocaine except to double the pleasure of "boy," which holds off "until the girl can operate." She described drugs as a form of self-completion: "You are all the things that you want to be because of the boy, so you're a whole person; and now you're a whole person plus these tremendous exciting feelings which are unique and unusual."[60] Janet represented her habit as "my mother, . . . the bottle the baby gets just before bed, . . . all the nourishment and comfort that I could find."[61] Heroin supplied the sense of completion Janet otherwise felt she lacked.

Relations between Janet and her mother were distinctly not the overindulgent, seductive, or overprotective relations on which male addiction was blamed. Janet's "mother complex" was explicitly, even vengefully, staged: "Love your mother! All mothers are good. All these cats have mother complexes. I have heard this from every mother-fucking cop. . . . You know, when they're scratching their head and figuring, 'Now what the hell can you tell this kid to do? What's gonna save her?' This is the obvious answer. And naturally, all I wanted to do was just get in a room with my mother for two minutes. Man! It was like a piece of iron inside me, hard and warped. Every time they just mentioned the word 'mother,' I wanted to regurgitate."[62] Addiction might be a route back to the mother for male addicts, but mothers reminded females of their failure to take up their proper places in the gender order. Gender failure was held responsible—in sociology and psychology, by narcotics agents and addicts—for producing drug-addicted sons, who transferred their dependencies from mothers to drugs. Drug-addicted daughters were another story.

Janet Clark's friend and confidant, sociologist Howard Becker, based *The Outsiders: Studies in the Sociology of Deviance*, on a 1947-to-1953 study of juvenile marijuana-using males conducted at the Institute for Juvenile Research and the Chicago Area Project. Seeking to counter the moral censure against drug addicts by displacing the analogy between drug use and disease, Becker proposed a socio-cultural explanation of drug use. Theorizing that the process of becoming a drug addict was a response to being labeled a deviant "outsider" by dominant "insiders," Becker exemplified the sociological project of listening to the addict.[63] To capture the intentional quality with which subjects committed to deviant careers, he sought an alternative to sociological functionalism and theories of psychological predisposition. He relied instead on Everett C. Hughes's largely anthropological construction of "culture" in urban sociology. Becker was fascinated by Hughes's notion of a "fantastic culture of the unfortunates who, having become addicted to the use of heroin, share a forbidden pleasure, a tragedy and a battle against the conventional world."[64] The recurrent notion that addict culture functions autonomously of and often at odds with mainstream reality linked psychological and sociological accounts. *The Fantastic Lodge* presented a window on the "fantastic culture" that drug addicts shared; the title drew parallels between the social hierarchies of the drug world and those of a fraternal lodge.[65] The inclusion/exclusion dynamic stabilized boundaries between "normal" and "deviant" cultures, making them separate enclaves worlds apart.

The Innocence of Babes
Fundamental Femininity and Neonatal Addiction

Addicted babies were not recognized as a social or medical problem until the late 1950s, when perinatal researchers noted the paucity of references to congenital addiction despite women's increased drug use.[66] Only one published article appeared on the topic in the 1940s, and it stressed its rarity.[67] Neonatal narcotics addiction was framed as a public health problem of possibly great but unknown extent in the late 1950s: "There is every reason to suspect that unrecognized and untreated neonatal addiction contributes to the total neonatal mortality rate in 'high incidence' areas of drug addiction throughout the nation. . . . Neonatal addiction is a public health problem potentially of serious magnitude in those areas of the country where a high incidence of addiction among females of child-bearing age is coupled with lack of adequate pre- and postnatal medical care for this group."[68] Rosenthal, Patrick, and Krug (1964) cited the rediscovery of methods for managing neonatal addiction and indicated that it was undoubtedly widespread and complex. They were interested in the "natural history of the disease, a way of assembling facts regarding the agent, host, and environment which influences the development of this entirely preventable complication of neonatal existence."[69] The knowledge and techniques to treat maternal drug abuse had disappeared from clinical practice for decades. Drug-addicted babies simply did not show up on most physicians' radar.

Physicians were reluctant to deal with "dope fiends" due to fear of Harrison Act prosecutions, which effectively barred addicts from medical care.[70] In the early 1960s the abandoned terrain was charted anew, as clinicians specified the signs of neonatal withdrawal: hyperactivity, trembling, twitching, convulsions; shrill, high-pitched, prolonged cry; and an "almost constant sucking and chewing on the hands and fingers as if hungry."[71] A survey of New York City's Metropolitan Hospital listed 66 cases between 1950 and 1959 and summarized the state of knowledge in 1966: addicted women averaged less than one prenatal visit per pregnancy; slightly over 40 percent experienced obstetrical complications; and 20 percent left the hospital early.[72] The average female addict was unconcerned with prenatal care: "She lives in conditions of poverty, her diet is poor, and she is liable to venereal disease and a multitude of infectious diseases. . . . Not only is her physical condition poor, but also she cares nothing about improving it as long as she can obtain enough heroin to stave off withdrawal symptoms and to give her the occasional lift above the conditions in which she lives."[73] Women who do not care about self-improvement are regarded as hardly women at all. While newborns were easily treated, controlling maternal behavior was difficult. According to Stern, addicted women were often "acute nursing problem[s]" who had to be tranquilized. Thus the emphasis initially fell on maternal behavior, a focus that shifted with the development of the perinatal profession.

Addicted women's abnormal psychological makeup prevented them from handling the "normal correlates of responsibility, tensions, feelings of inadequacy, [and] anxieties" of motherhood without narcotics.[74] Authors speculated that even "psychologically healthy females" would be unable to raise the unclaimed babies of addicts. They advised that the goal of public policy should be to "salvage the greatest number of infants possible while depending as little as possible on the voluntary cooperation of the pregnant addict."[75] Babies were immediately placed with adoption agencies, despite little knowledge about the effects of prenatal heroin exposure. The problem was immediately framed as a public matter caused by individual pathology.

Babies were used to redefine addiction in the law as "an illness which may be contracted innocently or involuntarily."[76] In *Robinson v. California* (1962), the U.S. Supreme Court cited the sparse medical literature on addicted babies in support of its position that addiction was an illness: "even one day in prison would be a cruel and unusual punishment for the 'crime' of having a common cold."[77] The Court found it "unlikely that any State at this moment in history would attempt to make it a criminal offense for a person to be mentally ill, or a leper, or to be afflicted with a venereal disease."[78] The case involved neither women nor babies but turned on a perennial question in deviance studies—the question of whether narcotics addiction was a status or an act. The Court held that the state of California could not criminalize the condition, status, or "affliction" of addiction even if an addicted person engaged in illegal acts such as narcotics purchase, sale, use, or "antisocial or disorderly behavior." Drug addiction was a condition or state of being—traffic, possession, or bad behavior were acts already regulated by a range of statutes.[79] While "not unmindful of the vicious evils of the narcotics traffic," the Court found that states already possessed enough means to attack them.

An analogy between drug addiction, insanity, and disease pervaded the *Robinson* decision. Justice Douglas argued against cruel and unusual punishment such as burning at the stake, "barbarous acts," or premodern methods of torture. Addicts, he stressed, were under the sway of compulsions they could not manage without professional help.[80] Unless jail sentences somehow became "medicinal" or prisons provided treatment, he argued, penal institutions could not be considered curative. Indeed, "prosecution for addiction, with its resulting stigma and irreparable damage to the good name of the accused, cannot be justified as a means of protecting society, where civil commitment would do as well."[81] Justice Douglas turned to the exemplary innocence of babies "who get the drug while in the womb from their mothers who are addicts."[82] Addicted babies' innocence was unquestioned and helped make the case for the short-lived civil commitment laws passed in many states during the 1960s.

Civil commitment policy resulted from a clinical parole model that resulted from a "rebirth of the Progressive penal vision" in the 1940s and 1950s as a result of the conjunction of a therapeutic literature with a public panic about narcotics addiction.[83] The narcotics addict was the perfect figure to embody the idea that parole officers could change a parolee's personality:

> Drug addiction, more than any other problem, exemplified the field in which the new clinical parole practice was taking shape. It brought into focus all of the major problems that plagued parole in its classical industrial guise. It tended to involve members of disadvantaged groups (primarily Hispanics and African-Americans) and others who lived in the hard-core poverty areas of the cities. The communities to which these parolees returned did not seem well organized enough to provide a context of control, particularly against the potent force of chemical dependence. Only if supervisory action could break the hold of addiction could real integration of the offender into the community take place. A parole supervision effort for addicts obviously had to do more than focus on community social control; it had to provide a direct and organizationally driven structure of control over the addict.[84]

Psychiatric and psychoanalytic constructions of addiction as a form of maladjustment played a direct role in expanding the criminal justice system into the clinical or therapeutic domains. Behavioral control was both a therapeutic dream and the hope of policy-makers. The addict was a representative figure for the desirability of behavioral control through clinical practice.

Civil commitment programs quietly disappeared in the early to mid-1970s just as pregnant addicts began to appear more frequently in the public eye. Mandatory treatment was suggested as the best way to control addicted women during pregnancy. "Unfortunately, no means exist at present for controlling the behavior of the pregnant addict in the interest of the unborn child," wrote advocates of compulsory commitment and mandatory treatment in 1972.[85] Densen-Gerber and her coauthors portrayed addicted women as both excessively and insufficiently feminine—driven by a "fundamental desire to become pregnant as a means of becoming normal feminine women." Pregnancy was their road to this desired state of normative femininity; they used children to affirm their female identity in the face of "poor sexual identity, . . . low self-esteem, hostility towards males, homosexuality coupled with brutality, and lack of heterosexual satisfaction." To protect unborn children from their mothers' overweening desires, the researchers advocated "narrowly drawn, closely defined statutes in every state providing for compulsory commitment and treatment of pregnant addicts for the duration of the pregnancy." The force of law would channel this fundamentally feminine drive.

The discursive construction of maternity as "fundamental" to femininity was no relic of the 1970s, as we will see in Chapter 7. "Maternal instinct" continues to be cast as fundamental to civilization and the very thing most eroded by illicit drug use. If addiction portended the breakdown of civilization, drug use by pregnant women symbolized the destruction of the society's capacity for biosocial reproduction. Babies were the focus of the medical and legal literature; mothers were points of intervention in sociological and psychological research. Babies were conduits to mothers in the law.

The Emerging Focus on Maternal Behavior

Autonomy from the mother and deferred gratification were class-marked signs of maturity in the mid-century. Parenting manuals and the culture and personality movement emphasized the mother's wise management of the child's "hunger tensions."[86] Breast-feeding and weaning could facilitate "emotional management" and play an important role in the adult capacity to manage social tensions.[87] If these crucial activities were improperly timed, a "mother fixation" would result—"continued dependence on the mother as the unique source of these auditory, if not tactile, stimuli for adjustment."[88] Problematic maternal behavior was thus implicated in the generation of addiction, a form of fixation on an unacceptable source of immediate gratification.

Psychoanalytic constructions of addiction that emphasized the mother's role were smuggled into the social and psychological sciences through a variety of routes. For example, a qualitative study on "The 'Pharmacogenic Orgasm' in the Drug Addict" was designed to predict addicts-to-be on the basis of relationships between adult addicts and their mothers.[89] To this end, Robert Chessick elicited phenomenological accounts of drug ingestion and its accompanying fantasies. His subjects described sensations of warmth, fullness, a "jolt," the feeling that something was forcefully put inside them, and the sense that their internal organs were displaced. One woman recounted feeling like "a hot iron was put in my vagina."[90] Addicts described "oral incorporative activities" and "autoerotic sexual activities"—warm baths, smoking, bowel movements, eating, vomiting, and erections.[91] Several patients reported a sense of fusion with the mother figure during heroin use, and often began the practice after a perceived or actual loss of maternal love.

The fantasy material expressed addicts' longing for intimacy with their mothers, in Chessick's view. He described a female subject who felt "that 'the monkey on my back' was her mother. She felt that shooting the drug meant feeding the monkey, her mother, and would think about this during the pharmacogenic orgasm." Chessick often found that drug use accompanied homosexuality in men because addicts' libido was improperly channeled into autoerotic or "regressive" activities. Women, too, felt "increased homosexual strivings," yet supposedly felt "revulsion at genital aspects of homosexuality." One subject reported, "I dream constantly that I am in a field of roses. One rose especially keeps swaying and the others make a path for me to this rose. I crawled up to it. It took human form and became my mother."[92] These dreams formed the basis for Chessick's interpretation of addicts' desire for a "mother-like figure" who could anticipate every disturbance and satisfy every need.[93] "The process of injecting the drug is equivalent to the introjection of the ambivalently loved mother, and results in the satisfaction of a primal love aim, where the breast is placed in the mouth and satiation after feeding occurs."[94] Interpretations along these lines were common in the social-psychiatric literature of the 1960s, despite the loss of prestige undergone by psychoanalysis.

Drug introjection was an efficient way to deny anger and disappointment at the loss of the mother-object. Therapy thus led the patient to redirect his or her anger toward its "proper object"—the mother—and was deemed successful when subjects overcame their mother fixations to express ill feelings toward their mothers. Brummit described a therapy session in which an inmate transferred her hatred for the house officer to her mother, "a rigid, religious fanatic and evangelist."[95] Paternal brutality or irresponsibility were rarely mentioned—the onus was placed on maternal behavior and the "rejecting home environment" she cultivated. Therapy for addiction diverted hatred from the "wrong authority figures"—

detention officers or law enforcement agents—to the "hypercritical" or "sadistic" mother. The mother was akin to a drug—it was as if addicts were first addicted to their mothers, a dependency that foreshadowed their dependency on drugs.

Therapeutic discourse continually positioned the mother as a causal factor in addiction. Sociologically, blame was also extended to mothers who nurtured antisocial behavior in "slum areas, where the Negro predominates."[96] Psychiatrists viewed racial discontent as a form of "self-contempt" that accompanied distrust and unwillingness to set aside the "folklore of hate" that augmented poverty.[97] White therapists struggled to overcome African-American women's rejection of therapy and supposed lack of self-expression. Therapists also encountered difficulty locating the actual mother in African-American kinship systems. Brummit recounted the story of an "illegitimate" woman who was "taught that her mother was her sister and that her grandmother was her mother. The same pattern was not only being repeated with her son but she again felt unwanted and twice the object of scorn."[98] Even in sociological writing that acknowledged racism and recognized its effects as real, problematic mothering remained the leading causal factor and was relayed to policy-makers.

Behavioral scientists represented women who used illicit drugs as more unstable and unruly than men. Marie Nyswander, groundbreaking architect of methadone maintenance,[99] observed that addicted women "seem to sink to a much lower level of degradation than the men."[100] Men could "better withstand the degrading effects or perhaps they do not represent as socially deteriorated a type as the females who succumb to drugs."[101] While all addicts, according to Nyswander, avoided maturity, responsibility, and competitive situations, male addicts were prone to the "ill-defined tension" of the "hungry infant whose desperation is appeased only by the breast or bottle."[102] The male addict's lack of paternal identification and "deep appreciation of his mother and sympathy for her as an individual and as the victim of his father" were evidence of a "mother fixation."[103] Although "mother fixations" and "father absence" were clearly drawn from the psychoanalytic vocabulary, they were translated into the more "scientific" language of psychodynamics or the even more acceptable sociological register.

Therapeutic discourse made the mother's causal role in generating addiction widely available as a popular explanation for addiction. Meanwhile, a greater number of addicted women began to give birth in the late 1960s, and social authorities recognized them as childbearers. Children's Bureau director Katherine Brownell Oettinger advocated removal of children from the homes of addicted parents in response to the bureau's 1967 report on neonatal narcotic addiction, which stated that "narcotic addiction in pregnant women cannot be a rare occurrence in this country and is certainly not so in areas where addiction is prevalent."[104] The report no longer assumed that neonatal addiction was a medical curiosity but instead that it was a common problem, based on the finding that 85 percent of female addicts were of childbearing age. New York City Hospital Commissioner Alonso S. Yerby reported that 800 addicted babies were born to addicted mothers in the city in 1965. According to the *New York Times*, the undiluted heroin sold in the past had acted as a contraceptive. Now that "the stuff [wa]sn't what it used to be," pregnancy occurred "indiscriminately," but not so randomly that it lacked logic: "Since many addicted women have confusion about their sexual roles as well as their low self-esteem, pregnancy may serve as proof of femininity or as compensation for a sense of inadequacy or of being aberrant. Often defiance and revenge are motivations toward pregnancy, or the desire to be a child again and become reunited with her parents or a lost love object."[105] Although somewhat buried, the psychoanalytic explanation was still present and popularly available.

Changing social conditions, "gender role strain," and family configuration were offered as reasons for increased addiction among women at this time. Addiction was initially constructed as a form of cultural sameness: the drug "impose[s] its own personality on that of the addict," and addicts, "despite original differences, take to acting as though they came from a common bin."[106] As gender and race became central categories of sociological analysis,[107] addiction researchers highlighted differences between addicts—between males and females, and "different kinds of females."[108] Women were still thought to "express their femininity in common ways"—they were law-abiding, indisposed toward violence, and passive, according to Cuskey and coauthors. Salient gender differences were related to different roles in social reproduction: "The differences are not only physical; they are also related to the roles, functions, and freedoms of females in our society, and to their abilities to cope with, or be defeated by, the problems that addiction raises. For instance, the effects of the addiction of a pregnant woman or a mother are generally a good deal more serious, both to society and the child, than the addiction of the father, who may have disappeared immediately after conception."[109] The above quotation clearly conveys that responsibility for social reproduction was the stake of research on gender differences in patterns of addiction.

Multicultural models of addiction were advanced to account for the proliferation of drug-using subcultures in the 1970s. Drug abuse researchers sought to integrate the new "psychology of women" in their misguided attempt to isolate the effects of "pure" gender difference.[110] Young women who used "reality-diluting drugs" were blamed for reproducing children with "cognitive and affective inadequacies."[111] A vintage 1970s study on female heroin use equated control over consumption with adequate female gender role performance, sexual behavior, and reproductive capacity.[112] In the remedial, so-called woman-centered studies of the 1970s, the cultural norms of femininity were explicitly policed, and deviance from them was attributed to the impact of social change.

Women's addiction was attributed to massive cultural shifts and ambiguous gender "role definitions" that left some women "neophytes in a new cultural universe."[113] Only maladaptive women succumbed to addiction. "The feminine mystique of the addict is petrified, for her mind and emotions become neutralized rather than sensitized. Drugs are the subtle betrayer of the feminine mystique in that they produce apathy and alienation, reduce ability to appreciate beauty and life and sharply curtail or destroy experiences of genuine concern, joy, warmth, and love."[114] The "free-floating anxiety" of female addicts was compounded by their female troubles: prostitution, abortion, childbearing, "reluctance to assume the specifically female role," and "psychological problems more devastating than those faced by the male addict."[115] Family configuration remained problematic, as addicted women grew up in families dominated by women who "deprecated" the father.[116] They learned at their mothers' knees the use of "passive qualities" to dominate men. The goal of drug rehabilitation was thus the achievement of feminine personhood through individuation. Foreshadowing the 1996 CASA report, Maureen McCarthy's "The Drug Addict and Her Feminine Mystique" suggested that "personhood rather than equality . . . be stressed so that the potential addict may realize her true feminine mystique."[117]

The role of maternal behavior in producing, transmitting, and reproducing addiction became an object of scrutiny by a range of academic, clinical, and therapeutic professions over the past 30 years. Although demographic shifts and social transformations partly account for this phenomenon, the meaning that we attribute to maternal drug use better accounts for it than the simple explanation that more women of childbearing age were using drugs. Our deeply held beliefs about women's morally fundamental position in "civilization" foreshadowed the concern about social reproduction that dominated the drug policy hearings of the 1980s and 1990s.

Reconfiguring "Heroin Mothers"
Three Models of Addiction

"Families and the future of the race depend more on women."[118] This statement encapsulates the cultural significance of women's drug use. However addiction is framed, women's overresponsibility for social reproduction places them in fundamentally causal roles. For instance, addiction was defined as a form of "adjustment to intolerable stress for maladjusted people" in the early 1970s.[119] The maladjustment model cast drug use as the outcome of growing up in homes characterized by "instability, emotional thwarting, and deprivation," whether parents were rich or poor. Addiction was associated with "urban areas, poverty, disturbed homes, and family life," environmental factors "perpetuated in subsequent generations as a result of effects on infants of maternal addiction or as a result of inadequate mothering by addict mothers."[120] Cuskey and his coauthors argued that in the 1920s, female addicts closely resembled nonaddicted women;

by the 1970s, increasing psychological disturbances and "malignant family structures" made addiction a "catch-all for misfits."[121] Addicts were rendered more
deviant, pathological, and maladjusted over time—but inadequate mothering
continued to be the source of the pathogen.

The contagious disease model posited a contagion within the family that spilled
into the "infected environment."[122] Women's behaviors as mothers allowed the contagion to take hold in vulnerable individuals from "sick environments" where health
is "under constant siege."[123] Echoing *The Road to H*, Cuskey and his coauthors
noted that women "almost seem[ed]" to seek out trouble," a "tendency [that] lies in
the nature of women, rather than of the drug."[124] Women stayed in unhealthy relationships longer than men, who were "apt to shake loose much more quickly."[125]
The "long term consequences of successive generations of such matings" were responsible for addiction.[126] In a passage similar to statements about the poor
prospects of the children of "morphinist mothers" of the nineteenth century,
Cuskey and his coauthors wrote: "Obviously, the typical addict, being unable to
concentrate on anything beyond the necessity of the next fix, would have great difficulty being a good mother. Many are saved the trouble, because the rates of prematurity, of stillbirths, and of other neonatal deaths are a good deal higher than in the
non-addict population."[127] The contagion model was not confined to biological
vulnerability but encompassed social transmission as well. Within the contagion
model, individuals were both agents of transmission and points of containment.

A "family configuration" model displaced the contagion and maladjustment
models, propelled by the rise of family systems theory—the application of cybernetics to family studies, social work, and therapy.[128] Family dysfunction was
increasingly accepted as the motor of addiction in the flurry of early-1970s hearings on addiction in upper- and middle-class youth. Permissive parenting was
often the culprit; "programs preparing people for parenthood" were the proposed
remedy.[129] Parents' stories about drug-using sons or daughters asserted that the
contagion was spread through peer pressure, not parental behavior. They proposed to segregate addicts on the theory that drug addiction was socially infectious.[130] The "dysfunctional family" was still considered the generative milieu
for addiction. Drug addiction occurred in families that were "cold or hostile, or
physically and sexually abusive; where there is much conflict and unhappiness
between the parents, and between them and the child; where the parents themselves abuse alcohol or drugs; and where discipline is inconsistent or harsh and
punitive."[131] But addiction was spawned especially in a "mother-dominated family system" that thwarted the self-definition and mastery necessary for independence.[132] Addicts fixated at a symbiotic level that resulted in a "lifelong
incestuous involvement with the mother."[133] Even nonaddicted mothers, it
seemed, could socialize their children into the drug culture if they perpetuated
infantile states, prevented individuation, or foreclosed the development of a ma-

ture heterosexuality. "Heroin mothers" were not only addicts themselves, but also mothers who "dominated" their households.

Alternative feminist constructions of addicted mothers soon emerged to counter the dire effects of "mother domination." Seventy percent of the heroin-addicted women in Marsha Rosenbaum's pathbreaking ethnographic work were mothers who "expressed concern, care, and often, guilt about their role as mothers and the well-being of their children."[134] Motherhood was so central to their identities that they accepted conventional gender role prescriptions and realized that their life options were narrowing precisely when their status as mothers was threatened.[135] Rosenbaum argued: "The women who were best able to combine heroin and children were those whose childcare responsibilities forced them to control their drug use; in fact, a woman would occasionally indicate that she had become pregnant and had a baby in order to control her use of heroin."[136] Mothering routines provided structure on which women could depend for a sense of identity and pride.[137] For Rosenbaum, gender differences were the product of women's differential responsibility for social reproduction: "in the areas of motherhood and the fear of losing children, women addicts differ greatly from addicted men but very closely resemble other women in the larger society."[138] Women addicts' "single claim to worthiness" lay in their enthusiastic embrace of the culturally prescribed role of the mother as the core of their feminine identity. Failing at this was tantamount to "failing at womanhood in general."[139] Fear of losing their children displaced women's focus on getting and taking drugs in ways that differed from men's. This fear also granted society more leverage over addicted women and more modes to regulate their lives, as their stake in conventional life opened them to disciplinary techniques.

Another influential article on heroin-addicted women represented them as both "product[s] of battering" and participants in a "generational cycle of abuse." Josette Escamilla-Mondanaro reported significant unmet needs and a "severe lack of resources both cognitive and affective" among pregnant addicts.[140] She described an "emotional battering syndrome" that encompassed physical violence and unrealistic mothering. Battered by parents, husbands, and boyfriends, heroin-addicted pregnant women were deprived of nurture by their own mothers and "groomed for failure" by parents. As a result, they entered relationships with dependent and immature men who used physical violence and threats. "Feeling powerless in the world, these men flex their muscles on the only people apparently more powerless than themselves: their wives and children."[141] These "typical male addicts" got themselves arrested, overdosed, or violated parole in the course of evading their parental responsibilities. This feminist version of male addiction mirrored the representation of addicted women as themselves irresponsible and powerless, yet controlling. Framed in terms of interest to the Women's Movement, addiction was theorized as the product of "strict sex-role socialization," low self-esteem, and parents who thought "girls were to be girls: i.e. passive, dependent, feminine, coy, and nonassertive."[142] The alternative discourse constructed addicted women's maternal instincts and femininity as too strong.

Researchers and policy-makers debated various policy approaches to the problem of "heroin mothers" and dysfunctional families. Some urged that policy-makers should prioritize young women as a distinct target population for treatment and prevention programs.[143] Others argued against "massive programs of social reform" because poor mothering and inadequate mother-child bonding was the root of addiction and could not be addressed through public policy.[144] In the early 1980s, NIDA advocated programs designed to transmit "mothering attitudes," despite identifying few differences between addicted and nonaddicted mothers.[145]

Dynamic Deflections

Dysfunctional families may be seen as an outcome of social practices, or as the sum of the pathological individuals within them. As a nation we prefer the latter explanation, locating "problematic mothering" as the source of our dysfunctionalities. Addiction discourse has become a haven for unabashedly racist and sexist claims about how women should conduct themselves. Like the discredited claim that women reproduce a "culture of poverty,"[146] the family configuration model assumes that women transmit addiction through mothering, sexuality, and reproductive practices. Mothers are present and thus have a far greater effect than absent fathers.

Certainly, "family values" ideologues hold to the family configuration model. But feminist family systems therapists, too, locate the dysfunctional family as the site of "patriarchal pain"—"any of a number of distressing ordeals women experience both publicly and privately in a gendered system of domination."[147] In their theory of addiction, gender has everything to do with why women use drugs, but this does not explain why most addicts are men. Equally problematic is the assertion that gender has nothing to do with licit or illicit drug use. According to this explanation, the social stress of economic dislocation and marginality outweighs all differences in "the worlds of endemic drug abuse."[148] These social conditions are, however, highly gendered. The historical reconstruction of the governing mentalities of discourse on drugs reveals how gendered, racialized, and sexualized claims saturate our notions of addiction.

Economic stratification, "dysfunctional families," and drug abuse have been historically structured through changing gender, class, and racial dynamics. Drug policy would be far more effective if we look at why people use drugs in problematic ways, instead of dwelling on who these people are and what elements of their personal history lead them to such behaviors. Here the "deflection dynamic" gets in our way, obscuring social-structural dynamics by casting into high relief the figures who embody them or the family configurations that we think produce them. All of the models discussed above render invisible the social context of systemic violence against women, economic injustice, and women's overresponsibility for social reproduction.

Regulating
Maternal Instinct

No example more fully demonstrates the slavery of drug addiction than the pregnant addict. To learn that the craving for drugs can override even essential maternal concern for the well-being of an unborn child is a frightening and tragic phenomenon.
—Opening Statement of Senator Brockman Adams (D-WA)[1]

"Mothers Still": Maternal Instinct and the Vulnerable Child
The "Double Whammy": Maternal Responsibility for Nature and Nurture

Policy-makers and witnesses from a wide political spectrum announced the erosion of "maternal instinct" in hearings on women's illicit drug use in the late 1980s and early 1990s. Members of Congress used the occasion to identify themselves with "America's most vulnerable citizens," giving voice to the "unborn child whose mother is a drug addict."[2] Women's behaviors and decisions were placed at the root of the drug problem: "Poor families are particularly hard hit, as their neighborhoods disintegrate into places of violence and fear. We, too, should feel fear and anger at what is happening to the vulnerable children growing up in this environment. *They are vulnerable because poor children often live in families headed by women.* And women seem particularly attracted to highly addictive crack cocaine. Many children experience physical, emotional, and psychological damage because of their parents' drug use, damage that sometimes begins before birth."[3] Women's peculiar attraction to crack-cocaine thus displaced poverty as the chief cause of damage.

Policy-makers dismissed the actual social, political, and economic conditions responsible for the increased number of female-headed households, dwelling instead on the decline of a universal maternal instinct. The logic was circular, for "drug abuse is not a crime that just affects the user, it is an enemy of nurture, it is an enemy of families, and it is an enemy of the helpless innocent."[4] Households headed by women were both the cause and the effect of drug abuse. By contrast, feminist researchers have found that female headship is both a collectively patterned coping strategy to which individuals resort, and a structural constraint.[5] In the crack-cocaine hearings, living in a family headed by a woman was assumed to produce vulnerable children. As I have argued throughout this book, the deflection of responsibility for social problems—which are often the consequences of policy decisions—onto figures that embody them is a consistent pattern in the policy-making apparatus of liberal democratic capitalism. In the governing mentalities of drug policy-makers, women who lack maternal instincts produce the structural effects of economic erosion and neighborhood disintegration.

Undertaken in the name of the "vulnerable child" or "from the point of view of the fetus,"[6] the hearings sought to answer whether drug-using women were victims or victimizers.[7] The answer to this question would in turn answer the policy question of whether the nation was best served by punitive policies or an expansion of the therapeutic state. The categorization of drug-using women as either victims or victimizers derived from an older sociological lexicon that categorized drug use as a consensual, and so "victimless," crime. The affirmation that "substance abuse is not a victimless crime, that in fact it is a growing threat to the health and well-being of our most vulnerable citizens, our children" was accomplished through the figure of the pregnant addict.[8] Mothers were identified as criminal perpetrators who left a "permanent imprint on the lives of a staggering number of drug-exposed infants" and practiced "child abuse through the umbilical cord."[9] Drug-using mothers typified the "victimizers," whose ranks were growing to "staggering" proportions. The "permanent imprint" established that the damage would affect future public policy, education, and social service delivery. With these ideas in mind, Congress set about crafting a national drug prevention policy to include "a generation of citizens as yet unborn."[10] Various policy approaches were debated in the hearings and reports of the 101st Congress between the summers of 1989 and 1990.

The "decline of maternal instinct" was the commonly identified source of the policy problem.[11] Women were represented as beyond the call of nature: "So powerful is the grip of addiction that it leaves many of them really unable to fulfill their maternal instinct."[12] Because mothers were rendered sovereign agents of social reproduction, they appeared guilty in narratives that traced the decline, disintegration, or displacement of the naturalized relations between mother and child. As agents of intergenerational transmission, mothers had produced a "lost generation" of "untouchable" newborns who would become the horrifying crack addicts who weighted "not just . . . our heart strings, but also . . . our purse strings, and . . . the kite strings that draw our national ambitions aloft."[13] An un-named NIDA psychologist was quoted as saying: "children of substance abusers become emotionally blunted, callous at a very young age."[14] Pregnant addicts were held rhetorically accountable for stalling historical progress: "the blunting of the human being, the blunting of the development and the growth and the maturation of the individual person."[15] Witness Reed V. Tuckson, Commissioner of Public Health for the District of Columbia, testified that women were "really the key to what is happening with our children and our families as it relates to substance abuse in so many cases."[16] Women who were "unable to manage their childcare responsibilities" were the "root etiological factors" because they sought to escape "the tensions, the pressures, the violence, the chaos, the family confusion, the dysfunctional people" of their lives.[17] They appeared to invite sexually transmitted diseases and pregnancies upon themselves, thereby increasing infant mortality rates.[18] The "decline of maternal instinct" bundled these problems together, making women appear to cause the effects of social inequality. I take issue with the discursive pattern of causation at work in the hearings—not the actuality of the harms of maternal drug use, overdrawn as they appear in the sober light of 1999. The dire intergenerational prediction did not materialize—as the crack-using cohort aged, they continued using crack but for the most part their sons and daughters never began.

Drug-using women were figured primarily as mothers in these hearings, which examined the social impacts, economic costs, and "child effects" of maternal behavior.[19] Needless to say, drug-using men were not figured primarily as fathers, nor was any decline in "paternal instinct" noted. Maternal instinct made a significant difference between male and female addicts in the minds of policymakers: "I think the thought that you are going to have an offspring, that you're carrying a child—well, who am I to be talking about it as just a male—but I think for a woman in that situation, knowing that she is going to give birth, has to make a difference—I just can't believe it doesn't have a more profound effect."[20] Pregnancy was thus regarded as a "special window of opportunity" for leveraging women into treatment,[21] and model programs showcased how they "capitalized on the profound maternal instincts of many of these mothers."[22] Maternal instinct was cast as a resource that the government could harness and train toward its goals.

Social service providers, ex-addicts, and drug researchers engaged in the project of humanizing female addicts by constructing them as mothers. They conveyed the higher social costs and greater complexity of women's addiction in order to argue for greater outlay of resources. One ex-addict, Donna Tice, testified: "Well, 5 years ago, I was a drug-addicted mother-to-be. And even though I wanted to quit, my need for the cocaine was greater than my maternal instinct, and I continued to abuse myself and my unborn baby. And as the guilt of what I was doing to myself became overwhelming, I sought drug treatment, and I was unable to find a treatment center that would accept me pregnant. So I had to lie to get into one. I also avoided prenatal care for fear of being pressured into an abortion or adoption of my child."[23] Maternal instinct provided a rhetorical resource for justifying targeted treatment for pregnant women. The "decline of maternal instinct" is a culturally resonant governing mentality used strategically, not only by conservatives seeking to roll back women's rights, but also by women's advocates.

The emotive resonance of "maternal instinct" also worked for Minnie Thomas, director of Mandela House, a residential treatment facility in Oakland, California, who pleaded:

> We are mothers still. We are loving, caring, forgiving, fighting, scolding, struggling but we are not all bad. We have just become a product of the environment, overwhelmed with life's perils, running away . . . to drugs. . . . I am a mother and I have given up. But you could help. How? Just love me, support me, stand by me as I try to be what you expect of me. And I know I can be, I am a mother. I love, I feel, I cry. But the pain is too great. I can't be what I need to be by myself. I am just a mother. No one taught me my role. Trial and error, that is me. Help me to be what I need to be, what I want to be. I am willing, but help me, I am a mother.[24]

Mothers and representatives of the human services sector sought state intervention to help women transcend their environments. The emotional force of these witnesses suggests that the appeal to maternity is powerful in a political arena set up on the premise that drug-using women are irresponsible mothers. By depicting themselves as indeed responsible for the transmission of cultural values, attitudes, and beliefs, women both countered and stabilized the notion that maternal instinct was in decline. They assumed women's responsibility for social reproduction, using it to gain resources and direct attention to the circumstances under which women mother.

"Maternal instinct" is a flexible signifier, open to interpretation from many political positions. A dominant interpretation emerged, however, in which "maternal instinct" signified women's dual responsibilities for both nature and nurture—and both social and biological reproduction. One witness declared that the nation had entered a new historical condition brought on by an "absolute epidemic of women who are doing [crack]" and the "absolute, extraordinary addiction" that occasioned the "loss of the maternal instinct." "We have never seen that, really, at this level of magnitude in the history of human experience with a substance that causes people to no longer care about being a mother, the most fundamental of drives that occurs."[25] The awkward phrase reminds us how strained gender-neutral policy talk can be when one gender is specifically impli-cated.[26] The hearings slipped between "women," "mothers," or "pregnant women" and "parents." For instance, Senator Joseph Biden (D-CT) gestured to "housing projects where more parents tonight will be cooking cocaine than will be cooking dinner for their children. And there are schools in this country where the phrase 'the iceman cometh' refers to the arrival of a methamphetamine dis-tributor and not a work of literature."[27] The "parents" of the projects neither discharged their daily responsibilities for cooking, nor engaged in the long-term project of enculturation represented by literature.

Crack-cocaine was represented as qualitatively different from its predecessors. Implicated in reproductive processes such as easing labor pains, inducing abor-tion, or hastening labor,[28] crack was represented as especially attractive to women.[29] According to Herbert Kleber, then Deputy Director for Demand Re-duction in the Office of National Drug Control Policy and later medical director at the National Center on Addiction and Substance Abuse (CASA): "Until re-cently, the majority of drug abusers have been male. The advent of crack has modified that, and although the majority of people using cocaine are still males, we now find in a number of areas of the United States that the number of female crack addicts exceeds that of male crack addicts."[30] The gradual but steady in-crease in women's use of illicit drugs since the 1950s was obscured by the sudden "advent" of crack-cocaine, a metaphor suggesting that women served as acolytes of the drug.

Metaphoric constructions of the drug epidemic represented the forces of order as about to be engulfed by an insidious tide that would "seep into every crack and crevice of American life."[31] Social service agencies were placed in the heroic position of plugging the hole in the dike—barely holding back the chaos of a natural disaster about to overwhelm them. Policy-makers' charge to the child welfare and drug treatment systems was to repair and unify "weak families": "I will be looking toward solutions that see the family as a seamless garment, solu-tions that address the family's problems comprehensively and seek to get at the underlying problems of poverty. . . . At a policy level, we often talk of multi-problem families, but our programs address individual needs, such as housing or parenting skills or drug treatment. Rarely do we seriously talk about looking at the family as a whole."[32] Holistic metaphors of solidity, stability, and surety—shoring up foundations, the "seamless garment," and returning to fundamental values—were asserted against fluid metaphors of a "tidal wave of drug abuse," the "flooding" of children into foster care, or the lack of definitive borders on an insidious problem.[33]

Women were at the center of this maelstrom of recurring metaphors, which ren-dered invisible a complicated history of the adverse effects of social and economic policy upon women who were often trying to hold families together. Maternal behavior was centered by policy-makers and therapeutic professionals as the cause of addiction, a position inhabited by addict witnesses themselves. For example, ex-addict Dawn Horrell testified to smoking crack with her mother in a perverse scenario of mother-daughter bonding.[34] The hearing in which she testified began with a senator echoing six-year-old Dooney Waters, who had voiced the position of the "crack baby" in a *Washington Post* story: "Drugs have wrecked my mother and if I am not careful, drugs are going to wreck me, too."[35] Horrell and Waters were exemplary figures of the "narrative wreckage" wrought by drugs.[36] Uncertainty pervaded their lives; the one person who should have been stable—their mothers—was wrecked by drugs. The "decline of maternal instinct" allowed for coherent claims about experiences that otherwise had no one cause or clear trajectory.

"Crack babies," according to then Senator Pete Wilson (R-CA), were "abandoned because of the particularly insidious effects of crack, the destruction of the maternal instinct."[37] The "sickly, inattentive, and inconsolable 'crack baby'" became a focal point for neurobehavioral research focused on identifying cognitive deficiencies and intellectual outcomes.[38] Researchers studied the subtle behavioral effects of cocaine exposure to discover "what kinds of interventions will work best . . . to soften the 'double whammy from nature and nurture' that these children have received."[39] Responsibility for both "nature" and "nurture" fell to women. This position effectively absolved social policy from doing anything other than controlling women in order to break the "intergenerational transmission of the disease of addiction. . . . As a country we have fostered a spiraling legacy of addicts giving birth to addicts. Must this generation and future generations suffer due to our unwillingness to act with urgency? We must make a sincere commitment that turns the course of this human tragedy."[40] Women were central to the socially transmitted disease model; they provided the environment that nurtures disease. "Addicts who give birth to addicts" were, after all, women. The figure of the pregnant drug addict served as a threatening portent of a cycle of contagion embodied by the compelling figure of the "hard case," the woman who was beyond the redemptive reach of the therapeutic state.

The "Hard Case": A Stubborn Fantasy

Considerable testimony was heard throughout these hearings on the lack of drug treatment available to pregnant women. For example, Judith C. Burnison, then executive director of the National Association of Perinatal Addiction, Research, and Education (NAPARE), testified that the lack of treatment slots meant that pregnant women who sought help were often turned away.[41] Despite this, William J. Bennett, then director of the National Office of Drug Control Policy, asked repeatedly, "What do we do with the hard case—and unfortunately, there is more than one—of the woman or parents who do not want to avail themselves of [treatment]?"[42] He pressed: "I want to know what you do in the hard case. . . . If you are looking at a situation where the damage that is going to be done is something you can't call back, it's there forever, what do you do in the hard case?"

Witnesses who dealt directly with pregnant addicts refused to dwell on the "hard case" and raised the more common figure of the pregnant woman refused treatment. In frustration, Bennett turned to the late Michael Dorris,[43] who offered an account of the "hard case": "If there was a person who was walking her child across the street without reference to lights and the first time she did it her child was killed and she did it again and again and again and each time her child was killed, is it the responsibility of society to simply stand on the sidelines and watch and bury the child? I don't think so. There has to be found some balance between the individual rights of the already living and those that are going to live because she has decided to carry to term."[44] The feminized figure of a stubborn woman was the "hard case" that underpinned the "truth of a representation, which ceases magically to have the status of a representation and emerges simply as the fact of the matter."[45] The "hard case" guaranteed the righteousness of sanctions and justified "some type of control over that individual's freedom of choice in terms of how they conduct their lives."[46]

The onslaught on freedom of choice was conducted in the name of "responsibility" and was part of the conservative agenda to lodge responsibility for social reproduction squarely with individuals. Bennett believed that "one of the fundamental obligations of any society is posed by the fact of natality."[47] According to Bennett, child care began "a long time before birth." He echoed Dorris, who remarked that "nurture begins not even with conception, it begins in the environment in which the society welcomes a new life."[48] The rollback of maternal responsibility to precede conception was linked to a conservative analysis of cultural decline marked by parental permissiveness. The figure of the "hard case" served those who sought to reduce the government's role in social provision and tighten control over resources. The "hard case" embodied infinite strain on finite resources and signaled the futility of trying to satisfy women's unnatural appetites through public policy. The female addict's condition resulted from her own stubbornness, rather than anything the government could remedy. In contrast, feminist lawyers, humanitarian physicians, and fatigued social workers counterpoised the figure of a pregnant woman desperately seeking treatment.

Attention to women's special needs has historically taken paternalistic and protective forms. Women have been constructed as a vulnerable and unique population that requires special protections and accommodations of difference. The pitfalls of special-needs arguments are apparent to anyone familiar with the voluminous feminist literature on the equality/difference dilemma.[49] Special-needs arguments assume a benevolent state devoted to the equality of its citizens. They appear attractive because they offer cultural recognition of the symbolic dimensions of a social problem without structural transformation.[50] Drug-using women foreground women's failures and open them to calls for moral values, "intact" families (which contain men), and personal responsibility. Not all women are held accountable to the same degree for all social ills—the racialization of drug problems heightens the visibility of women of color and situates them as scapegoats for the failures of the war on drugs.

Perceptions of blame and innocence are strategic moves that preserve the innocent from the dangerous. Blaming women—particularly poor women—for social problems holds women responsible for dynamics over which they exercise less control than most would like. Women who use drugs inhabit a conceptual category in U.S. political culture that encodes anxieties about social change. Attention to foster care and child abuse in particular expresses the fear that women have changed so much that they are neglecting their obligations as women. Similarly, the fear that persons of color will no longer occupy subordinate social positions causes great anxiety in an economic system dependent on a docile, low-wage labor force. The "hard case" embodies these fears, which rest on the long-standing governing mentality that women are more stubbornly addicted than men. The "hard case" deserves punishment—she is the stigmatized subject beyond the protective reach of pity. Stigma is "both the most consistent and most consequential similarity of the experiences of drug-involved women" because their behavior violates "female role expectations."[51] Thus women are the "hard cases."

The Meaning of Treatment in the Tutelary Complex

Policy-makers measure the strength of a woman's character by her resistance to drugs and her willingness to seek and undergo treatment. The perception that a mass of poorly nurtured individuals was growing up in families headed by women explained why drug addiction was "running rampant," spiraling, escalating, exponentially increasing, and skyrocketing out of control. Strengthening the family was policy-makers' solution. Parenting techniques became major components of drug treatment for women, who must "build the skills necessary to be a nurturing parent, leading to an ordered and productive life."[52] Treatment is an institutionalized discourse implicated in the work of cultural normalization and productive citizenship. The Senate Committee on Labor and Human Resources, which has jurisdiction over drug education, prevention, and treatment, serves as the center of a tutelary complex that governs response to drug addiction. The hearings allowed treatment professionals to consolidate their centrality to the enterprise of governance. Unlike the hearings of the 1950s, which set up polarized debates between law enforcement and medical approaches, these hearings largely segregated the two.

Treatment involves minute scrutiny of background and behavior. Social structure, economic deprivation, and sexual assault are considered mere contributing factors in addiction, which is portrayed as the outcome of an overwhelming set of pressures that converge on women who bear or raise children under difficult circumstances. Treatment might include counseling, day care, education in household management, shopping, cooking, nutrition, and parenting techniques, HIV/AIDS counseling, job training, and "influence [over] the development and socialization of children"—the skills necessary for social reproduction.[53] Treatment is a set of regulatory practices that attempts to bring individuals into conformity with the state's ideal of the productive citizen.[54] Its success is measured by the compliance and social adjustment of its subjects.

Current treatment modalities are designed to supply "essential life skills" to addicted women and increase their levels of social adjustment. Social service delivery to "pregnant and postpartum women and infants" (PPWIs, as the population is called) is administered as case management.[55] Loretta Finnegan, associate director of the Office for Treatment Improvement and joint-appointed to both the USPHS and ADMHA, noted that recidivism was the result of "low social adjustment" and physical, psychological, or social impairment. High social adjustment was defined in heteronormative terms—as being "married, older, better educated, better employed, with fewer arrests, and better psychological adjustment."[56] She listed the currently accepted profile of the "causes" of drug dependence:

1. "Problem behavior proneness or deviance syndrome";
2. Progressive development starting in adolescence and proceeding to hardcore use;
3. Psychopathology;
4. Impaired function, including "difficulty in emotional regulation, planning, problem solving, perceptual motor function, language and information processing, coping, and difficulty in interpersonal problem solving";
5. Familial or genetic components;
6. Environmental risk factors, including drug availability, family disruption, and "cultural norms";
7. Factors related specifically to drugs or their "routes of administration."

Addiction is still framed as individual deviance, maladjustment, and psychopathology. Genetic impairment is formed (and deformed) in response to familial dynamics, cultural norms, and environmental risks. The maladjustment framework now encompasses multiple causes.

Racial and class codes are embedded in the perennial idea that dominant cultural norms do not cause addiction; only "deviant" cultural norms do. For example, white women continue to explain their drug use in medicalized terms. Researchers interpret this tendency to their "reluctance to enter the criminal subculture," resistance to deviance, and preference for social conformity.[57] White women "feel a greater need than either black women or men to provide a socially acceptable justification for their behavior."[58] Conversely, drug use among persons of color entails the acceptance of deviant cultural norms:

> Minority group members may have a definition of socially acceptable norms that are [sic] different from those that are held by whites in American society. In a group which may well perceive itself as rejected members of the total society, general social codes that are enacted into law may have less meaning than they have for those members of society who are more involved in defining the law and other behavioral norms. This should not be interpreted to mean that narcotic use is socially acceptable behavior in the black community, but simply that the sanctions for use may not be as severe.[59]

The belief that formal or informal sanctions work better on white people is patently false. The woman who smoked marijuana in the 1940s or fifties "defined herself not only to her peers but also to herself as a person who was living outside the moral code of society."[60] Then her "willingness to violate social norms" was interpreted as a violation of her femininity. Today the "cultural norms" construct is used to write off the serious concerns of communities of color.

Women's drug use signals the breakdown of social norms, informal controls, and the reproductive power of normative social codes. Women of color were already understood to have stepped "outside" normative behavior in the 1960s and seventies: "The female black pattern appears to be more similar to the typical male pattern than does the white female pattern. Most white females in this society are conditioned to accept a normative social code that requires them to deny criminal or deviant activity."[61]

The 1970s studies divided women's drug use into an urban, black, criminal pattern, and a Southern, white, medical pattern.[62] Black women were said to engage in illicit activities for purposes of "self-support"; white women depended on others. These studies yielded a contradictory picture of how women manifested their "maladjustment." Addicted women whose psychosexual development was "disturbed" comprised two groups: transvestites and homosexuals, and women who had borne children out of wedlock. Since these behaviors had little in common, the explanation was strained. Both groups violated "conventional social norms for acceptable sexual behavior"; for both the underlying cause was the "failure to achieve a satisfactory heterosexual adjustment."[63] As in *The Road to H*, the maladjustment model associated drug use with nonnormative lifestyles. While the explicitly racist and heteronormative components of this discourse had disappeared by the time Finnegan advanced her seemingly straightforward list, they remain encoded in the "cultural norms" explanation and the persistent emphasis on psychopathology and deviance.

Governments worry about individuals "insofar as they are somehow relevant for the reinforcement of the state's strength: what they do, their life, their death, their activity, their individual behavior, their work, and so on."[64] As the state came to wield power over living beings as such, politics become what Foucault called "biopolitics." The discourse of the human sciences was increasingly used to justify state intervention into the habits of "troubled individuals."[65] The "decline in maternal instinct" positioned drug-using women as troubled in ways that concerned the tutelary complex. Their unwillingness, incapacity, or outright refusal to play their roles as "reproductive citizens" was a pressing issue in these hearings. A cultural diagnostics constructed addicted women as failures of femininity, conflating the regulatory fictions of ideal womanhood and motherhood. Because women "produce" children, women are responsible within public policy for their care. Women's failure to absorb the cost of care opened them to accusations of a widespread loss of maternal instinct. Maternal instinct served both practical and ideological purposes. On the one hand, it helped dispel public responsibility for the conditions under which women are likely to perform mother-work. On the other, it was metaphorically portrayed as a fundamental bulwark that wars, concentration camps, alcohol, and heroin could not "erode."[66] Crack appeared worse than myriad forms of political violence.

Policy-making consists of a series of ritual interactions rife with symbolism. Patterned descriptions of cause and effect give policy-makers an illusory sense of control. The interpretive frameworks invoked during the process affect policy outcomes and public response, but need not be factually accurate. For example, Tuckson maintained that:

> Crack users . . . will do almost anything to acquire that drug, particularly women. They will engage in sexual relationships as a means of bartering or financing their habits. Those sexual relationships combined with the stimulus for finances and getting the drugs, combined with the aphrodisiac effects of the drug, of course, now has [sic] become the single most important reason for the increase in sexually transmitted diseases that we find in this country.[67]

Despite reliable evidence that sex-for-crack exchanges are a small part of the problem, research is obsessively focused on it, as Chapter 8 contends.[68] Similarly, Senator Daniel Patrick Moynihan (D-NY) asserted invalid connections between "concentrations of crack babies," teen pregnancy rates, high illegitimacy rates, and welfare receipt.[69] He made unmarried women on public assistance discursively responsible for reproducing addiction, yet empirical research showed that rates of drug and alcohol problems among welfare recipients were similar to those of the unassisted population.[70] In drug policy discourse, women—especially poor women, women of color, and single women—spawn substance abuse and thus form points of intervention for the tutelary complex.

Changing Minds: Demand Reduction and Domestic Drug Control
The Moral Value of a "Priority Population"

Pregnant addicts first came to strategic prominence during a federal policy shift to "demand reduction" engineered by the National Office of Drug Control. Elected officials keenly felt the futility of the federal war on drug supply and in the mid-1980s shifted their attention to the costs of "this Nation's alarming and disturbing demand for illicit drugs."[71] The war on drugs was moved from the "cocaine jungles of South America where narco-terrorists prowl or on the inner-city street corners where the street gangs shoot it out" to the "battlefield of values" within the family.[72] Attorney General Dick Thornburgh urged a return to "law and order," self-respect, self-reliance, and integrity of mind and spirit.[73]

The demanding individual played a specific role in demand regulation: "We know that the drug crisis is also a crisis that affects individuals. On the demand side, it is a crisis of individual belief and behavior, a crisis of individual motivation and action, and without that, ultimately, we're not going to be successful. So our challenge is not just to destroy illegal substances. Our challenge is also to change minds. It is convincing individuals, especially our youths, that there is a drug-free standard that we expect and demand they meet, while we also provide compassionate rehabilitation for those who fail to meet it."[74] The policy shift to changing minds coincided with the heightened visibility of addicted women in the child welfare and drug treatment systems.[75] Pregnant women are vulnerable to the mechanisms of discipline—they are open to threats of child removal; most eventually present for obstetrical care; and they are susceptible to criminal prosecution if they are unresponsive to the techniques of discipline.

Pregnant drug users were the first population of women mentioned, much less prioritized in the nation's drug control strategy. By 1989 NIDA documented declining domestic drug use—except among "young women, teenage women, and certain small targeted groups and minorities."[76] As a practice of governance, focused priorities reduce the scope of the problem and position certain groups to receive behavioral interventions. The fact that most addicts are not pregnant, adolescent, incarcerated, or women did little to dispel the sense of control gained from the rhetorical targeting of "priority populations," which, policy-makers agreed, would yield "the greatest payoff in the largest sense for the country."[77] The drug crisis was paradoxically rendered a confined problem, and "America's number one domestic crisis." Priority populations afforded the seductive illusion that the state could regulate individual demand and manage family tensions.

Moral values supposedly inoculated against demand for drugs, which undermined the structure of values and caused "extreme entropy."[78] Bennett viewed "lack of civic courage" as the real problem, and parents as the "first line of defense," for "drug horror stories will not counteract youthful notions of invulnerability."[79] By locating the problem with youth and the solution with parents, demand was contained within the private domain. Demand reduction policy was not, however, solely the province of moral conservatives. Representative Charles Rangel (D-NY) argued against deflecting blame onto individuals. He represented addiction as an outcome of marginalization, claiming to have discovered a new class comprised of one in five Americans who had "no stake in the civic culture and conventional values that bind us together as one nation."[80] Living "on the edge of the American dream," this class threatened to "unspool the basic tenets of our economic and social infrastructure." Its growth paralleled increasing drug use. In a nostalgic and somewhat ahistorical hope, Rangel saw drug use and drug-related violence as "symptoms of a wholesale disintegration of essential social and economic infrastructures, which once created opportunity, assured public health, provided affordable housing, put food on the table, and extended to all our citizens the hope that they could share in the American dream."[81] For both moral conservatives and social liberals, demand reduction among women became a political priority because their drug use represented, in Rangel's words, the "subversion of traditional community values."

"Born Hooked": Compassion, Coercion, or "Choice"

Women are integrated into the state's utility through children, who are often manipulated through the child welfare apparatus to extract their mother's compliance. The welfare of the nation's children is one of the chief vehicles through which we talk about the material-symbolic differences that gender and race make. Neoconservative groups such as the Heritage Foundation or the American Enterprise Institute (AEI) used such policy debates as welfare reform, crime control, immigration, and illicit drug policy to gain an advantage in reproductive rights debates and cultural conversations about family formation. In this section, I examine one hearing rather than synthesizing several in order to stage the confrontation between advocates of reproductive freedom and "right to life" proponents who attempted to use the concern about drug-addicted women to "move back all prospective parents' responsibilities with respect to their future children to the point of conception."[82] Feminists and pro-choice legislators saw attempts to criminalize fetal abuse and consolidate the legitimacy of fetal rights as a roll-back of all women's reproductive rights.[83]

Like "responsibility," "choice" is a flexible term that triggers an emphasis on moral accountability. For the ranking Republican member of the House Select Committee on Children, Youth, and Families, Thomas J. Bliley, Jr. (R-VA): "Drug use makes a mockery of the principles of a free people. While a person always carries within him or her the freedom to choose particular courses of action, that person taking drugs ought to be held accountable for his or her actions. If we are led to believe that a person is not responsible for his or her actions in taking drugs, what does this mean for self-government?"[84] The separation between women who endanger children and women who protect children works in life and law as a basic distinction between women who make the "right" choices, and women who do not.

Participation in high-risk behaviors was used to justify the rollback of individual choice. Bliley implied that women engaged in risky behaviors while pregnant only because they knew abortion was available. For anti-choice conservatives, drug use resulted from the failure to teach "clear moral distinctions," a failure that originated with *Roe v. Wade* (1973). Bliley insinuated that the judiciary had granted women carte blanche to endanger "unborn babies." He cast doubt on all women's capacities to make good self-governing choices:

> We are forced to expose the veneer of life and liberty in America today. Our judicial system has determined that woman may make reproductive choices concerning the outcomes of their pregnancies. How does this affect the choices made by drug-addicted women who endanger the health and lives of the unborn babies by this high risk behavior? It is true enough that the purpose of law is to lead subjects to their own virtue. But do not search for the remedy to heal the wounds of drug abuse, it is nowhere other than within each of us. Victories will become elusive and public spirit will crumble if success is measured only by the size of drug busts or convictions. Victory will not come amidst blaring trumpets and smashing headlines, it is in the quiet humility of a million charitable and faithful homes.[85]

This version of demand reduction was linked to moral and cultural conservatism, and the containment of women's reproductive freedom.

Fetal rights advocate Jeffrey Parness, a law professor at DeKalb University, testified in both the Senate hearing, *Drug Addicted Babies: What Can Be Done?* and the House hearing, *Born Hooked.* He argued that women had asserted their constitutional rights so strenuously that laws protecting potential human life now involved only criminal conduct by third parties and excused that of the mother. He sought to extend such laws to maternal conduct, suggesting court-appointed fetal guardians who could sue mothers for "prebirth conduct" to revoke their parental rights. Parness favored paternalist legislation to guard the "unborn from the dangers posed by mom and others."[86] "To seek to assure that more humans are born with sound mind and body seems as American as apple pie," he noted in his written statement.[87] Thus we see the alignment between the health of the nation and fetal guardianship.

Testifying directly to the idea of "compassionate coercion," Harvard law professor Alan Dershowitz maintained the state's legitimate interest in fetal health once a woman had chosen to continue her pregnancy. "Simply stated, I think we have to say to ourselves that it is not punishment, rather it is prevention, to insist that a drug-addicted woman who has given birth to a drug-exposed infant submit to the kind of round-the-clock supportive treatment programs that are necessary to lead a drug-free life and thereafter to be able to give birth to healthy children. It can't be seen as cruel to subject a woman who needs that kind of support and that kind of reinforcement to a caring and supportive living environment where she can in fact learn to resist the temptation of drugs."[88] This is an excellent example of the redefinition of coercive measures as compassionate rehabilitation—and the perceived inevitability of punitive sanctions. I call this reconfiguration "postmodern Progressivism," distinguishing the expansive Progressivism of the earlier twentieth century from today's version, which takes place in the context of the ideological contraction of the state's responsibility for social provision.

Postmodern Progressivism takes the form of a dream that the state will or can provide comprehensive social services under the guise of "compassionate coercion." As Representative George Miller (D-CA), who chaired the hearing, said, it was a "fantasy" to think that the state was going to "take this [drug-using] woman away to society's breast and we're going to harbor her in a fashion that will change the outcome of the pregnancy in her life."[89] The question of whether criminal sanctions were coercive or compassionate was a key issue in *Born Hooked.*[90] The chair believed that policy-makers turned to criminal sanctions out of frustration and political expediency (law enforcement was perceived as a legitimate public expense, while drug treatment for pregnant women was not). Sanctions did not work: "we've tried essentially a decade of this mode which is intense sanctions on almost all behavior and yet there's no indication that we're changing behavior."[91] Drug abuse would only increase as long as Congress failed to spend money on drug rehabilitation, and that, he knew, was not going to happen.[92] When the chair tried to move the conversation beyond sanctions, the hearing became a philosophical debate on the failure of language to represent coercion as the "positive intervention" or "leverage" that it really was.[93] Concluding that neither sanctions nor treatment alone would work, the committee reframed coercion in the more palatable terms of postmodern Progressivism. Loathe to appear "soft on addicts," policy-makers then slid into "protecting potential human life"—whatever their views on reproductive rights might be. Dissenting beliefs—and different realities—are foreclosed from policy-making on valence issues, in which all values must converge.

Women's rights advocates were well aware how intertwined the antiabortion agenda was with the antidrug agenda. *Born Hooked* was so strongly biased toward the "fetal rights" position that Molly McNulty of the National Health Law Program submitted a corrective critique of legal measures to protect "potential human life," the "right to be born with a sound mind and body," and maternal duty toward unborn children.[94] She argued: "The principle inherent in these newly expressed state interests ultimately would force all women of child-bearing age to live as though they were perpetually pregnant, with the most extreme restrictions on their liberty."[95] Rangel was similarly wary about the woman-blaming of the fetal rights agenda. He argued that women could not be blamed for "bumper crops" in producer nations, the influx of drugs into the United States, or lack of federal funds for drug education and prevention. He constructed drug-using women as themselves vulnerable, and drug use as "one of the saddest indictments of a civilization."[96] While Rangel did not support harm reduction measures such as needle exchange, he supported gender-focused treatment and urged those who wanted "comparable treatment of the born and the unborn" to show "equal concern about life after birth."[97] The hearing presented a "balanced" set of viewpoints, in the sense that both pro-choice and antiabortion testimony was heard.

Feminist advocates feared that the antiabortion movement's strategic opposition between maternal and fetal interests would direct policy toward sanctions. Wendy Chavkin, M.D., M.P.H., testified to the lack of available drug treatment for pregnant women and located U.S. drug policy at a crossroads on the question of therapy or sanctions. She argued for therapeutic services, without which "an addict cannot conform her behavior to the requirements of the law."[98] Drug treatment is a hybrid mode that exhibits both compassion and coercion. For instance, Neal Halfon, M.D., director of the Center for the Vulnerable Child in Oakland, California, testified to the use of the motherhood experience as a "therapeutic lever" to get women into recovery.[99] He described addicted mothers in terms that neatly accorded with the governing mentalities: as ignorant, unrealistic, unstructured, and insatiably needy.[100] The mother-infant pair would be jeopardized if the child's demands for "total commitment to his/her physical, development, and emotional needs" were not met. The "vulnerable child" was figured as totally demanding, while mothers were either totally committed or totally incapable of commitment. "A child's irritable temperament, fluctuating behavioral state, hypersensitivity and inconsolability is very demanding even for the most competent caretaker."[101] Thus mothers needed to be taught the "knowledge, skills, and qualities associated with good mothering." The politics of this position are complex and contradictory, playing into the very constructions of ideal motherhood that underlie the vilification of female addicts.

At the same time, the Center for the Vulnerable Child reunified mothers and babies by "fast-tracking" babies out of foster care and back to their biological mothers, where they were used as "carrots" to get drug-abusing women to remain in treatment.[102] Given the circumstances surrounding women's use of drugs— lives of abuse, poverty, and neglect within "horrible environments," Halfon argued that "having a baby is a natural healing response" that enhanced women's lives and represented a potential success for the mother.[103] The center included treatment for physical and sexual abuse, emphasized developmental issues and parenting, and de-emphasized medical modalities.[104] Its clients were not "chemical dependents," a term that erased factors other than the "chemical." Rather, they were addicts for environmental and social reasons, and thus required an "ecological approach" to treatment that combined medical, public health, and social models. The Center for the Vulnerable Child, I would argue, has fashioned a political response that is neither simple compassion nor naked coercion. Its approach cannot be broken down into "crime" or "disease," but instead fits the framework of postmodern Progressivism, which replies to the fear that women will no longer perform the tasks of social reproduction. This fear pervaded *Born Hooked* and was most evident in the perennial question of who would take care of the kids.

The novel strain of the crack-cocaine epidemic on child welfare and protective services was because "grandmothers would no longer take care of the problem."[105] "Heroin," social workers explained, "did not produce a generation of grandmothers who are not able to take care of their mothers [daughters]. . . . We did not have a problem."[106] Crack's appeal to women meant that grandmothers were themselves young (28 to 35 years old) addicts who could not "step in to provide the social contact as in the past."[107] The real problem was that mothers and grandmothers could no longer care for the escalating numbers of drug-exposed infants. "Infinite programs" could not "stem the flow of drug-addicted women and babies."[108] This is compelling evidence for the claim that drug policy makes audible the concern that women are no longer fit or willing to absorb the tasks and costs of social reproduction. Postmodern Progressivism is designed to make sure they do.

The social reproduction calculus was presented as a zero-sum game, in which some populations benefited at the expense of others. In revealing testimony, Haynes Rice, Director of Howard University Hospital in Washington, D.C., stated that overcrowded neonatal units and increased maternal and infant mortality threatened middle-class women. Poor women absorbed more than their share of health care resources; boarder babies displaced the "normal deliveries" of the middle classes.[109] The emphasis on overcrowding constructed low-income and drug-using women as direct threats to middle-class, non-drug-using women. Poor women were depicted as the kind of women who walk away from infants; poor children—"not the most wantable product"—displaced the wanted children of the middle classes.[110]

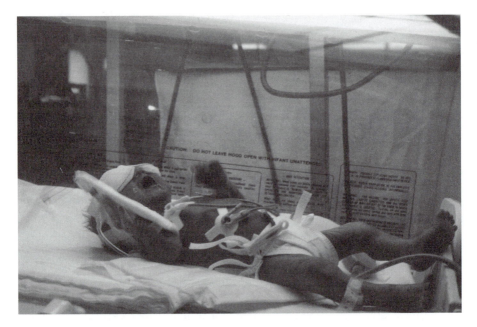

Figure 23   Photograph captioned "lifelong casualty of drug abuse," 1990.

Reprinted, with permission, from Gamma-Liaison, New York, New York.

Boarder babies fell unseen "through the cracks," yet were the "most expensive citizens of all."[111] They became lost children who "drift into the foster care system and they can drift into the institutional system and they can drift into the criminal justice system."[112] Their movements were the random motion of a refugee population, floating unguided on the seas of chance (see Figure 23). Drugs fueled a pervasive sense of futility, for which there was no limit or remedy. Even those who situated drug use in the context of structural unemployment, the feminization of poverty, or the collapse of local economies did not propose to remedy these larger, structural problems. The increasing number of children on welfare in the mid-1980s was blamed on drug exposure.[113] The symptom was attacked, the cause displaced.

As these policy images circulated, feminists and civil rights advocates found themselves defending rollbacks of rights that once seemed settled. For many, the criminal prosecution of pregnant women who used drugs, disproportionately low-income women of color, encrypted the elements of a feminist issue. A coalition of feminists, public health activists, and legal scholars argued vociferously—and successfully—against criminal prosecution of individual pregnant addicts. Because punitive laws or threats to custody deter women from prenatal care, they do not promote health in babies or mothers. Policies that aim "to protect fetuses by denying the humanity of their mothers will inevitably fail."[114] The hearing provided fetal rights and women's rights advocates a stage on which to dramatize their disagreement. The gap between them was bridged in *Born Hooked* by postmodern Progressivism—the redefinition of coercion as compassion in the context of declining state support for social provision.

The governing mentalities that guide our understanding of the social factors and cultural norms that lead to drug use have a racialized effect. Coercive measures are directed toward persons of color, and therapeutic measures primarily toward whites. The crack-cocaine crisis illustrated that women of color in the United States are but grudgingly offered social services. Public provision has been attacked since African-American women first gained parity in welfare benefits, and over time public support for social provision has eroded. Yet the charge in these hearings was that unreasonable paranoia made "nontraditional populations refuse to enter systems."[115] African-Americans' well-founded suspicions toward the social organization of health research, health care, and social services were deflected onto stubborn individuals who refused treatment or evaded prenatal care out of willful disregard and ignorance.[116] The political discourse aired in the hearings legitimated both coercive and compassionate state intervention, the two faces of postmodern Progressivism.

"Irreconcilable Differences": The Divorce between Maternal and Fetal Rights
Figurative Prosecutions

Public discourse constructs individual women as if they alone control the circumstances under which they use drugs, become pregnant, get or stay married, decide whether or not to carry to term, or raise children. Such voluntarism contradicts most women's experience. Feminists have documented how the stratified social terrain of social and biological reproduction in the United States belies individual agency and constrains the reproductive autonomy of all but a few women.[117] Drug policy discourse obscures social stratification, deflecting its effects onto individual figures. There is no better illustration of the effects of a racially uneven policy than the wave of criminal prosecutions that engulfed pregnant women of color in the late 1980s and early 1990s. These women literally and figuratively embodied the "hard case."

Court intervention into the lives of pregnant women is not novel—since the 1960s courts have compelled pregnant women to undergo medical treatment such as blood transfusions and surgery from which men are exempt.[118] But in the 1980s, convergence between the war on drugs and the growing legal and cultural recognition of fetal rights made maternal drug use an example of the stark conflict between the pregnant woman and the fetus. Women's rights began to be understood as opposed to fetal rights, with the state sandwiched in the nonexistent space between a pregnant woman and the fetus she carries. Even more disturbing, "the rights of women as persons and the obligations of women as mothers emerge[d] . . . as irreconcilable differences that serve to generate issues and debates that are central to women and the treatment accorded them by the criminal justice system.[119] Drug use during pregnancy became the paradigmatic example of the figurative divorce between maternal rights and fetal rights.

The "irreconcilable differences" framework assumes an adversarial relationship between woman and fetus, but also separates women's rights as persons from their maternal duties and obligations.[120] This separation predicates (some) women's rights as persons on their behaviors and decisions as mothers. Women's rights as persons are made conditional—rights are purchased by women's good behavior as mothers and forfeited in the case of bad behavior. Mothers are bound by obligation; "persons" are "free," possessing unencumbered rights and entitlements.[121] The logic of "irreconcilable differences" supports the idea that the government is not compelled to lessen, remove, or even attend to social obstacles that block the exercise of rights.

Anti-choice advocacy moved onto the terrain of the war on drugs through the opening provided by the separation of women's rights from maternal obligations. Portraying the relationship between maternal and fetal rights as a conflict widens the gulf between women's rights as persons, and their obligations as mothers. To place such conditions on women's rights of personhood imposes an undue responsibility on women and encodes an asymmetric power relation in the law that denies women "equivalent" respect, freedom, and imagination.[122] Women's overresponsibility for absorbing the tasks of social reproduction presents a similar problem. Setting women's rights against maternal duties and pitting women against the very potential lives they are carrying places women in an impossible position. The discursive trap that feminists found themselves negotiating was very real for approximately 200 women who were prosecuted in some form for drug use during pregnancy.

The wave of prosecutions had largely spent itself by the mid-1990s, and punitive state and federal sanctions were forestalled in all states with the exception of South Carolina. Most states interrupted the cycle of "blaming the victim," and saw through the logic of punitive measures. Prenatal drug exposure was institutionalized as a medical and social problem rather than as the criminal matter it had threatened to become. When the deck was stacked against them, women's advocates prevailed. Sociologist Laura E. Gomez credits the 1987 prosecution of Pamela Rae Stewart with galvanizing the movement. The Stewart case illustrates that how you tell a story matters. Whether we see Stewart as a callous woman who flouted physician's orders or as an abused woman whose actions were severely constrained by a violent husband matters for how we interpret the death of their recently born child.[123] Charged with "failing to follow her doctor's advice to stay off her feet, to refrain from sexual intercourse, to refrain from taking street drugs, and to seek immediate medical attention," Pamela Rae Stewart failed to take proper prenatal precautions. Unlike 80 percent of prosecuted women, Stewart was white and not a crack-cocaine user. She was poor, dependent on a violent husband, and living where methamphetamine was regularly available. Although her case was eventually dismissed on grounds that the criminal child support statute was not meant to penalize pregnant drug users, the case mobilized a feminist opposition that linked the policing of pregnant women's conduct to encroachments on women's reproductive rights. "Pro-life" organizations supported criminal prosecutions of pregnant women; feminists and the ACLU, which became a major player in this struggle, opposed them.

National and state ACLU organizations worked in concert, providing lawyers, surveying the number of available treatment slots in the United States, and attracting media attention. Drug treatment professionals also became deeply involved in work against punitive laws in California, forming the California Advocates for Pregnant Women (CAPW) to work through lobbying and consciousness-raising.[124] Through the Stewart case and the legislative battles that ignited in its wake, CAPW worked with physicians' organizations and other lobbies such as the Consumers' Union and the March of Dimes. This coalition provides an example of a non-identity-based social movement working with addicted women to convince legislators that punitive sanctions were not in anyone's best interest.

Prosecutors, on the other hand, operated in a differently charged symbolic arena to place blame on the shoulders of mothers whose instincts were widely noted to be in decline.[125] Gomez identified two prosecutorial strategies—one very punitive, and the other, one of "inaction." The paucity of cases in mid-range categories—"hard" or "soft" diversion—showed that the symbolic dimension of prenatal drug exposure produced gaps between the prosecutor's "high interest in and strong language about the social problem" and their relative inaction. Gomez found that many constraints on prosecutors mitigated against prosecution (such as proscription against filing weak cases, workload, dismissals, and the emerging consensus against criminalization in the state legislature). Where cases were prosecuted, outcomes tended to be harsh and coupled with the prose-cutor's moral outrage.[126] "Outrage" suggests that cultural processes enter legisla-tive outcomes and prosecutorial decisions, but the social problems approach did not allow Gomez to get at the governing mentalities that drive such processes.

While the perennial features of political discourse on drugs were present in this case, the political conditions were novel due to the struggle over the rights of the fetus. The blurring of "fetus" into "child" and the widening chasm between ma-ternal interests and fetal rights were countered by arguments that the state should play a facilitative rather than an adversarial role.[127] Both sides endlessly repeated "worst case scenarios"; stories of human rights atrocities provided lurid fodder for the press and fueled a full-scale moral panic among the public. The diffusion of interest to lawmakers, who generally confine themselves to issues that play well to their constituents, suggests that the imperatives of the issue derived from the media to a greater degree than usual.[128] These prosecutions were partly attempts to gain symbolic purchase over a much wider political and cultural domain. As Gomez notes, the "issue engages larger debates about the changing role of women and motherhood, including debates about parenting practices, moral standards, women's equality, and reproductive rights."[129] What these debates share is the anxiety that women may not be willing or able to continue to perform as "women" to provide the services they have in the past. Social reproduction is the issue—"maternal instinct" is the name we use to signal this concern.

The success of the feminist coalition that argued against criminal sanctions is rarely recognized as "feminist" because drug-using women occupy a peripheral position to organized feminism. The Women's Movement has been rightfully criticized for allowing privileged and professional women to speak as if they speak for all women. As much as race and class have divided feminism, issues of reproductive autonomy have also split racial-ethnic communities. These dual ex-clusions obscure how a movement for the reproductive liberty of women of color and poor women could revitalize both struggles. This is Dorothy Roberts's point in *Killing the Black Body*—she redefines "reproductive liberty" as a relationship between liberty and equality, rather than liberty at the expense of equality.[130] Such a redefinition would guard against the separation between abstract rights of choice and the concrete means to exercise them. As feminists have long main-tained, a choice means nothing in the absence of the means to make one.

Public policy impacts women differently in ways that greatly affect political affinities (and disaffinities) between groups and individuals. It sometimes appears that the project of building a movement for reproductive liberty asks more of (white) feminism than it can give. Yet the drug prosecutions suggest otherwise. Punitive drug laws negatively impact poor women and women of color most, yet the movement consisted largely of white, professional-class women. "In order to successfully oppose criminalization, the feminist coalition had to recast the social problem as affecting *all* women, rather than the subset of drug-addicted women (or poor women of color presumed to be candidates for drug addiction). This crucial step converted the policy problem from one that fell under the jurisdiction of the criminal justice system to one that more properly belonged in the medical-public health domain."[131] By redefining prenatal drug exposure as a "generic women's problem,"[132] the movement de-emphasized racial-ethnic and class specificity but foregrounded the threat to all women's reproductive freedom. Thus it provided a counterexample to Roberts's pessimistic view of the potential for cross-race, cross-class political alliances among feminists.

Feminist organizations "bracketed" racial and class-specific differences between women in order to navigate the waters of liberalism. The African-American legislators who first opposed punitive legislation sought more resources for poor women of color. The feminists who later took up the cause made a more universal case and may have thereby given up resources that might have made a material difference in some women's lives. Their trade-off "succeeded in shifting the discourse from one about bad women who need to be punished to one about sick women who needed help by focusing on drug-using women in general."[133] Did the shift from villain to victim, from bad to sick, from specific to generic occur at the expense of poor women of color? Or did the universal appeal gain heightened protection for a highly vulnerable group?

Conclusion

Pregnancy might be viewed not as creating special needs, but as exemplifying basic needs that, if met, would provide a measure of social justice for women. By contrast, the "decline of maternal instinct" justified disciplinary and punitive approaches, ranging from child removal to incarceration, that have resulted in miscarriages of justice. Under such circumstances, feminists had to argue for increased access to treatment, gender-specific treatment, and parenting education, even though these techniques lend themselves to a form of social discipline and surveillance. By broadening the analysis of what pregnant drug users need from the state and society, feminists were paradoxically placed in the position of arguing for an expansion of postmodern Progressivism as the lesser of two evils.

The fetal-rights context made this dangerous terrain. The state's overidentification with the fetus evokes the "male fetal identification syndrome."[134] The syndrome renders pregnant women increasingly less equal as pregnancy progresses — less self-determining, less rights-bearing, less competent, less. Rather than policies that assume a convergence between women's interests and those of a potential child, the state's vigorous pursuit of maternal-fetal "equality" has exacerbated the disjunction between women's self-care and their care for the other within. Feminists often take right-to-lifers to task for ignoring the rights of the already-born in favor of the "unborn." Drug policy debates value potential life over the actual life of woman or child—but the value of potential life evaporates with birth. Low birth weight, the crack-baby cry, behavioral problems, and the unlovability of an aggressive child pierce the bubble of potential. Actual life is so much messier. Actual babies—particularly babies of color, with their overpresent mothers and absent fathers—are devalued and dehumanized after they exit the "hostile climate" of their mothers' wombs. This dynamic clearly indicates the degree to which the right-to-life argument rests on a putative equality that obscures how fundamental women's inequality is to fetal rights. For this reason, the goal of drug policy targeted toward women should be to strengthen women's autonomy in the decisions that bear on their own lives. The appeal to maternal instinct does little to advance this more substantive goal.

A Politics of
Social Justice

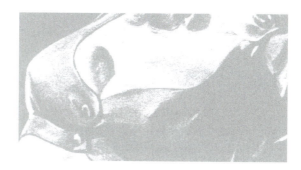

A COMPLETE BOOK-LENGTH
TRUE CRIME NOVEL.

A Politics of
Social Justice

Representative Figures

Predators or prey, drug-using women deviate from the norms of modern femininity. Women were symbolically overdetermined in the contagion model, the maladjustment model, and the family configuration model because they were positioned to relay addiction from its "hidden" confines in the family to the larger society. The residual power of governing mentalities is never fully displaced, which is why the historical repository of representative figures traced in Part II remains significant. Social change, however, transmutes older conceptualizations to fit new circumstances, as we saw in Part III. When demographic and economic shifts produced more female-headed households, the old family configuration model guided policy-makers' alarm. Material factors, in other words, are not so threatening without the governing mentalities that frame their meaning.

Congressional hearings, scientific studies, and addicted women's self-representations—ranging from witness testimony to memoirs—form a fascinating archive. Despite at least 30 hearings on drug use and traffic a year since 1969,[1] a sea of data, and an incitement to discourse, addiction remains undertheorized. Policy approaches are frozen in an undoubtedly frustrating state of amnesia, uncertainty, and contradiction. I chose to analyze specific events that aired public discourse on drugs, rather than turn to extensive archival research unavailable to the public. Public constructions of drug addiction remain a significant barrier to the critical interrogation of drug policy, and so I have confined my object of study to the dominant discourse, with occasional forays into contending alternatives. My study is by no means exhaustive, for I have left contending counterdiscourses to others. Feminists have long been more interested in resistant or critical discourse, but I believe that in separating the "resistant" from the "hegemonic," we miss the cross-fertilization between these modes. Echoes of the dominant discourse resonate through resistant claims; dominant discourses prevail by incorporating elements appropriated from contending claims. In emphasizing the governing mentalities that prevail in our political imaginary, I do not mean to dismiss the efforts of those who work to displace their rule. Chapter 8 considers representations of women addicts that are specifically designed to unsettle prevailing images. By reading drug ethnography just as we read the historical narratives and more recent public policy, we can discern the elements of a counterdiscourse with the potential to displace the governing mentalities.

Ethnography represents another way of telling the stories through which addicted women make sense of their lives. Like any storytelling mode, ethnography operates according to a set of generic conventions that make promises—in this case to reveal the real conditions of drug-using women's lives. A contingent of drug ethnographers has begun to counter the "rhetoric of contempt" directed toward addicted women.[2] In their texts, the figure of the pregnant drug user illustrates the limits of the criminal model, the absurdity of fetal rights claims, and the continued subordination of women along the differential axes of race, class, and sexuality. For a substantial group of feminist scholars, health professionals, prison activists, legal scholars, and medical practitioners, the pregnant drug addict symbolizes social policy gone awry.

Chapter 8, "Reading Drug Ethnography," attests to another of my preoccupations in *Using Women*. Although knowledge does not force the hand of governance, knowledge shapes the form that it can take. Ethnography becomes relevant to policy-makers when other methods of knowledge production fall short—when reliable numbers are lacking, when the confabulatory narratives cannot explain "cause," or when there is a vacuum of sociological studies that connect statistical data to interpretive frames. Ethnographic texts reveal that women's lack of autonomy (or, we might say, the presence of constraint) is a major determinant of which women use drugs, how they initiate use, and why they remain users. Ethnography potentially rearticulates knowledge claims in ways that are useful to a movement for socially just drug policy and a feminist movement for women's autonomy.

Strange Bedfellows

The politics of illicit drug policy have, however, fostered odd alliances. Child welfare advocates and neoconservatives struck a troubling alliance in the mid-1990s. Neoconservatives are paradoxically interested in rolling back social provision and returning to state guardianship and institutional care. To illustrate their influence, I will briefly compare two publications by the Child Welfare League of America (CWLA). The first emerged from a symposium on "Crack and Other

Addictions: Old Realities and New Challenges for Child Welfare" held on March 12 and 13, 1990. At the time the league was seeking a role for child welfare in the drug war.[3] According to David S. Liederman, CWLA Executive Director, crack-cocaine placed child welfare workers "under siege" and forced them to question "tried-and-true methods."[4] He lamented that "large gaps in existing knowledge . . . precluded rational decision making."[5] The drug problem was depicted as overwhelming and elusive, the solutions vague and remote.[6] "Where were the 'facts' which would clearly show the right direction?" Leiderman asked.

Women were not the source of the drug problem in the 1990 publication. The drug was responsible—the drug fundamentally transformed the meanings of motherhood, womanhood, and childhood, as evident in the three opening vignettes. The first read: "Other drugs have plagued our society since the 1960s but cocaine and especially crack pose a threat to many more young children. According to Dr. Jin Ja Yoon, Bronx Lebanon Hospital, 'Crack is destroying people—I have never seen mothers like this before. Children aren't being fed, mothers sell their food stamps. Young women sell their bodies in front of their children. Even when heroin was at its worst, it wasn't like this.'"[7] The second epigraph was a *New York Times* excerpt titled "Poor Families Are Dying of Crack," which depicted a twelve-year-old boy selling crack from an upturned crate while his mother drank beer nearby. As the "head of the family," he brought in several thousand dollars a week at his makeshift stand. The third vignette extended the allusion to old-fashioned lemonade stands, recounting the discovery of a playground "drug stand" where children sold bags of sugar and grass clippings. The images associated a child's first business and a woman's oldest profession, setting the stage for the league's exploration of the toll exacted by crack-cocaine on the child welfare system. These fantastic figures—mothers who encourage children to deal drugs, women who sell their bodies in front of their children, children whose play presages doom—indicate that the rationality project is inseparable from the images that propel its agenda.

Social inequality framed the symposium, which characterized the "drugs of the 90s" as especially devastating for communities of color.[8] Physician Ira J. Chasnoff presented research indicating that white women showed higher levels of positive urine toxicologies (15.4%) than black women (14%) in a study of 500 white women and 200 African-American women in Pinellas County, Florida.[9] Despite Florida's mandatory reporting law, women of color were ten times more likely to be reported: "When a woman walks into a hospital in Pinellas County, and this is not, I can guarantee you, only in Pinellas County, if she walks into a hospital and has just used drugs, a black woman has a ten times higher chance of being reported into the [child protection] system than a white woman."[10] Chasnoff rhetorically asked: "Could it be that physicians have a preconception that substance abuse in pregnancy is a problem of the minority, of the indigent class, of black women and their systems, and so they are much more ready to take histories from black women than white women and are much more ready to do urine toxicologies and make the diagnosis and report [black] women?"[11] Punishing individual women did not address social inequality and was the wrong "investment strategy," he argued, because it would drive women beyond the reach of "the system." Far from improving children's lives, it would turn them into "battlefields in the war on drugs."[12]

The recognition of gender inequality and racism, a critique of punishment and child removal, a concern with service provision, and an attempt to treat addicted women fairly were integral to the CWLA's approach to the problem in the early 1990s. The political orientation of the CWLA was liberal, rationalist, and pragmatist at that time. Four years later, the league copublished *When Drug Addicts Have Children: Reorienting Child Welfare's Response* with the American Enterprise Institute (AEI), a neoconservative and antifeminist think tank. Douglas Besharov, resident scholar at AEI and former director of the National Center on Child Abuse and Neglect, edited the second collection. *When Drugs Addicts Have Children: Reorienting Child Welfare's Response* differed markedly in tone, portraying its agenda as "realistically" and "radically" recognizing that cure is elusive and relapse the rule.[13]

The "radical" reorientation of child welfare meant recognizing addiction as a chronic and relapsing disorder—and not as a disease that can be cured.[14] Visual cues helped make the case (see Figure 24). The cover photo depicted a young girl of uncertain ethnicity in a white dress, barrettes, and tennis shoes, pensively swinging in a playground. Her hair is straight, suggesting a child who is not African-American. The book jacket wrapped to the back, where a much less focused African-American child grins as she swings in a baseball cap, braids hanging down her back. Readers can make out little detail on the back photo, but the gleeful, toothy grin is unmistakable amid the ominous shadows. The cover touches on the theme of the drug culture's colonization of childhood and corruption of innocence. This time, the title is clearly gendered—drug addicts are "having" children rather than "raising" them. The cover girls embody the threat that they, too, will reproduce. The African-American girl is out of focus and moving faster; the "white" girl seems more controlled. The swing suggests a pendulum, which promotes the idea that the racial face of "drugs" changes cyclically but they remain a gendered problem.

The editor argued that long-term responses to parental addiction should assume it was incurable. Social management—terminating parental rights through permanent guardianship arrangements and warehousing children in large, residential-care facilities—should displace treatment.[15] This reinstitutionalization of the children of drug-addicted women was suggested in the context of declining social provision and state responsibility for the welfare of its citizens. While this

Figure 24   Cover photograph by Lloyd Wolf. *When Drug Addicts Have Children*, 1992.

Reprinted, with permission, from Lloyd Wolf.

initially appears paradoxical, it indicates the neglect of the issue of social inequality in favor of an emphasis on managing those who cannot govern themselves—and will, supposedly, never be able to do so. This is the polar opposite of support for women's autonomy. Instead, it is a form of postmodern Progressivism.

Conclusion

Hostility and moral outrage remain the dominant registers through which women's drug use is regarded, with the occasional intrusion of ethnographic pathos. For the most part, drug-using women are constructed without pity or entitlement. Racial hostility, sexually and racially discriminatory practices, and opposition to women's political autonomy augment the hostility toward women addicts. The results are potent and volatile fantastic figures that evoke some of our deepest cultural fears and our most intense repudiations. These images work against the drug policy reform movement's becoming a movement for social justice. For it to do so, the unequal burden of social reproduction would have to be acknowledged rather than disavowed. I do not mean to confine redistribution to the level of the household or "biological" family. As Nancy Folbre concludes, men have generally been able to minimize their contribution to the costs of social reproduction in historically specific ways.[16] As I have shown throughout *Using Women,* women are held to higher standards of performance. Some women have passed this burden to other, less-fortunate women; today there is widespread commercial "outsourcing" of these tasks. Because women are ultimately responsible for keeping families "intact," they are blamed for the failure to do so. Even where women do this on their own with little social provision, they do so in absence of the recognition that they in fact provide a social service by privately absorbing the cost of care.

More and more people in modern economies live and parent outside biological kin networks. Thus a movement for social justice must broadly and deeply redefine and redistribute responsibilities for social reproduction. There cannot be social justice if undue burdens are placed on some of us. Just as an unjust measure of responsibility for productive labor falls to workers, an unjust portion of the costs of social reproduction falls to mothers. Drug-using women remind us of this equation—but "deserve" the blame that is directed toward them. As representative figures they permit us to disavow social injustice. We might instead "use" them to call for the recognition and remedy of social injustice.

Reading Drug Ethnography

It is because subjects do not, strictly speaking, know what they are doing that what they do has more meaning than they know.
—Pierre Bourdieu, Outline of a Theory of Practice, *79*

Feminist Nightmares in the Realist Text
Empowerment or Degradation?

Policy-relevant research has recently taken an ethnographic turn. Proliferating ethnographic accounts of drug-using women convey social worlds at distinct odds with one another. Some situate their subjects in a feminist nightmare world of degradation; others emphasize women's empowerment and agency. All challenge the long-standing blindness to gender subordination within "the broader structure of drug markets . . . as a variable influencing women and drugs."[1] Ethnography provides accounts of addiction that often work as discursive counterweights to the governing mentalities amplified in the hearings. Ethnography enriches our understanding of the material and cultural conditions that drug-using women confront daily. This chapter considers "state ethnographies" funded by government agencies to supplement quantitative data, and popular accounts that take journalistic form. Building on my claim that how we "know" drug-using women matters for how we govern them, the chapter recounts how the governing mentalities shape knowledge production, the cultural practices of governance, and popular understandings through the ethnographic form.

The drama of drug ethnography unfolds against the backdrop of suburbanization, urban tax flight, infrastructural decline, and deindustrialization. This careful context-setting, a feature of ethnographic texts, guards against the deflection dynamic so often glimpsed in drug policy discourse. For instance, Fagan's recent study of gender in New York City drug markets identified two social worlds—in one, women experienced the established pattern of narrowing options in which "gender roles still weigh[ed] significantly." In the other world, women's incomes from drug selling buffered them from health risks and exploitative prostitution; they were less restricted in terms of gender. "But the changing gender composition of inner cities that host active drug markets suggest that partnerships with males will be a declining part of these social and economic worlds."[2] In the context of policy-making, however, such a statement is the stuff of nightmares because of policy-makers' entrenched belief that female-headed households and skewed sex ratios somehow "cause" addiction.

The ethnographic evidence shows that women who exercise some measure of agency within their own lives do "better"—even within the brave new world of the informal economy. Women distributors obtained a sense of autonomy and occupational mobility that they had never before experienced—and with it increased control over their own consumption. They expressed this as "the feeling that they are their 'own person.' "[3] The drug economy was the only sphere in which they experienced a sense of effectiveness, pride, and independence. Although small numbers of women were involved in distribution, they "claimed to work when they wanted and how they wanted. Others claimed to work for whom they wanted and some of them were clearly able to work for themselves."[4] The centrality of the female distributor counters the tendency for drug research to focus on women solely as out-of-control consumers, reinforcing "excessive sexual scripts."[5] These ethnographies present women as economic actors who gained autonomy and occupational mobility from their participation in the informal economy.[6] Of course, the results are not uniformly beneficial, for women who develop profiles in the illicit market may not develop skills useful in the legitimate economy.[7]

Women involved in drug sales are portrayed as more masculine—as "toughening up" to compensate for being female.[8] Their gender performance is tied to the uniquely violent aspects of their work.[9] Both Fagan's team and Dunlap, Johnson, and Maher emphasized their female subjects' self-sufficiency and enhanced self-esteem. In contrast to the vast majority of drug ethnographies, studies of female distributors show that the lack of legitimate, well-paying jobs for women of color drives them into the more accessible informal sector. This suggests that women who use illicit drugs do not need pity, compassion, life skills, or social services designed to help them to adjust to the worlds they inhabit. They need different worlds to inhabit.

The feminist ethnographic vein was developed to counter the masculinist slant of the ethnography of crime and deviance.[10] One of its earliest practitioners,

Marsha Rosenbaum, remains actively committed to the field; an emerging co-hort of feminist scholars now contributes to its development. Well intentioned and often explicitly feminist and antiracist, drug ethnographies supply context, fill in caricatured outlines, and "humanize" drug users.[11] Still, most cannot help but reinforce the prevailing narrative constructions of drug-involved women—even when they explicitly try not to do so. The narrative conventions of ethno-graphic realism, the necessity for identified "victims" in our political rationality, and a "routinization of caricature"[12] overpower the complexity and nuance that drug ethnographers work so hard to convey.

All ethnographic projects take shape around an originary failure: words in-evitably fall short of the actual encounter, and the result is a slippage between context and figure, economy and behavior, action and interpretation. Secondly, the conventions of social science "make the basic unit of the analysis the kind of person, treated analytically as if that's what he or she is, that's all he or she is, and as though what such people do or are likely to do makes sense, has been 'ex-plained' causally, by the kind of person they are."[13] While researchers may intend the terms "opiate users" or "crack addicts" to be value-neutral descriptions of "or-dinary people who happen to do [this] particular thing a lot,"[14] readers impute moral judgments to such figures. Ethnography individualizes the subject, impli-cating individual circumstances that include early childhood experiences, family structure, or personality dynamics in the "causation" of addiction. Systemic and structural variables that apply more broadly are not offered as accounts of why individuals behave as they do, although they appear as background.

Explanations that rely on individual deviance marginalize the systematic and everyday aspects of drug use and addiction. As Reinarman and Levine argue, "a core feature of drug war discourse is the *routinization of caricature*—worst cases framed as typical cases, the episodic rhetorically crafted into the epidemic."[15] As a mode of knowledge production, ethnography generates frames of reference that confirm the governing mentalities and become the nightmares writ large in the media and popular consciousness. Ethnographers are not to blame for this translation process—like other authors, they exercise little control over the inter-pretation of their work. The current practice of ethnography leaves the govern-ing mentalities intact, reinscribing the very effect of otherness that most ethnographers seek to displace. With greater attention to the conventions of real-ism and the effects of pathos, this reinscription need not take place.

Hypotyposis: Fictions of Authenticity

Ethnographic texts tend to display their subjects when the author is establishing the warrant for the project, a process crucial to the narrative contract. Agreement is often achieved through the use of a rhetorical figure called "hypotyposis": "the use of a highly graphic passage of descriptive writing, which portrays a scene or action in a vivid and arresting manner. It is used to conjure up the setting and its actors, and to 'place' the implied reader as a firsthand witness."[16] Authors convey authority, credibility, and the sense of having been there through the use of intense imagery that arouses empathy or outrage. Readers who enter into an ethnographic contract are asked to accept this fiction of authenticity.

Moments of hypotyposis are strategically placed throughout realist texts to achieve the effect of authority where it might otherwise be questioned—where the narrative seems to founder. They often occur within exemplary narratives that mark transitions, reinforce the author's credibility, and align readers with a desired perspective. The reader becomes witness to the author, attributing mastery to the author's interpretation and cultural competence to the subjects' performance. Ethnography depends on a series of pacts—between subject and ethnographer, between the ethnographer as witness and as writer, and between the writer and the reader. Hypotyposis overrides readerly resistance and produces the effect of empathy through exemplary narratives, which provide the indexes to the reader's world so essential to meaning.[17] Exemplars are especially powerful because they allow knowledge claims to be smuggled in via narrative. For example, consider "Two Women Who Used Cocaine Too Much," Murphy's and Rosenbaum's contribution to an anthology assembled to debunk the stereotypes of crack users.[18]

Monique is introduced in the deteriorated physical surroundings of a dark, smelly, and previously firebombed apartment in a public housing complex.[19] Her bodily sensations—hunger, dry mouth, and headache—are dominant, and then the setting is described. The action begins with Monique sitting on a filthy mattress, when a man who offers her "a rock for some head" approaches her.[20] Her race and class status are unmentioned—readers, it is assumed, will visualize a young, African-American woman living in a social world where she is nothing more than a means to a man's end. Snippets of dialogue in which Monique and the unnamed man call each other "bitch" and "baby" categorize them as African-American. Neither party upholds their end of the deal. When he leaves, "again Monique began crying silent tears while her stomach growled."[21] It is hard to imagine a more abject and degraded femininity. The authors are well aware of this effect, noting: "No doubt some readers were shocked and dismayed by the stigmatizing image of a young black woman in our opening narrative."[22] They defend the decision to lead with a "worst-case scenario" as an act of narrative heroism that allows them "to show the importance of class and racism in shaping the setting, mind-sets, and consequences or [sic] drug use."[23] Their readers are thus to agree that the opening accurately renders "[Monique's] lived experience as she described it to us"—a lived experience "profoundly affected by the poverty, racism, and sexism that shaped her life."[24] The essay proceeds to narrate

Monique's life history, initiation into drug use, and eventual descent into depression and homelessness.

Monique's story contrasts to that of Becky, a middle-class, white teenager who works as a coat checker in a nightclub. Becky's cocaine use is socially congenial—an inconsequential way to bond with friends and coworkers. Her drug use is a weekend diversion that does not interrupt the progress of her life—she is in college by the end of her story. Although the ethnographers claim that neither girl is "necessarily 'typical' of their socioeconomic or ethnic groups," both are "real women" whose lives illustrate the essay's main point: "that class, race, and gender are more important in shaping these different experiences with and consequences of cocaine than the cocaine itself."[25] These girls are situated within a framework of interlocking oppressions that condition their drug experiences. Class and race privilege protect white women—even if they use illicit drugs—but render women of color vulnerable to detection, abuse, and further degradation. Additionally, Murphy and Rosenbaum depict power relations between the genders as more symmetric among whites, and less symmetric among persons of color. They suggest that men who use crack—predominantly men of color at present—use a masculine form of power to control the drug supply and gain sexual access to women.[26] Enmeshed in this "web of gender and power relations," women of color are subjected to more consequential forms of drug use and have fewer resources to respond than do white women.

The phenomenological display of Monique's despair at the essay's outset contrasts with Becky's innocent fun. Crack is the center of Monique's devastated world; cocaine is a minor prop in the drama of Becky's life. The hypotyposis of Monique's story contrasts to the matter-of-fact account of Becky's. The hypotyposis establishes one kind of relationship between the reader, the authors, and Monique—and a different kind between the reader, the authors, and Becky. Readers who have experimented with recreational drug use will generally identify with the middle-class account—the "respectable" middle-class can have fun without becoming addicted. Few readers will identify with the unrelenting, predictable abjection of Monique, who is emotionally and financially ruined by the end of the story, although she no longer uses crack. Becky has returned to the protected fold of middle-class life.

The mode of relationality central to the ethnographic form reinforces the governing mentalities. While such accounts are intended to disabuse outsiders of erroneous notions about drug-using women, they effectively reinforce existing power relations, social antagonisms, and divisions. They reproduce the very problems that the ethnographers set out to dispel, and disserve the very political positions they seek to affirm. Like accounts of illness and disability, narrative reconstructions of drug use allow the healthy, able, and non-drug-using population to convert the undesirability reflected in the "corrupt" body into a sign of its own wholeness, purity, and value. Illness and disability stories are often restorative, seeking to make sense of chaos and contingency through quest and restitution. Some attribute to such narratives the power to disassemble the "relations of ruling."[27] Addiction stories work differently—relapse always threatens, "the life" always beckons; the lapsed self is always ready to overwhelm the recovering self. The governing mentalities, so central to the "relations of ruling," are buttressed by addiction stories as we tell them. Ethnographic texts might momentarily destabilize the governing mentalities, but they do not dislodge them. The unstable effects of pathos and outrage generate both empathy and resistance, identification and distance.

Ethnographic Prescriptions
Realism Revisited

"State ethnographies" are funded out of the recognition that quantitative data cannot track rapidly changing practices in drug subcultures and noninstitutional populations.[28] Drug ethnography has recently taken on a clinical cast, spurred by U.S. government attempts to understand and end HIV transmission through intravenous (IV) drug use by studying the actual practices of drug users. NIDA regards qualitative research as "particularly useful for studying emergent and little-understood phenomena and for learning more about hidden populations: the homeless and transient, chronically mentally ill, high school dropouts, criminal offenders, prostitutes, juvenile delinquents, gang members, runaways, and other 'street people.'"[29] The assumption is that ethnographers achieve rapport with their subjects that places them beyond the "stereotyped and manipulative responses that drug users often develop for professional ears."[30] Funders, producers, and readers assume that ethnography tells us something we do not already know because the ethnographer "penetrates" hidden regions of social life.

During the drug crises of the late 1960s and 1970s, ethnographers began to challenge assumptions and stereotypes about the lifestyles of drug users.[31] Early studies elicited the folk definitions and rituals of "the addict subculture."[32] For instance, Michael Agar contrasted addicts' "folk" schema with the professional approaches of "squares"—police, treatment professionals, and policy-makers. Such studies observed drug users in their natural setting and were confined almost entirely to male subjects until the pathbreaking 1981 publication of Marsha Rosenbaum's *Women on Heroin*, which supplied knowledge about the day-to-day lives of women who used heroin. *Women on Heroin* achieved a moral reversal through Rosenbaum's descriptions of women's narrowing options, which eked humanity out of an apparent domain of inhumanity, order out of chaos, an ethics out of a seemingly brutal social world. "The contrast between the insider's precise knowledge and the outsider's erroneous common sense constructs a major warrant for the authoritative claim of the ethnography."[33] Insider knowledge is presented as a systemic ordering of an otherwise unintelligible world. Rosenbaum sought to convince readers that women addicts are "more oppressed than other women," situating her subjects as disadvantaged by virtue of their reduced options and social isolation.[34]

Rosenbaum argued that the woman addict's career was "inverted": "She begins with somewhat reduced but still viable life options. The longer she remains in the heroin life, however, the more her choices begin to narrow, both subjectively and objectively and primarily in the areas of family and work."[35] Neither option traditionally open to women was open to women on heroin. Rosenbaum painted a sympathetic portrait of her heroin-using subjects: their ethical choices were based on values similar to those of "straight" women. She argued against child removal on grounds that it was often destructive for the "addict-mother."[36] She also promoted "affirmative action" policies to strengthen addicted women's occupational skills. "Women on heroin" became women, first and foremost, who were oppressed because they were women. The framework of oppression allowed for a critical narrative that disrupted the prevailing images of heroin-using women.

Ethnographic texts work realist effects in their readers, and they are successful when a reader experiences the text as congruent with his or her own governing mentalities and sense of reality. The realist text is a "predominantly conservative form" even when it sets out to counter a dominant representation. According to literary critic Catherine Belsey, "the experience of reading a realist text is ultimately reassuring, however harrowing the events of the story, because the world evoked in the fiction, its patterns of cause and effect, of social relationship and moral values, largely confirm the patterns of the world we seem to know."[37] Ethnographic constructions of crack-cocaine use represent a feminist nightmare world that confirms alarmist claims about the decline and degradation of women in low-income urban environments. Because drug ethnographers focus on how individual subjects construct meaning under conditions of extreme deprivation, they sketch structural conditions in evocative yet highly phantasmatic ways.

Qualitative research attempts to achieve the effect of realism. Consider a presentation by street ethnographers based in Hartford, Connecticut.[38] By capturing the structures and dynamics of "high risk locations," they sought the natural history of frequent behaviors in "high risk settings." The settings were used as "metaphors for the people with whom [they] come into contact," metaphors that signaled the social disorganization of "group drug consumption arenas." Women, who comprised one quarter of Hartford's illicit drug users, were complicated subjects for the ethnographers because they were reluctant to show up in these settings due to reasonable fears of legal complications concerning sex work or child custody. Thus the research team had to penetrate women's more deeply hidden and privatized activities. The job of the "high-risk site ethnographer" was to represent the complex behavior of the "target pop" (as it was affectionately dubbed). They subjected drug-using women to higher levels of scrutiny and surveillance because of women's role in social reproduction. The study was intended to suggest "interventions" into the rules and behaviors that govern "high risk settings." Drug ethnography is a science of conduct designed to investigate the moral universe within which illicit drug use takes place.

The dominant "amoral" image of intravenous drug users (IVDUs) influences researchers to focus on the differences between "target populations" and the rest of "us."[39] With an emphasis on moral dilemmas indigenous to the context of street drug use, ethical reflections among drug users are revealed as not dissimilar from those of non-drug users. For instance, IVDUs differentiate between "bad addicts" and "good abusers" (who regard limits, do not harm others, and follow standards of conduct such as breaking off the tips of used needles). Women face certain perplexing moral dilemmas—for instance, how to seek treatment without losing custody of their children. Ethnographers make apparent the complexity their subjects face in negotiating their lives; therein lies their merit. Drug ethnographers are well aware that their texts are read as reflections of reality. Fearing that readers might be misled into thinking that "exchanging sex for crack is typical of crack smokers," Mitchell S. Ratner, editor of a multisite ethnography, elaborated: "This study went looking for a particular phenomenon—regular crack users who exchanged sex for crack—found it, comprehensively described and analyzed its many variations. . . . While looking for individuals who exchanged sex for crack, study researchers also encountered many individuals whose crack use was not compulsive and/or whose sexual behavior was extremely circumscribed."[40] Secondly, he warned readers not to think that "the sex-for-crack phenomenon arises from the moral failing, poor judgment, inadequate socialization, or depravity of the participants." These problematic behaviors were to be contextualized in their full complexity, the aim of this fine and subtle ethnography. Yet the disclaimers of the preface were soon submerged beneath the weight of the "reality" recorded in thorough ethnographic detail. What reader resists the "crack pipe as pimp," a sexualized and racialized image that crowds out all others, or the phantasmatic visions of "Crackworld"? Even the most confabulatory numbers cannot compete with the nightmarish visions that inhabit the streets of "broken windows, broken dreams."

Living in a Phantasmatic State: Life in "Crackworld"

Crackworld was portrayed as an "emerging culture of resistance and refusal of ideologies that honor existing power relations" in a journalistic ethnography, *Crackhouse: Notes from the End of the Line.*[41] This popular genre lacks authority but is important to drug studies because of beliefs that addicts reflect something "essential" about America:

> The crackheads represent a rebellion, a refusal to accept sobriety and safe sex as standards of behavior; the people in the crackhouse consistently challenge, ridicule, and reject accepted notions of moral action. Americans often ignore signals from the underground, but the drug culture represents an extreme response to the most intractable problems of our day—including family instability, AIDS, teenage and adult unemployment, and crime.[42]

The book confronted readers with their own narrow views, and drew attention to connections between crack use and mainstream cultural texts such as *Star Trek*. According to Williams, crack addicts look as though they want to escape reality—"beam me up, Scotty"[43]—but secretly long to be "absorbed into a meaningful way of life." Fully 40 percent of Williams's subjects were described as "lost girls," products of "incestuous and argumentative famil[ies]."[44]

Adopting the hackneyed pose of an anthropologist studying "crack culture," Williams employed a primitivizing rhetoric far beyond that tolerated within postmodern anthropology. He likened crack users to a "tribe" or an "aboriginal society, its members busying themselves with the rudiments of day-to-day survival, like hunter-gatherers."[45] The pipe was a fetish used in rituals of total absorption. Women and girls were exposed to particular risks in this society—they were exploited on sex-for-crack "missions." One subject, Shayna, said: "It's a macho thing all the way, where the men think a woman should be in a woman's place. The whole drug business is a macho thing," but claimed she was an exception because men respected her brain "over being just a woman."[46] She criticized the misrepresentation that young girls are willing to do anything for crack, noting that women were acting on the basis of individual desires and strategically using their sexuality to get drugs.[47] Shayna continued: "Certainly, the girls and women play power games around the use of crack. Men come into the crackhouse for sex, and they usually bring drugs as the medium of exchange. So sex is like money for women."[48]

"Women love this drug" was echoed by many of Williams's male subjects. Women both confirmed and contradicted this, constructing crack as drawing out an essential self: "This drug brings out what you are, what you really think of yourself. . . . This drug brings out the one you don't want others to see. But it makes you not care one way or the other."[49] Whether women do or do not in actuality "love this drug" was immaterial to what the construction says about gender relations in Crackworld. This pseudo-ethnographic text purported to listen to crack for what it tells us about our culture. The interpretations that emerge shape our reading of the "reality" of this form of ethnographic data and this genre of inquiry.

Crackworld also named the "social decay" that pervaded Sue Mahan's ethnography of women crack-cocaine users.[50] Setting Crackworld apart is a common move.[51] Such texts assume that most of the U.S. population poorly understands Crackworld, and fears it will generate "crisis and chaos," a "coming anarchy," a "feared future crime wave that has no point,"[52] or a state of "entropy" where "nothing is happening."[53] These constructs convey an uncertain but violent future ushered in by the advent of crack-cocaine. Curiously, the violent climate surrounding crack is portrayed as having little to do with guns or the illegality of the drug, and much to do with its "pharmacological omnipotence."[54] The demonization of the substance itself extends to its users and the social world they inhabit.

This social world is one shaped by less-than-benign neglect by policy-makers. Mahan predicted that the costs would be high if the "systems that are in chaos in the neighborhoods where crackworlds thrive" were not reordered.[55] She redefined treatment as the restoration of order in the form of social support systems and services, thus displacing the goal of systemic social change with the goal of changing social services and their delivery systems. Cadres of outreach workers, she suggested, might scour laundromats, grocery stores, and crackhouses to encourage pregnant addicts to seek prenatal care and drug treatment.[56] This faith that "the system" of social service delivery once enhanced community life, imbuing neighborhoods with order where chaos now reigns, is a misplaced belief central to postmodern Progressivism.

Mahan based her version of Crackworld on interviews with a mere seventeen subjects who, she claims, had so much in common that the causes of crack addiction itself could be deduced from her findings. First, she argued that addiction was basically the "abuse of self."[57] Secondly, women's dependency was problematic in the context of a "violent and male dominated" market subculture. While her respondents claimed to be capable of supporting themselves and their children by working in low-paying clerical, food service, janitorial, or hospital jobs, Mahan found that most depended on a man to supply drugs, food, housing, and clothing. "The lifestyle of crack addicts often involves relationships of dependency and domination by men who use access to drugs for control."[58] All the women recounted a history of violence ranging from rape to battering to living in fear, leading Mahan to speculate that Crackworld was more "degrading and depraved" than other drug-using subcultures. Crackworld was an "authoritarian subculture dominated and controlled by men" where submission is coerced with fear and violence, where relationships with men are "based on exploitation and objectification."[59] Not only do these women abuse themselves, but they allow others to use them as objects. This feminist nightmare world, I suggest, is the contemporary version of the world invoked by early-twentieth-century moral-reformists who fought "white slavery" with an equal share of moral conviction.

"Street culture is profoundly sexist," according to Mahan.[60] Sex-for-crack exchanges so disadvantaged women that they lacked even the rights of sex workers. Unlike non-crack-using prostitutes, crack-addicted women were in a poor position to barter sex for drugs and are widely represented as deserving their degradation and victimization even by their male, crack-using clients.[61] The figure who haunts this nightmarish world is the "rock star" ("rock" is another name for crack). The "rock star" crystallizes the elements and patterns brought to light in Mahan's self-described "penetrating look at Crackworld."[62] The story of S., a "rock monster," resembled the narratives of the pseudonymous Beverly Lee Roman and Janet Clark. All were intelligent, articulate, and insightful observers of their social worlds. All were ethical subjects of their time, and each submitted to an apparatus of knowledge production bent on "penetrating" the individual circumstances of their degradation.

S. was a 28-year-old Native American woman who had injected cocaine for five years before Mahan's interview. She described the bodily effects of cocaine and the deterioration of her central nervous system. Physical symptoms and social effects such as unemployment, after which she turned to prostitution, accompanied her mental pain. S. recounted incidents of childhood sexual abuse by her father, two brothers, and a neighbor, in addition to domestic violence in adulthood. Her second husband, a nonusing crack dealer, beat her to get her to stop using crack: "But he said it was for my own good. Afterward he would feel guilty, and then he gave me dope. . . . I saw him for what he really was for the way he treated addicts. He had a power trip over them, like little slaves to him. He would degrade them, treated them really bad, and they would beg him. . . . My husband was one of those who used crack to buy women."[63]

S. constructed her experience of Crackworld in racial terms: it was, according to her, a world "run by blacks" through a strict sexual hierarchy that Mahan referred to as male domination. S. cast it as "reverse racism": "Blacks dominate, so whites get used and abused. They say, 'Since white men used black women for ages, now we are going to get back' . . . like revenge. Dominating white women seems to give them a feeling of power. It's a euphoria. They 'dog out the whites.' White guys will pay a white woman $50 (for sex). But they will pay a black woman $10 for the same thing. Then, the black guys will sell crack cheaper to their black sisters."[64] Racial and sexual meanings of crack-cocaine were associated with the first wave of responses to it in the mid- to late 1980s. They form an available discursive resource for ethnographic informants. S. constructed a world in which black men used aggressive techniques to exact racial revenge through sexual domination—a kind of "payback for slavery." This construction is not idiosyncratic to S. but recurs and is mirrored in white fears of crack invading their neighborhoods.

The dominant classes tend to displace responsibility for drug use and traffic onto low-income African-Americans. Race and ethnicity need not be mentioned in order for this displacement to take place, because certain drugs are "racialized"—associated with specific racial-ethnic groups or attributed racial meanings. These associations shift across time and space. For instance, "angel dust" (PCP) shifted from being a "white" drug to its current status as a drug used primarily by African-Americans and Latinos.[65] Crack-cocaine is demographically and symbolically coded "black," taking on the reputation of a "women's drug" relatively early. As the introduction showed, methamphetamine, a "white" drug, was becoming a "women's" drug as this book was being written. Additionally, certain sites and geographic spaces are gendered, racialized, or associated with particular substances. Crackworld is a feminist dystopia where women allow their bodies to be controlled by crack, men, and pleasures that ultimately betray them. Mahan's study resembles the "crack pipe as pimp" construct certified by the NIDA, which also analyzes the "sex/gender system" of Crackworld. The figures who populate the political imaginary of drug policy in the late twentieth century are hybrid constructions that combine elements of predator and prey. Where once women were innocent prey, they are now carrion feeders, waiting for the scraps to fall. For the most part they are portrayed as "victims" until they transmute into the "victimizers" of babies and children. Sexuality is the main route of victimization.

The Ethnographic State: "For Them a Woman Is a Commodity"

Ironically, *Crack Pipe as Pimp* set out precisely to dispel the sensationally sexualized view conjured by its very title. The contributing ethnographers encountered many variations on crack use and exchange, but ascribed common "personality structures" to their informants: the "low value they place on human life"; self- and other-devaluation; the commodification of women and sex; and an inability to limit the power that crack exerted over their lives "as a pimp, demon, or devil might."[66] The collection employed Norman E. Zinberg's framework on the interaction between drug, set, and setting.[67] "Drug" referred to pharmacological properties; "set" referred to the personality attributes of "crack-using sexual providers" and "crack-using sexual receivers"; and "setting" referred to factors both internal and external to the crack-using subculture such as the market structure of sex work.[68]

Race and class did not appear as "set" or "setting," although economic dislocation, "degradations of inner-city services," and "concentrations of poverty and pathology in the inner cities" formed the backdrop against which male exploitation of "desperate [female] crack users" took place.[69] Because sex-for-crack transactions were identified mainly in urban African-American neighborhoods, 72 percent of the sample was black.[70] Whites and Spanish-speakers were "peripheral members of the African-American dominated networks."[71] The research focused on low-income African-American women aged 26 to 35. Two thirds of the 340 subjects were not on government assistance. The findings that sex-for-crack exchanges take place only in a "defined subcultural space" effectively isolated that environment.[72] Because the sampling occurred where researchers could find what they were looking for, we gain little sense of the larger economy of crack-cocaine use. The persistent scrutiny of low-income African-Americans in drug studies has left us with wide gaps in our knowledge, suggesting that the intensity with which this population is investigated is symptomatic.

"Culture," "cultural difference," sexuality, or race were not directly named in the study, but substitute forms proliferated. "Setting" stood in for subcultural patterns and in some cases even sexuality. For instance, *Crack Pipe as Pimp* quoted an official from the Centers for Disease Control (CDC): "the crack house of today has become what the gay bathhouse was yesterday with regard to all sexually transmitted diseases."[73] Socially transmitted contagions inhabited places supposedly unknown to "mainstream" (straight, non-crack-using) society. These sites concentrated disease and effectively located individual behavior as its source. This formulation of "setting" signaled that disease transmission is not pervasive but local, not normal but deviant.

Gender appeared in the difference between "crack-using sexual providers," depicted as women beyond control, and "crack-using sexual receivers," who are "men who control resources (especially crack and money)." Women comprised two thirds of the taped respondents because women "provide" sexual services whereas men simply receive them. Women "provide" sexual services more often than men "receive" them.[74] Thus men who "seek" sexual services were rendered passive "recipients," while women actively "provide." There is no sense of extraction or exploitation in this economy—desperation becomes the engine of desire. Men and women alike shared an "inability to set limits on drug use."[75]

Crack Pipe as Pimp took the sociological constructs of gender and the family as the "set" in which personality structures conducive to drug use were formed. The family was but one of many institutions that failed to nurture the future crack addict; it was the originary site for the devaluation of women who became "sexual providers." Early sexual experience took place in the family, often in the form of rape. Women who grew up under these conditions were "deeply ambivalent about traditional female gender roles"—partly because "traditional female gender roles" were not so traditional for them. Caught in the contradictions of their "freedom" and fast-paced lives, they longed for "a future when they would be loving wives and mothers."[76] The studies considered their "desire to be more responsible and effective as mothers" as the the strongest internal deterrent of crack use—thus family therapy was recommended as the only social support for women who are raising children under conditions of severe deprivation.

Men and male sexuality were equally caricatured—men were represented as simple creatures with unambivalent desires. "Men desire sexual services for their own sake and to complement the drug high. But the desire to humiliate and degrade the provider—male or female—was also implicit in many of the actions and openly mentioned by many respondents."[77] The researchers interpreted this desire as compensatory—in crack-for-sex exchanges, men obtained the sense of mastery and control denied them elsewhere. Their violence, fueled by the ever-naturalized construct of "sexual frustration," was the masculine outcome of "backgrounds similar to those of the women offering the services." The "generalized use of violence and intimidation in the inner cities" was intensified within the crack-using subculture. The "generalized violence" and chronic dissatisfaction resulted from "the ubiquitous message in American society that one needs something from outside oneself to feel good."[78] The dynamics of the illicit drug economy, joblessness in the legitimate economy, and increasing poverty still did not appear as forces that propelled the "downward spiral of drug use and degradation."[79]

Like many social ills, crack-cocaine use and its effects were portrayed as trapping drug users in a vicious cycle oscillating between euphoria and self-disgust. Illicit drug use initially appeared as a form of "self-medication" that "allayed feelings of ill ease and lack of self-esteem."[80] The tighter the fit between psychological and pharmacological states, the less room there was for social and economic conditions to enter the text except as contextual background against which the gendered and racially marked figures of female crack addicts emerged. The crack user sprang into high relief against the ground of the family—not the "culture of poverty," a "culture of violence," or even the "larger reign of terror governing inner-city street life" described by Bourgois and Dunlap.[81] *Crack Pipe as Pimp* reduced culture to mere context, foregrounded gendered "personality structures," and located responsibility for drug use fully within the family.

Crack Pipe as Pimp was framed as "agnostic" in terms of treatment approach and policy recommendations. However, the text conformed to NIDA's priorities. Understanding how funding sources shape research programs to align with the governing mentalities is a step toward mapping the complex relations between public policy, social values, and cultural ideals:

Scientific claims and ideas have an influence on public (governmental) policies, on the social values informing policy, on informal policies, and on cultural ideals. By informal policies I mean institutional practices or policies of action that are generally accepted but not legally or administratively articulated or prescribed. . . . Informal policies have their source in social values. . . . By cultural ideals I mean norms of behavior or types of individual behavior accepted as desirable within a culture. . . . While there may be no official sanctions attached to failing to satisfy or to aspire to satisfy such ideals, one runs the danger of en-countering derision and discrimination by such refusal.[82]

"State ethnography," conducted to gain useful knowledge about drug-using be-haviors, produces knowledge about target populations that policy-makers use to develop mechanisms to manage and control them more efficiently. "Contain-ment must be accomplished by behavioral modification," stated one "high-risk ethnographer" who was developing culturally specific strategies "to truly change behavior, not just study it."[83]

In *Drug, Set, and Setting*, Zinberg found that informal social controls were the most effective in controlling drug use so that it exacted minimal social costs. Un-controlled use, on the other hand, was "dysfunctional, intensified, and compul-sive, and therefore has high social costs."[84] Informal controls appeared "naturally in the course of social interaction among drug-takers," and thus could not be im-posed through social policy. In fact, drug policy might have adverse effects on in-formal controls, as Ethel Gore once noted in the Washington, D.C., Daniel hearings. Drug-control polices in the mid-1950s dried up marijuana supplies, and users turned to heroin because they could get it. There are many similar ex-amples of the unintended consequences of drug interdiction. Similarly, Zinberg opposed certain forms of treatment because he equated them with noxious forms of social control over minority groups. Bureaucratic paternalism was not the route to better drug policy, in his view. Over the years, however, his work has been transmuted from a substantive political critique of drug policy to a struc-tural model devoid of political purchase. While the absence of informal social controls was striking to the contributors to *Crack Pipe as Pimp*, this observation did not make them critics of formal social control. Indeed, it made them even more prone to postmodern Progressivism.

Monsters Abound: Women, Crime, and Drugs
Sameness or Difference?

Women's initial experiences, motives, consequences, and experiences of stigma appeared to make little difference in their experience of addiction. One of the first ethnographic reports on crack, *Women and Crack-Cocaine* by James A. Inciardi, Dorothy Lockwood, and Anne E. Pottieger, was written to dispel stereotypes about crack-using women. They presented women's drug experiences as "strik-ingly similar regardless of the drug's legal status or psychopharmacological prop-erties" or demographic differences between women.[85] Drug-using women appeared united across lines of class, race, and age: "Such behavior violates fe-male role expectations so seriously that it can result in social isolation, cultural denigration, and feelings of shame that help to perpetuate the very behavior at issue."[86] Any drug ethnography risks confirming stereotyped expectations of drug users; I suspect that this putative similarity is a defense against criticisms that the work is racist or sexist. The "striking similarity" of women's drug experiences deflects from the variety of drug experiences in the United States, where gendered patterns of use are highly overdetermined by race, ethnicity, class, and geographic and cultural location.

The conceptual practice of reading female drug use as a universal violation of femininity contrasts with the compatibility drawn between masculinity and male drug use. Drug use in men is understood as a risk-taking behavior that falls within culturally appropriate expressions of masculinity—unless and until it becomes extreme. Girls who use drugs are figured as out of control—promiscuous, emotionally disturbed, and psychopathological. Deviant behavior in women is always gender deviance, perennially raising questions about women's gender performance and their moral and psychological fitness for motherhood. Sociologists name this gender difference "male role compatibility" and "female role incompatibility." Drug use certifies proper gender-role performance in men; in women it can "spoil a woman's entire social identity, stigmatizing her as wild, promiscuous, unstable."

Women are localized to "the family" in drug ethnographies. A higher incidence of so-called family problems—violence, child abuse, alcoholism, drug addiction, suicide, mental illness—was identified among female users.[87] *Women and Crack-Cocaine* noted that women use drugs to cope with family situations, life events, and psychological distress that attended women's cultural devaluation—low self-esteem, personal trauma, and serious economic pressures compounded by inadequate training and education and higher rates of unemployment. Women cocaine users also showed "impaired sexual functioning," which men did not.[88] Inciardi and his coauthors questioned whether this impairment derived from women's gender role deviance, the conditions of sex work, the outcome of childhood sexual abuse, or their generalized shame. Women appeared far more complicated than men, making it difficult to separate the effects of drugs from women's other problems, among them complications of pregnancy and fetal damage.[89]

Cocaine was portrayed in scientific and popular literatures as a novel drug with particular appeal to women in the mid- to late 1980s. This feminine preference was not borne out by research findings. Inciardi and his coauthors argued that heroin should appeal to women seeking relief from caretaking, yet no one claimed it was the "perfect trap for women" (a claim widely made about crack-cocaine).[90] Women's cocaine use was seen as more alarming than men's because of old ideas about sexual corruption, newer pressures from women's workforce participation, and anxieties about women taking on male characteristics.[91] Sex-for-crack behavior was truly unique to female crack addicts: "the incredible degradation of women surrounding much of its routine enactment is like nothing ever seen in the annals of drug use, street life, prostitution, or domestic women-battering."[92] "Neither the 'strawberries,' 'skeezers,' 'head hunters,' or 'toss-ups' (the crack 'house girls' who provide oral sex for just a few cents' worth of drugs) nor the crack-house 'freaks' (the 'house girls' who have public sex with other women for similarly small amounts of drugs) have any parallel in either the heroin subculture or that of the old-style brothels."[93]

Under these novel conditions, women were treated as "virtual slaves of the crack house owner, providing sexual services on demand in return for 'room and board'—typically, a mattress, junk food, and ready access to crack."[94] Their "hypersexual behavior," according to Inciardi and his coauthors, had less to do with psychopharmacology than with the cultural expectations and economic arrangements of crack use. Sex-for-crack exchanges were a means to survive a violent and abusive environment.[95] Still, women gave up any semblance of "choice" in their bid for survival: "Women in crack houses resign all control of their bodies and their sexual self-determination to the crack-house owner and customer. Unless they can purchase crack on their own, they are permitted no input into either the fee or the act. What constitutes sex is decided by the customer."[96] Despite their focus on sex-for-crack exchanges, Inciardi and his coauthors included a caveat: "Regardless of whether the hypersexuality of crack is real or imagined, the overwhelming majority of the women encountered in this study were not bartering sex for crack for the sake of sensual pleasure."[97] *Women and Crack-Cocaine* offered a portrait of women's participation in the crack economy that emphasized the similarity of women's victimization in drug-using subcultures while at the same time countering the sexual stereotypes of the mainstream.

Women's Drugs, Women's Crimes

A book on women's drug use would be incomplete without some acknowledgment that illicit drug use is classified as a crime. Paradoxically, the field of criminology paid little attention to women's illicit drug use:

> Even as fields of study, women's drug use and women's crime have a number of striking similarities and interconnections. First, both had extremely small literatures until the early 1970s, when both were given major boosts by the impact of the women's movement on social science research. Second, each has traditionally been conducted as if the other didn't exist. Criminology—whether concerned with studying males or females, adults or adolescents—has been especially prone to ignoring drug use as a topic, and reference to crime in research on female drug users has only rarely been more than a mention."[98]

Guided by "startlingly sexist assumptions and viewpoints," criminology explained women's crimes—shoplifting, prostitution, and promiscuity or "sexual ungovernability"—as the outcome of biology or emotion.

Prior to the 1970s, female addicts served as examples of inadequate personality adaptation, gender deviance, or sexual/social maladjustment in the criminological literature. This literature existed for males, but comprised a smaller proportion of criminological research on addicted men. Sociocultural factors were thought to protect women from "deviance" by making the punishments for nonconformity more severe for them. Sociologists of deviance, who came to prominence in the 1960s, subjected the concept of psychological predisposition to heavy critique.[99] Howard Becker criticized psychological explanations because they did not account for psychologically "normal" users or for the changes over time implied by his "career" model. The shift to "the street" as a research site also rendered certain drug interactions more visible—low-level dealing, relations between men, and streetwalking—but rendered others less so. Current ethnographies do much the opposite, leaving the street for interior spaces and recirculating psychological states and sexual ambivalence as "predispositions" to addiction. The ethnographic shift from the street to the hidden spaces of women's addiction parallels a shift in drug policy—street-level sweeps are no longer common. Instead an obsession with controlling women's sexuality, reproductive capacity, and parenting practices has emerged.

Ethnographic studies reveal a tension between individuality and the claim that these subjects represent whole populations in an empirically robust way. Although Inciardi and coauthors found significant correlation between women's drug involvement and criminal involvement,[100] they concluded that crack did not lure girls into lives of crime.[101] The assumed connection between drugs and crime is elusive, notoriously difficult to understand, and counterintuitive, as Lawrence Kolb showed as early as 1925. On the other hand, the cultural effect of that assumption is concrete, brutally evident in the criminal and juvenile justice systems, and responsible for the incarceration of enormous numbers of nonviolent offenders. Incarceration is a particularly problematic response to women's largely nonviolent involvement in illicit drug use and traffic.

Gender both enables and constrains thought, perception, expression, and action within historically and socially situated limits. Men who use illicit drugs are not constructed as "monsters," for their actions fall within the gendered parameters of masculinity. Women who use drugs were and are constructed as "monsters," especially when they are unwilling or unable to meet "their" responsibilities for social reproduction. *Women and Crack-Cocaine* argued that drug use is overdetermined for some: "Drug abuse is a disorder of the whole person; the problem is the person and not the drug, and addiction is but a symptom and not the essence of the disorder."[102] The disordered person is both cause and cure—the person is the problem, and the problem is "essential" to that person. "What became apparent, as well, was that women had become special victims of crack-cocaine, and that the levels of human suffering within the ranks of women drug users had surpassed those of any previous era of epidemic."[103] Crack appeared exceptionally harmful to women—not because of their activities and responsibilities, but because of their "essential" traits.

Drug use and policy have greater effects on women—not because women are more disordered or essentially troubled,[104] but because of women's social responsibilities. The war on drugs enacts multiple traumas within the lives of our most vulnerable populations, making it more difficult for women to carry out the activities of social reproduction. Nor should the state's role in inscribing its rules on women's bodies be discounted—policies of segregation and exclusion exacerbate the existing tensions in women's lives. Additionally, the monstrous figure of the drug-addicted woman of color bears witness to the micropolitics of everyday oppression.[105] There is little doubt that addicted women are subjugated even if they are "successful" in Fagan's terms and are not constructed as "victims" but as "monsters." They remain caught in a gendered and sexualized scene of degradation that provides a nightmarish countermemory to the feminist political imaginary. Crackworld is a world apart in which drug-using women represent a concrete form of oppression—"the real." At the same time, they are the fantastic "monsters" who abound in our political imaginary.

Feminist ethnography counters the criminological construction of addicted women as disordered persons. Drug-addicted women occupy a place in feminist discourse among the most degraded, exploited, and "used" of women—and the most difficult to defend. Lisa Maher's ethnographic work yields a theoretically nuanced feminist account of how crack-using women are deployed in the formal and informal regulation of motherhood. She argues: "Attempts to define these issues exclusively in terms of the formal legal discourse of regulation and control via the rhetoric of 'rights' encourages individualization and in effect, privatization and the attendant disqualification from public discourse and political agendas. By framing these social issues in terms of individual reproductive rights we not only occlude the social and cultural origins [and the role of the state in defining and reproducing them], but encourage the disparity that results from private solutions."[106] Additionally, "women who use crack are subject to informal regulation and control by virtue of their status as women and mothers."[107] Formal and informal sanctions are differentially applied, and thus a focus on individual reproductive rights will miss this uneven application. In contrast to white and/or middle-class women, poor women of color are more likely to be prosecuted or subjected to administrative sanctions (child removal and loss of custody, loss of eligibility for or reduction of welfare benefits, and subjection through the health care system). Unlike formal sanctions, the administrative and therapeutic axis of state power is not so constrained by due process or procedural safeguards.

Feminists must thus pay attention to multiple political arenas as we take on drug policy. These include the more spectacular cases of draconian punishment; the more pervasive and fully regularized forms of discipline that predominate in drug-using women's lives; and the broadening of campaigns for individual reproductive rights into a movement for social justice. Ethnographic projects contribute to the project of understanding the everyday conditions of drug-using women's lives, including the role of the state's policies and procedures in producing and perpetuating those conditions. They also increase women's vulnerability to subjection and thus present an ethical dilemma that can be offset only by explicit safeguards on women's rights within the bureaucratic-administrative apparatus of government. Additionally, ethnographers' tendency to disclaim policy recommendations, political positions, or normative commitments leaves their work entirely too open to interpretation.

What, then, should feminists committed to a politics of gender and racial justice do to dislodge the power of the governing mentalities? My short answer is to make them explicit—they are less likely to garner consensus when fully spelled out. But the more difficult task is to frame them within a movement for social justice that exposes how the guiding assumptions of policy-making reproduce structural inequality. Our social policies undermine the very autonomy that might give some women a sense of control over their own lives. Ethnographic research has produced ample knowledge about the beneficial effects of political and economic autonomy for women. The current policies of incarceration and many treatment approaches undermine women's attempts to live their own lives. What remains to be addressed is the larger project of articulating a policy direction that upholds women's rights to their own lives.

Conclusion
Postmodern Progressivism

A new drug policy begins in our own hearts.
— *Sher Horosko,* The Drug Policy Foundation Newsletter, *1998*

Coercive Compassion

Illicit drugs cause social problems; licit drugs, it seems, solve them. Illicit drug use signals nonconformity; licit drug use represents compliance with cultural norms. Illicit drug use among women—especially women of color—is a political shorthand by which our culture anxiously encodes notions of social decay and deviance. "The birth of a drug-damaged child is not only a tragedy; it can also be considered a crime against humanity."[1] As I have amply demonstrated, by this calculus, women's crimes outweigh men's. My work began from a sense that public discourse on drugs revealed deeply held governing mentalities about women as political persons.

Whose problem are drug-using women and their hapless babies and children? What is the proper role of government in regulating "demand"? Policy-makers must adjudicate between competing answers to these questions. To do so, they bring to bear their political frames, store of cultural representations, and personal experiences. They construct the drug problem as intractable yet subject to the manipulation of minor adjustments in social services.[2] Some argue that drug epidemics are not Washington's problem. Others take the position that the problem is bigger than us all and argue that the solution rests fundamentally on eradicating ignorance, poverty, and disease. The metaphor of the body politic invokes an immune-system logic in which the nation resists foreign substances to become drug-free. This common metaphor requires an antidote to deter bad behavior but encourage good behavior. Maternal instinct was that antibody in the recent past; its absence was "part of that pattern of the natural defenses breaking down."[3]

Maternal instinct is a naturalized—and naturalizing—assessment of the strength of a woman's character. Some women have "sufficient strength of maternal instinct and sufficient strength of character"; others "simply cannot summon the kind of strength that will be required to voluntarily submit to the rehabilitation that is necessary to get them clean."[4] Mandatory measures are redefined as a project of rehabilitation to take place in the "compassionate State."[5] The redefinition of coercion as compassion is a disciplinary mechanism to which women are highly vulnerable because of their responsibility for social reproduction.[6] The "compassionately coercive" state is a social regime that I call "postmodern Progressivism"—the dream that a salvationist state will strengthen families and stimulate the qualities of productive citizenship.

Drug policy discourse shifts blame to mothers for the effects of policy decisions, social change, and structural phenomena of the late twentieth century. Two policy directions arise from this deflection: expand the public health apparatus and social provision—especially universal access to health care—or continue to punish women for their crimes against humanity. Women addicts and their advocates emphasize the first approach, resting on the idea that women's drug use can be prevented and fetal damage mitigated. This was construed as a special demand on behalf of an undeserving group of disposable persons by Representative Curt Weldon (R-PA), who argued against federal programs for "pregnant women on drugs" because by the time women discover they are pregnant, the "damage has already been done to the fetus."[7] The consignment of the damned to what they deserve is the flip side of the salvationist plot.

Rather than expand social provision, policy-makers urge the citizenry to encourage healthy habits among pregnant women through informal means: "The best thing a pregnant woman can do is to stay healthy while pregnant, to avoid drugs, avoid alcohol, avoid tobacco, and any other substance which will harm her baby. We must do all that we can as Government, as private organizations, and most importantly as individuals to encourage healthy habits among our citizens. I am asking our fellow citizens to help. Anyone who knows a drug or alcohol using pregnant woman has a duty to warn her away from these substances, and if necessary to help her toward treatment. This is especially the responsibility of the baby's father."[8] I am not arguing against "healthy habits" but showing how the emphasis on personal responsibility creates an atmosphere of public surveillance and minimizes public responsibility for structural change and redistributive social policy. Postmodern Progressivism devolves to the individual and attributes too much therapeutic value to the state without expanding social provision. "Coercive compassion," like "compassionate conservatism," is a mode of social regulation that is ultimately more coercive than compassionate.

Because the form of drug use that our society has judged socially problematic is an effect of the converging structures of social subordination, political exclusion, and economic inequality, structural changes in labor practices, redistributive social policies, and support for women's autonomy would go far toward reducing women's addiction and its associated harms.[9] The postmodern state structures the constraints within which we live, but the polity decides where those constraints will be placed and whom they will affect. For women—yet to achieve privacy rights, equal protection, economic parity, or the constitutional guarantees to bodily integrity that men can assume—postmodern Progressivism leads to increased social vulnerability. The women whose very existence "violates" the normalizing projects of the therapeutic state will feel the most scrutiny and constraint. White, middle-class, heterosexual women will largely escape notice, while women of color and poor women live subject to postmodern Progressivism. The cycles of scrutiny I traced through this book are the product of our governing mentalities. Changing them is our responsibility, and a project that I hope this book inspires feminists to take up. The question remains. Who will have access to the processes of democratic governance when the conditions of possibility for a policy "lurch" next come around?

Reinventing a Feminist Political Imaginary

Feminist theory is a critical practice that can dislodge unthinking adherence to the governing mentalities and self-evident patterns of thought, perception, and practice. It returns to a set of normative commitments based on the recognition of social inequality, economic dislocation, and political exclusion. The state became a focus for feminists because of its ambivalent role in social provision and the installation of inequality. What, then, is the place of the state—which disciplines, punishes, and "protects" in the same breath—in feminist projects of freedom? Can women's claims for political autonomy, bodily integrity, and full participation in the polity be realized if "gender difference" is recognized? Can we keep "policy" within our sights without fetishizing the state or its powers? The case of illicit drug policy suggests that we can and indeed must engage the state but be wary of how our own governing mentalities and those of others converge with the regulatory agenda of postmodern Progressivism.

Where do rights reside? Do rights attach to the body, the political category of the person, or the performance of a particular social identity? Do they arise from the discharge of duty? Should they be conditioned on meeting obligations? Or are rights the basis on which relationships of obligation are built and sustained? How do rights structure relationships and institutions? Can strategic constructions of rights be used to claim entitlements and elicit reciprocity where none has existed? Finally, what are feminists to do when confronted by the governing mentalities of actors within state institutions?

Using Women answers this cascade of questions by considering the type of threat that drug-addicted women pose to social reproduction. "The family" plays a large role in policy-makers' vision of what civil society ought to be and do, for moral values transmitted by the family supposedly "inoculate" against desire for drugs. Drugs undermine the edifice of values, collapsing family structure and engendering a state of entropy in which "there is no basis in the organism for improvement because . . . there's nothing to build on."[10] As one witness put it, "people who sense an opportunity for their future . . . have a much better likelihood of taking care of themselves and taking care of their children and *doing all the things we want them to do.*"[11] Policy-makers want women to absorb the costs of social reproduction—without commitment of social resources. The fundamental policy problem is how to change individual behavior without changing anything else.

Policies designed to privatize the social context of reproduction tie women's rights to their "proper" discharge of duty, effectively contain the feminist critique of heterosexual normativity, the gendered division of labor, women's lack of political autonomy, and gendered forms of economic insecurity. What is at stake, I have argued, is women's responsibility for social reproduction—despite the lack of support for women's full participation in social life that a more mutual and reciprocal relationship between rights and obligations entails. "Mothers on drugs" conjure up the specter that rights-bearing women will refuse to act as "women."

Rights-talk cannot fully capture all values, meanings, and experiences significant in the political imaginary of a given moment.[12] There is an "agonistics" to rights-talk: "universal" rights are never truly so, but partial rights can never be enough. The false antithesis between women's rights as persons and their maternal duties is even more serious and consequential. The language of individual rights can contest exclusion and denial, but may backfire—rights-talk positions "good" women against "bad" women because it individualizes both problem and solution. A discourse of social justice more effectively contests the distribution of duty, obligation, and participation in public matters without devolving to the reductive form of rights. The state is limited as an agent of social change, and to appeal to the state as the ultimate arbiter of rights gives too much power over to it.

Some women encounter the punitive reach of the criminal justice system; others find themselves in the therapeutic arms of child welfare and social services (which are predicated on disciplinary norms that subject women to myriad forms of social control but appear relatively benign in contrast to criminal justice). The state promises to ensure "good" citizens against risk and vulnerability.[13] Feminists often counterpoise the "good," therapeutic state to the bad state that incarcerates and withholds treatment. This buys into postmodern Progressivism, and I hope to make feminists more wary of its pitfalls for women. If the state conditions rights on women's behavior as women, broad social entitlements, such as a real right to privacy or the recognition that social reproduction is a shared responsibility, will never come about.

State-centered modes of feminist activism and policy studies paradoxically unfolded in the midst of an academic and activist critique of liberal feminism.[14] Feminist theorists eschewed policy recommendations that smacked of overidentification with the state or reproduced "statist discourse."[15] Others implied that feminists were political wimps, suggesting that fear prevented us from developing a politics appropriate to our historical moment.[16] My thinking assumes that the governing mentalities inhabit us all to varying degrees—we both collude and collide with the state. Feminists should resist the charms of the state in its postmodern Progressive mode but not give up on state-centered organizing. Such organizing always takes place, however, to get the state to act on behalf of (some) women—thus the most socially vulnerable women should be prioritized in ways that do not call for heightened discipline and greater intervention. Women's autonomy should be the priority. This position flies in the face of the panic over female-headed households and skewed sex ratios, but will ultimately yield a population that is "self-governing."

Awareness of the discursive nature of the gendered state can only bolster feminist strategy—that is not a reformist position so much as a pragmatic one. Women's policy research and advocacy organizations deployed "insider" tactics to respond to the backlash of the 1980s, becoming sophisticated users of the "language of liberal individualism" to prevent further marginalization: "Most of the organizations that did survive the 1980s maintained their credibility while keeping feminist claims—for women's economic rights, overcoming violence and sexual assault against women, abortion rights, civil rights, and political empowerment—on the policy agenda, albeit not always in their purest form."[17] Yet women who conform to prevailing notions of gender formation, self-discipline, and right conduct are still awarded citizenship rights; women who do not, find their fundamental rights threatened. Drug-using women embody a threat that must be contained within political discourse—and some women's lives are still held hostage to that threat.

Introduction

1. In 1964 Congress addressed the "menace of pep pills" but declined to examine the decreasing availability of meaningful labor, Cold War anxieties, increased mobility, and amplified stress that contributed to their use. See U.S. Senate. Committee on Labor and Public Welfare. Subcommittee on Health. *Control of Psychotoxic Drugs.* 88th Cong., 2d sess., 3 August 1964.

2. Christopher S. Wren, "The Illegal Home Business: 'Speed' Manufacture," *New York Times,* July 8, 1997, A8. Former user Bruce Fowler was quoted as saying: "Meth just makes you want to go. You go out to mow the lawn and end up manicuring it."

3. Carey Goldberg, "Way Out West and Under the Influence," *New York Times,* March 16, 1997, E16. Quotation attributed to Michael Gorman, University of Washington.

4. Milton C. Regan, Jr., *Family Law and the Pursuit of Intimacy* (New York: New York University Press, 1993) contrasts the modernist "acontextual self" to the postmodern "relational self."

5. See Nancy Folbre, *Who Pays for the Kids? Gender and the Structures of Constraint* (New York: Routledge, 1994). Women's disproportionate share of the work of social reproduction is an effect of structural forms of power that represent the collective interests of men. Folbre identifies them as "structures of constraint." I employ the shorthand "structure" throughout the book.

6. U.S. Congress. House Select Committee on Children, Youth, and Families. *Law and Policy Affecting Addicted Women and Their Children.* 101st Cong., 2d sess., 17 May 1990, 22. These are direct quotes of Senator Pete Wilson (R-CA).

7. House Select Committee. *Law and Policy Affecting Addicted Women,* 21–22.

8. "Women in Prison: Some Facts and Figures" (Washington, DC: National Women's Law Center, 1996).

9. Nearly half of women were incarcerated for violent offenses in 1979. That proportion has fallen to less than one third. See Bureau of Justice Statistics 1988 and 1994 quoted in Meda Chesney-Lind, "Sentencing Women to Prison: Equality without Justice," in *Race, Gender, and Class in Criminology,* eds. Martin D. Schwartz and Dragan Milovanovic (New York: Garland Publishing, 1996), 130.

10. Ilene H. Nagel and Barry L. Johnson, "The Role of Gender in a Structured Sentencing System,"

The Journal of Criminal Law and Criminology 85, no. 1 (1994): 216.

11. Chesney-Lind, "Sentencing Women," *Race, Gender, and Class in Criminology,* 130.

12. Most incarcerated women "face the potential if not actual loss of their children"; male prisoners report that others are caring for their children. See Chesney-Lind, "Sentencing Women," *Race, Gender, and Class in Criminology,* 130.

13. In 1984 drug offenders served an average sentence of 27 months; under "neutral" sentencing guidelines, the average sentence lengthened to 67 months.

14. Karen J. Swift, *Manufacturing "Bad Mothers": Critical Perspectives on Child Neglect* (Buffalo, NY: University of Toronto Press, 1995), 122.

15. What counts as truth changes over time, depending on the knowledge-production practices of the moment. The sociology of knowledge provides a useful perspective, as do historical and cultural studies of law, science, and medicine.

16. Critical legal studies, critical race theory, and critical race feminism emphasize the narrative power and political scripting of law. See Thomas J. Kaplan's essay in *The Argumentative Turn in Policy Analysis and Planning,* eds. Frank Fischer and John Forester (Durham, NC: Duke University Press, 1993). Kaplan asserts that each element of narrative analysis—agent, act, scene, agency, and purpose—can be connected to achieve a level of coherence and thus establish truth (178). He fails to see that "what counts as truth" emerges from social interaction.

17. Not all cultures consider addiction permanent or transformative. See Marilyn Strathern, "Relations without Substance," in Lamont Lindstrom, ed., *Drugs in Western Pacific Societies: Relations of Substance* (Lanham, MD: University Press of America, 1987), 231–254.

18. See Philippe Bourgois and Eloise Dunlap, "Exorcising Sex for Crack: An Ethnographic Perspective from Harlem," in *Crack Pipe as Pimp: An Ethnographic Investigation of Sex-for-Crack Exchanges,* ed. Mitchell S. Ratner (New York: Lexington Books, 1993), 129.

19. The "culture of no culture" is Donna Haraway's summary of Sharon Traweek, *Beamtimes and Lifetimes: The World of High Energy Physicists* (Cambridge, MA: Harvard University Press, 1988).

20. Eva Bertram, Morris Blackman, Kenneth Sharpe, and Peter Andreas, *Drug War Politics: The Price of Denial* (Berkeley, CA: University of California Press, 1996), 56.

21. See Frank R. Baumgartner and Bryan D. Jones, *Agendas and Instability in American Politics* (Chicago: University of Chicago Press, 1993).
22. Mary E. Hawkesworth, *Theoretical Issues in Policy Analysis* (Albany, NY: SUNY Press, 1988); Adrian Howe, *Punish and Critique* (New York: Routledge, 1994); Sanford Schram, *Words of Welfare* (Minneapolis, MN: University of Minnesota Press, 1995); Dorothy E. Smith, *Texts, Facts, and Femininity: Exploring the Relations of Ruling* (New York: Routledge, 1990); Deborah Stone, *Policy Paradox and Political Reason* (Glenview, IL: Scott, Foresman, and Company, 1988).
23. Catherine S. Marshall, ed. *Feminist Critical Policy Analysis.* (Washington, DC: The Falmer Press, 1997).
24. Emery Roe, *Narrative Policy Analysis* (Durham, NC: Duke University Press, 1994), 2.
25. See Michel Foucault, "Theatrum Philosophicum," in *Language, Counter-Memory, Practice*, trans. Donald F. Bouchard (Ithaca, NY: Cornell University Press, 1977), 169–170. The phantasm is not a mere sign but an "incorporeal materiality": Phantasms must be allowed to function at the limit of bodies; against bodies, because they stick to bodies and protrude from them, but also because they touch them, and multiply their surfaces; and equally, outside of bodies, because they function between bodies according to laws of proximity, torsion, and variable distance—laws of which they remain ignorant. Phantasms do not extend organisms into an imaginary domain; they topologize the materiality of the body.
26. Foucault, "Theatrum Philosophicum," *Language, Counter-Memory, Practice*, 177.
27. Drug prohibition worked better than alcohol prohibition because the law-abiding professionals who regulated narcotics wanted to maintain their social authority. See Joseph F. Spillane, "Doctors and Drug Laws: Defining 'Legitimate' Sale and Use," paper presented at the National Policy History conference, Bowling Green State University, Bowling Green, Ohio, June 5–7, 1997.
28. Michael Omi and Howard Winant, *Racial Formation in the United States: From the 1960s to the 1980s* (New York: Routledge and Kegan Paul, 1986), 57. Racialization is a cultural process by which racial meanings are extended to previously "unclassified" relations and social practices.
29. Bertram et al., *Drug War Politics*; Craig Reinarman and Harry G. Levine, *Crack in America: Demon Drugs and Social Justice* (Berkeley, CA: University of California Press, 1997). Feminist organizations and the ACLU deterred most policy-makers from punitive measures in the maternal crack-cocaine crisis of the early 1990s. As Laura E. Gomez documents in *Misconceiving Mothers: Legislators, Prosecutors, and the Politics of Prenatal Drug Exposure* (Philadelphia, PA: Temple University Press, 1997), feminists recast

maternal drug use from a narrow issue to one that implicated all women. This political redefinition was as much a reframing of drug discourse as a series of policy arguments.

The Politics of Women's Addiction and Women's Equality

1. The National Center on Addiction and Substance Abuse (CASA), *Substance Abuse and the American Woman* (New York: The National Center on Addiction and Substance Abuse at Columbia University, June 1996). Funded by Bristol-Meyers Squibb Foundation and the Pew Charitable Trusts.
2. Elliott Currie, *Reckoning: Drugs, the Cities, and the American Future* (New York: Hill and Wang, 1993), 100–103.
3. This explanation preceded the 1967 Moynihan Report. The family dysfunction model derived from Talcott Parson's views on gender roles in the nuclear family, in which fathers contributed the dominant values of "structure" and discipline, while mothers were responsible for the subordinate emotional or "expressive" domain.
4. This is the central protagonist in feminist political theorist Wendy Brown's "unlivable world, a world without basis for connection or bonding, and a world without security for the needy and dependent." See Wendy Brown, *States of Injury: Power and Freedom in Late Modernity* (Princeton, NJ: Princeton University Press, 1995), 158–160.
5. Bruce Bullington and Alan Block, "A Trojan Horse: Anti-Communism and the War on Drugs," *Contemporary Crises: Law, Crime, and Social Policy* 14, no. 1 (1990): 39–55; Peter Lupsha, "Towards an Etiology of Drug Trafficking and Insurgent Relations: The Phenomenon of Narco-Terrorism," *International Journal of Comparative and Applied Criminal Justice* 13, no. 2 (1989): 61–75; U.S. Senate. Committee on Labor and Human Resources. Subcommittee on Alcoholism and Drug Abuse. *Drugs and Terrorism.* 98th Cong., 2d sess, 1984.
6. David Campbell, *Writing Security: U.S. Foreign Policy and the Politics of Identity* (Minneapolis: University of Minnesota Press, 1992).
7. See Frank R. Baumgartner and Bryan D. Jones, *Agendas and Instability in American Politics,* (Chicago: University of Chicago Press, 1993), 150. Their influential model of agenda-setting proposes that policy "solutions" float in political space until they are connected to "uniformly agreed-upon problems."
8. Baumgartner and Jones, *Agendas and Instability in American Politics,* 151.
9. See Peter Reuter, "Hawks Ascendant: The Punitive Trend of American Drug Policy," in *Drug Use*

and Drug Policy, eds. Marilyn McShane and Frank P. Williams (New York: Garland, 1997), 365. Reuter argues for a three-way discussion modeled on the images of hawks, doves, and owls drawn in U.S. foreign policy debates.

10. The "market model" dangerously oversimplifies, according to Eva Bertram, Morris Blackman, Kenneth Sharpe, *Drug War Politics* (Berkeley, CA: University of California Press, 1996), 30–31. They identify three flaws in antidrug strategy: (1) the profit paradox, in which drug policy raises consumer prices but grossly inflates traffickers' profits; (2) the hydra effect, in which new production and distribution routes open in the wake of "successful" interdiction; and (3) the war against consumer demand, which punishes but does not affect the social context in which drug use occurs. Although I concentrate on demand reduction, "supply-side" policies also harm communities and negatively impact women (who serve in the lowest levels of the drug trade as agrarian producers, "mules," or "swallowers").

11. Bertram et al., *Drug War Politics*; Michael Tonry and James Q. Wilson, eds., *Drugs and Crime* (Washington, DC: National Institute of Justice, 1990); Franklin E. Zimring and Gordon Hawkins, *The Search for Rational Drug Control* (New York: Cambridge University Press, 1992).

12. Baumgartner and Jones, *Agendas and Instability*, 161.

13. U.S. Congress. House Select Committee on Children, Youth, and Families. *Born Hooked: Confronting the Impact of Perinatal Substance Abuse.* 101st Cong., 1st sess., 27 April 1989, 150.

14. P. A. O'Hare, R. Newcombe, A. Matthews, Ernst R. Buning, and Ernest Drucker, eds., *The Reduction of Drug-Related Harm* (New York: Routledge, 1992).

15. Nancy E. Stoller, *Lessons from the Damned: Queers, Whores, and Junkies Respond to AIDS* (New York: Routledge, 1998), 98, 105.

16. Sheigla Murphy and Marsha Rosenbaum, *Pregnant Women on Drugs* (New Brunswick, NJ: Rutgers University Press, 1999); Marsha Rosenbaum, *Women on Heroin* (New Brunswick, NJ: Rutgers University Press, 1981).

17. Cynthia R. Daniels, *At Women's Expense: State Power and the Politics of Fetal Rights* (Cambridge, MA: Harvard University Press, 1993); Laura E. Gomez, *Misconceiving Mothers: Legislators, Prosecutors, and the Politics of Prenatal Drug Exposure* (Philadelphia, PA: Temple University Press, 1997); Dorothy Roberts, *Killing the Black Body: Race, Reproduction, and the Meaning of Liberty* (New York: Pantheon Books, 1997).

18. Gomez, *Misconceiving Mothers*, 121.

19. Peter Reuter, "Hawks Ascendant," *Drug Use and Drug Policy*, 393.

20. For a clear summary, see *The Drug Policy Letter* (Washington, DC: The Drug Policy Forum, January/February 1999), 6–7.

Chapter 1

1. John Bowersox, "Cocaine Affects Men and Women Differently," *NIDA Notes* 11, no. 1 (1996). At http://www.nida.nih.gov/NIDA_Notes/NNVol 11N1/CocaineGender.html.

2. Donna Haraway, *Simians, Cyborgs, and Women* (New York: Routledge, 1991), and *Modest_Witness@Second_Millennium.FemaleMan_Meets_OncoMouse: Feminism and Technoscience* (New York: Routledge, 1997); Sandra Harding, *The Science Question in Feminism* (Ithaca, NY: Cornell University Press, 1986) and *Whose Science? Whose Knowledge?* (Ithaca, NY: Cornell University Press, 1991); Helen Longino, *Science as Social Knowledge* (Princeton, NJ: Princeton University Press, 1990); E. Doyle McCarthy, *Knowledge as Culture: The New Sociology of Knowledge* (New York: Routledge, 1996).

3. Cora Lee Wetherington, quoted in Bowersox, "Cocaine Affects Men," *NIDA Notes*, 2.

4. NIDA, a U.S. government agency, funds approximately 85 percent of the world's addiction research. Its preoccupations are consequential for the type of research that takes place.

5. The text presents a highly condensed version of claims about the truths and consequences of women's addiction, as it synthesizes 1,700 articles on the topic.

6. Dorothy E. Smith understands "textually mediated social organization" as an essential form of the "relations of ruling" in the late twentieth century. See Dorothy E. Smith, *Texts, Facts, and Femininity: Exploring the Relations of Ruling* (New York: Routledge, 1990), 212. The social organization of knowledge and decision-making that circulates in and through formal organizations exceed individual intent.

7. Only one CASA staff member, medical director Herbert D. Kleber, has tenure at Columbia. In 1989 erstwhile drug czar William J. Bennett lured Kleber from the Yale University psychiatry department to Washington, D.C., where he served as deputy director for demand reduction in the Office of National Drug Control Policy. He then went to CASA.

8. William N. Elwood, *Rhetoric in the War on Drugs: The Triumphs and Tragedies of Public Relations* (Westport, CT: Praeger, 1994), 143.

9. The National Center on Addiction and Substance Abuse (CASA), *Substance Abuse and the American Woman* (New York: The National Center on Addiction and Substance Abuse at Columbia University, June 1996), 3.

10. CASA, *Substance Abuse and the American Woman*, 2.

11. Elizabeth Ettore, *Women and Substance Abuse* (New Brunswick, NJ: Rutgers University Press, 1992); Marsha Rosenbaum, *Women on Heroin* (New Brunswick, NJ: Rutgers University Press, 1981).

12. CASA, *Substance Abuse and the American Woman,* 142.

13. CASA, *Substance Abuse and the American Woman,* 3.

14. CASA, *Substance Abuse and the American Woman,* 4.

15. CASA, *Substance Abuse and the American Woman,* 5.

16. CASA, *Substance Abuse and the American Woman,* 10.

17. CASA, *Substance Abuse and the American Woman,* 42.

18. CASA, *Substance Abuse and the American Woman,* 43.

19. CASA, *Substance Abuse and the American Woman,* 44.

20. CASA, *Substance Abuse and the American Woman,* 136.

21. CASA, *Substance Abuse and the American Woman,* 136.

22. CASA, *Substance Abuse and the American Woman,* 8.

23. CASA, *Substance Abuse and the American Woman,* 75.

24. See Dorothy C. Holland and Margaret A. Eisen-hart, *Educated in Romance: Women, Achievement, and College Culture* (Chicago: University of Chicago Press, 1990).

25. See William F. Skinner, "The Prevalence and Demographic Predictors of Illicit and Licit Drug Use among Lesbians and Gay Men," *American Journal of Public Health* 84, no. 8 (August 1994): 1307–1310.

26. CASA, *Substance Abuse and the American Woman,* 17.

27. CASA, *Substance Abuse and the American Woman,* 5, 68.

28. "Pharmacological omnipotence" displaces the social context in which drug use takes place. Drugs exercise physiological effects; such effects are really felt, but differences in the social context of use modulate our interpretations of them.

29. CASA, *Substance Abuse and the American Woman,* 1–2.

30. CASA, *Substance Abuse and the American Woman,* 1–2.

31. CASA, *Substance Abuse and the American Woman,* 136.

32. CASA, *Substance Abuse and the American Woman,* 95.

33. Peter D. Kramer, *Listening to Prozac* (New York: Penguin Books, 1993), 64.

34. CASA, *Substance Abuse and the American Woman,* 89.

35. Deborah Stone, *Policy Paradox and Political Reason* (Glenview, IL: Scott, Foresman, and Company, 1988), 156. Stone sees risk as a means by which policy-makers assign responsibility for problems and empower agents to "fix" them.

36. Robert Castel, "From Dangerousness to Risk," in *The Foucault Effect: Studies in Governmentality,* eds. Graham Burchell, Colin Gordon, and Peter Miller (Chicago: University Of Chicago Press, 1991), 289.

37. Castel, "From Dangerousness to Risk," *The Foucault Effect,* 288.

38. CASA, *Substance Abuse and the American Woman,* 39–40.

39. CASA, *Substance Abuse and the American Woman,* 67.

40. Bridget F. Grant and Deborah A. Dawson, "Alcohol and Drug Use, Abuse, and Dependence among Welfare Recipients," *American Journal of Public Health* 86, no. 10 (1996): 1450–1454. The study's goal was to identify high-risk subgroups of the welfare population. Alcohol use/abuse was more prevalent among men; no statistically significant sex differences were found for drug use/abuse; and no statistically significant racial differences were found for either alcohol or drug use/abuse among the population receiving AFDC, WIC, food stamps, SSI, and Medicaid.

41. This racially selective metaphor does not reflect the historical experience of women of color, whose presence in the labor force has been strong over time.

42. CASA, *Substance Abuse and the American Woman,* 17.

43. CASA, *Substance Abuse and the American Woman,* 6.

44. See Elizabeth Ettore and Elianne Riska, *Gendered Moods: Psychotropics and Society* (New York: Routledge, 1995).

45. See Leonard S. Brahen, "Housewife Drug Abuse," *Journal of Drug Education* 3, no.1 (1973): 13–24; and C. D. Chambers and D. Schultz, "Housewives and the Drug Habit," *Ladies' Home Journal,* December 1971, 66–70.

46. Maureen McCarthy, "The Female Drug Addict and Her Feminine Mystique," *Psychiatric Opinion* 9 (1972): 30–35. Mature female identity "means enlightened acceptance of the essentially female core," and a recognition that women are "distinctly different creature[s who] evade interpretation or analytical definitiveness" (31).

47. McCarthy, "The Female Drug Addict," *Psychiatric Opinion,* 31.

48. CASA, *Substance Abuse and the American Woman,* 19.

49. CASA, *Substance Abuse and the American Woman,* 58.

50. CASA, *Substance Abuse and the American Woman,* 19.

51. CASA, *Substance Abuse and the American Woman,* 20.

52. CASA, *Substance Abuse and the American Woman,* 97–98.

53. CASA, *Substance Abuse and the American Woman,* 11.

54. CASA, *Substance Abuse and the American Woman,* 21.

55. CASA, *Substance Abuse and the American Woman,* 12.

56. CASA, *Substance Abuse and the American Woman,* 12.

57. CASA, *Substance Abuse and the American Woman,* 12.

58. Ira J. Chasnoff, "The Prevalence of Illicit-Drug or Alcohol Use During Pregnancy and Discrepancies in Mandatory Reporting in Pinellas County, Florida," *New England Journal of Medicine* 322, no. 17 (April 26, 1990): 1202–1206. This oft-quoted study found health care professionals ten times as likely to test women of color than white women. The fiction that "mandatory" reporting laws are evenly applied parallels the fiction that "mandatory" sentences are fair.

59. CASA, *Substance Abuse and the American Woman,* 14.

60. CASA, *Substance Abuse and the American Woman,* 14.

61. CASA, *Substance Abuse and the American Woman,* 52.

62. CASA, *Substance Abuse and the American Woman,* 52.

63. CASA, *Substance Abuse and the American Woman,* 52.

64. CASA, *Substance Abuse and the American Woman,* 123.

65. The message was similar in Muriel Nellis's popular book, *The Female Fix* (Boston: Houghton Mifflin, 1980), in which women's addiction resulted from lack of preparation for motherhood. Nellis depicted mothering as a "combat zone of self-definition" that tore women between traditional and nontraditional roles and resulted in stress and drug abuse. Women's stress originated in struggles over self-definition, a "deeply felt need for support," and the search for approval (32). For men, stress was "related to jobs, careers, economic advancement, and other tangible dilemmas" (53).

66. *The Chemically Dependent Woman,* proceedings of a conference at the Dogwood Institute (Toronto: Addiction Research Foundation, 1977), 7.

67. CASA, *Substance Abuse and the American Woman,* 130.

Chapter 2

1. Throughout this book, "we" signals membership in a polity that includes both citizens and noncitizens affected by U.S. public policy. While individuals may dissent from the governing mentalities, my argument is based on a politics of shared responsibility for social reproduction that requires acknowledging "our" mutual membership in the polity.

2. Michael J. Shapiro, *Language and Political Understanding: The Politics of Discursive Practices* (New Haven, CT: Yale University Press, 1981), 124. Foucault's concept of discursive practice gets at the "things and activities that we speak of, . . . the rules which prescribe distinctions we make, distinctions that reside in our language in general and speech practices in particular, . . . the commitments to meanings that we make [which] have the effect of allocating power, authority, and legitimacy."

3. Hayden White, *Tropics of Discourse* (Baltimore, MD: Johns Hopkins University Press, 1978), 2.

4. Kathleen Jones, *Compassionate Authority: Democracy and the Representation of Women* (New York: Routledge, 1993), 10.

5. Jones, *Compassionate Authority,* 10.

6. Donna Haraway, *Modest_Witness@Second_Millennium.FemaleMan_Meets_OncoMouse: Feminism and Technoscience* (New York: Routledge, 1997), 11.

7. Haraway, *Modest_Witness,* 41–42.

8. Haraway, *Modest_Witness,* 23. Haraway's notion of "situatedness" emphasizes multiple literacies and hybrid constructs: "I learned early that the imaginary and the real figure each other in concrete fact, and so I take the actual and the figural seriously as constitutive of lived material-semiotic worlds" (2).

9. See *The Anthropology of Policy,* eds. Chris Shore and Susan Wright (New York: Routledge, 1997), 4–6; Foucault, "Technologies of the Self" and "The Political Technology of Individuals" in *Technologies of the Self,* eds. Luther H. Martin, Huck Gutman, and Patrick H. Hutton (Amherst, MA: University of Massachusetts Press, 1988); and Foucault's essays on "governmentality" in *The Foucault Effect,* eds. Graham Burchell, Colin Gordon, and Peter Miller (Chicago: University of Chicago Press, 1991).

10. See Dorothy E. Smith, *The Conceptual Practices of Power: A Feminist Sociology of Knowledge* (Boston, MA: Northeastern University Press, 1990), 66. If the "relations of ruling" are a set of discursive and material relationships, the "governing mentalities" are the discursive imperatives that drive "rulers" and inhabit the "ruled."

11. Mary E. Hawkesworth, *Theoretical Issues in Policy Analysis* (Albany, NY: SUNY Press, 1988), 61–62. By accepting the intertwinement of "fact" and "value," normative policy analysts produce good reasons to adopt proposed policies that may include compatibility between value commitments and policy decisions.

12. John S. Dryzek, *Discursive Democracy: Politics, Policy, and Political Science* (New York: Cambridge University Press, 1990); Frank Fischer and John Forester, *The Argumentative Turn in Policy Analysis and Planning* (Durham, NC: Duke University Press, 1993); Emery Roe, *Narrative Policy Analysis* (Durham, NC: Duke University Press, 1994).

13. Hawkesworth, *Theoretical Issues.*

14. Sandra Harding, *Whose Science? Whose Knowledge?* (Ithaca, NY: Cornell University Press, 1991).

15. Fischer and Forester, *The Argumentative Turn,* 37.

16. Monica J. Casper, *The Making of the Unborn Patient* (New Brunswick, NJ: Rutgers University Press, 1998); George L. Dillon, *Contending Rhetorics* (Bloomington, IN: Indiana University Press, 1991); Nigel Gilbert and Michael Mulkay, *Opening Pandora's Box: A Sociological Analysis of Scientists' Discourse* (Cambridge: Cambridge University Press, 1983); Joseph Gusfield, *The Culture of Public Problems* (Chicago: University of Chicago Press, 1981); Haraway, "Situated Knowledges" in *Simians, Cyborgs, and Women* (New York: Routledge, 1991) and *Modest_Witness*; Harding, *Whose Science? Whose Knowledge?*; Helen Longino, *Science as Social Knowledge* (Princeton, NJ: Princeton University Press, 1990); John S. Nelson, Allan Megill, and Donald M. McCloskey, *The Rhetoric of the Human Sciences* (Madison, WI: University of Wisconsin Press, 1987).

17. Arthur Frank, *The Wounded Storyteller: Body, Illness, and Ethics* (Chicago: University of Chicago Press, 1995), 146.

18. See Catherine S. Marshall, ed., *Feminist Critical Policy Analysis I* (Washington, DC: The Falmer Press, 1997), which "dismantles and reconstructs" policy analysis in these terms.

19. Hawkesworth, *Theoretical Issues*, 191.

20. I borrow the idea of "confabulation" from Deborah Stone, *Policy Paradox and Political Reason* (Glenview, IL: Scott, Foresman, and Company, 1988), especially Chapter 7.

21. M. Dicker and E. A. Leighton, "Trends in Diagnosing Drug Problems among Newborns," *Drug and Alcohol Dependence* 28, no. 2 (1991): 151–165.

22. Dicker and Leighton, "Trends in Diagnosing Drug Problems," *Drug and Alcohol Dependence*; H. Hurt et al., "Cocaine-Exposed Children: Follow-Up through 30 months," *Journal of Developmental and Behavioral Pediatrics* 16, no. 1 (1995): 29–35; Cora Wetherington, Vincent Smeriglio, and Loretta Finnegan, "Behavioral Studies of Drug-Exposed Offspring: Methodological Issues in Human and Animal Research," *NIDA Research Monograph* 164 (Rockville, MD: NIDA, 1996).

23. Quoted in Gretchen Vogel, "Cocaine Wreaks Subtle Damage on Developing Brains," *Science* 278, no. 5335 (October 3, 1997), 38.

24. There are many critiques of the model. Mitchell Dean, in *The Constitution of Poverty* (New York: Routledge, 1991), examines the economic roots of Darwinism in relation to British poor laws; Nancy Folbre, *Who Pays for the Kids?: Gender and the Structure of Constraint* (New York: Routledge, 1994) examines the inapplicability of the masculine figure of *Homo economicus* to women's situation; and Hawkesworth notes convergence between applied pluralist and systems analytic approaches on this historically

specific individual whom policy-makers seek to affect in *Theoretical Issues*, 24–25.

25. Douglas J. Besharov, ed., *When Drug Addicts Have Children: Reorienting Child Welfare's Response* (Washington, DC: Child Welfare League of America/American Enterprise Institute, 1994).

26. Rather than falsely divide structure and agency, Anthony Giddens suggests that structural principles and institutions guide individual action: "All social interaction is expressed at some point in and through the contextualities of bodily presence." See Philip Cassell, ed., *The Giddens Reader* (Stanford, CA: Stanford University Press, 1993), 165. For instance, the discourse of liberal individualism and personal responsibility bridges the gap between the Democratic and Republican parties. Overemphasizing structure—as Democrats are wont to do—hides how individuals negotiate structures. This is as much an analytical and political error as the fetishization of individual agency of the Republican Party, which obscures structure. The product of this ideological convergence is the emphasis on changing individual behavior but retaining existing structures of power.

27. Stone, *Policy Paradox*, 81.

28. U.S. Congress. Senate. Subcommittee on Children, Family, Drugs, and Alcoholism of the Committee on Labor and Human Resources. *Adolescent Substance Abuse: Barriers to Treatment.* 101st Cong., 1st sess., 2 May 1989.

29. Senate Subcommittee. *Adolescent Substance Abuse*, 72. The model consists of interventions to break down "resistance to change," reestablish parental control, interrupt "dysfunctional behavioral sequences and patterns," and provide assertion skills. See Terry S. Trepper, Fred P. Piercy, Robert A. Lewis, Robert J. Volk, Douglas H. Sprenkle, "Family Therapy for Adolescent Alcohol Abuse" in *Treating Alcohol Problems: Marital and Family Interventions,* ed. Timothy J. O'Farrell (New York: Guilford Press, 1993), 261–278.

30. Senate Subcommittee. *Adolescent Substance Abuse*, 73.

31. Senate Subcommittee. *Adolescent Substance Abuse*, 6.

32. Senate Subcommittee. *Adolescent Substance Abuse*, 66.

33. U.S. Congress. Senate. Committee on Labor and Human Resources. *Role of Treatment and Prevention in the National Drug Strategy.* 101st Cong., 2d sess., 24 April 1990.

34. Senate Committee. *Role of Treatment and Prevention*, 6.

35. Senate Committee. *Role of Treatment and Prevention*, 4.

36. Senate Committee. *Role of Treatment and Prevention*, 6.

37. Senate Subcommittee. *Adolescent Substance Abuse*, 62.

38. Senate Committee. *Role of Treatment and Prevention*, 1.

39. Senate Committee. *Role of Treatment and Prevention*, 2.

40. Senate Committee. *Role of Treatment and Prevention*, 2.

41. Douglas J. Besharov, "The Children of Crack," *Public Welfare* 54, no. 1 (1996): 32–38; Besharov, *When Drug Addicts Have Children*, 1994.

42. Elliott Currie, *Reckoning: Drugs, the Cities, and the American Future* (New York: Hill and Wang, 1993), 216.

43. Besharov *When Drug Addicts Have Children*, xxii.

44. Besharov, *When Drug Addicts Have Children*, ix.

45. Lisa Maher, "Punishment and Welfare: Crack Cocaine and the Regulation of Mothering," *Women and Criminal Justice* 3, no. 2 (1992): 35–70; Sheigla Murphy and Marsha Rosenbaum, *Pregnant Women on Drugs* (New Brunswick, NJ: Rutgers University Press, 1999); Marsha Rosenbaum, *Women on Heroin* (New Brunswick, NJ: Rutgers University Press, 1981).

46. Stone, *Policy Paradox*, 94.

47. "Redeemable" addicts go to treatment—an example of how values enter public policy and affect individuals. Juvenile justice works on two racial tiers—white girls are diverted to treatment; girls of color remain untreated in the custody of the criminal justice system (Meda Chesney-Lind, *The Female Offender* [Thousand Oaks, CA: SAGE, 1997], 177). Rehabilitation is both a process of social control through which deviant girls are managed into conformity, and a positive therapeutic intervention that brings them into the state's orbit. Girls often become involved with the illicit drug trade under circumstances of abuse and violence (177). Women work as low-level drug dealers and couriers, coming from communities where legitimate jobs are scarce and even prostitution markets have collapsed (178). The political efficacy of feminist claims lies in their ability to show that women use drugs as survival strategies, rather than out of a taste for risk, disregard for harm, "low cognitive abilities," or lack of maternal instinct.

48. Avram Goldstein, *Addiction: From Biology to Drug Policy* (New York: W.H. Freeman, 1994).

49. Hawkesworth, *Theoretical Issues*, 66. She argues that attempts to provide a "rational ideology" are ultimately unpersuasive and self-defeating: "As arguments in the sociology of knowledge have so clearly demonstrated, claims that all belief systems are ideological support unending rounds of ideological unmasking, but they afford little room for the rational assessment of the merits of arguments."

50. Eva Bertram, Morris Blachman, Kenneth Sharpe, and Peter Andreas, *Drug War Politics: The Price of Denial* (Berkeley, CA: University of California Press, 1996) demonstrates that policy-makers distance themselves from policies they have been instrumental in forging.

51. Hawkesworth, *Theoretical Issues*, 185.

52. See Kirstie McClure, "The Issue of Foundations: Scientized Politics, Politicized Science, and Feminist Critical Practice," in *Feminists Theorize the Political*, eds. Judith Butler and Joan W. Scott (New York: Routledge, 1992), 341–368.

53. William Connelly, *Identity/Difference: Democratic Negotiations of Political Paradox* (Ithaca, NY: Cornell University Press, 1991); Ernesto Laclau and Chantal Mouffe, *Hegemony and Socialist Strategy* (London: Verso Books, 1985).

54. Alan Hunt and Gary Wickham, *Foucault and the Law: Towards a Sociology of Law as Governance* (Boulder, CO: Pluto Press, 1994), 88.

55. Sanford Schram, *Words of Welfare* (Minneapolis: University of Minnesota Press, 1995), xxvi. Schram proposes that an "economistic-therapeutic-managerial discourse" operates to neutralize social science research and open it to political appropriation.

56. See Frank R. Baumgartner and Bryan D. Jones, *Agendas and Instability in American Politics* (Chicago: University of Chicago Press, 1993), and Anne Griffin, "Women's Health and the Articulation of Policy Preferences," in *Forging a Women's Health Research Agenda: Policy Issues for the 1990s*, eds. Jeri A. Sechzer, Anne Griffin, and Sheila M. Pfafflin (New York: Annals of the New York Academy of Sciences vol. 736, 1994), 205–216.

57. John W. Kingdon, *Agendas, Alternatives, and Public Policies*, 2d ed. (New York: HarperCollins, 1995).

58. Mary Douglas, *How Institutions Think* (Syracuse, NY: Syracuse University Press, 1986), 67.

59. Norman E. Zinberg, *Drug, Set, and Setting: The Basis for Controlled Intoxicant Use* (New Haven, CT: Yale University Press, 1984).

60. Pierre Bourdieu, *Outline of a Theory of Practice*, trans. Richard Nice (Cambridge: Cambridge University Press, 1977), 29.

61. Lorraine Code, *Rhetorical Spaces: Essays on Gendered Locations* (New York: Routledge, 1995), 58.

62. Code, *Rhetorical Spaces*, 59–60.

63. For the pathbreaking feminist argument against the "unassailability" of experience, see Joan W. Scott, "Experience," in *Feminists Theorize the Political*, eds. Butler and Scott (New York: Routledge, 1992), 22–40.

64. Frank, *Wounded Storyteller*, 8–10.

65. Norman K. Denzin, *Symbolic Interactionism and Cultural Studies* (Oxford: Basil Blackwell, 1992), 90.

66. Code, *Rhetorical Spaces*, 142; Nancy Naples, "The 'New' Consensus on the Gendered 'Social Contract': The 1987–1988 U.S. Congressional Hearings on Welfare Reform." *Signs* 22, no. 4 (1997): 907–945.

67. Code, *Rhetorical Spaces*, 64.

68. U.S. Congress. Senate. Committee on Appropriations. *The Drug Problem in Iowa*. 101st Cong., 1st sess., 17 July 1989, 105.

69. Senate Committee. *The Drug Problem in Iowa*, 98.
70. Senate Committee. *The Drug Problem in Iowa*, 95.
71. Senate Committee. *The Drug Problem in Iowa*, 100.
72. Senate Committee. *The Drug Problem in Iowa*, 102.
73. Senate Committee. *The Drug Problem in Iowa*, 104.
74. Senate Committee. *The Drug Problem in Iowa*, 105.
75. Senate Committee. *The Drug Problem in Iowa*, 97.
76. Code, *Rhetorical Spaces*, 52.
77. Code, *Rhetorical Spaces*, 66.
78. Code, *Rhetorical Spaces*, 68.
79. See Nancy Fraser, "Rethinking the Public Sphere," in *Justice Interruptus* (New York: Routledge, 1997), 69–98.
80. U.S. Congress. Senate Committee on Governmental Affairs. *Missing Links: Coordinating Federal Drug Policy for Women, Infants and Children*. 101st Cong., 1st sess., 31 July 1989, 5.
81. Senate Committee on Governmental Affairs. *Missing Links*, 5.
82. See Hawkesworth, *Theoretical Issues*, 90–92, on the implications of cognitive theory.
83. William N. Dunn, *Public Policy Analysis* (Englewood Cliffs, NJ: Prentice-Hall, 1981), 19–23.
84. Lasswell popularized his ideas in the paperback best-seller *Politics: Who Gets What, When, How* (Cleveland, OH: World Publishing, 1958), 20-21.
85. Lasswell, *Who Gets What*, 133.
86. Fischer and Forester, *The Argumentative Turn*, 24–25.
87. Feminist philosophers have argued that "postpositivist" policy studies includes ethics. See Hawkesworth, *Theoretical Issues*; Rosemarie Tong, *Ethics in Policy Analysis* (Englewood Cliffs, NJ: Prentice-Hall, 1986); and *Daring to Be Good: Essays in Feminist Ethico-Politics*, eds. Bat-Ami Bar On and Ann Ferguson (New York: Routledge, 1998).
88. Fischer and Forester, *The Argumentative Turn*, 37.
89. Burchell, Gordon, and Miller, eds., *The Foucault Effect*, 79.
90. Pierre Bourdieu and Loic J. D. Wacquant, *An Invitation to Reflexive Sociology* (Chicago: University of Chicago Press, 1992), 114. This form of capital "trumps" all others; "it follows that the construction of the state goes hand in hand with the constitution of the field of power understood as the space of play in which holders of various forms of capital struggle in particular for power over the state, that is, over the statist capital that grants power over the different species of capital and over their reproduction" (115).
91. Pierre Bourdieu, *In Other Words* (Stanford, CA: Stanford University Press, 1990), 63–65.
92. Jane Jenson, "Rebel Sons: An Interview with Alain Lipietz," *French Politics and Society*, September 1987, 18.
93. Jenson, "Rebel Sons," *French Politics and Society*, 18.
94. Jenson, "Rebel Sons," *French Politics and Society*, 18. Emphasis in original. As J. K. Gibson-Graham

explain in *The End of Capitalism as We Knew It* (Oxford: Basil Blackwell, 1996), the regulationist project posits that a "regulatory complex" of social norms, practices, and institutions "mediate" or "stall" the effects of crisis or contradiction, thus permitting capital accumulation to occur smoothly (note 15, p. 32).
95. Jenson, "Rebel Sons," *French Politics and Society*, 20.
96. Kingdon, *Agendas, Alternatives, and Public Policies*, 96–98. Kingdon's quantitative data suggests that personal experience serves as reinforcement rather than primary impetus.
97. Bourdieu, *Outline of a Theory of Practice*, 165.
98. Kingdon, *Agendas, Alternatives, and Public Policies*, 116–117.
99. Linda Gordon, *Pitied but Not Entitled: Single Mothers and the History of Welfare* (Cambridge, MA: Harvard University Press, 1994), 297.
100. Dean, *The Constitution of Poverty*, 176.
101. Michael Shapiro, *Language and Political Understanding: The Politics of Discursive Practices* (New Haven, CT: Yale University Press, 1981), 124.

Gendering Narcotics

1. David R. Buchanan and Lawrence Wallack, "This Is the Partnership For a Drug-Free America: Any Questions?" *Journal of Drug Issues* 28, no. 2 (1998): 332.
2. Judith Butler, *The Psychic Life of Power* (Stanford, CA: Stanford University Press, 1997), 27; Lorraine Kenny, "Amy Fisher, My Story: Learning to Love the Unlovable," *Socialist Review* 24, no. 3 (1994): 81–127.
3. Susan Bordo, *Twilight Zones* (Berkeley, CA: University of California Press, 1997), 113.
4. See Gail Bederman, *Manliness and Civilization* (Chicago: University of Chicago Press, 1995). " 'Civilization' was protean in its applications. Different people used it to legitimize conservatism and change, male dominance and militant feminism, white racism and African-American resistance" (23). In my material, "civilization" entails racial and sexual distinctions that narcotics erode. Drugs threaten "civilization" by breaking down the differentiations on which it is based.
5. H. S. Middlemiss, ed., *Narcotic Education*, edited report of the proceedings of the First World Conference on Narcotic Education (Washington, DC: 1926), 264.
6. Quoted in Michael Starks, *Cocaine Fiends and Reefer Madness* (New York: Cornwall Books, 1982), 42. See also Eric Schaefer, *"Bold! Daring! Shocking! True!" A History of Exploitation Films, 1919–1959* (Durham, NC: Duke University Press, 1999): 217–252.
7. U.S. Congress. House. Committee on Education. *Conference on Narcotic Education*. 69th Cong., 1st sess., 16 December 1925, 148.

8. David Courtwright, *Dark Paradise: Opiate Addiction in America before 1940* (Cambridge, MA: Harvard University Press, 1982) confirms that Second Wave immigrants were "relatively immune to heroin addiction," although their children were not (89).
9. House Committee on Education. *Conference on Narcotic Education*, 148.
10. H. S. Middlemiss, ed., *Narcotic Education*, 21–28, 145–157.
11. Richmond Pearson Hobson to the New York Academy of Medicine, January 6, 1926, Committee on Public Health Folder 1913–1929, Library of the New York Academy of Medicine.
12. H. S. Cumming to the New York Academy of Medicine, February 12, 1926, Committee on Public Health Folder 1913–1929, Library of the New York Academy of Medicine.
13. Alba B. Johnson of the Committee on Public Health to Richmond Pearson Hobson, March 23, 1926, Committee on Public Health Folder 1913–1929, Library of the New York Academy of Medicine.
14. House Committee on Education. *Conference on Narcotic Education*, 149.
15. House Committee on Education. *Conference on Narcotic Education*, 149.
16. Widely reported by Hearst newspapers, the conference influenced public perceptions of the drug problem. Speeches by Hobson and Wallis at the 1926 conference were reprinted almost verbatim in Philadelphia Police Department narcotics squad training materials as late as the 1950s. Luminaries William B. McKinley, then U.S. Senator from Illinois, and Gifford Pinchot, then governor of the state of Pennsylvania, attended. Speakers included government officials, corrections personnel, college professors, mystics, and physicians.
17. H. S. Middlemiss, ed., *Narcotic Education*, 251.
18. H. S. Middlemiss, ed., *Narcotic Education*, 251.
19. H. S. Middlemiss, ed., *Narcotic Education*, 264.
20. H. S. Middlemiss, ed., *Narcotic Education*, 264. "Men are not the same as they were before the war"; thousands irradiated "waves of pain" (263).
21. H.S. Middlemiss, ed., *Narcotic Education*, 264.
22. H.S. Middlemiss, ed., *Narcotic Education*, 262, 264.
23. David Langum, *Crossing over the Line: Legislating Morality and the Mann Act* (Chicago: University of Chicago Press, 1994).
24. See Mara L. Keire, "Dope Fiends and Degenerates: The Gendering of Addiction in the Early Twentieth Century," *Journal of Social History* 31, no. 4 (1998): 809–822.
25. For instance, a soft-core magazine pitched to law enforcement officers featured Molly Wendt, the "oriental queen of drug smuggling." Nat Perlow, "Movie Stars and Moguls Worshipped Her," *National Police Gazette*, July 7, 1940 (Box 9, Anslinger Papers).

26. *New York American*, March 8 and September 25, 1934; *Seattle Post-Intelligencer*, November 10, 1933; *Washington Herald*, July 18, 1934 (Box 9, Anslinger Papers).
27. Dixie Dixon, "Trapped by the Poison Gas in Her Jeweled Vanity Case," *American Weekly*, September 1931. The occasional "dashing, black-eyed woman animated by the fire of Latin blood" appeared, as in Lawrence Sullivan, "How Government Sleuths, Starting in Washington, Smashed the Big 'Dope Ring,'" *Washington Star*, September 28, 1930 (Box 9, Anslinger Papers).
28. Sara Graham-Mulhall, *Opium: The Demon Flower* (New York: Howard Vinal, 1926), 62–63.
29. Ralph M. Crowley, "Psychoanalytic Literature on Drug Addiction and Alcoholism," *Psychoanalytic Review* 26 (1939): 39–54; Edward Glover, "Common Problems in Psychoanalysis and Anthropology: Drug Ritual and Addiction," *British Journal of Medical Psychology* 12 (September 1932): 109–131.
30. Stewart Robinson, "Dope on Dope," *The Family Circle*, October 24, 1945, 10–11, 16, 20 (Box 12, Anslinger Papers). See Douglas Clark Kinder, "Bureaucratic Cold Warrior: Harry J. Anslinger and Illicit Narcotics Traffic," *Pacific Historical Review* 50 (1981): 169–191; with William O. Walker, III, "Stable Force in a Storm: Harry J. Anslinger and United States Narcotic Foreign Policy," *Journal of American History* 72 (1986): 918–927.
31. Robinson, "Dope on Dope," *The Family Circle*, 16 (Box 12, Anslinger Papers).
32. Eli Marcovitz and Henry J. Meyers. "The Marijuana Addict in the Army," *War Medicine* 6, no. 6 (1944): 385.
33. Marcovitz and Meyers, "The Marijuana Addict in the Army," *War Medicine*, 385–386.
34. Marcovitz and Meyers, "The Marijuana Addict in the Army," *War Medicine*, 391.
35. Herbert S. Gaskill, "Marijuana: An Intoxicant," *American Journal of Psychiatry* 101, no. 2 (1945): 202–204. This study located its subjects among U.S. soldiers stationed in India and Burma. The ratio of "white to colored" was 1:20.
36. Marcovitz and Meyers, "The Marijuana Addict in the Army," *War Medicine*, 390; Sol Charen and Luis Perelman, "Personality Studies of Marijuana Addicts," *American Journal of Psychiatry* 102, no. 5 (1946): 674–682.
37. Marcovitz and Meyers, "The Marijuana Addict in the Army," *War Medicine*, 387.
38. Marcovitz and Meyers, "The Marijuana Addict in the Army," *War Medicine*, 382.
39. Gaskill, "Marijuana: An Intoxicant," *American Journal of Psychiatry*, 204.
40. Charen and Perelman, "Personality Studies," *American Journal of Psychiatry*, 682.
41. According to Charen and Perelman, "strong homosexual tendencies are also present in many

addicts" (682). Homosexuality was thought to emerge from early childhood conflicts that arrested subjects in infantile stages of development.

42. Harold J. Lawn, "The Study and Treatment of Alcoholism in the 5th S.C. Rehabilitation Center," *American Journal of Psychiatry* 102, no.4 (1946): 479–482. This 700-case study deflected charges that the army caused or exacerbated drinking.

43. Charen and Perelman, "Personality Studies," *American Journal of Psychiatry*, 684.

44. Marcovitz and Meyers, "The Marijuana Addict in the Army," *War Medicine*, 385. The evidence for "homosexual trends" was inability to identify figure drawings as male or female.

45. Charen and Perelman, "Personality Studies," *American Journal of Psychiatry*, 677.

46. Charen and Perelman, "Personality Studies," *American Journal of Psychiatry*, 677.

47. Charen and Perelman, "Personality Studies," *American Journal of Psychiatry*, 677.

48. Charen and Perelman, "Personality Studies," *American Journal of Psychiatry*, 682.

49. Harry J. Anslinger, audiotape of radio address, WFBR Baltimore, MD, 10:00 A.M., February 18, 1942. Anslinger Archives.

50. Albert Q. Maisel, "Getting the Dope on Dope," *Liberty*, November 24, 1945, 28–29, 95–99 (Box 12, Anslinger Papers).

51. For a more thorough examination of "communist narcotic aggression," see Nancy D. Campbell, "Cold War Compulsions: U.S. Drug Science, Policy, and Culture," Ph.D. diss., University of California at Santa Cruz, 1995.

Chapter 3

1. For works that take seriously the symbolic dimensions of policy, see Cynthia Daniels, *At Women's Expense: State and the Politics of Fetal Rights* (Cambridge, MA: Harvard University Press, 1993); Joseph R. Gusfield, *The Culture of Public Problems* (Chicago: University of Chicago Press, 1981); Kristin Luker, *Dubious Conceptions: The Politics of Teenage Pregnancy* (Cambridge, MA: Harvard University Press, 1996); Barbara Nelson, *Making an Issue of Child Abuse* (Chicago: University of Chicago Press, 1984); and Dorothy Roberts, *Killing the Black Body: Race, Reproduction, and the Meaning of Liberty* (New York: Pantheon, 1997).

2. The three major federal legislative efforts of the Progressive period were the 1910 Mann Act, which regulated the "white slave trade"; the 1914 Harrison Act, which regulated the sale of narcotics; and Prohibition.

3. For accounts of the development of the U.S. public health bureaucracy, see Katherine Ott, *Fevered Lives: Tuberculosis in American Culture Since*

1870 (Cambridge, MA: Harvard University Press, 1996), and Zachary Gussow, *Leprosy, Racism, and Public Health* (Boulder, CO: Westview Press, 1989).

4. Stephen R. Kandall, M.D., *Substance and Shadow: Women and Addiction in the United States* (Cambridge, MA: Harvard University Press, 1996), 179. See also William L. White, *Slaying the Dragon: The History of Addiction Treatment and Recovery in the United States* (Bloomington, IL: Chestnut Health Systems/Lighthouse Institute, 1998), a true compendium of treatment technologies.

5. The hospitals opened in 1935 and 1938 respectively, and operated until the 1970s.

6. Harris Isbell and William R. Martin, *Drug Addiction and the U.S. Public Health Service* (Rockville, MD: U.S. Department of Health, Education, and Welfare, Public Health Service, National Institute on Drug Abuse, 1978), 251–259.

7. Isbell and Martin, *Drug Addiction*, 254.

8. David Courtwright, *Dark Paradise* (Cambridge, MA: Harvard University Press, 1982) named this shift the "transformation of the opiate addict" (115).

9. David Musto, *The American Disease: Origins of Narcotic Control*, 2d ed., (New York: Oxford University Press, 1987), 184.

10. There was little evidence of concern about narcotics use by African-American women, although African-Americans were associated with heroin use during the Harlem tuberculosis epidemic and with cocaine use in the South (Musto, *The American Disease*, 5–8).

11. Quoted in Charles E. Terry and Mildred Pellens, *The Opium Problem* (1928; reprint, Montclair, NJ: Patterson Smith, 1970), 470.

12. See Martin I. Wilbert, "Efforts to Curb the Misuse of Narcotic Drugs," *Public Health Reports* 30, part 1 (1915): 893–923. Wilbert soberly calculated that the total number of opiate users could not exceed 187,000; however, he was also convinced that drug addiction had reached "gigantic proportions" in the United States (894).

13. H. S. Middlemiss, ed., *Narcotic Education* (Washington, DC: 1926), 232–267.

14. Middlemiss, *Narcotic Education*, 249, 264.

15. Middlemiss, *Narcotic Education*, 250.

16. Musto, *The American Disease*, 17.

17. U.S. Congress. House Committee on Ways and Means. *Importation and Use of Opium*. 61st Cong., 1st and 2d sess., 14 December 1910 and 11 January 1911, 11.

18. House Committee on Ways and Means. *Importation and Use of Opium*, 15–16.

19. House Committee on Ways and Means. *Importation and Use of Opium*, 16, 20.

20. Musto, *The American Disease*, 32, 96.

21. House Committee on Ways and Means. *Importation and Use of Opium*, 22.

22. House Committee on Ways and Means. *Importation and Use of Opium*, 23.
23. House Committee on Ways and Means. *Importation and Use of Opium*, 20.
24. House Committee on Ways and Means. *Importation and Use of Opium*, 12.
25. House Committee on Ways and Means. *Importation and Use of Opium*, 13. Professionals comprised a small part of the picture. Koch listed the proportion of "dopes" among certain occupations: nearly half of criminals; 21.6 percent of "lewd women"; 2.06 percent of physicians; 1.32 percent of nurses; 0.844 percent of other adults.
26. Restrictions were passed as the U.S. State Department sought to break British control over opium traffic in its new protectorate, the Philippines. Moral crusading was not solely accountable for anti-opium policies in China, the Philippines, or the United States. Diplomacy was also a factor. Seeking leverage in China, the U.S. State Department fastened on opium consumption, which had become a significant domestic issue in an increasingly antiforeign China. "In the absence of a deterioration in Sino-American relations during the first decade of the century the consumption of opium for non-medical purposes would not have become an *international* social problem, necessitating the introduction of a complex system of controls; at least not during the first decade of the twentieth century," according to S. D. Stein, *International Diplomacy, State Administrators, and Narcotics Control* (Hampshire, England: Gower Publishing, 1985), 49.
27. Jerald W. Cloyd, *Drugs and Information Control* (Westport, CT: Greenwood Press, 1982) classified the passage of the Harrison Act as a racial and class conflict and explored the figure of Hamilton Wright as a "moral entrepreneur" from a dominant group that practiced "racial isolation" to assure continued access to the professional labor market.
28. Quoted in Musto, *The American Disease*, 43, n. 82.
29. Gail Bederman, *Manliness and Civilization* (Chicago: University of Chicago Press, 1995), points out, strong gender differentiation was an "essential component of civilization" (25). Advanced civilizations had supposedly evolved "pronounced sexual differences"; gender differences among the less advanced races were blurred. Bederman showed that "civilization" was a racialized concept by the 1890s in that only whites were thought to have evolved to the "civilized" stage.
30. Middlemiss, *Narcotic Education*, 262.
31. Middlemiss, *Narcotic Education*, 254.
32. Arthur Woods, *Dangerous Drugs: The World Fight Against Illicit Traffic in Narcotics* (New Haven, CT: Yale University Press, 1931), 43.
33. See Orlando Patterson, *Freedom* (New York: Basic Books, 1991). Thanks to Eileen Julien for directing me to Patterson's work. Paul Gilroy discusses slavery as an integral part of modernity in *The Black Atlantic* (Cambridge, MA: Harvard University Press, 1993).
34. Middlemiss, *Narcotic Education*, 15.
35. *Congressional Record*. 61st Cong., 2d sess., 1910, 45, pt. 1, 546.
36. *Congressional Record*, 547.
37. *Congressional Record*, 1040.
38. Middlemiss, *Narcotic Education*, 16.
39. Clifford Griffith Roe and B. S. Steadwell, *The Great War on White Slavery, or, Fighting for the Protection of Our Girls* (United States, 1911), 97.
40. Middlemiss, *Narcotic Education*, 17.
41. Middlemiss, *Narcotic Education*, 75.
42. Middlemiss, *Narcotic Education*, 71.
43. Middlemiss, *Narcotic Education*, 172, 175.
44. House Committee on Education. *Conference on Narcotic Education*, 151.
45. House Committee on Education. *Conference on Narcotic Education*, 156.
46. Middlemiss, *Narcotic Education*, 153.
47. House Committee on Education. *Conference on Narcotic Education*, 177, 191.
48. Quoted in Starks, *Cocaine Fiends*, 45.
49. Box 9, Anslinger Papers. News clippings appeared in a series of scrapbooks maintained at the FBN. Sources were rarely identified, although the scrapbooks were categorized by year.
50. Bret Wood, ed., *Marijuana, Motherhood, and Madness* (Lanhan, MD: Scarecrow Press, 1998), 189. The book contains three screenplays and letters of appeal to the censorship boards.
51. Quoted in Starks, *Cocaine Fiends*, 103.
52. Woods, *Dangerous Drugs*, 48–49.
53. Middlemiss, *Narcotic Education*, 149.
54. Middlemiss, *Narcotic Education*, 187.
55. Graham-Mulhall, *Opium: The Demon Flower* (New York: Howard Vinal, 1926), 57, 62.
56. Graham-Mulhall, *Opium: The Demon Flower*, iii.
57. Graham-Mulhall, *Opium: The Demon Flower*, iii.
58. Graham-Mulhall, *Opium: The Demon Flower*, 29.
59. Graham-Mulhall, *Opium: The Demon Flower*, 31–32.
60. Graham-Mulhall, *Opium: The Demon Flower*, 29–31. According to her, addicted babies were born with weak constitutions, high susceptibility to pain, and low resistance to disease. Physicians who maintained them exacerbated these effects. Like her future "zero-tolerance" compatriots, Graham-Mulhall argued against all drug maintenance.
61. Graham-Mulhall, *Opium: The Demon Flower*, 39.
62. Graham-Mulhall, *Opium: The Demon Flower*, 43.
63. Graham-Mulhall, *Opium: The Demon Flower*, 49.
64. Graham-Mulhall, *Opium: The Demon Flower*, 56.
65. Graham-Mulhall, *Opium: The Demon Flower*, 57.
66. Graham-Mulhall, *Opium: The Demon Flower*, 58.
67. Graham-Mulhall, *Opium: The Demon Flower*, 98–99.
68. The deflection dynamic was already apparent in Progressive attempts to change maternal behavior,

which primitivized the child-rearing practices of recent immigrants and Southern African-Americans. (See Bruce Bellingham and Mary Pugh Mathis, "Race, Citizenship, and the Bio-Politics of the Maternalist Welfare State: 'Traditional' Midwifery in the American South under the Sheppard-Towner Act, 1921–29," *Journal of Social Politics* 1, no. 2 (1994): 157–189.

69. Graham-Mulhall, *Opium: The Demon Flower*, 61.

70. Graham-Mulhall, *Opium: The Demon Flower*, 61.

71. Graham-Mulhall, *Opium: The Demon Flower*, 61.

72. Lawrence Kolb, "Drug Addiction and Its Relation to Crime," *Mental Hygiene* 9 (1925): 74–89; "Types and Characteristics of Drug Addicts," *Mental Hygiene* 9 (1925): 300–313; "Pleasure and Deterioration from Narcotic Addiction," *Mental Hygiene* 9 (1925): 699–724.

73. Kolb, "Drug Addiction and Its Relation to Crime," *Mental Hygiene*, 87–88.

74. Kolb, "Drug Addiction and Its Relation to Crime," *Mental Hygiene*, 80.

75. Kolb, "Drug Addiction and Its Relation to Crime," *Mental Hygiene*, 75.

76. Kolb, "Drug Addiction and Its Relation to Crime," *Mental Hygiene*, 88.

77. Kolb, "Pleasure and Deterioration," *Mental Hygiene*, 712.

78. Kolb, "Pleasure and Deterioration," *Mental Hygiene*, 712.

79. Kolb, "Pleasure and Deterioration," *Mental Hygiene*, 715.

80. Kolb, "Pleasure and Deterioration," *Mental Hygiene*, 715.

81. Allusions to homosexuality illustrate the continued "feminization" of addiction even among men. See Mara L. Keire, "Dope Fiends and Degenerates," *Journal of Social History*, 31, no. 4 (1998): 809–822.

82. Kolb, "Pleasure and Deterioration," *Mental Hygiene*, 717.

83. Kolb, "Types and Characteristics," *Mental Hygiene*, 304.

84. Bingham Dai, *Opium Addiction in Chicago* (1937; reprint Montclair, NJ: Patterson Smith, 1970).

85. Dai, *Opium Addiction in Chicago*, 187.

86. Dai, *Opium Addiction in Chicago*, 56.

87. Dai, *Opium Addiction in Chicago*, 187.

88. Dai, *Opium Addiction in Chicago*, 122–123.

89. John C. McWilliams, *The Protectors* (Newark, DE: University of Delaware Press, 1990), 88.

90. McWilliams, *The Protectors*, 88.

91. Wooster Taylor, "Father Seeks Help for Girl Against Narcotics," *San Francisco Examiner*, November 6, 1933 (Box 9, Anslinger Papers).

92. See Marie-Christine Leps, *Apprehending the Criminal: The Production of Deviance in Nineteenth-Century Discourse* (Durham, NC: Duke University Press, 1992), which traces how criminology came to speak for criminals.

93. On the sexualization of Asian women and the "feminization" of Asian men, see King-Kok Cheung, "The Woman Warrior Versus the Chinaman Pacific," in *Conflicts in Feminism*, eds. Marianne Hirsch and Evelyn Fox Keller (New York: Routledge, 1990), 234–251.

94. Wooster Taylor, *Los Angeles Examiner*, November 3, 1933. Taylor reported that female agents sold white girls of the ages 16 to 20 into "dope and slavery" (Box 9, Anslinger Papers).

95. Wooster Taylor, "Dope Ring Linked to Traffic in Girls," *San Francisco Examiner*, November 3, 1933 (Box 9, Anslinger Papers).

96. Wooster Taylor, "Hospital, Jail Reveal Horror of Dope Peril," *Washington Herald*, November 9, 1933 (Box 9, Anslinger Papers).

97. Winifred Black, "Father Sent Girl of 12 into Slums to Sell Dope," *Washington Herald*, November 27, 1933 (Box 9, Anslinger Papers).

98. Box 9, Anslinger Papers.

99. National Archives, Great Lakes Region. Records of the District Courts of the United States, Northern District of Ohio, Eastern Division. Narcotic Case Report 0–1162.

100. Charles M. Conway, "Dope Raiders Nab 4 Girls, Chinese," *Cleveland Plain Dealer*, January 11, 1931.

101. Narcotic Case Report 0–1162, 5.

102. Narcotic Case Report 0–1162, 6.

103. Narcotic Case Report 0–1162, 7.

104. Narcotic Case Report 0–1162, 9.

105. Narcotic Case Report 0–1162, 10.

106. Narcotic Case Report 0–1162, 10.

107. Jack Heil, "Chinese Bluebeard," 6 (File 14, Box 4. Anslinger Papers).

108. "Gets 10 Years for Dope Den Where Girls Were Lured," *Cleveland Plain Dealer*, February 4, 1931.

109. National Archives, Great Lakes Region. Records of the District Courts of the United States, Northern District of Ohio, Eastern Division. Criminal Case 16409.

110. National Archives, Criminal Case 16409.

111. Jack Heil, "Chinese Bluebeard."

112. Heil, "Chinese Bluebeard."

113. File 23, Box 9, Anslinger Papers.

114. Heil, "Chinese Bluebeard," 8.

115. Heil, "Chinese Bluebeard," 10.

116. Harry J. Anslinger, *The Murderers: The Story of the Narcotics Gangs* (New York: Farrar, Straus and Cudahy, 1961), 25.

117. Harry J. Anslinger, "Underworld Slaves" (File 14, Box 4, Anslinger Papers).

118. Anslinger, "Underworld Slaves," 1.

119. Anslinger, "Underworld Slaves," 2.

120. Anslinger, "Underworld Slaves," 2.

121. Anslinger, *The Murderers*, 25.

122. Anslinger, *The Murderers*, 27.

123. Anslinger, *The Murderers*, 31.

124. Anslinger, "Underworld Slaves," 3.

125. Anslinger, "Underworld Slaves," 4.

126. Anslinger, "Underworld Slaves," 11.
127. Anslinger, "Underworld Slaves," 12.
128. Heil, "Chinese Bluebeard," 12.
129. Heil, "Chinese Bluebeard," 14.
130. Anslinger, "Underworld Slaves," 14.
131. See Marianna Torgovnick, *Primitive Passions* (Chicago: University of Chicago Press, 1997).
132. Michel Foucault, *The History of Sexuality,* vol. 1, trans. Robert Hurley (New York: Vintage Books, 1980), 141.

Chapter 4

1. Victor H. and Virginia E. Vogel. *What Teenagers Should Know about Narcotics* (Washington, DC: Science Research Associates/United States Public Health Service, 1950). The text was also published in *Look* magazine in September 1951, 99–102.
2. The psychoanalytic grip on the concept of addiction loosened as new cybernetic and sociological models took hold. For instance, the World Health Organization (WHO) offered "drug dependence" to move away from the outmoded psychoanalytic concept of "addiction." Psychoanalysis was labeled "nonscientific," propping up the scientificity of the newer explanations derived from systems theory. Like any repressed other, the psychoanalytic material was subject to return and repetition, as its concepts were smuggled into knowledge systems seemingly opposed to it.
3. This signal is still broadcast by those who regard the flow of drugs into rural or small-town communities as an "urban" invasion of pastoral life.
4. Mayor's Committee on Drug Addiction, "Report of Study on Drug Addiction among Teenagers" (New York: City of New York, December 11, 1950), 40. A New York City school district survey conducted for the committee employed a sample of 30 adolescent drug users among whom a "chain reaction" occurred. How to stimulate resistance to peer pressure remains a central question in antidrug education efforts even today.
5. U.S. Congress. Senate Special Committee to Investigate Organized Crime in Interstate Commerce. *Investigation of Crime in Interstate Commerce: Hearings on S. Res. 202 and S. Res. 129.* 82d Cong., 1st sess., 1951. See also Estes Kefauver, *Crime in America,* ed. Sidney Shalett (Garden City, NY: Doubleday, 1951), 10.
6. Kefauver, *Crime in America,* 330.
7. See William H. Moore, *The Kefauver Committee and the Politics of Crime* (Columbia, MO: University of Missouri Press, 1974). Kefauver won presidential primaries in California, Illinois, New Hampshire, and Nebraska in 1952. In 1956 he lost the Florida and California primaries to Adlai Stevenson, ending his presidential hopes.
8. *Public Law No. 255.* 82d Cong., 1st sess., 2 November 1951. Debate on the Boggs Act is contained in the *Congressional Record,* 82d Cong., 1st sess., 16 July 1951, 8195–8211.
9. Nathaniel L. Goldstein, attorney general of the state of New York, *Narcotics: A Growing Problem, a Public Challenge, a Plan for Action, Report to the Legislature Pursuant to Chapter 528 of the Laws of 1951, 175th Session* (Albany, NY: Legislature of the State of New York, 1952) 3, no. 25–28, 30.
10. American Bar Association, Joint Legislative Committee on Narcotic Study, November 25, 1957, 58.
11. Malachi Harney, "Mandatory Sentences for Narcotic Law Offenses," reprinted in the *Congressional Record,* 16 July 1951, 8201. An Assistant Commissioner of the FBN, Harney was Anslinger's right-hand man and sometime coauthor.
12. *Congressional Record.* 16 July 1951, 8204.
13. Robert C. Doty, "New Tactics Urged in Narcotic Battle—Present Weapons Are Wholly Inadequate to Curb Evil, Legion Parley Is Told," *New York Times,* June 19, 1951. Reprinted in the *Congressional Record,* 16 July 1951, 8199. Anslinger compared the current wave to the epidemic of addiction after World War I, and declared that Communist China was the "unreachable source" of heroin.
14. "Crime: The Junkies," *Time,* June 25, 1951. Reprinted in the *Congressional Record,* 16 July 1951, 8198.
15. *Congressional Record.* 16 July 1951, 8209.
16. Historians claim otherwise. The vast majority of prosecutions under the Mann Act involved consensual sex, according to David Langum, *Crossing over the Line: Legislating Morality and the Mann Act* (Chicago: University of Chicago Press, 1994).
17. *Congressional Record,* 84th Cong., 1st sess., 18 March 1955, 3187. Senator Ellender said: "I presume there will be a little more television and a little more radio to follow the committee around the country. I am sure the chairman of the subcommittee . . . will probably get quite a bit of advertising out of it. And this problem needs no more advertising; it cries for immediate remedial action. If the amount herein were to be used in actually correcting some of the evils of juvenile delinquency, I would support it with all my strength. But these are not action funds, they are advertising funds."
18. *Congressional Record.* 18 March 1955, 3182–3187.
19. Musto, *The American Disease,* 232. During "red scares" (1919–1920 and 1950–1951), sanctions against drug use and traffic were increased as a means to contain domestic subversion.

20. Citizens' Advisory Committee to the Attorney
General on Crime Prevention in the State of
California, *Report to Attorney General Edmund
G. Brown*, March 26, 1954, 8–12.

21. U.S. Congress. Senate Subcommittee to Investigate Juvenile Delinquency of the Committee on
the Judiciary. *Hearings on S. Res. 173 and S. Res.
303*. 84th Cong., 2d sess., 1956, 7.

22. Senate Special Committee. *Investigation of Crime
in Interstate Commerce*, 307.

23. The Reagan administration and right-wing think
tanks reiterated the link between narcotics export and communism in the 1980s, calling it
"narcoterrorism."

24. The New York City Welfare Council report used the
state's figures, which indicated a 700 percent increase in the number of known addicts in 1950
over 1946, although the total number of teenagers
involved remained unknown. No one knew how
many addicts there were. The figures came from
the Research Center for Human Relations, New
York University (NYU), then conducting the
study published by Isidor Chein, Donald L. Gerard, Robert S. Lee, and Eva Rosenfeld, *The Road
to H: Narcotics, Delinquency, and Social Policy*
(New York: Basic Books, 1964).

25. Robert L. McFarland and William A. Hall, "A
Survey of One Hundred Suspected Drug Addicts," *Journal of Crime, Criminology, and Police
Science* 44 (1953–54): 308–319. The authors,
from the Psychiatric Institute of Chicago, noted
"tremendous public pressure had been brought
to bear on the city officials to do something
about a suspected increase in drug addiction."
They felt the narcotics drive was "an impulsive
gesture designed to rid the city at once of a
problem which is deep-rooted in the very nature of our western civilization" (318). This resembled the situation in New York City.

26. James R. Dumpson, who authored the Welfare
Council report, aired this admission at the New
York Academy of Medicine conference "Drug
Addiction among Adolescents" (New York:
New York Academy of Medicine with the Josiah
Macy, Jr., Foundation, November 30, 1951, and
March 13–14, 1952), 105.

27. Howe was a clinical professor of neurology at Co-
lumbia-Presbyterian Medical Center. He explained the factions not as "crime versus
disease," but as "social versus psychiatric."

28. U.S. Congress. Senate Subcommittee on Improvement to the Criminal Code of the Committee
on the Judiciary. *Hearings on the Illicit Narcotics
Traffic*. 84th Cong., 1st sess. (Washington, DC:
GPO, 1955–1956).

29. *Drug Addiction: Crime or Disease? Interim and
Final Reports of the Joint Committee of the Amer-
ican Bar Association and the American Medical
Association on Narcotic Drugs* (Bloomington,
IN: Indiana University Press, 1961).

30. Most practicing lawyers and physicians were not
part of this alliance because they realistically
feared reprisal from the FBN. Among its enemies the FBN listed Lindesmith, Kolb, Howe,
and King. The latter published *The Drug Hang-
Up: America's Fifty-Year Folly* (New York: W.W.
Norton, 1972).

31. James R. Dumpson, *The Menace of Narcotics to the
Children of New York: A Plan to Eradicate the
Evil*, interim report to the Welfare Council
Committee on the Use of Narcotics by Teenage
Youth (New York: August 1951).

32. Paul Zimmering, James Toolan, Renate Safrin, and
S. Bernard Wortis. "Heroin Addiction in Adolescent Boys," *Journal of Nervous and Mental
Disease* 114 (1951): 19–33. This study was conducted at the Bellevue Hospital Psychiatric Division on 22 male adolescent heroin addicts.
Prior to 1950, only six cases of heroin use were
admitted to Bellevue. The number increased
more than tenfold in early 1951.

33. Dumpson, *The Menace of Narcotics*, 46.

34. Dumpson, *The Menace of Narcotics*, 36.

35. Baldwin mentioned three antidrug education films
produced between 1951 and 1952 for public
schools and parent groups: *H: The Story of a
Teenage Drug Addict*, *The Terrible Truth*, and
Drug Addiction. The academy criticized *The
Terrible Truth*, which was about a female heroin
addict, because it portrayed drug addiction as
the spread of communism.

36. New York Academy of Medicine, *Drug Addiction
Among Adolescents* (New York: New York Academy of Medicine, 1952).

37. The Macy Foundation's efforts ranged from improving medical education to serving as a CIA
cover for LSD research. Fremont-Smith organized three sets of conferences relevant to drug
studies: Problems of Consciousness (1950–1954);
Neuropharmacology (1954–1959); and Use of
LSD in Psychotherapy (1956 and 1959).

38. See Steve Heims, *Constructing a Social Science for
Postwar America: The Cybernetics Group,
1946–1953* (Cambridge, MA: MIT Press, 1991).

39. New York Academy of Medicine, *Drug Addiction
among Adolescents*, 145.

40. New York Academy of Medicine, *Drug Addiction
among Adolescents*, 145.

41. New York Academy of Medicine, *Drug Addiction
among Adolescents*, 140.

42. New York Academy of Medicine, *Drug Addiction
among Adolescents*, 109.

43. New York Academy of Medicine, *Drug Addiction
among Adolescents*, 170.

44. New York Academy of Medicine, *Drug Addiction
among Adolescents*, 193. The allusion to an "impotent" masculinity contrasted to the talk about
"vigor" in antidrug rhetoric.

45. Theoretical constructs of male adolescent drug use
were indebted to the psychoanalytic theory that

problems of masculine identification generated addiction and delinquency.

46. ABA, Committee on Narcotic Study, 58.

47. ABA, Committee on Narcotic Study, 80.

48. ABA, Committee on Narcotic Study, 91–92.

49. ABA, Committee on Narcotic Study, 93.

50. ABA, Committee on Narcotic Study, 93–94.

51. ABA, Committee on Narcotic Study, 1048.

52. ABA, Committee on Narcotic Study, 418.

53. ABA, Committee on Narcotic Study, 419.

54. ABA, Committee on Narcotic Study, 419.

55. ABA, Committee on Narcotic Study, 428–429.

56. ABA, Committee on Narcotic Study, 682.

57. ABA, Committee on Narcotic Study, 679.

58. ABA, Committee on Narcotic Study, 694.

59. ABA, Committee on Narcotic Study, 855.

60. ABA, Committee on Narcotic Study, 971.

61. ABA, Committee on Narcotic Study, 971.

62. New York Academy of Medicine, *Drug Addiction among Adolescents*, 5. Resources were directed toward "innocently addicted" persons.

63. Judges and probation officers pointed out that New York City's facilities for addicted girls were already insufficient in 1951.

64. See Arthur Schlesinger, "The Crisis of Masculinity," *Esquire,* November 1958.

65. Chein et al., *The Road to H.*

66. Elliott Currie, *Reckoning: Drugs, the Cities, and the American Future* (New York: Hill and Wang, 1993), 37. Currie refers to aspects of that study on social networks and economic position. He used *The Road to H* to counter psychological models of addiction, which he considered as problematically prevalent in the 1990s as in the 1950s. His reading of *The Road to H* was produced by an inattention to how gender pervades drug policy history and research. While Chein and his coauthors located individual psychological problems in community "pathologies," their model remained strikingly psychiatric.

67. Chein et al., *The Road to H*, 5. Suspicious of scientific detachment, the authors compared "neutral" scientists to psychopaths: "It is his responsibility to keep his feelings from intruding into his determination of the facts; it is not his responsibility to deny himself as a human being by indifference to the facts, and it is only scientific irresponsibility to conceal from his readers the fact that he does have feelings."

68. Chein et al., *The Road to H*, 365. "We have reason to believe that, even if there were no sanctions against opiate use, we would regard or would learn to regard the people who become opiate addicts as seriously disturbed in their relationships with themselves, with their families, and in the complexities of their relationships with what is loosely called 'reality.'. . . We have reason to be concerned with opiate addiction because of its human significance as an indicator of trouble within the individual and, because of the endemic nature of opiate addiction, as an indicator of trouble within many individuals in our society."

69. Chein et al., *The Road to H*, 14. The authors listed these common symptoms: inability to enter intimate relations, difficulties in assuming a masculine role, futility, depression, and intolerance of anxiety or frustration. The list elaborated on the "patterned disturbance or syndrome" found in Donald L. Gerard and Conan Kornetsky, "Adolescent Opiate Addiction," *Psychiatric Quarterly* 28, nos. 1 and 3 (1954), and 29, no. 1 (1955): 457–486. Gerard's and Kornetsky's addicts displayed: (1) dysphoria; (2) problems of sexual identification; and (3) disturbed interpersonal relations.

70. Chein et al., *The Road to H*, 365.

71. Chein et al., *The Road to H*, 365.

72. Chein et al., *The Road to H*, 366–367. The authors used the metaphor of a "monstrous neonate," a victim of unfavorable prenatal environments that cannot be restored to normalcy.

73. Chein et al., *The Road to H*, 195–196.

74. Gerard and Kornetsky, "Adolescent Opiate Addiction," *Psychiatric Quarterly*, indicated excessive personality malfunction in addicts but not in controls. The NYU researchers used nonaddict friends of addict patients at Riverside Hospital as controls.

75. Gerard and Kornetsky critically cited Howard Becker, *The Outsiders* (New York: The Free Press, 1963), Alfred Lindesmith, *Opiate Addiction* (Bloomington, IN: Principia Press, 1947), and David W. Maurer and Victor H. Vogel, *Narcotics and Narcotic Addiction* (Springfield, IL: Charles C. Taylor, 1954).

76. Experimental psychology used the aforementioned techniques to gain the discursive effect of facticity, repressing its basis in psychoanalysis and the project of cultural normalization.

77. Human figure drawings were used to determine levels of maturity, flexibility, and conventionality. Addicts drew rigid, childlike figures that lacked "adequate psychosexual differentiation" and occupied "culturally unacceptable" gender roles. They refused to make up stories about the figures they produced. On the basis of test data and "the most objectifiable, categorical statements offered by the subjects" in unstructured interviews—in an extremely small sample—the researchers defined diagnostic categories. My point is not to question the empirical validity of these tests, but to note the frequency with which regression, arrested development, and inadequate object relations appear as foundational categories in claims about drug addiction.

78. Gerard and Kornetsky, "Adolescent Opiate Addiction," *Psychiatric Quarterly,* 483–484.

79. Chein et al., *The Road to H*, 213.

80. Chein et al., *The Road to H*, 199.

81. E. Bibring, "The Mechanism of Depression," in *Affective Disorders*, ed. Phyllis Greenacre (New York: International Universities Press, 1953). For a useful genealogy of "self-esteem," see Martin Hoffman, "Drug Addiction and Hypersexuality: Related Modes of Mastery," *Comprehensive Psychiatry* 5, no. 4 (1964): 262–270.

82. Chein and his coauthors cited Otto Fenichel, *The Psychoanalytic Theory of Neurosis* (New York: W.W. Norton, 1945), who categorized addiction as an "impulse neurosis." Addicts used drugs to "satisfy an archaic oral longing which is sexual longing, a need for security, and a need for the maintenance of self-esteem simultaneously." They "never estimated object relations very highly. . . . Objects are nothing to them but deliverers of supplies" (376).

83. Leon Brill, "Some Notes on Dynamics and Treatment in Narcotic Addiction," *Journal of Psychiatric Social Work* 23, no. 2 (1954): 67–81. Chein et al. quoted Brill; both accepted Fenichel's categorization of addiction as a "perversion and impulse neurosis." Brill noted higher incidence among "certain minority groups where broken homes, deteriorated slum environment, and racial discrimination interlock with psychological factors." Brill's paper was reproduced in the record of the Daniel hearings.

84. Judith Butler, *Gender Trouble* (New York: Routledge, 1990), 17.

85. Emphasis fell on gratifying oral needs in compulsive reenactments of "the drama of getting and losing." Although Freud was not cited, the *fort/da* game relied on the "compulsion to repeat overrid[ing] the pleasure principle." See Sigmund Freud, *Beyond the Pleasure Principle*, trans. James Strachey (New York: W.W. Norton, 1961), 217.

86. Chein et al., *The Road to H*, 223.

87. Chein et al., *The Road to H*, 262.

88. Chein et al., *The Road to H*, 263.

89. Chein et al., *The Road to H*, 264.

90. Chein et al., *The Road to H*, 264. Cf. n. 8. Chein and his coauthors believed that normative pressures were acute in U.S. society due to the emphasis on strong sexual differentiation, "many degrees of freedom with an associated breakdown in traditional lines of differentiation," and no "third-sex option."

91. Chein et al., *The Road to H*, 230. In constructing this decidedly Western version of "Eastern" philosophy, they admitted "we may only be displaying our own culturocentrism."

92. Chein and his coauthors differentiated between "Western" pleasures—quick satisfaction, remounting desire, and ready-to-hand gratification—from "Eastern" concepts of pleasure such as nirvana, absence of desire, postponement of orgasm, and what they described as "frustration."

93. Chein et al., *The Road to H*, 256.

94. Chein et al., *The Road to H*, 272–273. Only 45 percent of nonaddict controls experienced weak relations with their fathers.

95. Chein et al., *The Road to H*, 274.

96. The investigators mentioned disciplinary competition at the Research Center for Human Relations over what addicts were "really like."

97. ABA, Committee on Narcotic Study, 321–322. Isidor Chein reported on the ongoing study.

98. Chein et al., *The Road to H*, 49.

99. All comparative statistics are found in Chein et al., *The Road to H*, 52–53.

100. Chein et al., *The Road to H*, Appendix L, 465.

Chapter 5

1. David Musto, *The American Disease: Origins of Narcotics Control*, 2d ed. (New York: Oxford University Press, 1987), 252.

2. Robert DuPont, M.D. *Perspective on an Epidemic* (Washington, DC: Special Action Office For Drug Abuse Prevention, 1973), 18. Many thanks to Robert DuPont for his remarks on the 1950s at the conference "One Hundred Years of Heroin," Yale College, September 20, 1998.

3. Rufus King, *The Drug Hang-Up: America's Fifty-Year Folly* (New York: W.W. Norton, 1972), 113. In a scathing critique of the Kefauver hearings, King noted that the 1951 Boggs Act was the only Crime Committee recommendation to become law.

4. U.S. Congress. Senate Subcommittee on Improvements to the Criminal Code of the Committee on the Judiciary. *Hearings on the Illicit Narcotics Traffic*. 84th Cong., 1st sess., 1955 (Washington, DC: GPO).

5. Incidents and threats of violence toward witnesses, relatives, or committee members occurred when the hearings were televised (Senate Subcommittee, *Illicit Narcotics Traffic*, Part 7, 3402, and Part 8, 4008).

6. Alfred R. Lindesmith, in *The Addict and the Law* (Bloomington, IN: Indiana University Press, 1965), aimed to demonstrate that drug law enforcement was "cruel in its effects."

7. Frank R. Baumgartner and Bryan D. Jones, *Agendas and Instability in American Politics* (Chicago: University of Chicago Press, 1993), 25–26.

8. Baumgartner and Jones, *Agendas and Instability*, 4.

9. Baumgartner and Jones, *Agendas and Instability*, 250.

10. Several sources document this phenomenon relative to drug issues: Baumgartner and Jones, *Agendas and Instability*, 1993; Eva Bertram, Morris Blackman, Kenneth Sharpe, and Peter Andreas, *Drug War Politics: The Price of Denial* (Berkeley, CA: University of California Press, 1996); Laura E. Gomez, *Misconceiving Mothers: Legislators, Prosecutors, and the Politics of Prenatal Drug Exposure* (Philadelphia, PA: Temple University Press, 1997); and Elaine B. Sharp,

The Dilemma of Drug Policy in the United States (New York: HarperCollins, 1994).

11. Baumgartner and Jones, *Agendas and Instability*, 160.

12. Barbara J. Nelson, *Making an Issue of Child Abuse* (Chicago: University of Chicago Press, 1984), 137. She concluded that U.S. citizens have only two choices—supporting gradual change, or hoping for major change that may never come.

13. Baumgartner and Jones, *Agendas and Instability*, 159. They classify hearings according to "enforcement" or "education" topics to present empirical evidence for this claim.

14. Baumgartner and Jones, *Agendas and Instability*, 38.

15. George Rossman, "The Testimony of the Drug Addict," *American Law Review* 58 (1924): 196–228.

16. Rossman, "The Testimony of the Drug Addict," 203–204.

17. Quoted in Rossman, "The Testimony of the Drug Addict," n. 21, 205.

18. Quoted in Rossman, "The Testimony of the Drug Addict," 197.

19. Rossman, "The Testimony of the Drug Addict," 207–208.

20. Rossman, "The Testimony of the Drug Addict," 222.

21. Rossman, "The Testimony of the Drug Addict," 223.

22. Rossman, "The Testimony of the Drug Addict," 222.

23. Rossman, "The Testimony of the Drug Addict," 223.

24. Quoted in Rossman, "The Testimony of the Drug Addict," 196.

25. Nancy Fraser, *Unruly Practices* (Minneapolis, MN: University of Minnesota Press, 1989), 168.

26. Douglas Clark Kinder, "Shutting Out the Evil: Nativism and Narcotics Control in the United States," *Journal of Policy History* 3, no. 4 (1991): 468–493.

27. Senate Subcommittee. *Illicit Narcotics Traffic*. Part 1, 34.

28. John C. McWilliams, *The Protectors: Harry J. Anslinger and the Federal Bureau of Narcotics, 1930–1962* (Newark, DE: University of Delaware Press, 1990), 151. In 1953–1954, eight senators mentioned communist drug trafficking on the floor and hundreds of popular references appeared in publications as far-ranging as *True Crime Detective* to *The Saturday Evening Post*.

29. McWilliams, *The Protectors*, 152. U.S. intelligence encouraged southeast Asian heroin cultivation and traffic. Covert operations sought to control Third World liberation movements, a goal that led to alliances with drug producers and traffickers. See Alfred W. McCoy, *The Politics of Heroin* (New York: Lawrence Hill Books, 1991).

30. Senate Subcommittee. *Illicit Narcotics Traffic*, Part 1, 33.

31. Senate Subcommittee. *Illicit Narcotics Traffic*, Part 1, 34.

32. Alan A. Block and John C. McWilliams, "On the Origins of American Counterintelligence: Building a Clandestine Network," *Journal of Policy History* 1, no. 4 (1989): 353–372.

33. According to King, Senator Daniel exploited his status as an antidrug crusader to political advantage in his gubernatorial campaign. King, *The Drug Hang-Up*, 1972.

34. Anslinger copublished *The Traffic in Narcotics* with William F. Tompkins (New York: Funk and Wagnalls, 1953); *The Murderers: The Story of the Narcotics Gangs* with Will Oursler (New York: Farrar, Straus and Cudahy, 1961); and *The Protectors: The Heroic Story of the Narcotics Agents* with J. Dennis Gregory (New York: Farrar, Straus, 1964).

35. See Joost A. M. Meerloo, "Artificial Ecstasy: A Study of the Psychosomatic Aspects of Drug Addiction," *Journal of Nervous and Mental Disease* 115 (1952): 246–266; "Pavlovian Strategy as a Weapon of Menticide," *American Journal of Psychiatry* 110 (1954): 809–813; and "Medication into Submission: The Danger of Therapeutic Coercion," *Journal of Nervous and Mental Disease* 122, no. 4 (1955): 353–360. See also Louis Lasagna, John M. von Felsinger, and Henry K. Beecher, "Drug Induced Mood Changes in Man," *JAMA* (March 19, 1955): 1006–1020, and (March 26, 1955): 1113–1119.

36. U.S. Congress. House Committee on Un-American Activities, *Soviet Total War: "Historic Mission" of Violence and Deceit*. 85th Cong., House Doc. no. 227, September 23, 1956; Jan Karski, "War by Argument in Asia," 734–741.

37. House Committee on Un-American Activities, *Soviet Total War*, 735.

38. Anslinger and Tompkins, *The Traffic in Narcotics*, 8. Supposedly, the Japanese deployed drugs as "chemical warfare" against mainland Chinese, who adopted the tactic. "This time the free people of the world, fighting against communism and its spread, was the objective, with an enemy who was spreading addiction to swell its coffers and finance a war."

39. "A turn of the judicial wheel" was necessary to avoid the coming anarchy, according to Malachi Harney, then Superintendent of the Division of Narcotic Control, Illinois Department of Public Safety. See "The Requirement for Law Enforcement," in *Narcotic Drug Addiction Problems*, Proceedings of the Symposium on the History of Drug Addiction Problems, ed. Robert B. Livingston (Bethesda, MD: National Institute of Health and Washington, DC: U.S. Department of Health, Education, and Welfare, 1958), 84–99. Harney advised taking addicts "out of society . . . let[ting them] back into circulation with a string attached" (93).

40. U.S. Congress. Senate Subcommittee to Investigate Juvenile Delinquency of the Committee on the Judiciary. *Juvenile Delinquency: Treatment and Rehabilitation of Juvenile Drug Addicts.* 84th Cong., 2d sess., December 17–18, 1956 (Washington, DC: GPO, 1957). See Charles Winick, "Narcotics Addiction and Its Treatment," *Law and Contemporary Problems* (Winter 1957): 24.

41. Senate Subcommittee. *Juvenile Delinquency: Treatment and Rehabilitation*, 42. Winick cited an article by Herbert Krugman, "The Role of Hostility in the Appeal of Communism in the United States," *Psychiatry* 16, no. 3 (1953): 253–261, which identified psychodynamic similarities between parents of communists and parents of addicts.

42. Senate Subcommittee. *Juvenile Delinquency: Treatment and Rehabilitation*, 20–21.

43. See Winick, "Narcotics Addiction," 24.

44. Senate Subcommittee. *Juvenile Delinquency: Treatment and Rehabilitation*, 87.

45. Senate Subcommittee. *Illicit Narcotics Traffic*, Part 2, 597–605.

46. For ample evidence that Driscoll quoted directly from a speech by Frederick A. Wallis, "The Curse of Civilization," compare to H. S. Middlemiss, *Narcotics Education* (Washington, DC: 1926), 145–157.

47. The Philadelphia PD's resourcefulness was not confined to its literature: Driscoll recounted that a "colored" undercover agent, Burdell Beaman, worked South Street in drag.

48. Senate Subcommittee. *Illicit Narcotics Traffic*, Part 2, 521.

49. Senate Subcommittee. *Illicit Narcotics Traffic*, Part 2, 521.

50. See Alan A. Block and Bruce Bullington, "A Trojan Horse: Anti-Communism and the War on Drugs," *Contemporary Crises* 14, no.1 (1990): 39–55; and Simon Davies, "International Law: The Final Solution?" in *The Reduction of Drug-Related Harm,* eds. P. O'Hare, R. Newcombe, A. Matthews, Ernst C. Buning, and Ernest Drucker (New York: Routledge, 1992), 62–70. The latter discusses obstacles to instituting "harm minimization" policy in a political culture shaped by prohibition and antidrug discipline.

51. Robert Felix, "The Technique of Mass Approach to the Problems of Mental Health," *Neuropsychiatry* 2, no. 1 (1952): 48–62.

52. Musto, *The American Disease*, set out the parameters within which all drug policy historians work. I am not disagreeing with Musto but reading claims about drug addiction for what they can tell us about (post)modern regimes of truth and subject formation, and how policy operates as a form of cultural production.

53. The following federal employees testified: Kenneth W. Chapman, National Institute of Mental Health (NIMH); Robert H. Felix, Director,

NIMH; Clifton K. Himmelsbach, NIMH; G. Halsey Hunt, USPHS; Harris Isbell, USPHS; James V. Lowry, USPHS; and John A. Trautman, USPHS.

54. Senate Subcommittee. *Illicit Narcotics Traffic*, Part 4, 1466.

55. Senate Subcommittee. *Illicit Narcotics Traffic*, Part 4, 1465.

56. Senate Subcommittee. *Illicit Narcotics Traffic*, Part 4, 1468. Robert Felix considered the addict an "inadequately adjusted individual not radically different from his non-addicted fellows, who has at some time discovered that drugs either dulled the sense of discomfort produced by his difficulties, or gave him a subjective feeling of mastery over his situation. In either case he experienced a release and emotional uplift which compensated for the attitude of society toward him." See "An Appraisal of the Personality Types of the Addict," *American Journal of Psychiatry* 100, no. 4 (1944): 462–467. Felix found that men "repress much that they would like to express" under stress.

57. Senate Subcommittee. *Illicit Narcotics Traffic*, Part 4, 1479.

58. Senate Subcommittee. *Illicit Narcotics Traffic*, Part 4, 1487.

59. John Marks, *The Search for the Manchurian Candidate: The CIA and Mind Control* (New York: W.W. Norton, 1979), 66–70. CIA-contract drug experimentation occurred on an order of magnitude parallel to the Tuskegee syphilis studies and those at the Holmesburg prison. This will most likely continue to be unverifiable as Isbell refused interviews; the Macy Foundation records are closed; and surviving subjects are difficult to locate.

60. Quoted in Marks, *The Manchurian Candidate*, 69. Much of Isbell's research concerned hallucinogens and was not restricted to narcotics addiction.

61. Senate Subcommittee. *Illicit Narcotics Traffic*, Part 4, 1466.

62. Senate Subcommittee. *Illicit Narcotics Traffic*, Part 4, 1496.

63. For an opposing view, see Lindesmith, *The Addict and the Law*, 266. He suggested that the FBN and USPHS converged on policy. "The consensus among them inevitably suggests that the apparent uniformity of views is artificially imposed from above or that it arises from the nature of the institutional environment within which the officials deal with addicts."

64. In 1955, the only other health care the USPHS delivered was treatment for leprosy. The narcotics "farms" treated felons, voluntary patients, and Veterans' Administration hospital overflow. Institutional facilities were originally prisonlike, complete with "bars and grills," but were remodeled to achieve a more hospital-like atmosphere in the 1960s. The metaphor for addiction

had implications for the very architecture of treatment facilities.

65. Judge Carroll's tough reputation convinced federal authorities to allow local prosecution.

66. Senate Subcommittee. *Illicit Narcotics Traffic*, Part 2, 433.

67. Senate Subcommittee. *Illicit Narcotics Traffic*, Part 2, 372. Philadelphia Police Lieutenant Thomas McDermott presided over the FBN/Philadelphia PD narcotics raid prior to the hearing.

68. Senate Subcommittee. *Illicit Narcotics Traffic*, Part 2, 382.

69. Senate Subcommittee. *Illicit Narcotics Traffic*, Part 2, 434.

70. Senate Subcommittee. *Illicit Narcotics Traffic*, Part 2, 560.

71. Senate Subcommittee. *Illicit Narcotics Traffic*, Part 2, 561.

72. Senate Subcommittee. *Illicit Narcotics Traffic*, Part 2, 563.

73. Senate Subcommittee. *Illicit Narcotics Traffic*, Part 2, 564.

74. Senate Subcommittee. *Illicit Narcotics Traffic*, Part 2, 564.

75. Senate Subcommittee. *Illicit Narcotics Traffic*, Part 2, 566.

76. Senate Subcommittee. *Illicit Narcotics Traffic*, Part 2, 562.

77. Senate Subcommittee. *Illicit Narcotics Traffic*, Part 2, 563.

78. Senate Subcommittee. *Illicit Narcotics Traffic*, Part 2, 566.

79. Senate Subcommittee. *Illicit Narcotics Traffic*, Part 2, 566.

80. Senate Subcommittee. *Illicit Narcotics Traffic*, Part 9, 4201.

81. Senate Subcommittee. *Illicit Narcotics Traffic*, Part 9, 4201.

82. Senate Subcommittee. *Illicit Narcotics Traffic*, Part 3, 751.

83. Senate Subcommittee. *Illicit Narcotics Traffic*, Part 2, 610.

84. Senate Subcommittee. *Illicit Narcotics Traffic*, Part 9, 4205.

85. Senate Subcommittee. *Illicit Narcotics Traffic*, Part 9, 4208.

86. Senate Subcommittee. *Illicit Narcotics Traffic*, Part 9, 4208.

87. Senate Subcommittee. *Illicit Narcotics Traffic*, Part 3, 1005.

88. Senate Subcommittee. *Illicit Narcotics Traffic*, Part 3, 1014.

89. Senate Subcommittee. *Illicit Narcotics Traffic*, Part 7, 2427.

90. Senate Subcommittee. *Illicit Narcotics Traffic*, Part 8, 3654.

91. Senate Subcommittee. *Illicit Narcotics Traffic*, Part 9, 4214–4215.

92. Senate Subcommittee. *Illicit Narcotics Traffic*, Part 9, 4221.

93. Senate Subcommittee. *Illicit Narcotics Traffic*, Part 9, 4222.

94. Senate Subcommittee. *Illicit Narcotics Traffic*, Part 9, 4232.

95. Senate Subcommittee. *Illicit Narcotics Traffic*, Part 9, 4275.

96. Senate Subcommittee. *Illicit Narcotics Traffic*, Part 9, 4276.

97. Senate Subcommittee. *Illicit Narcotics Traffic*, Part 9, 4277.

98. Senate Subcommittee. *Illicit Narcotics Traffic*, Part 9, 4280.

99. Senate Subcommittee. *Illicit Narcotics Traffic*, Part 10, 4523.

100. Senate Subcommittee. *Illicit Narcotics Traffic*, Part 10, 4527.

101. Senate Subcommittee. *Illicit Narcotics Traffic*, Part 10, 4528.

102. Senate Subcommittee. *Illicit Narcotics Traffic*, Part 10, 4529.

103. Patrick J. Kelley, *Reaching the Teenage Addict* (New York: New York City Youth Board, 1966).

104. Lauretta Bender, "Drug Addiction in Adolescence," *Comprehensive Psychiatry* 4, no. 3 (1963): 190. Her review of social-psychiatric research on adolescent addicts to date approvingly summarized Kelley's efforts with 15 "main-liners" in a heroin-using gang.

105. Kelley, *Reaching the Teenage Addict*, 45.

Mother Fixations

1. U.S. Congress. Senate Committee on Labor and Human Resources. Subcommittee on Children, Families, Drugs and Alcoholism. *Children of Substance Abusers.* 101st Cong., 2d sess., 5 February 1990, 5.

2. See Timothy Egan, "A Drug Ran Its Course, Then Hid with Its Users," *New York Times,* September 19, 1999, A1, 46. The article cites the effects of declining crack use among women: decreased arrests, murder rates, and numbers of children in foster care. Whether drug policy and policing were responsible for these effects was unclear. The article credited "human resiliency" and the fact that children of crack users found it repulsive. While use was steady in the adult cohort from 1989 to 1999, it declined precipitously among persons aged 15 to 20, especially among urban African-American youth.

3. The first part of the statement summarizes the position of Robert Blank, *Regulating Reproduction* (New York: Columbia University Press, 1990); the second part directly quotes House Select Committee on Children, Youth, and Families. *Born Hooked: Confronting the Impact of Perinatal Substance Abuse.* 101st Cong., 1st sess., 27 April 1989, 104.

4. U.S. Congress. House Select Committee on Children, Youth, and Families. *Born Hooked.*

5. Gwendolyn Mink, *Welfare's End* (Ithaca, NY: Cornell University Press); Nancy A. Naples, "The 'New Consensus' on the Gendered 'Social Contract': The 1987–1988 U.S. Congressional Hearings on Welfare Reform," *Signs* 22, no. 4 (1997): 907–945; Sanford Schram, *Words of Welfare* (Minneapolis, MN: University of Minnesota Press, 1995).

6. Mink, *Welfare's End*, 69–101.

7. Blank, *Regulating Reproduction*, 51.

8. Franklin E. Zimring and Gordon Hawkins, *The Search for Rational Drug Control* (New York: Cambridge University Press, 1992), 168.

9. Zimring and Hawkins, *The Search for Rational Drug Control*, 170.

10. See Karen J. Swift, *Manufacturing "Bad Mothers": Critical Perspectives on Child Abuse* (Buffalo, NY: University of Toronto Press, 1995); and Nancy Fraser, *Unruly Practices* and *Justice Interruptus* (Minneapolis, MN: University of Minnesota, 1989).

11. Michelle Boulous Walker, *Philosophy and the Maternal Body* (New York: Routledge, 1998), 135. Walker understands metaphors and images as "the point in the text where the (artificial) distinction between reality and fiction breaks down" (34), a useful way to think about moments when figurative language interrupts "rational" political discourse.

12. Although maternity is central to Part III, the meaning of femininity cannot and should not be reduced to the maternal. That reduction is, however, quite evident in the discursive construction of drug-using mothers and pregnant addicts in U.S. political discourse.

Chapter 6

1. Linda Gordon, *Pitied but Not Entitled: Single Mothers and the History of Welfare, 1890–1935* (New York: Free Press, 1994); Gwendolyn Mink, *The Wages of Motherhood: Inequality in the Welfare State, 1917–1942* (Ithaca, NY: Cornell University Press, 1995); Theda Skocpol, *Protecting Soldiers and Mothers: The Political Origins of Social Policy in the United States* (Cambridge, MA: Harvard University Press, 1992).

2. Molly Ladd-Taylor, *Mother-Work: Women, Child Welfare, and the State, 1890–1930* (Urbana, IL: University of Illinois Press, 1994).

3. Sara Ruddick, *Maternal Thinking* (New York: Ballantine Books, 1989), 111.

4. Dorothy E. Roberts, *Killing the Black Body: Race, Reproduction, and the Meaning of Liberty* (New York: Pantheon Books, 1997).

5. Quoted in Stephen R. Kandall, *Substance and Shadow: Women and Addiction in the United States* (Cambridge, MA: Harvard University Press, 1996), 53.

6. Quoted in Kandall, *Substance and Shadow*, 56.

7. Quoted in Charles E. Terry and Mildred Pellens, *The Opium Problem* (1928; reprint, Montclair, NJ: Patterson Smith, 1970), 414.

8. Quoted in Terry and Pellens, *The Opium Problem*, 416.

9. Terry and Pellens, *The Opium Problem*, 428.

10. Paul Zimmering, James Toolan, Renate Safrin, and S. Bernard Wortis, "Heroin Addiction in Adolescent Boys," *Journal of Nervous and Mental Disease* 114 (1951): 19–30.

11. Michael J. Pescor asserted that adolescent addiction only occurred among "hedonists" or in broken homes with a "history of a tyrannical father and an overindulgent mother" (1953, 471–488).

12. Stewart Robertson, "Dope on Dope," *The Family Circle*, October 26, 1945 (Box 12, Anslinger Papers).

13. See Michael J. Pescor, "A Comparative Study of Male and Female Drug Addicts," *American Journal of Psychiatry* 100 (1944): 771–774.

14. Houston Brummit, "Observations on Drug Addicts in a House of Detention for Women," *Corrective Psychiatry and Journal of Social Therapy* 9, no. 2 (1963): 62–70.

15. See Carl D. Chambers, R. Kent Hinesley, and Mary Moldestad, "The Female Opiate Addict," in *The Epidemiology of Opiate Addiction in the United States*, eds. John C. Ball and Carl D. Chambers (Springfield, IL: Charles C. Thomas, 1970): 222–239. The authors criticized studies that ignored the "known effect of race as a significant independent variable in addiction." See also Chambers and Arthur D. Moffett on "Negro Opiate Addiction," in Ball and Chambers, 178–201.

16. Michael Starks, *Cocaine Fiends and Reefer Madness* (New York: Cornwall Books, 1982), 55. The 1946 revision to the Motion Picture Production Code forbade any portrayal that "stimulate[d] curiosity concerning the use or traffic in such drugs."

17. "Drug Addiction Film Guide 579," *Drug Addiction* 1951.

18. "Drug Addiction Film Guide 579," *Drug Addiction* 1951.

19. N. R. DeMexico, *Marijuana Girl* (New York: Softcover Library, 1960).

20. DeMexico, *Marijuana Girl*, 64–65.

21. DeMexico, *Marijuana Girl*, 136.

22. DeMexico, *Marijuana Girl*, 139.

23. Lauretta Bender, "State Care of Emotionally and Socially Disturbed Adolescents," in *Planning and Action for Mental Health*, ed. E. M. Thornton (London: World Federation for Mental Health, 1961): 200–215; and "Drug Addiction in Adolescence," *Comprehensive Psychiatry* 4, no. 3 (1963): 181–194. The first peak was in 1918 and 1919.

24. Bender, "Drug Addiction in Adolescence," *Comprehensive Psychiatry*, 185.

25. Bender, "Drug Addiction in Adolescence," *Comprehensive Psychiatry*, 192.

26. Bender, "Drug Addiction in Adolescence," *Comprehensive Psychiatry*, 190.

27. New York Academy of Medicine, *Drug Addiction among Adolescents* (New York: New York Academy of Medicine, 1952), 139 (emphasis mine).

28. Bender, "Drug Addiction in Adolescence," *Comprehensive Psychiatry*, 190.

29. Isidor Chein, Donald L. Gerard, Robert S. Lee, and Eva Rosenfeld, *The Road to H: Narcotics, Delinquency, and Social Policy* (New York: Basic Books, 1964), 300.

30. Chein et al., *The Road to H*, 310–311.

31. Chein et al., *The Road to H*, 311.

32. Chein et al., *The Road to H*, 312.

33. Despite no data on women from other racial-ethnic backgrounds, the researchers did not restrict their claims to the African-American female drug-using population.

34. Chein et al., *The Road to H*, 300.

35. Brummit, "Observations on Drug Addicts," *Corrective Psychiatry and Journal of Social Therapy*, 64.

36. Jeremy Larner and Ralph Tefferteller, eds., *The Addict in the Street* (New York: Grove Press, 1964), 109. This subject estimated that one third of addicts were female.

37. Chein et al., *The Road to H*, 305. Heroin use among women occurred only "in the setting of prolonged and pervasive maladjustment."

38. Chein et al., *The Road to H*, 307. Emphasis in the original.

39. Chein et al., *The Road to H*, 313.

40. Judith Allen, *Sex and Secrets* (Oxford: Oxford University Press, 1990) emphasizes the under-policing of "women's" crimes. Understanding the process by which we "charge" acts or identities with gendered, racialized, or sexualized meanings is crucial to understanding the history of social processes and cultural figurations. Defining whether gender, race, class, or sexuality is most salient is not as important as defining their interarticulation.

41. See Linda Singer, *Erotic Welfare* (New York: Routledge, 1993), 43–44. Both those who seek to control behavior and those who call for humanitarian treatment call on similar "logics of contagion." "Both rationalize power as management . . . in the production of addiction, then, regulatory power preserves and increases the very criminality that it claims to oppose, becoming the paradigm for the contagious criminality that justifies its own interventionist strategies ad infinitum."

42. For instance, Florrie Fisher, *The Lonely Trip Back* (Garden City, NY: Doubleday, 1971); Emily Hahn, *Times and Places* (New York: Crowell, 1970); Diane di Prima, *Memoirs of a Beatnik* (San Francisco: The Last Gasp, 1969); and Barbara Quinn, *Cookie* (New York: Bartholomew House, 1971; also published under the title *Junkie*). Excerpts of the above appear in Michael Horowitz and Cynthia Palmer, *Shaman Woman, Mainline Lady: Women's Writings on the Drug Experience* (New York: William Morrow, 1982).

43. Social reproduction never functions in an uninterrupted or total way, as members of "deviant" categories interrupt the processes of normalization. Historiographically tracing these "conflict[s] within dominant accounts" can attribute meaning to moments when girl subjects interrupt normalizing constructions proffered by judges, congressmen, parents, scientific investigators, or the press. See Jennifer Terry, "Theorizing Deviant Historiography," *differences* 3 (1991): 59. The interruptions, however, also work to shore up the sense of superiority among the "normal." They are often opportunities for the governing mentalities to contain or defuse the disruption.

44. Colonel Frank J. Smith, Chief of Narcotic Control, New York State Department of Health, believed that girls merely posed as addicts to gain special treatment and privileges. New York Academy of Medicine, *Drug Addiction among Adolescents*, 140–141.

45. See Evelyn Nakano Glenn, "From Servitude to Service Work: Historical Continuities in the Racial Division of Paid Reproductive Labor," *Signs* 18, no. 1 (1992): 1–43, for a relational model to replace additive models of race, class, and gender, thereby offering a theoretical "corrective to feminist theories of gendered thought that posit universal female modes of thinking growing out of common experiences such as domesticity and motherhood."

46. The rebellion aspect was important to female addicts of the 1950s and 1960s, but addiction cannot be considered simply a form of adolescent rebellion. Addiction's racial and sexual economics have changed radically over the past decades. Perhaps a restricted group of upper- and middle-class white women who use heroin today can claim to "resist the dominant discourse" or "reject restrictive gender and class expectations." See Jennifer Friedman and Marisa Alicea, "Women and Heroin: The Path of Resistance and Its Consequences," *Gender and Society* 9, no. 4 (August 1995): 432–449.

47. Bender, "Drug Addiction in Adolescence," *Comprehensive Psychiatry*, 191. Howard Becker was the unnamed sociologist.

48. Bender, "Drug Addiction in Adolescence," *Comprehensive Psychiatry*, 191.

49. This project brings historical sociology and cultural studies into conversation, adding a historical dimension to Angela McRobbie's critique of sociology and cultural studies in *Postmodernism and Popular Culture* (New York: Routledge, 1994), 180.

50. Janet Clark, *The Fantastic Lodge: Autobiography of a Girl Drug Addict*, ed. Helen MacGill Hughes

(Boston: Houghton Mifflin, 1961). For the text's convoluted publication history, see James Bennett, *Oral History and Delinquency: The Rhetoric of Criminology* (Chicago: University of Chicago Press, 1981).

51. Clark, *The Fantastic Lodge*, vii.
52. Clark, *The Fantastic Lodge*, 220.
53. Clark, *The Fantastic Lodge*, 49.
54. Clark, *The Fantastic Lodge*, 49.
55. See Rickie Solinger, *Wake Up Little Susie: Single Pregnancy and Race before Roe v. Wade* (New York: Routledge, 1992), 61. "Culture" operated as a "dignified cover for biological racism." White culture was presented as benign and protective, failure being an individual matter; black culture as deviant and dangerous, failure being a collective matter.
56. Clark, *The Fantastic Lodge*, 54. Her doctor suggested she read Philip Wylie, "very unusual for an obstetrician, I think—I hope; if it isn't, God help all poor women."
57. Within psychoanalytic discourse, addiction resulted from abrupt weaning, a "frustrating, denying, seductive mother," oral fixation, and the ongoing search for the breast. According to Robert J. Chessick, "To the addict the drug has become equivalent to the milk and love he received as an infant" ("The 'Pharmacogenic Orgasm' in the Drug Addict," *Archives of General Psychiatry* 3, no. 5 [1960]). Male addicts reported dreams in which huge bottles of morphine and heroin represented their mothers' breasts none too subtly. Such representations appeared in films depicting intoxication, which often conflated women and drugs. *Reefer Madness* (1937) contained a scene equating feminine disarray with marijuana use. *The Lost Weekend* (Best Motion Picture of 1945), the first Hollywood movie to portray alcoholism, contained a fantasy sequence in which women and bottles were superimposed.
58. Clark, *The Fantastic Lodge*, 126.
59. Clark, *The Fantastic Lodge*, 129.
60. Clark, *The Fantastic Lodge*, 131.
61. Clark, *The Fantastic Lodge*, 132.
62. Clark, *The Fantastic Lodge*, 141–142.
63. Howard S. Becker, *The Outsiders* (New York: Free Press, 1963), 43. He wanted to remedy the fragmentary and amateurish "data" of social science by replacing it with a precise and detailed "social anatomy."
64. Becker quoted Hughes's *Students' Culture and Perspectives: Lectures on Medical and General Education* (Lawrence, KS: University of Kansas School of Law, 1961) in *The Outsiders*. Both Everett C. Hughes and his wife, Helen MacGill Hughes (who edited the transcripts that became *The Fantastic Lodge*), were students of sociologist Robert E. Park, who studied the "marginal man" in the 1920s. The "outsider" figure was a hybrid construction of mid-century sociology that was primarily masculine.
65. Becker thought that deviant subcultures formed to respond to social isolation—an idea shaped by his experience as a white, middle-class, jazz musician in a largely African-American milieu. He shared that experience of cultural difference with Janet and Bob Clark.
66. Ralph H. Kunstadter, M.D., Reuben I. Klein, M.D., Evelyn C. Lundeen, R.N., Winifred Witz, R.N., and Mary Morrison, R.N., "Narcotic Withdrawal Symptoms in Newborn Infants," *JAMA* 165 (October 25, 1958): 1008–1010. The article presented data on five infants "born of addicted mothers," four African-American and one white.
67. M. A. Perlstein, "Congenital Morphinism: Rare Cause of Convulsions in Newborn," *JAMA* 135 (November 8, 1947): 633. Perlstein presented a short history of references in the medical literature from 1875 to 1934. He reported on a 1941 case of an infant girl born to a known morphine addict. The girl showed "normal development" after one month of age.
68. Theodore Rosenthal, M.D., Sherman W. Patrick, M.A., and Donald C. Krug, M.A., "Congenital Neonatal Narcotics Addiction: A Natural History," *American Journal of Public Health* 54, no. 8 (August 1964): 1252–1262. Babies were the one "segment of the total addiction population where 'cure' is attainable" (1253). Neonatal addiction was presumed highest among African-Americans, who were reported addicted more frequently than white women, particularly in public hospitals, even then.
69. Rosenthal, Patrick, and Krug, "Congenital Neonatal Narcotics Addiction," *American Journal of Public Health*, 1253.
70. Rosenthal, Patrick, and Krug, "Congenital Neonatal Narcotics Addiction," *American Journal of Public Health*, 1260–1261. "Most general practitioners, if faced with an illegally addicted patient, probably are only concerned in getting the addict out of the office as soon as possible. The historical developments leading to this situation are well documented."
71. Kunstadter et al., "Narcotic Withdrawal Symptoms," *JAMA*, 1010. The authors also wrote a chapter to be incorporated into a textbook edited by Kunstadter and Lundeen, *Care of the Premature Infant* (Philadelphia: J.B. Lippincott, 1958), 267.
72. Roy Stern, "The Pregnant Addict," *American Journal of Obstetrics and Gynecology* 94 (1966): 253–257.
73. Stern, "The Pregnant Addict," *American Journal of Obstetrics and Gynecology*, 255.
74. Rosenthal, Patrick, and Krug, "Congenital Neonatal Narcotics Addiction," *American Journal of Public Health*, 1261.

75. Rosenthal, Patrick, and Krug, "Congenital Neonatal Narcotics Addiction," *American Journal of Public Health*, 1261. "Complexity" quickly becomes the justification for coercion.
76. The U.S. Supreme Court cited five studies on neonatal addiction in *Robinson v. California* 370 U.S. 554 (1962).
77. *Robinson v. California*, 667.
78. *Robinson v. California*, 666.
79. *Robinson v. California*, 665.
80. Self-control was the crux of the matter. Justice Clark's dissent argued that addicts were "commonly recognized as a threat to the State and to the individual" and presented a "grave threat of future harmful conduct" (*Robinson v. California*, 683). The California Health and Safety Code defined an addict as "a person who habitually takes or otherwise uses to the extent of having *lost the power of self-control* any opium, morphine, cocaine, or other narcotic drug." Controlled users were not legally defined as addicts and could not be committed under California law. Clark argued the appellant should be criminally charged because he was "redeemable" and so could not be committed (*Robinson v. California*, 688).
81. *Robinson v. California*, 677.
82. Earl Ubell, *New York Herald Tribune*, April 25, 1962, 25. Saul Krugman, a Bellevue physician, claimed to have seen more than one hundred heroin-addicted babies across two years. Thorazine, the major tranquilizer employed in mental institutions, was used to control their symptoms. Cited in *Robinson v. California*, 670–671.
83. Jonathan Simon, *Poor Discipline: Parole and the Social Control of the Underclass, 1890–1990* (Chicago: University of Chicago Press, 1993).
84. Simon, *Poor Discipline*, 72. The shift to clinical parole was also a shift from work discipline to treatment designed to facilitate individual adjustment and productive citizenship.
85. Judianne Densen-Gerber, M. Wiener, and R. Hochstedler, "Sexual Behavior, Abortion, and Birth Control in Heroin Addicts," *Contemporary Drug Problems* 1, no. 4 (1972): 72. Densen-Gerber founded Odyssey House, a residential treatment center in New York City. The subjects were 27 white, 23 African-American, and seven Puerto Rican women.
86. Lawrence K. Frank, *Society as the Patient* (New Brunswick, NJ: Rutgers University Press 1948), 118.
87. Frank, *Society as the Patient*, 120–121.
88. Frank, *Society as the Patient*, 123.
89. Robert J. Chessick, "The 'Pharmacogenic Orgasm' in the Drug Addict," *Archives of General Psychiatry* 3, no. 5 (1960): 117–128. Conducted at the USPHS hospital in Lexington, Kentucky, the study involved 50 heroin addicts (including eight women). It set out to test psychoanalyst

Sandor Rado's theory of the "pharmacogenic orgasm," advanced in "The Psychic Effects of Intoxicants," *International Journal of Psychoanalysis* 7 (1926): 396–413; "The Psychoanalysis of Pharmacothymia," trans. Bertram D. Lewin, *The Psychoanalytic Quarterly* 2 (1933): 1–23; and "Narcotic Bondage," *American Journal of Psychiatry* 114, no. 2 (1957): 165–170.
90. Chessick, "The 'Pharmacogenic Orgasm,'" *Archives of General Psychiatry*, 120.
91. Chessick, "The 'Pharmacogenic Orgasm,'" *Archives of General Psychiatry*, 121.
92. Chessick, "The 'Pharmacogenic Orgasm,'" *Archives of General Psychiatry*, 122.
93. Chessick, "The 'Pharmacogenic Orgasm,'" *Archives of General Psychiatry*, 122.
94. Chessick, "The 'Pharmacogenic Orgasm,'" *Archives of General Psychiatry*, 127.
95. Brummit, "Observations on Drug Addicts," *Corrective Psychiatry*, 67.
96. Brummit, "Observations on Drug Addicts," *Corrective Psychiatry*, 63.
97. Brummit, "Observations on Drug Addicts," *Corrective Psychiatry*, 63, 66–67.
98. Brummit, "Observations on Drug Addicts," *Corrective Psychiatry*, 69.
99. Methadone maintenance is a harm-reduction practice in which synthetic methadone is substituted for heroin to allow users to regulate aspects of their lives (and bodies) that heroin does not. Nyswander's work was pathbreaking.
100. Marie Nyswander, *The Drug Addict as Patient* (New York: Grune and Stratton, 1956).
101. Nyswander, *The Drug Addict as Patient*, 88.
102. This analogy is drawn from Otto Fenichel, *The Psychoanalytic Theory of Neurosis* (New York: W.W. Norton, 1945).
103. Nyswander, *The Drug Addict as Patient*, 79.
104. Prepared by Jane S. Lin-Fu, pediatric consultant to the Division of Health Services, Children's Bureau, Welfare Administration (Washington, DC: U.S. Department of Health, Education, and Welfare, 1967), 2.
105. "Yerby notes 15% rise in babies born with narcotics addiction," *New York Times*, March 18, 1966, 40.
106. Walter R. Cuskey, T. Premkumar, and Lois Sigel, "Survey of Opiate Addiction among Females in the United States between 1850 and 1970," *Public Health Reviews* 1 (1972), 7.
107. See Chambers et al., "The Female Opiate Addict." Heroin use predominated among the African-American women subjects, 93 percent of whom used it and 81 percent of whom preferred it to other drugs. Only 37 percent of the white women subjects preferred heroin and only 33 percent used it often. White women offered "medical or quasi-medical" reasons for use; African-American women "spoke of 'kicks' or 'curiosity' and addiction through the pressure of peers."

108. Cuskey, Premkumar, and Sigel, "Survey of Opiate Addiction among Females," *Public Health Reviews*, 7.

109. Cuskey, Premkumar, and Sigel, "Survey of Opiate Addiction among Females," *Public Health Reviews*, 7.

110. Janee Bemko and Virginia Davidson, "International Review of Women and Drug Abuse (1966–1975)," *Journal of the American Women's Medical Association* 33, no. 12 (1978): 507–518.

111. Josette Escamilla-Mondanaro, "Women: Pregnancy, Children, and Addiction," *Journal of Psychedelic Drugs* 9, no. 1 (1977): 62. The study was done at the Pregnant Addicts' Program in San Francisco. "Methadone mothers" were demonstrated to reproduce "the generational cycle of abuse" in children who became "needy, dependent, asocial adults."

112. Densen-Gerber, Wiener, and Hochstedler, "Sexual Behavior, Abortion, and Birth Control," *Contemporary Drug Problems*, 72.

113. Maureen McCarthy, "The Drug Addict and Her Feminine Mystique," *Psychiatric Opinion* 9 (1972): 31. McCarthy quoted Nyswander at length.

114. McCarthy, "The Drug Addict and Her Feminine Mystique," *Psychiatric Opinion*, 32.

115. McCarthy, "The Drug Addict and Her Feminine Mystique," *Psychiatric Opinion*, 33.

116. McCarthy, "The Drug Addict and Her Feminine Mystique," *Psychiatric Opinion*, 34.

117. McCarthy, "The Drug Addict and Her Feminine Mystique," *Psychiatric Opinion*, 35.

118. Cuskey, Premkumar, and Sigel, "Survey of Opiate Addiction among Females," *Public Health Reviews*, 7–39.

119. Cuskey, Premkumar, and Sigel, "Survey of Opiate Addiction," *Public Health Reviews*, 23.

120. Cuskey, Premkumar, and Sigel, "Survey of Opiate Addiction," *Public Health Reviews*, 30.

121. Cuskey, Premkumar, and Sigel, "Survey of Opiate Addiction," *Public Health Reviews*, 23, 27. Age of onset decreased between 1929 and 1970, especially among women of color.

122. Cuskey, Premkumar, and Sigel, "Survey of Opiate Addiction," *Public Health Reviews*, 27.

123. Cuskey, Premkumar, and Sigel, "Survey of Opiate Addiction," *Public Health Reviews*, 27–28.

124. Cuskey, Premkumar, and Sigel, "Survey of Opiate Addiction," *Public Health Reviews*, 30.

125. Cuskey, Premkumar, and Sigel, "Survey of Opiate Addiction," *Public Health Reviews*, 30.

126. Cuskey, Premkumar, and Sigel, "Survey of Opiate Addiction," *Public Health Reviews*, 30.

127. Cuskey, Premkumar, and Sigel, "Survey of Opiate Addiction," *Public Health Reviews*, 31.

128. See S. L. Zimmerman, *Understanding Family Policy*, 2d ed. (Thousand Oaks, CA: SAGE Publications, 1995).

129. U.S. Congress. House Select Committee On Crime. *Drugs in Our Schools*. 92 Cong., 2d sess., 21 June 1972, 315.

130. House Select Committee. *Drugs in Our Schools*, 619. A psychiatrist ordered Shirley Fletcher to stop cooking breakfast for her 21-year-old son—as if the withdrawal of bacon, eggs, and "overprotective" mothering would avert his heroin overdose. Frank Brasco (D-NY) recast her testimony: "Drug addiction, while not infectious bacteriologically, we know that it is socially infectious. . . . Do you believe we should allow drug addicts to remain in a healthy school population, or should we take them out of the school population and treat them and educate them in a separate program?" Mrs. Fletcher agreed that addicts had to be removed so they could not contaminate others through "peer pressure."

131. Currie, *Reckoning*, 41.

132. Ann Singer, "Mothering Practices and Heroin Addiction," *American Journal of Nursing* 74, no. 1 (1974): 77–82. Singer directed a program for pregnant addicts in New York City from 1967 to 1970.

133. Singer, "Mothering Practices," *American Journal of Nursing*, 79, 81.

134. Marsha Rosenbaum, *Women on Heroin* (New Brunswick, NJ: Rutgers University Press, 1981), 93. Parts of the book appeared in article format in the late 1970s. I discuss this work in greater depth in Chapter 8.

135. Rosenbaum, *Women on Heroin*, 94.

136. Rosenbaum, *Women on Heroin*, 95.

137. Rosenbaum, *Women on Heroin*, 96.

138. Rosenbaum, *Women on Heroin*, 99.

139. Rosenbaum, *Women on Heroin*, 100.

140. Escamilla-Mondanaro, "Women: Pregnancy, Children, and Addiction," *Journal of Psychedelic Drugs*, 60.

141. Escamilla-Mondanaro, "Women: Pregnancy, Children, and Addiction," *Journal of Psychedelic Drugs*, 60.

142. Escamilla-Mondanaro, "Women: Pregnancy, Children, and Addiction," *Journal of Psychedelic Drugs*, 62.

143. George M. Beschner and Kerry G. Treasure, "Female Adolescent Drug Use," in *Youth Drug Abuse: Problems, Issues, and Treatment*, eds. George M. Beschner and Alfred S. Friedman (Lexington, MA: Lexington Books, 1972).

144. H. P. Coppolillo, "Drug Impediments to Mothering Behavior," *Addictive Diseases* 2, no.1 (1975): 201–208.

145. Thomas J. Glynn, Helen Wallenstein Pearson, and Mollie Sayers, *Women and Drugs*, DHHS Pub. No. (ADM) 83–1268 (Rockville, MD: NIDA, 1983).

146. See Leith Mullings, *On Our Own Terms: Race, Class, and Gender in the Lives of African-American Women* (New York: Routledge, 1997); Mar-

garet Weir, "From Equal Opportunity to 'The New Social Contract,'" in *Racism, the City, and the State*, eds. Malcolm Cross and Michael Keith (New York, Routledge, 1993): 93–107; Maxine Baca Zinn, "Family, Feminism, and Race in America," in *Race, Class, and Gender*, eds. Esther Ngan-Ling Chow, Doris Wilkinson, and Maxine Baca Zinn (Thousand Oaks, CA: SAGE Publications, 1996): 169–183.

147. Elizabeth Ettore, *Women and Substance Abuse* (New Brunswick, NJ: Rutgers University Press, 1992), 103.

148. Currie, *Reckoning*, 122.

Chapter 7

1. U.S. Congress. Senate Subcommittee on Children, Family, Drugs, and Alcoholism of the Committee on Labor and Human Resources. *Falling through the Crack: The Impact of Drug-Exposed Children on the Child Welfare System*. 101st Cong., 2d sess., 8 March 1990, 3. The subcommittee served as a "forum for discussing the most tragic and frightening aspects of our national drug abuse problem: the use of cocaine, heroin, and other illegal drugs by pregnant women and women of childbearing age."

2. U.S. Congress. House Select Committee on Children, Youth, and Families. *Born Hooked: Confronting the Impact of Perinatal Substance Abuse*. 101st Cong., 1st sess., 27 April 1989, 2 and 11. This chapter is based on a discourse analysis of the hearings. All phrases placed in quotation marks indicate that these exact words appeared in the hearings.

3. U.S. Congress. Senate Committee on Labor and Human Resources and Committee on the Judiciary. *Impact of Drugs on Children and Families*. 101st Cong., 1st sess., 9 November 1989, 5 [emphasis mine].

4. Senate Subcommittee on Children. *Falling through the Crack*, 5.

5. Faye Ginsburg and Rayna Rapp, *Conceiving the New World Order* (Berkeley, CA: University of California Press, 1995), 3, 133; Arlene Geronimus, "The Weathering Hypothesis," in *Power and Decision: The Social Control of Reproduction*, eds. Gita Sen and Rachel Snow (Boston: Harvard School of Public Health, 1994).

6. U.S. Congress. House Subcommittee on Human Resources of the Committee on Ways and Means. *Impact of Crack Cocaine on the Child Welfare System*. 101st Cong., 2d sess., 3 April 1990, 6.

7. Witness Barry Zuckerman, M.D., asked: "At what age did we stop feeling sorry for her as a victim and become angry at her as the victimizer? If we were as willing to spend as much money when [the mother] was a child, as some people would

now have us spend in order to put her in jail, we might have prevented this continuing cycle of pain and destruction." House Subcommittee on Human Resources, *Impact of Crack Cocaine*, 8.

8. Senate Subcommittee on Children. *Falling through the Crack*, 5. Sociologists once represented adult drug use as a "victimless crime" involving two consenting adults—a buyer and a seller. See Edwin M. Schur, *Crimes without Victims: Deviant Behavior and Public Policy* (Englewood Cliffs, NJ: Prentice-Hall, 1965). Schur cited three examples of the sociological problem of unenforceable law—abortion, homosexuality, and addiction.

9. Senate Subcommittee on Children. *Falling through the Crack*, 5.

10. Senate Subcommittee on Children. *Falling through the Crack*, 8.

11. "Maternal instinct" is a dangerously naturalized construction of women's culturally assigned role in social reproduction. The term is not used even in fields where it initially came into being. It is surprising that it so commonly crops up in congressional hearings of the late twentieth century. Maternal instinct designates a normative construction of womanhood specific to liberal, democratic, capitalist states. The "loss of maternal instinct" taps into the threat that addicted women represented in the earlier part of the century.

12. U.S. Congress. Senate Committee on Governmental Affairs. *Missing Links: Coordinating Federal Drug Policy for Women, Infants, and Children*. 101st Cong., 1st sess., 31 July 1989, 21.

13. Committee on Labor and Human Resources and Committee on the Judiciary. *Impact of Drugs on Children and Families*, 4–5.

14. Committee on Labor and Human Resources and Committee on the Judiciary. *Impact of Drugs on Children and Families*, 5.

15. Committee on Labor and Human Resources and Committee on the Judiciary. *Impact of Drugs on Children and Families*, 24.

16. Committee on Labor and Human Resources and Committee on the Judiciary. *Impact of Drugs on Children and Families*, 23.

17. Committee on Labor and Human Resources and Committee on the Judiciary. *Impact of Drugs on Children and Families*, 24–25.

18. See Senate Committee on Governmental Affairs, *Missing Links*, 8, in which Tuckson stated: "There can be no question that the numbers of women who abuse drugs such as crack cocaine and the resultant increase in sexually transmitted disease, HIV disease, infant mortality, disabled and neglected infants and children, has now reached the level of a true public health emergency."

19. The Congressional Information System (CIS) database lists these hearings under "child effects," and not "women," "pregnancy," or "mothers."

20. Senate Subcommittee on Children. *Falling through the Crack*, 201.
21. National Center on Addiction and Substance Abuse (CASA), *Substance Abuse and the American Woman* (New York: The National Center on Addiction and Substance Abuse at Columbia University, June 1996), 1227; House Subcommittee on Human Resources, *Impact of Crack Cocaine*, 7; House Select Committee on Children, *Born Hooked*, 49.
22. Senate Committee on Governmental Affairs. *Missing Links*, 11.
23. Senate Subcommittee on Children. *Falling through the Crack*, 164.
24. Senate Committee on Governmental Affairs. *Missing Links*, 14–15.
25. Committee on Labor and Human Resources and Committee on the Judiciary. *Impact of Drugs on Children and Families*, 38.
26. The gender-neutral "parenting" obscures the fact: that the work implied by proper parenting is virtually all done by women. Second, it sets standards that appear classless and culture-free, thus obscuring the very different conditions in which the work is done. Third, parenting takes account of the entry of women into the labor force during the past generation. In moving away from the more simple and clearly gendered idea of motherhood, it allows the mother who is not devoting herself full time to her children to be a "proper" parent, through the hiring out, with proper supervision, of parenting tasks. . . . This form of parenting is geared to the requirements of the labor force, focused as it is on skill development, independence, and the creation of social habits such as punctuality and task completion. Culturally different attributes enter this scheme only peripherally, and race and racializing processes are entirely absent from view. (Swift 1995, 177)
27. Committee on Labor and Human Resources and Committee on the Judiciary. *Impact of Drugs on Children and Families*, 3.
28. Senate Committee on Governmental Affairs. *Missing Links*, 4, 31; Committee on Labor and Human Resources and Committee on the Judiciary. *Impact of Drugs on Children and Families*, 38.
29. See Senate Committee on Governmental Affairs, *Missing Links*, 8, in which Tuckson stated: "Crack users we know . . . will do almost anything to acquire that drug, particularly women." This "fact" was disproved by James A. Inciardi, Dorothy Lockwood, and Anne E. Pottieger, *Women and Crack-Cocaine* (New York: MacMillan, 1993), 36–39.
30. Senate Committee on Governmental Affairs. *Missing Links*, 18–19. See the introduction of this book for McCaffrey's similar remarks on white women's use of methamphetamines. Both illustrate how claims about drug use among women tip the balance toward crisis.
31. U.S. Congress. Senate Committee on Labor and Human Resources. *Role of Treatment and Prevention in the National Drug Strategy*, 101st Cong., 2d sess., 24 April 1990, 3.
32. U.S. Congress. Senate Committee on Labor and Human Resources. *Children of Substance Abusers*. 101st Cong., 2d sess., 5 February 1990, 2. The "seamless garment" was a recurring metaphor in this set of hearings.
33. U.S. Congress. Senate Subcommittee on Children, Family, Drugs, and Alcoholism of the Committee on Labor and Human Resources. *Drug Addicted Babies: What Can Be Done?* 101st Cong., 1st sess., 9 October 1989, 2.
34. Senate Committee on Governmental Affairs. *Missing Links*, 15.
35. Senate Committee on Governmental Affairs. *Missing Links*, 1.
36. Arthur Frank uses this term to delineate a "condition of perpetual uncertainty . . . endemic to postmodern times." See Arthur W. Frank, *The Wounded Storyteller: Body, Illness, and Ethics* (Chicago: University of Chicago Press, 1995), 69.
37. Senate Committee on Governmental Affairs. *Missing Links*, 9. The Committee on Governmental Affairs first heard witnesses on this "most troubling aspect of drug use" in 1989.
38. See Cora Wetherington, Vincent Smeriglio, and Loretta Finnegan, *Behavioral Studies of Drug-Exposed Offspring: Methodological Issues in Human and Animal Research*, NIDA Research Monograph 164 (Rockville, MD: NIDA, 1996), 192. "There has been a longstanding bias in the research community, influenced in part by funding and public policy issues, that cognitive and intellectual outcomes are of primary importance." As in early studies on prematurity, researchers were pessimistic about infants' potential recovery from prenatal injury. Later, "doom was replaced by optimism for the developing preterm infant" (196). Almost all data on drug use in pregnancy come from women who live in poverty, which affects cognitive development. Thus it is impossible to know what difference drug use makes.
39. Gretchen Vogel, "Cocaine Wreaks Subtle Damage on Developing Brains," *Science* 278, no. 5335 (October 3, 1997), 39.
40. Senate Committee on Governmental Affairs. *Missing Links*, 8. Testimony of Teresa Hagan, supervisor of clinical services at The Family Center, Jefferson Medical College, Philadelphia, Pennsylvania. She argued that policy-makers ignored the broad lack of support for poor

women, and lacked the "holistic" sociological and cultural knowledge to solve the problem.

41. Senate Subcommittee on Children. *Drug Addicted Babies: What Can Be Done?* 18.

42. Senate Subcommittee on Children. *Drug Addicted Babies: What Can Be Done?* 18.

43. Dorris appeared in the role of an adoptive father of an FAS child, professor of Native American Studies at Dartmouth College, and the author of *The Broken Cord: A Family's Ongoing Struggle with Fetal Alcohol Syndrome* (New York: Harper and Row, 1989).

44. Senate Subcommittee on Children. *Drug Addicted Babies: What Can Be Done?* 19.

45. See Donna Haraway, *Modest_Witness@Second_Millennium.FemaleMan@Meets_OncoMouse: Feminism and Technoscience* (New York: Routledge, 1997), 33.

46. Senate Subcommittee on Children. *Drug Addicted Babies: What Can Be Done?* 20.

47. Senate Subcommittee on Children. *Drug Addicted Babies: What Can Be Done?* 21.

48. Senate Subcommittee on Children. *Drug Addicted Babies: What Can Be Done?* 21.

49. Carol Bacchi, *Same Difference: Feminism and Sexual Difference* (Boston: Allen and Unwin, 1990); Martha Minow, *Making All the Difference* (Ithaca, NY: Cornell, 1990); Lise Vogel, *Mothers on the Job: Maternity Policy in the U.S.* (New Brunswick, NJ: Rutgers University Press, 1993); Gisela Bock and Susan James, *Beyond Equality and Difference: Citizenship, Feminist Politics, and Female Subjectivity* (New York: Routledge, 1992).

50. Nancy Fraser's schematic model in *Justice Interruptus: Critical Reflections on the "Postsocialist" Condition* (New York: Routledge, 1997) generates a useful typology for thinking about modes of addressing the "recognition-redistribution" dilemma.

51. James Inciardi, Hilary L. Surratt, and Christine A. Saum, *Cocaine-Exposed Infants: Social, Legal, and Public Health Issues* (Thousand Oaks, CA: SAGE Publications, 1997), 13.

52. Senate Committee on Governmental Affairs. *Missing Links*, 12.

53. Senate Committee on Governmental Affairs. *Missing Links*, 8, 12.

54. Michel Foucault, *Technologies of the Self*, eds. Luther H. Martin, Huck Gutman, and Patrick H. Hutton (Amherst, MA: University of Massachusetts Press, 1988), 161–162; Iris Marion Young, "Punishment, Treatment, Empowerment: Three Approaches to Policy for Pregnant Addicts," *Feminist Studies* 20, no. 1 (Spring 1994): 43–48.

55. U.S. Congress. House Select Committee on Children, Youth and Families. *Law and Policy Affecting Addicted Women and Their Children*. 101st Cong., 2d sess., 17 May 1990, 81. "Touted as the panacea for all problems in almost every human service system," case management is a vague but all-encompassing attempt "to help women hold their lives together as they went through the up and down recovery process," according to Neil Halfon, director of the Center for the Vulnerable Child in Oakland, California.

56. House Select Committee on Children, Youth and Families. *Law and Policy*, 321.

57. These meanings derive from older concepts articulated in John O'Donnell, "The Rise and Decline of a Subculture," *Social Problems* 15, no. 1 (1967): 73–84; Carl D. Chambers, R. Kent Hinesley, and Mary Moldestad, "The Female Opiate Addict," in *The Epidemiology of Drug Addiction in the United States*, eds. John C. Ball and Carl D. Chambers (Springfield, IL: Charles C. Thomas, 1970), 222–239; and "The Female Opiate Addict," *Toward a Typology of Opiate Users*, eds. William Bates and Betty Crowther (Cambridge, MA: Schenkman, 1974).

58. Bates and Crowther, *Toward a Typology of Opiate Users*, 97–98.

59. Bates and Crowther, *Toward a Typology of Opiate Users*, 97–98.

60. Bates and Crowther, *Toward a Typology of Opiate Users*, 100.

61. Bates and Crowther, *Toward a Typology of Opiate Users*, 101.

62. Bates and Crowther attributed these differences to individual lifestyle preferences. If white women "associate[d] with a criminal subculture" or led "antisocial" lifestyles, they might be as likely to use drugs as African-American women were.

63. Bates and Crowther, *Toward a Typology of Opiate Users*, 106.

64. Foucault, *Technologies of the Self*, 152.

65. Foucault, *Technologies of the Self*, 160–161.

66. House Select Committee on Children. *Born Hooked*, 168.

67. Senate Committee on Governmental Affairs. *Missing Links*, 8.

68. See Mitchell S. Ratner, ed., *Crack Pipe as Pimp: An Ethnographic Investigation of Sex-for-Crack-Exchanges* (New York: Lexington Books, 1993), a prime example of how research parameters dictated by funding agencies restrict research. Ratner points out that "sex-for-crack exchanges" represent a small portion of behaviors in which crack users engage. Yet the seven ethnographies that comprise the book focus on this tiny piece, because that was the knowledge NIDA sought and funded.

69. U.S. Congress. Senate Committee on Finance. *Infant Victims of Drug Abuse*. 101st Cong., 2d sess., 24 June 1990, 38.

70. Bridget F. Grant and Deborah A. Dawson, "Alcohol and Drug Use, Abuse, and Dependence among Welfare Recipients," *American Journal of Public Health* 86.10 (1996), 1453.

71. U.S. Department of Justice, Office of the Attorney General, *Drug Trafficking: A Report to the*

President of the United States (Washington, DC: GPO, 1989), 1.

72. U.S. Department of Justice, *Drug Trafficking*, 2.

73. U.S. Department of Justice, *Drug Trafficking*, 2–3.

74. Senate Committee on Labor and Human Resources. *Role of Treatment and Prevention*, 4.

75. House Select Committee on Children. *Born Hooked*, 49.

76. Senate Committee on Labor and Human Resources. *Role of Treatment and Prevention*, 2.

77. Senate Committee on Labor and Human Resources. *Role of Treatment and Prevention*, 32. On "priority populations," see Cynthia Daniels, "Between Fathers and Fetuses: The Social Construction of Male Reproduction and the Politics of Fetal Harm," *Signs* 22, no. 3 (1997): 608.

78. House Select Committee on Children. *Born Hooked*, 146.

79. Senate Committee on Labor and Human Resources. *Role of Treatment and Prevention*, 31. For an evaluation of the effectiveness of William J. Bennett's tenure as the "drug czar," see Franklin E. Zimring and Gordon Hawkins, *The Search for Rational Drug Control* (New York: Cambridge University Press, 1992), 184.

80. U.S. Congress. House. *Report of the Select Committee on Narcotics Abuse and Control, "On the Edge of the American Dream: A Social and Economic Profile in 1992."* 102d Cong., 2d sess. (Washington, DC: GPO, 1992), 3.

81. House. *Report of the Select Committee on Narcotics Abuse and Control, "On the Edge of the American Dream,* 3.

82. Senate Subcommittee on Children. *Drug Addicted Babies: What Can Be Done?* 51.

83. Laura E. Gomez, *Misconceiving Mothers: Legislators, Prosecutors, and the Politics of Prenatal Drug Exposure* (Philadelphia, PA: Temple University Press, 1997), 38.

84. House Select Committee on Children. *Born Hooked*, 12.

85. House Select Committee on Children. *Born Hooked*, 12.

86. House Select Committee on Children. *Born Hooked*, 103.

87. House Select Committee on Children. *Born Hooked*, 104.

88. Senate Subcommittee on Children. *Falling through the Crack*, 17–18.

89. House Select Committee on Children. *Born Hooked*, 152.

90. House Select Committee on Children. *Born Hooked*, 152–153.

91. House Select Committee on Children. *Born Hooked*, 151.

92. House Select Committee on Children. *Born Hooked*, 153.

93. House Select Committee on Children. *Born Hooked*, 153.

94. House Select Committee on Children. *Born Hooked*, 239.

95. House Select Committee on Children. *Born Hooked*, 240.

96. House Select Committee on Children. *Born Hooked*, 89.

97. House Select Committee on Children. *Born Hooked*, 89.

98. House Select Committee on Children. *Born Hooked*, 112.

99. House Select Committee on Children. *Born Hooked*, 49.

100. House Select Committee on Children. *Born Hooked*, 46, 61–62.

101. House Select Committee on Children. *Born Hooked*, 61–62.

102. Child Welfare League of America, *Crack and Other Addictions: Old Realities and New Challenges for Child Welfare* (Washington, DC: Child Welfare League of America [CWLA], 1990), 33.

103. CWLA, *Crack and Other Addictions*, 33.

104. CWLA, *Crack and Other Addictions*, 25–26.

105. House Select Committee on Children. *Born Hooked*, 21, 155.

106. House Select Committee on Children. *Born Hooked*, 139.

107. House Select Committee on Children. *Born Hooked*, 121.

108. House Select Committee on Children. *Born Hooked*, 133, 140.

109. House Select Committee on Children. *Born Hooked*, 121.

110. House Select Committee on Children. *Born Hooked*, 121.

111. House Select Committee on Children. *Born Hooked*, 123.

112. House Select Committee on Children. *Born Hooked*, 225.

113. House Select Committee on Children. *Born Hooked*, 47.

114. Dorothy Roberts, "Punishing Drug Addicts Who Have Babies: Women of Color, Equality, and the Right of Privacy," *Harvard Law Review* 104 (1991): 1419–1482. "Drug addicts who have babies" appear as figures whose privacy rights have been historically proscribed on the basis of race, gender, and sexuality. Roberts adopted Catherine MacKinnon's analysis of *Harris v. McRae,* in which MacKinnon argued that reproductive freedom had become a matter of "private privilege" rather than a public right. A decision that enjoined the state to ensure that even indigent women could exercise choice would have construed reproductive freedom as a right. Instead, *Harris* denied one of the state's basic obligations to its citizens: to provide "the social conditions and resources necessary for self-determination and autonomous decisionmaking" (1478).

115. House Select Committee on Children. *Born Hooked*, 173.

116. This resembles the portrayal of women who refuse medical treatment as "backward" or irrational. See Cynthia R. Daniels, *At Women's Expense: State Power and the Politics of Fetal Rights* (Cambridge, MA: Harvard University Press, 1993).

117. Faye D. Ginsburg and Rayna Rapp, eds., *Conceiving the New World Order: The Global Politics of Reproduction* (Berkeley, CA: University of California Press, 1995); Kristin Luker, *Dubious Conceptions: The Politics of Teenage Pregnancy* (Cambridge, MA: Harvard University Press, 1996).

118. Daniels, *At Women's Expense*; Renee M. Popovits, "Criminalization of Pregnant Substance Abusers: A Health Care Perspective," *Journal of Health and Hospital Law* 24, no. 6 (June 1991): 169–181.

119. Roslyn Muraskin and Ted Alleman, *It's a Crime: Women and Justice* (Englewood Cliffs, NJ: Regents/Prentice Hall, 1993), 75. This undergraduate criminology textbook is an accessible introduction to the topic of women and crime.

120. See Nancy J. Hirschmann and Christine Di Stefano, *Revisioning the Political* (Boulder, CO: Westview Press, 1996): 157–180. Obligation, Hirschmann argues, is a limitation on behavior to which an actor consents. Duty exists without explicit choice or consent. Hirschmann extends obligation to encompass connection, need, and vulnerability, all of which are recognized by persons who enter into states of obligation (which parenting doubtless is). The privatization of the tasks and costs of social reproduction imposes a duty on mothers under the guise of a chosen obligation.

121. Wendy Brown, *States of Injury: Power and Freedom in Late Modernity* (Princeton, NJ: Princeton University Press, 1995), 154–156.

122. Drucilla Cornell, *The Imaginary Domain: Abortion, Pornography and Sexual Harassment* (New York: Routledge, 1995).

123. Michelle Oberman, "Sex, Drugs, Pregnancy, and the Law: Rethinking the Problems of Women Who Use Drugs," *Hastings Law Journal* 43 (March 1992): 505–548.

124. Gomez, *Misconceiving Mothers*, 46.

125. See Nancy D. Campbell, "Regulating 'Maternal Instinct': Governing Mentalities of Late Twentieth-Century U.S. Illicit Drug Policy," *Signs* 24, no. 4 (Summer 1999): 895–923.

126. Gomez, *Misconceiving Mothers*, 101.

127. Dawn Johnsen, "The Creation of Fetal Rights: Conflicts with Women's Constitutional Rights to Liberty, Privacy, and Equal Protection," *Yale Law Journal* 95 (1986).

128. Gomez, *Misconceiving Mothers*, 31.

129. Gomez, *Misconceiving Mothers*, 35.

130. Dorothy E. Roberts argues that the "degrading mythology about Black mothers influences public policy as long as government officials do not explicitly act on the basis of race." *Killing the Black Body: Race, Reproduction, and the Meaning of Liberty* (New York: Pantheon Books, 1997). Roberts suggests using African-American women's reproductive liberty as a yardstick against which to measure all women's reproductive liberty. If African-American women have the least reproductive autonomy, then a guarantee of privacy, liberty, and equality for them would ensure that others did as well or better.

131. Gomez, *Misconceiving Mothers*, 122.

132. Gomez, *Misconceiving Mothers*, 122.

133. Gomez, *Misconceiving Mothers*, 123.

134. See Mary Daly, *Gyn/Ecology* (Boston, MA: Beacon Press, 1978), 58.

A Politics of Social Justice

1. Frank R. Baumgartner and Bryan D. Jones, *Agendas and Instability in American Politics* (Chicago: University of Chicago Press, 1993), 159. Most drug hearings focus on law enforcement approaches. Considerably less attention is paid to educative efforts, prevention, or treatment. Hearings that focus on women's drug use and its impact on the fetus, babies, or children exhibit a tension between punitive and therapeutic approaches.

2. See the special issue on "The Rhetoric of Reproduction: Pregnancy and Drug Use," *Contemporary Drug Problems*, eds. Sheigla Murphy and Marsha Rosenbaum, 22, no.4 (1995). Katherine Irwin's article exemplifies the turn to rhetorical analysis. Here drug-using women appear properly guilty, fearful, and concerned about fetal well-being in well-intentioned but misinformed ways. The rehabilitated image of the drug-using woman is offered as if that will be sufficient to deter policy-makers from their own "ideologies."

3. CWLA, *Crack and Other Addictions: Old Realities and New Challenges for Child Welfare* (Washington, DC: Child Welfare League of America, 1990), 4. The effort was supported by the J.C. Penney Company.

4. CWLA, *Crack and Other Addictions*, vi.

5. CWLA, *Crack and Other Addictions*, vii.

6. CWLA, *Crack and Other Addictions*, vii.

7. "Crack Babies: The Worst Threat Is Mom Herself," *Washington Post*, August 6, 1989.

8. CWLA, *Crack and Other Addictions*, 9.

9. CWLA, *Crack and Other Addictions*, 12.

10. CWLA, *Crack and Other Addictions*, 19.

11. CWLA, *Crack and Other Addictions*, 19.

12. CWLA, *Crack and Other Addictions*, 20.

13. Douglas J. Besharov, ed., *When Drug Addicts Have Children: Reorienting Child Welfare's Response* (Washington, DC: Child Welfare League of America/American Enterprise Institute, 1994), xiii.

14. Besharov, *When Drug Addicts Have Children*, ix, xiii, xviii, xxv.

15. See also Besharov, "Children of Crack," *Public Welfare* 54, no. 1 (1996): 32–38.
16. Nancy Folbre, *Who Pays for the Kids? Gender and the Structures of Constraint* (New York: Routledge, 1994), 254.

Chapter 8

1. Jeffrey Fagan, "Women and Drugs Revisited: Female Participation in the Cocaine Economy," *Journal of Drug Issues* 24, no. 2 (1994): 182.
2. Fagan, "Women and Drugs Revisited," *Journal of Drug Issues*, 212.
3. Eloise Dunlap, Bruce D. Johnson, and Lisa Maher, "Female Crack Sellers in New York City: Who They Are and What They Do," *Women and Criminal Justice* 8, no. 4 (1997): 37.
4. Dunlap, Johnson, and Maher, "Female Crack Sellers," *Women and Criminal Justice*, 53.
5. Dunlap, Johnson, and Maher, "Female Crack Sellers," *Women and Criminal Justice*, 26, 52.
6. Dunlap, Johnson, and Maher, "Female Crack Sellers," *Women and Criminal Justice*, 42.
7. Dunlap, Johnson, and Maher, "Female Crack Sellers," *Women and Criminal Justice*, 49.
8. Dunlap, Johnson, and Maher, "Female Crack Sellers," *Women and Criminal Justice*, 42, 50.
9. Dunlap, Johnson, and Maher, "Female Crack Sellers," *Women and Criminal Justice*, 50–51.
10. The masculinist bias is still evident; see Jeff Ferrell and Mark S. Hamm, eds., *Ethnography at the Edge: Crime, Deviance, and Field Research* (Boston, MA: Northeastern University Press, 1998). Set up as a series of "true confessions," the collection recounts the masculine adventure stories of field researchers and their vicarious identification with militarists and crack dealers. The anthology confines feminist work to the "sex work" section. I bring this up not to cast aspersion on this vein of research, but to show what feminist ethnography was designed to counter.
11. Because I am convinced of the need for a fuller picture of the day-to-day humanity of drug-involved women, I admire the ethnographers and their subjects. However, the ethnographies invite a continued categorization of drug-using subjects as "not like us" by dwelling on the degraded circumstances of (some) users, who come to stand for all users and become the prevailing figurations for drug addiction because they confirm the governing mentalities.
12. Craig Reinarman and Harry G. Levine, *Crack in America: Demon Drugs and Social Justice* (Berkeley, CA: University of California Press, 1997), 24.
13. Howard S. Becker, *Tricks of the Trade* (Chicago: University of Chicago Press, 1998), 44.
14. Becker, *Tricks of the Trade*, 46.
15. Reinarman and Levine, *Crack in America*, 24.

16. Paul Atkinson, *The Ethnographic Imagination* (New York: Routledge, 1990), 71.
17. Atkinson, *The Ethnographic Imagination*, 86. The exemplar is an iconic representation that indexes to the reader's social world. The author relies on the reader's familiarity with the embedded indexes, for the text fails if the reader does not share the writer's frame of reference.
18. Reinarman and Levine, *Crack in America*, 98–112. The essay makes a point congruent with both my analysis and my political stance. Thus I am a sympathetic reader, grateful to the ethnographers for presenting a picture that reinforces my own governing mentalities.
19. Reinarman and Levine, *Crack in America*, 98.
20. Reinarman and Levine, *Crack in America*, 98.
21. Reinarman and Levine, *Crack in America*, 99.
22. Reinarman and Levine, *Crack in America*, 101.
23. Reinarman and Levine, *Crack in America*, 101.
24. Reinarman and Levine, *Crack in America*, 101.
25. Reinarman and Levine, *Crack in America*, 100.
26. Reinarman and Levine, *Crack in America*, 107.
27. Arthur W. Frank, *The Wounded Storyteller: Body, Illness, and Ethics* (Chicago: University of Chicago Press), 144; Dorothy E. Smith, *The Conceptual Practices of Power: A Feminist Sociology of Knowledge* (Boston, MA: Northeastern University Press, 1990).
28. NIDA emphasizes the public health consequences of drug users' individual behavior and moral decisions, such as needle-sharing and discard practices. The HIV/AIDS movement initially linked safe sex practices to drug use practices, and achieved some legitimation of harm-reduction measures even where "condoning" safe use means "condoning" drug use.
29. Elizabeth Lambert and W. Wayne Weibel, *The Collection and Interpretation of Data from Hidden Populations*. NIDA Research Monograph 98 (Rockville, MD: National Institute on Drug Abuse, 1990), 1.
30. Mitchell S. Ratner, ed., *Crack Pipe as Pimp: An Ethnographic Investigation of Sex-for-Crack Exchanges* (New York: Basic Books, 1993), 4.
31. Edward Preble and John J. Casey, "Taking Care of Business: The Heroin User's Life on the Street," *International Journal of the Addictions* 4 (March 1969): 1–24.
32. Michael Agar, *Ripping and Running* (New York: Seminar Press, 1973).
33. Atkinson, *The Ethnographic Imagination*, 165.
34. Marsha Rosenbaum, *Women on Heroin* (New Brunswick, NJ: Rutgers University Press, 1981), 136.
35. Rosenbaum, *Women on Heroin*, 131.
36. Rosenbaum, *Women on Heroin*, 137.
37. Catherine Belsey, *Critical Practice* (New York: Methuen, 1980), 51. Belsey uses the term realism to distinguish between writing that effaces its own textuality and *refuses* its "existence as dis-

course," and writing that draws explicit attention to its status as discourse.

38. Margaret Weeks and Kim Radda, "Broken Windows, Broken Dreams: Street Ethnography of IVDUs," paper presented at the annual meeting of the American Anthropological Association, Washington, DC, November 22, 1997.

39. Pellegrino Luciano, Toni Marisa Gallo, and Michael C. Clatts, "The Moral Actions of IVDUs," paper presented at the annual meeting of the American Anthropological Association, Washington, DC, November 23, 1997.

40. Ratner, *Crack Pipe as Pimp*, viii.

41. Terry Williams, *Crackhouse: Notes from the End of the Line* (Reading, MA: Addison-Wesley, 1992).

42. Williams, *Crackhouse*, 3.

43. Williams, *Crackhouse*, 35.

44. Williams, *Crackhouse*, 12.

45. Williams, *Crackhouse*, 40.

46. Williams, *Crackhouse*, 68.

47. Williams, *Crackhouse*, 113.

48. Williams, *Crackhouse*, 114.

49. Williams, *Crackhouse*, 116.

50. Sue Mahan, *Crack, Cocaine, Crime, and Women: Legal, Social, and Treatment Issues* (Thousand Oaks, CA: SAGE, 1996).

51. Adele Harrell and George Peterson, eds., *Drugs, Crime and Social Isolation: Barriers to Urban Opportunity* (Washington, DC: Urban Institute Press, 1992); Mahan, *Crack, Cocaine, Crime, and Women*, 77.

52. Senate Subcommittee on Children, *Drug Addicted Babies: What Can Be Done?* 19.

53. House Select Committee on Children, *Born Hooked*, 146.

54. For an argument to the contrary, see Franklin E. Zimring and Gordon Hawkins, *Crime Is Not the Problem: Lethal Violence in America* (New York: Oxford University Press, 1997).

55. Mahan, *Crack, Cocaine, Crime, and Women*, 78.

56. Mahan, *Crack, Cocaine, Crime, and Women*, 48.

57. Mahan, *Crack, Cocaine, Crime, and Women*, 17.

58. Mahan, *Crack, Cocaine, Crime, and Women*, 17.

59. Mahan, *Crack, Cocaine, Crime, and Women*, 22.

60. Mahan, *Crack, Cocaine, Crime, and Women*, 14.

61. Mahan, *Crack, Cocaine, Crime, and Women*, 14.

62. Mahan, *Crack, Cocaine, Crime, and Women*, 23.

63. Mahan, *Crack, Cocaine, Crime, and Women*, 25.

64. Mahan, *Crack, Cocaine, Crime, and Women*, 26.

65. Harvey W. Feldman, Michael H. Agar, and George M. Beschner, *Angel Dust: An Ethnographic Study of PCP Users* (Lexington, MA: Lexington Books, 1979).

66. Ratner, *Crack Pipe as Pimp*, 17–18.

67. Norman E. Zinberg, *Drug, Set, and Setting: The Basis for Controlled Intoxicant Use* (New Haven, CT: Yale University Press, 1984). Zinberg advanced his model to make sense of the experience of heroin-addicted Vietnam veterans who ceased heroin use upon return to the States. He posited an unconscious "set" of preparatory expectations. The pharmacological experience of the drug, informal knowledge transmission about its use, and the cultural transmission of new rituals and informal social sanctions to control use impacted the social experience of the drug (12). The controlled (male) heroin users in Zinberg's study avoided "addict culture" because it negatively affected their lives. Heterosexuality was one of the strongest "social controls"—Zinberg found that male heroin users depended on girlfriends to help them abstain (143). Zinberg's model remains one of the chief ways by which "discredited" psychoanalytic constructions of addiction are smuggled into sociological constructions today. He cited psychoanalytic theorists such as Sandor Rado, who saw intoxicant use as driven by the need to substitute for an unloving mother.

68. Ratner, *Crack Pipe as Pimp*, 14–22. See Zinberg, *Drug, Set, and Setting*.

69. Ratner, *Crack Pipe as Pimp*, 15.

70. Ratner, *Crack Pipe as Pimp*, 8.

71. Ratner, *Crack Pipe as Pimp*, 9.

72. Ratner, *Crack Pipe as Pimp*, 19.

73. Ratner, *Crack Pipe as Pimp*, 2.

74. Ratner, *Crack Pipe as Pimp*, 7.

75. Ratner, *Crack Pipe as Pimp*, 18.

76. Ratner, *Crack Pipe as Pimp*, 18.

77. Ratner, *Crack Pipe as Pimp*, 18–19.

78. Ratner, *Crack Pipe as Pimp*, 21. Television was implicated as the promulgator of that message and as a "mind-altering substance."

79. Ratner, *Crack Pipe as Pimp*, 18.

80. Ratner, *Crack Pipe as Pimp*, 18.

81. Ratner, *Crack Pipe as Pimp*, 129.

82. Helen Longino, *Science as Social Knowledge* (Princeton, NJ: Princeton University Press, 1990), 164.

83. Elizabeth W. Dowling, "Sex, Drugs, and HIV: An Ethnographic Approach," paper presented at the annual meeting of the American Anthropological Association, Washington, DC, November 22, 1997.

84. Zinberg, *Drug, Set, and Setting*, 203.

85. James A. Inciardi, Dorothy Lockwood, and Anne E. Pottieger, *Women and Crack-Cocaine* (New York: MacMillan, 1993), 21.

86. Inciardi, Lockwood, and Pottieger, *Women and Crack-Cocaine*, 22.

87. Inciardi, Lockwood, and Pottieger, *Women and Crack-Cocaine*, 26.

88. Inciardi, Lockwood, and Pottieger, *Women and Crack-Cocaine*, 27.

89. Inciardi, Lockwood, and Pottieger, *Women and Crack-Cocaine*, 28.

90. Inciardi, Lockwood, and Pottieger, *Women and Crack-Cocaine*, 36.

91. Inciardi, Lockwood, and Pottieger, *Women and Crack-Cocaine*, 38.

92. Inciardi, Lockwood, and Pottieger, *Women and Crack-Cocaine*, 39.
93. Inciardi, Lockwood, and Pottieger, *Women and Crack-Cocaine*, 96.
94. Inciardi, Lockwood, and Pottieger, *Women and Crack-Cocaine*, 40.
95. Inciardi, Lockwood, and Pottieger, *Women and Crack-Cocaine*, 63.
96. Inciardi, Lockwood, and Pottieger, *Women and Crack-Cocaine*, 76.
97. Inciardi, Lockwood, and Pottieger, *Women and Crack-Cocaine*, 98.
98. Inciardi, Lockwood, and Pottieger, *Women and Crack-Cocaine*, 109–110.
99. Becker, *The Outsiders*, 42.
100. Inciardi, Lockwood, and Pottieger, *Women and Crack-Cocaine*, 112.
101. Inciardi, Lockwood, and Pottieger, *Women and Crack-Cocaine*, 130. Crack was unavailable until two years after their juvenile female informants began selling drugs or sex. The study also found that crack dealing was not profitable for juveniles, although it did open drug markets to them.
102. Inciardi, Lockwood, and Pottieger, *Women and Crack-Cocaine*, 145.
103. Inciardi, Lockwood, and Pottieger, *Women and Crack-Cocaine*, 19.
104. See Clarence Lusane, *Pipe Dream Blues: Racism and the War on Drugs* (Boston, MA: South End Press, 1991): 55–66.
105. Lisa Maher, "Punishment and Welfare: Crack Cocaine and the Regulation of Mothering," *Women and Criminal Justice* 3, no. 2 (1992): 52.
106. Maher, "Punishment and Welfare," *Women and Criminal Justice*, 50–51.
107. Maher, "Punishment and Welfare," *Women and Criminal Justice*, 53.

Conclusion

1. Avram Goldstein, *Addiction: From Biology to Drug Policy* (New York: W. H. Freeman, 1994), 275.
2. U.S. Congress. Senate Committee on Finance. *Infant Victims of Drug Abuse*. 101st Cong., 2d sess., June 28, 1990, 13–14. This hearing considered the COSA (Children of Substance Abusers) Act.
3. Senate Committee on Finance. *Infant Victims of Drug Abuse*, 38.
4. U.S. Congress. Senate Subcommittee on Children, Family, Drugs, and Alcoholism of the Committee on Labor and Human Resources. *Falling through the Crack: The Impact of Drug-Exposed Children on the Child Welfare System*. 101st Cong., 2d sess., 8 March 1990, 12.
5. Senate Subcommittee on Children, Family, Drugs, and Alcoholism. *Falling through the Crack*, 14.
6. See Andrew J. Polsky, *The Rise of the Therapeutic State* (Princeton, NJ: Princeton University Press, 1991), for a thoroughgoing critique of the

feminist contribution to the development of "normalizing" agencies in the Progressive period. Second Wave feminism criticized gender "bias" in state programs and developed alternative agencies (many of which were coopted by the state and for-profit concerns). Polsky is critical of therapeutic discourse on grounds that it is exclusionary, mystifying, and fixated on "obscure behavioral sciences" (222). Feminists have sometimes sought alliances within the "therapeutic state," but have also sometimes rejected them.

7. U.S. Congress. House Select Committee on Children, Youth, and Families. *Born Hooked: Confronting the Impact of Perinatal Substance Abuse*. 101st Cong., 1st sess., 27 April 1989, 235.
8. Senate Committee on Finance. *Infant Victims of Drug Abuse*, 20. Fathers were rarely mentioned. Senator Moynihan later assumed a correlation between concentrations of crack babies in areas "where the illegitimacy ratios are 80 percent" (38). The presumption of father absence reminds us how effectively fathers have disappeared from these conversations. Despite ample evidence to the contrary, "intact" families — nuclear and structured by heterosexual pair bonds — are assumed not to produce drug addiction.
9. As I emphasize throughout, our construction of the "problem" obscures white and middle-class drug use, which is not considered problematic in social terms, although it may be understood as problematic for individuals engaged in it.
10. House Select Committee on Children. *Born Hooked*, 146.
11. House Select Committee on Children. *Born Hooked*, 146. Emphasis mine.
12. Mary Lyndon Shanley and Uma Narayan, eds., *Reconstructing Political Theory* (University Park, PA: Pennsylvania State University Press, 1997).
13. Vulnerability is articulated through the pervasive language of "being at risk." See Mary Douglas, *Risk and Blame: Essays in Cultural Theory* (New York: Routledge, 1992); and *Purity and Danger: An Analysis of Conceptions of Pollution and Taboo* (London: Routledge and Kegan Paul, 1966). The shift from "danger" (which lacks the "aura of science") to "risk" heightens the sense of vulnerability to potential harm caused by others, but preserves the innocence of the self (Douglas, 1992: 28–30).
14. Categorizing feminism as a set of stable ideological varieties (cultural feminism, socialist or materialist feminism, liberal feminism, radical feminism, or multicultural feminism) is no longer a useful exercise (if it ever was). The category "liberal feminism," for instance, is used to dismiss state-centered reforms within existing institutions. This delegitimates some feminists as mainstream, reformist, conformist, or simply

unambitious. Epistemological ruptures within feminism are breaks between states of thinking, knowing, and acting in the world—modes of expressive style or symbolic action. The deepest rifts in feminism are epistemological—how we know the world and act on our knowledge. My conceptual bridge-building is not designed to "heal our wounds," nor smooth generational conflict, but to build a political constituency capable of resisting containment by the variety of hostile forces arrayed against women's political

autonomy—only some of which are interred in "the state."

15. Judith Butler, *Excitable Speech: A Politics of the Performative* (New York: Routledge, 1997), 77.

16. Wendy Brown, *States of Injury: Power and Freedom in Late Modernity* (Princeton, NJ: Princeton University Press, 1995), 33.

17. Myra Ferree and Patricia Martin, eds., *Feminist Organizations: Harvest of the New Women's Movement* (Philadelphia, PA: Temple University Press, 1995), 125.

INDEX